ACCLAIM FOR THE STUNNING SUSPENSE OF THE CHRIST CLONE TRILOGY

"BeauSeigneur knows how to write, deploying a tough, driving style in perfect cadence.... The paranoia he evokes is a perfect fit for these times."
—*Booklist* (starred review)

"A lively, three-part novel dramatizing the End Time events described in Revelation."
—*New York Times*

"This extraordinary trilogy is nothing short of incredible. These End Time books will knock your socks off."
—**Ted Dekker,**
bestselling author of *Thunder of Heaven* and *Three*

"Tremendous.... I couldn't stop, and I must tell you, I was overwhelmed."
—**Wayne Watson,**
Dove Award-winning singer/songwriter

"Intelligent, well-researched, and flawlessly executed.... By far the most exciting, true-to-life portrayal of End Time events I've ever read."
—**John Ter**

ACTS
of
GOD

THE CHRIST CLONE TRILOGY

In His Image
Birth of an Age
Acts of God

ACTS of GOD

THE CHRIST CLONE TRILOGY   BOOK THREE

JAMES BeauSeigneur

WARNER BOOKS

NEW YORK   BOSTON

This is a work of fiction. All of the characters, incidents, and dialogue, lexcept for incidental references to public figures, products, or services, are imaginary and are not intended to refer to any living persons or to disparage any company's products or services.

Unless otherwise noted, Scriptures are taken from the HOLY BIBLE: NEW INTERNATIONAL VERSION®. Copyright © 1973, 1978, 1984 by International Bible Society. Used by permission of Zondervan Publishing House. All rights reserved.

Scriptures noted KJV are taken from the King James Version of the Bible.

Cover design by Kirk Douponce UDG/Design Works
Photo by Peter Holst/The Image Bank

Warner Books

Time Warner Book Group
1271 Avenue of the Americas New York, NY 10020
Visit our Web site at www.twbookmark.com

Printed in the United States of America

Originally published in hardcover by Warner Books
First Paperback Printing: October 2004

10 9 8 7 6 5 4 3 2 1

*For Gerilynne, Faith, and Abigail, who sacrificed so much
to allow this trilogy to become a reality.*

*But most of all for Shiloh, who sacrificed far more.
May it serve you well.*

Acknowledgments

While writing *The Christ Clone Trilogy*, I called upon the support of specialists in many fields of endeavor to ensure the accuracy and plausibility of my work. Others provided editorial direction, professional guidance, or moral sustenance. These include: John Jefferson, Ph.D.; Michael Haire, Ph.D.; James Russell, M.D.; Robert Seevers, Ph.D.; Peter Helt, J.D.; James Beadle, Ph.D.; Christy Beadle, M.D.; Ken Newberger, Th.M.; Eugene Walter, Ph.D.; Clement Walchshauser, D.Min.; Col. Arthur Winn; Elizabeth Winn, Ph.D.; Ian Wilson, Historian; Jeanne Gehret, M.A.; Linda Alexander; Bernadine Asher; Matthew Belsky; Wally & Betty Bishop; Roy & Jeannie Blocher; Scott Brown; Dale Brubaker; Curt & Phyllis Brudos; Dave & Deb Dibert; Estelle Ducharme; Tony Fantham; Georgia O'Dell; Mike Pinkston; Capt. Paul & Debbie Quinn; Doug & Beth Ross; Doris, Fred, & Bryan Seigneur; Mike Skinner; Gordy & Sue Stauffer; Doug & Susy Stites.

ACTS
of
GOD

"Are these the shadows of things that will be, or are they the shadows of things that may be, only?"

CHARLES DICKENS, *A Christmas Carol*

"For false Christs and false prophets will appear and perform great signs and miracles to deceive even the elect—if that were possible."

MATTHEW 24:24

"There's no place like home."

L. FRANK BAUM, *The Wizard of Oz*

Prologue

Behold the Hosts of Heaven

Jerusalem

THE SCENE AT THE TEMPLE was not much different than it had been at the airport. Even from a distance, immense crowds could be seen. The Temple was usually a swarm of activity, but now, despite the number of people in the streets, the Temple itself was empty. The inner and outer courts, usually bustling with priests and worshipers, were abandoned, and the steps leading up to the front of the Temple were equally barren, with two exceptions. As the helicopter circled, Christopher Goodman, Robert Milner, and Decker Hawthorne could see two men standing on the steps, both clothed in sackcloth and covered with gray ash.

Farther away, two hundred to three hundred priests and Levites huddled near High Priest Chaim Levin, who stood a safe distance away in a tableau of mock defiance toward the men on the steps. A little farther back, the crowds watched from behind a line of armed Israeli soldiers. Reporters from the international news media, unable to leave the country and aware that Jerusalem was Christopher's destination, stood ready to cover every second of the event. The unexpected arrival of the oracles John and Cohen an hour earlier and their subsequent clearing of the Temple while Christopher was en route from New York only intensified the level of expectation. Into this, but more specifically between the line of military personnel and the steps of the Temple, Christopher directed the pilot to set the helicopter down.

With television cameras rolling, Christopher was the first to disembark the aircraft. His hair and long robes tossed wildly about him in the swirling winds of the helicopter's rotating blades, painting a striking portrait for television viewers and magazine covers as he stood unflinching before the challenge that faced him. Looking out as he waited to exit the helicopter, Decker could see that John and Cohen had expected Christopher's arrival.

Once they were all on the ground, Milner turned and signaled for the pilot to withdraw. Standing there face to face with John and Cohen, Decker could not ignore the sudden twinge of anxiety that swept over him. Was any of this feeling the result of animosity borne between him (in his previous incarnation as Judas) and John two thousand years earlier, as Christopher had told him? To Decker's surprise, despite all else that was going on, Christopher turned to him and put his hand on his shoulder. "It's all right," he said, and somehow Decker understood that it was.

John was the first to speak. *"Hiney ben-satan nirah chatat haolam!"* he shouted in Hebrew, meaning: "Behold the son of Satan who manifests the sin of the world."

"So we meet again at last," Christopher answered in an ironic turn of the phrase, ignoring John's comment.

"You are mistaken," John replied. "I never knew you."

"No, Yochanan bar Zebadee," Christopher responded, using the Hebrew form of John's full name. "It is I who never knew you!"

For a long moment neither spoke, but only stared at each other. Then Christopher dropped his gaze to the ground. "It's not too late," he said finally, addressing both John and Cohen. His voice had a sense of pleading but at the same time the tone indicated that he knew the attempt was in vain.

Quite uncharacteristically, John smiled and then began to laugh. In a moment Cohen joined in. Christopher looked back at Decker with an expression that seemed to say, "this is for both of us." Then, taking a deep breath and with no sign of anger but every ounce of conviction, he looked back at the two men and then shouted above their laughter, "As you will!"

Then raising his right hand, he made a quick sweeping motion, and immediately John and Cohen's laughter stopped as they were thrown backward through the air at incredible, almost unbelievable speed, their bodies slamming against the front walls of the Temple on either side of the entrance. The crunch of breaking bones was loud enough to be heard throughout the vast multitude and left no doubt as to their fate. Their blood splattered liberally on the wall and remained there as witness of where they had hit. As Christopher brought his hand back down, the two lifeless bodies fell and, with a sweep of his hand, they tumbled down the steps toward the street below, leaving two long trails of blood to mark their paths.

Those assembled watched in stunned silence as

Christopher, Milner, and Decker climbed the steps to the Temple while the crumpled bodies rolled on either side of them. As soon as the crowd realized that John and Cohen were actually dead, a shout went up from civilians and military alike. A spontaneous celebration began and was soon joined by people all around the world cheering the news as they watched on television or listened on radio. Members of the media quickly pushed through the lines of Israeli soldiers to get a better look at the bodies.

❑

In Chieti, Italy, a man whose nostrils were filled with the rank smell of burning sulfur and whose heart was filled with the madness by which he had thus far made blood-ied carnage of all but one member of his family, held a gory meat cleaver above his head and was about to bring it down upon his only remaining son when, as quickly as it had come upon him . . . the madness was gone. Carefully the man lowered the cleaver and laid it aside, and there among the dismembered bodies of his family, he dropped to his knees to hold his terror-filled son, and wept. In Rudnyj, Turskaja, an old woman choked and gasped for breath as she pulled her head from a barrel of rain water in which she had tried to drown herself. In Baydhabo, Somalia, a teenage boy stopped only seconds before striking a match to set fire to his four gasoline-soaked younger siblings.

Throughout the affected areas, at the moment John and Cohen died, the madness ceased.

❑

When they reached the top stair of the Temple, Christopher turned to the gathering. "No one must touch the bodies," he shouted, pointing at John and Cohen. "There is still great power within them. It will not be safe for anyone to touch or dispose of the bodies for at least four days." Nodding to Decker to imply that he should reinforce the warning, Christopher turned back and then, together with Robert Milner, he continued into the Temple.

As they had planned before their arrival, Decker remained outside. Pulling a folded piece of paper from his jacket pocket, he waited for the press who would, no doubt, descend on him as soon as they finished taking pictures of the two dead oracles. Decker was pleased to see that the press were heeding Christopher's advice and not venturing too close to the bodies. There was no need to fear that the priests or Levites would touch them: Their laws forbade contact with dead bodies. The only real problem might come from onlookers who for now were still held back behind police lines.

❑

Inside the Temple, Robert Milner and Christopher walked side by side. Crossing the floor of the normally bustling Court of the Gentiles, the only sound came from the column-lined portico that surrounded the court. There, animals meant for sacrifices had been brought to the Temple for sale to worshipers. They had been left there untended by the shepherds and merchants when everyone was driven out.

A hundred and fifty yards ahead of Christopher and Milner, the buildings of the Inner Court and the Sanctuary within it towered more than two hundred feet above them.

❏

Outside the southern entrance and framed on either side by the blood of John and Cohen, Decker waited as the members of the press hurried up the steps to find what light he could shed on the events they were witnessing.

❏

Christopher and Milner reached the *soreg,* the low stone wall that separated the Court of the Gentiles from the inner courts of the Temple and that formed a sacred balustrade, or enclosure, into which no Gentile was permitted to enter. Inscriptions on the soreg, harking back two thousand years to signs in Herod's Temple, warned visitors in more than a dozen languages, "No foreigner may enter the enclosure around the Temple. Anyone doing so will bear the responsibility for his own ensuing death." It was convenient that the Temple had been cleared, for the priests and Levites would never have permitted Christopher and Milner passage beyond the balustrade without an altercation.

Intentionally going out of their way to enter from the east, the men walked to the middle opening of the eastern end of the soreg. Quickly spanning the distance between the soreg and the first of three short flights of steps, Christopher and Milner ascended to the *Chel,* or rampart, a flat area 15 feet wide from which the massive stone walls of the Inner Court rose 37 feet above them.

❏

"Ladies and Gentlemen," Decker shouted above the din of the reporters. "I have a brief prepared statement, and then I'll be available for a few questions."

Someone yelled out a question but Decker ignored it. "Forty-five years ago I was a part of a scientific team from the United States that went to Italy to examine the Shroud of Turin, a piece of cloth bearing the image of a crucified man," Decker began, reading from the statement he had prepared on the plane. In the limited time available, he provided as much detail as he could about the events that had followed the Turin expedition and which had led to this moment. He told them how, eleven years after the expedition, he had been contacted by a member of that team, Professor Harold Goodman, who asked him to come to UCLA to witness a discovery he had made concerning the Shroud.

"Professor Goodman," Decker said, "had discovered that among the samples taken from the Shroud was a microscopic cluster of human dermal skin cells. To my amazement . . . ," Decker paused, still awed as he recalled what he had seen those many years before, "the cells from the Shroud were still alive." For some in the assembly, that piece of the puzzle and Christopher's resurrection were all that was needed to make sense of the whole incredible picture, but though there was an audible gasp, no one spoke. "Tests of the cells showed them to be incredibly resilient and possessing a number of unique characteristics," Decker continued. "It was from cultures grown of these cells that Professor Goodman conducted his cancer research.

"Unknown to me on that occasion, Professor Goodman had already performed a number of experiments with the cells," Decker paused as if to give the reporters a chance to brace themselves, "including implanting the DNA from one of the cells into the embryo of an unfertilized human egg and then replacing that egg into the donor, thus . . . cloning the person whose cells were on the Shroud. From that cloning, a male child was born." For those who had not yet figured it out, this revelation provided the missing link; for those who had guessed earlier, it was undeniable confirmation. Christopher Goodman was the clone of Jesus Christ.

It was an incredible story, but nothing else could explain Christopher's resurrection only hours before or what they had just witnessed on the Temple steps. "That child was named Christopher," Decker said, adding further confirmation. "He was raised by Professor Harry Goodman and his wife Martha until their untimely deaths in the Disaster. At that time," Decker went on, "Christopher Goodman was fourteen years old and, having been directed by Professor Goodman to turn to me in the case of emergency, Christopher came to live with me. The rest of the story, at least the important parts, you know."

The inflection in Decker's voice let it be known that his prepared statement had drawn to a close, and as he folded the paper to return it to his pocket he was surprised that no one seemed to have any questions. He needn't have been, for the reporters had plenty; they were all still processing what they had been told.

Looking around at their blank stares, Decker should have realized the problem, but instead started to excuse himself. His movement was just enough stirring of the waters for the dam to break. Someone in the back started to shout a question and then a flurry of queries were suddenly hurled at him. No particular arrangements had been made, so Decker simply answered first the question that had been yelled the loudest.

Yes, Christopher had really been dead.

Yes, he was indeed saying that Christopher was the clone of Jesus Christ.

Yes, he *was* saying that Christopher was God's son, just as Jesus was. (This did not set well with the Jewish reporters in the group, but it was not a point that was currently open to argument.) No one had any reason to suspect or ask for the specific details of that relationship—which Christopher had revealed to Decker on the plane—and Decker had no intention of volunteering them. Christopher would explain all of that soon enough.

"What about his arm and eye?" a reporter called.

"Though Christopher has the power to restore his arm and sight," Decker answered, "he has pledged not to do so until his mission is complete."

"What is that mission? Why has Ambassador Goodman come to the Temple?" someone yelled. Most of the rest of the reporters fell silent, also wanting to know the answer to that question.

Decker thought for a moment. "There are a number of reasons, actually," he said. "The first and most important reason was to end the reign of terror of the two men, John and Saul Cohen. That, as you have all just witnessed, he has done. Also, he came to the Temple because, I suppose, it is the most appropriate place for the announcement that he intends to make."

"What announcement is that?" someone yelled, while someone else called, "Can you tell us what Ambassador Goodman intends to say?"

"He will be addressing the people of the world on the subject of the destiny of Humankind."

❑

Christopher and Milner climbed three more short flights of stairs through the Beautiful Gate and entered the Court of the Women. Only hours before, this court had been the center of activity in the Temple. Now it was silent except for the hollow echo of footfalls on the stone floor as Christopher and Milner walked without speaking toward the broad semicircular steps at the western end of the court. At the top of these steps, the magnificent Nicanor Gate, sixty feet wide and seventy-five feet high, extended far above the walls themselves, forming an arch, and opened into the Court of Israel.

Only Jewish men and boys were allowed to enter this part of the Inner Court. Unlike the Court of the Women, which was square and open to the sky, the Court of Israel was narrow and roofed, encircling the innermost court, and crowded with numerous columns. A series of rooms used for storage and small meetings lined the walls of the Court of Israel, further reducing the open space.

The third and final court, the Court of the Priests, rose four feet above the Court of Israel. Though adjoining and fully open to the Court of Israel, admittance to this court was permitted only to laymen bringing a sacrifice. At all other times only the priests and Levites could enter. In the gateway to the Court of the Priests were four tables of hewn stone, on which lay the blood-drained carcasses of a half-dozen lambs and goats, abandoned there when the priests and Levites were driven from the Temple. The smell of blood, incense, and charred animal fat still hung heavy in the air. To the north and south of the gateway stood eight more tables in a similar state.

In the center of the easternmost part of the Court of the Priests, the Altar of Sacrifice rose twenty feet in stair-stepped pyramid form in a series of four immense, unfinished stones, which by commandment had never been touched by metal tools.[1] Steps on the eastern edge of the altar provided access to the upper stones. The capstone, which was called *Ariel* by the priests and Levites, was twenty-one feet square and, like the stone immediately below it, was seven feet thick. On this stone was the fire of sacrifice, which consumed the burnt offerings. Unattended by the priests, the fire had been reduced to embers.

From the four corners of the altar's capstone, horn-like projections, each twenty-one inches long, reached skyward. On these horns and upon the altar itself, the priests would pour out the blood of the recently slaughtered animals as a sacrificial offering. Around the base of the altar was a gutter, twenty-one inches wide and twenty-one inches deep, with a containing rim of nine inches and a total capacity of more than three thousand gallons to accommodate the huge amounts of blood that were poured upon the altar during the busier days. The

[1] Exodus 20:25.

priests and Levites had been driven from the Temple only a little more than an hour into their day and so only a few inches of blood now settled in the altar's gutter, coagulating and drawing flies.

Directly behind the altar, in the westernmost portion of the Court of the Priests, stood the Sanctuary. This was Christopher's ultimate goal, but there was a mission he and Milner needed to accomplish before continuing. Quickly he found what he was looking for and nodded his intention to Milner. "We must see to it that no more animals are slaughtered here to satisfy Yahweh's blood thirst. We must desecrate the altar so that it cannot be used again."

Followed closely by Milner, Christopher went to where he had spotted a number of brass shovels used by the priests for removing ashes. They each picked up one of the shovels and went to a spot near the slaughter tables where a hill of animal dung had been collected for later removal. As best he could with the use of only one arm, Christopher scooped up a shovel full and then walked over and slung it against the sides of the altar. Again and again Christopher and Milner repeated the act until there was no dung left and the altar had been liberally splattered. Next they beat the brass shovels against each of the altar's four stones.

"That should do it," Christopher said finally, knowing that Jewish law would forbid ever again using these desecrated stones as an altar.

After finishing their chore, Christopher and Milner proceeded on to the Sanctuary. From above, the shape of the Temple proper formed a huge T—the result of the compromise between those who wanted to rebuild the

Temple according to the plans of the prophet Ezekiel and those who wanted to recreate the design of Herod's Temple. It was 175 feet across at the widest point, 105 feet at the narrowest, and stood 175 feet above the Court of the Priests. To the right and left of the entrance stood two tremendous free-standing bronze pillars, called by the priests respectively Jachin and Boaz.

Here Milner stopped. The rest of the way, Christopher would go alone.

Looking back only to nod to Milner, Christopher ascended the final set of steps to the Vestibule, or Porch. Directly in front of him were immense double doors six feet wide and thirty-five feet tall made of olive wood, decorated with carvings of cherubim, palm trees, and flowers and covered entirely in pure gold. Suspended above the doors, a spectacular multicolored tapestry displayed a panorama of the universe. And above that, the full width of the wall was covered with huge carvings of grape vines and leaves with clusters of grapes as tall as a man and nearly that distance across, entirely covered with gold.

Christopher took a deep breath and continued. Pushing open one of the huge doors and then the other, he let in the bright light of day and stepped through into the next chamber, called the *Hēkhāl,* or Holy Place. The ceiling of the Holy Place dropped 40 feet from the ceiling of the Porch to a height of 105 feet. The floor was covered with cypress wood. The walls were wainscoted with cedar, above which they were covered with gold. A golden altar for incense still smoldered, releasing the fragrant smell of frankincense. Another altar for shewbread (holy bread) sat undisturbed with twelve sheets of unleavened bread laid out in rows. The candles of a golden menorah, though nearly consumed by the flame, provided the only interior light.

❑

Still outside the Sanctuary, Robert Milner turned and walked back the way they had come in. There was a matter outside the Temple that awaited his attention.

❑

In front of Christopher, suspended from the ceiling at the western end of the Holy Place was the Veil, a divider between the Holy Place and the final chamber, the *Dᵉbhīr,* or Holy of Holies. Beyond the Veil, where only the high priest was allowed to go—and he, only once a year on the Day of Atonement—sat the ancient Ark of the Covenant. The Veil was actually two richly decorated curtains, which hung parallel to each other with about five feet of clearance between the two, forming an entry corridor that prevented any light from reaching the windowless Holy of Holies.

Walking to the northern edge of the curtain nearest the Holy Place, Christopher took hold and pulled sharply until, bit by bit, it broke loose from the ceiling. He continued this until only a few yards of the curtain remained hanging. He then did the same with the other curtain, pulling it loose from the southern edge, thus leaving a wide entrance through the middle of the Veil and exposing the Holy of Holies to the light of day, which poured in through the Sanctuary's huge doors.

Before him in the Holy of Holies two enormous winged cherubim, each eighteen feet tall, carved from olive wood and covered with pure gold, stood watch over the Ark of the Covenant. Their outstretched wings each spanned half the width of the chamber and met in the center of the room directly over the Ark.

Christopher entered the Holy of Holies and approached the Ark.

❑

Outside, as Decker took another question from the press, a low rumbling began that shook the steps where he and the others stood. It seemed to come from inside the Temple. Without explanation, Decker calmly announced that he would take no more questions and that the press conference was concluded. "I suggest that you may want to move to the bottom of the steps and away from the Temple at this point," he added in obvious understatement. Decker was beginning to enjoy himself.

❑

Inside the Holy of Holies, Christopher stood before the Ark and after a moment's pause, gripped the Ark's cover and slid it back, revealing its contents.

❑

"What's happening?" several of the reporters shouted at Decker as the Temple shook again.

"Ladies and Gentlemen, if you'll be patient, I'm sure

you'll have answers to all of your questions, but for your own safety, I must insist that you move away from the Temple immediately." The resolve in Decker's voice and the urgency of his steps convinced the others to follow.

❑

Reaching into the Ark, Christopher found the items he was looking for.

❑

A thunderous rumble many times louder than the first two rolled through the Temple like a freight train, sending reporters and onlookers running. A moment later Robert Milner emerged. He was alone. Resolutely, he descended about a quarter of the way down the steps. Looking out over the thousands of people and the dozens of cameras that broadcast the event around the world, he began to speak. It was his own voice, but it was different; at least Decker could tell there was a difference.

"'See, I will send you the prophet Elijah before that great and dreadful day of the Lord comes. He will turn the hearts of the fathers to their children, and the hearts of the children to their fathers; or else I will come and strike the land with a curse,'" Milner said, quoting the prophet Malachi.[2] The words were familiar to many but especially to the priests and Levites. "Hear, O Israel," Milner said, no longer quoting, "for this day, this very hour, your

---

[2] Malachi 4:5–6.

lamentation is ended. This is the day of which the prophet spoke. Elijah has come! I am he!"

There was a great stirring from the Jewish priests and Levites at this proclamation and all eyes turned to see how the high priest would respond. It was bad enough that they had been run out of their own Temple, but now for this Gentile to claim that he was the prophet Elijah, while it wasn't exactly blasphemy, it was a tremendous offense. No one was quite sure how to respond and they looked to Chaim Levin, the high priest, to follow his lead. Had they even an inkling that at that very moment Christopher stood within the Holy of Holies before the Ark of the Covenant, they would not have waited for the high priest, but already would have been tearing their clothes and dumping dust on their heads in Jewish ceremonial outrage.

Surprisingly, Chaim Levin was very calm. Dressed in the traditional Temple raiment of his office, the high priest wore a bulbous blue hat with a band of solid gold engraved with the Hebrew words ליהוה קדש, meaning "Holy to Yahweh." Over the standard white linen tunic of the ordinary priest, which hung down to his ankles, revealing only his bare feet, he wore a richly embroidered robe that reached below his knees and was decorated at the bottom by golden bells that jingled musically as he walked. Over this, he wore a vest-like garment that hung to his hips and was lavishly embroidered with thick threads of gold, purple, blue, and crimson. In the middle of his chest, supported by heavy chains of gold attached to broad epaulets upon his shoulders and around his waist by scarlet strips of cloth, was the ephod, a thick square linen breastplate decorated with gold brocade and inset with twelve large gemstones in four rows of three each, representing the twelve tribes of Israel.

Whether Chaim Levin's tolerance of Milner was borne of gratitude for Christopher's dispatch of John and Cohen or because he simply did not want to ruin a perfectly good set of robes, he remained unruffled by Milner's claim. Instead, he looked him in the eye and very politely but with skeptical amusement asked, "By what sign shall we know that you are who you claim?"

"By that same sign by which I, Elijah, proved myself to King Ahab and to the people of Israel on Mount Carmel,"[3] Milner answered, loud enough for everyone to hear.

Chaim Levin raised an eyebrow and frowned a bit. The boldness of Milner's claim impressed him, though he did not for a minute think that Milner could carry it out. "And when shall we see this sign?" he asked after a moment.

"This very hour," answered Milner. Then, turning away from Levin and toward the crowd, Milner continued. "For 1,260 days Israel has suffered drought. Today it ends!" With that, Milner's hands shot skyward and from somewhere beyond the Temple a low rumbling was heard, which in just seconds grew in intensity to an earth-shaking peal of thunder. Faster than anyone could imagine possible, the sky grew dark, as out of nowhere heavy gray clouds began to fill the heavens. In fear, the crowds and all but a few of the priests nearest the high priest drew back. No sooner had an area of a few hundred square feet been cleared than a bolt of lightning struck the

[3] 1 Kings 18:19–40.

earth and a deafening crack of thunder sent people running, clasping their hands over their ears. In the larger clearing that resulted from the evacuation, the first bolt of lightning was quickly followed by three more, each more powerful than the previous one. And then it began to rain.

It came down in a torrent, pouring down upon Milner, the high priest, and everyone else except a very few who had made it to cover. Most stood there looking up with their hands upraised, thankful for the rain. Some began to dance.

For the crowd, who knew the biblical story of Elijah, the verdict was clear: This truly must be the prophet. What other explanation could there be? Although the high priest was unconvinced, he could offer no more believable explanation and so he remained silent, staring at Milner as the rain turned his impeccably elegant attire to dripping disarray. Soon many of the priests and Levites joined in with the crowds, proclaiming Milner as the promised Elijah who, according to the prophecy, would come before the Messiah.[4]

It came as no surprise, therefore, when after a few minutes of drenching rain, Milner announced, "Behold your Messiah!"

With rain still pouring down, Milner turned and seemed to be pointing with his outstretched hand toward the Temple, but no one could see exactly what he expected them to find. Then above the southeastern corner, a break appeared in the clouds, allowing a single brilliant shaft of sunlight to shine through. "There he is!" someone shouted.

[4] Malachi 4:5–6; Matthew 17:10–13.

At the top of the wall, on the very edge of the south-eastern corner of the Temple, 180 feet above them, at a point which by tradition is called the pinnacle, stood Christopher, robes blowing in the wind and completely dry as the shaft of light shone down like a spotlight. Quickly the beam broadened, as from that point the clouds retreated in all directions, bringing rain to the parched countryside around Jerusalem. In just moments the area around the Temple was in full daylight again with the sun shining brightly overhead.

By now nearly every network in the world was carrying the events in Jerusalem live. Every camera was on him, broadcasting his words and image to the most distant corners of the planet.

"People of earth," Christopher began slowly with a serene, peaceful tone calculated to restore calm. "For millennia the prophets and soothsayers, the astrologers and oracles, the shamans and the revelators have all foretold the coming of one who would bring with him the olive branch of peace for all the world. By a hundred different names the world has known him. And by a hundred different names this promised peace bringer has been petitioned to come quickly to those in distress. For the Jews, he is Messiah; for the Christians, the returning Christ; for the Buddhists he is the Fifth Buddha; for the Muslims, the Thirteenth Heir to Mohammed or Immam Mahdi. The Hindus call him Krishna; the Eckankar call him Mahanta. The Bahá'í look to the coming Most Great Peace. To the Zorastrians he is Shah-Bahram; to others he is Lord Maitreya, or Bodhisattva, or Krishnamurti, or Mithras, or Deva, or Hermes and Cush, or Janus, or Osiris.

"By whatever name he is known," Christopher declared, "in whatever tongue he is entreated, this day I say to you: The prophecies have been fulfilled! This day the promise has been kept! This day the vision has been realized for all Humankind!" Christopher paused as the anticipation rose.

"For on this day I have come!" he shouted triumphantly, surprising no one—for the conclusion was obvious—and yet astonishing all, for no one could have been truly prepared for such a declaration.

Christopher's voice quickly picked up speed and fervor. "I am the promised one!" he chanted. "I am the Messiah, the Christ, the Fifth Buddha, the Thirteenth Heir to Mohammed; I am the one who brings the Most Great Peace; I am Krishna, Shah-Bahram, Mahanta, Lord Maitreya, Bodhisattva, Krishnamurti, and Immam Mahdi; I am Mithras, Deva, Hermes and Cush, Janus, and Osiris! There is no difference. They are all one. All religions are one. And I am he of whom all the prophets spoke! This is the day of the earth's salvation!"

To the displeasure of the high priest, many in the assembly in Jerusalem roared their approval and the response was echoed around the world. They had all seen Christopher die at the hands of an assassin, and they had seen his resurrection. They had witnessed him powerfully dispatching John and Cohen, who had called down terrible plagues upon the earth. They had watched in amazement as Robert Milner called down lightning and brought rain to the drought-stricken holy land. But more than anything else they cheered because they were *ready* for a savior.

"I have not come to make pious religious pronouncements," Christopher said. "Nor have I come to demand your worship or insist that you pay me homage. I do not seek your praise and adoration or demand your devotion. It is not my intent that you venerate or adulate me or that you pay me your tribute. Nor do I wish you to glorify, deify, idolize, extol, exalt, or revere me.

"I have come instead to tell you to look to yourselves. For within each of you is all the deity, all the divinity, that you will ever need. You may call me a god, and I do not deny it: I am a god! But I call *you* gods. All of you! Each of you!"

High Priest Chaim Levin had heard all that he needed to. This was obvious blasphemy and, new robes or not, he was obligated to tear his garments and throw dust upon his head. And so he began with a vengeance, though he had to settle for mud. Some of the other priests and Levites near him immediately followed his lead. But others, many others, were far too interested in what this man who had risen from the dead had to say.

"It is not my own godhood that I have come here to proclaim," Christopher continued. "It is yours!

"I have not come to threaten or punish," he said reassuringly, undistracted by the actions of the high priest so far below him. "I have come to offer to Humankind life everlasting and joy unimagined. I bring you the opportunity to build a tomorrow of abundance and life from a yesterday of hunger and death. Come with me. Follow me. And I will lead you into a millennium of life and of light."

The high priest's overdramatic rending of cloth and hurling of mud distracted Decker from Christopher's speech just long enough for him to notice that despite the distance between Christopher and the street, he could hear him clearly. Christopher's voice seemed to be coming from right next to him or, perhaps . . . even from inside of him. It was as though he was hearing Christopher's voice from within himself. This discovery was quickly followed by another, even more startling: Decker suddenly realized that Christopher was not speaking English; nor had he since he began to speak. Decker was not sure what language it was, but he was certain he had never heard it before; yet he clearly understood every word. Apparently, so did those all around him, and as Decker correctly assumed, so did every other person on earth, no matter what their native tongue.

He wondered if others had noticed that the language Christopher spoke was not their own. Under his breath, Decker tried to recall and repeat a few of the words, but discovered that though he understood everything Christopher said, he could not for the life of him duplicate a single word or even a syllable. Later Christopher would explain that he had been speaking in the root language of all human languages, one that was as universal and instinctive to humans as animal sounds are to the given type of animal. It was, as Christopher would explain later, the language spoken by all humans prior to the confusion of language, which Yahweh used to scatter the people of the earth when they built the Tower of Babel.[5] This language did not need translation. It *was* the translation.

"Three and a half days ago," Christopher continued, "before the eyes of the whole world, a follower of John and Cohen and the Koum Damah Patar fired a bullet into my brain and killed me. Less than twelve hours ago,

[5] Genesis 11:1–9.

again with the entire planet as witness, I was resurrected from the dead!

"But my resurrection is not a symbol of *my* victory over death. It is, rather, a symbol of *Humankind's* victory of life. My resurrection, my release from the chains of death, occurred because the time has at last come for Humankind to break the chains that have bound it and to claim the glorious future that awaits.

"Let there be no mistake: The afflictions that have befallen the earth over these past three and a half years have not been accidental or the result of natural disasters. They have been cold, calculated acts of supernatural oppression, enacted through the men John and Cohen, against all Humankind. But John and Cohen did not act alone. They were, in fact, merely the conduit for an oppressive, evil force—a spiritual entity whose savage, barbaric, selfish goal has been and continues to be to prevent the human race from fulfilling its destiny and attaining its proper place in the universe.

"The power that directed my assassination and the entity that has brought the world to the brink of annihilation are one and the same. But my resurrection is proof that this entity *can* be defeated, that the earth can be restored, and that Humankind is ready to throw off the yoke of bondage and to take the ultimate evolutionary step toward spiritual completion.

"I have returned to lead the world out of this age of destruction and death and into a new and transcendent age where suffering and death are no longer a fact of life, an age borne out of the trials that the earth has suffered, and into a time of individual harmony with the universe. You, the ones who have outlasted the disasters, the floods, the earthquakes, you are the survivors and you shall be the victors!

"The human race has tasted the worst of this evil entity's spiritual oppression and has stood defiant. It is the power of this defiance that has restored my life. It is the power of this defiance that has weakened the enemy. It is this defiance and Humankind's self-reliance that have ushered in the New Age.

"Let there be no doubt: The New Age is not about replacing one religion with another. Quite the opposite. This is *not* about reliance upon or faith in some distant, isolated god. This is about Humankind coming to rely upon itself, upon the power and god that is within each of us. This is *not* about a limited few self-righteous, self-serving oppressors bent on self-aggrandizement. This is about individuals taking control of their own lives, their own environment, and their own destinies.

"For two thousand years calendars have been based upon the birth of the Christian messiah. My resurrection from the dead has marked the commencement of the New Age. The estimated date of Jesus' birth is now irrelevant and the calendars of the Christian era have been relegated to history. A New Age has begun. Therefore, let the calendars of the world mark the day of my resurrection as the first day of the first year of the New Age." Christopher raised his right hand and shook his head as he offered an explanation for his directive. "It is not that I wish you to mark the date of my resurrection for *my* sake," he explained. "Rather, it is to mark the beginning of your own liberation from the hands of the one who has tried to crush your spirit and to destroy your soul.

"Let this date also mark the end of claims to exclusive

truth that are held by backward religions such as that practiced by the KDP. To the members of the Koum Damah Patar, I extend my hand in peace. John and Cohen are dead, their self-righteous claims lay barren and lifeless with their bodies. I appeal to you to abandon your offensive ways; abandon your sanctimonious claims to exclusive truth and join us. We must purge ourselves and our world of such intolerant philosophies and religions. From this day forward, the religion of Humankind shall be Humankind!

"Let no one boast that their way to god is better, for it is not a god we should seek at all. It is the power that lies within us. Let us no longer excuse ourselves as being '*only* human.' *Human* is all we *need* to be!

"It is in our humanity that divinity resides. Humanity stands poised on the brink of the final great evolutionary stride. But it is not through physical evolution that divinity and immortality will be achieved. It is through spiritual evolution. For some, this evolution will take only a few decades. For others, it may take much longer. But even if it takes a thousand years it will have been time well spent." Christopher paused to allow that thought to sink in. He wanted his audience to fully understand what he was saying. "Do not wonder," he continued, "that I say that it may take a thousand years. It will not matter if it takes ten years or two hundred years or even a thousand years! Immortality is yours to take! Through the same power by which the man John lived more than two millennia, the same power by which I was raised from the dead, the same power by which we shall overcome the evil entity that opposes us, you shall live! To those who follow me, I will give the power to live for a thousand years! After that, you shall take your rightful place as evolved beings and shall never die!

"Again I extend the hand of peace to the Koum Damah Patar. Turn from your error and follow me and you shall be the vanguard of the evolutionary process. You, who have already begun to experience the evolutionary metamorphosis, as evidenced by your advanced extrasensory abilities, do not use your powers for oppression. Use them instead to look inside yourself. Turn from serving the evil entity who claims to be God and instead serve Humankind. Cease your worship of the one who seeks to destroy the world and instead glorify Humankind, and together we shall restore the world.

"Worthy are they who work for the advancement of Humankind, for the universe shall be theirs. Worthy are they who have learned first to love themselves, for they shall be as gods. Worthy are they who do not deny themselves the desires of their hearts, for they have understood that to do so is to deny themselves. Worthy are they who draw their strength and hope from within themselves, for they shall be strengthened. Worthy are they whose spirit is strong and defiant, for they shall be first in the kingdom of the universe. Worthy are they who forbid intolerance and crush that which restricts growth, for they will be called beacons of truth and guideposts to fulfillment.

"Hear me and believe! Honor truth and growth with your allegiance!

"Yet a third time to the Koum Damah Patar, I offer the open arms of brotherhood. Understand, however, that there is no place for you in the New Age if you continue your onerous ways. Unto whom much is given, much shall be expected. If you, who are the first to exercise the power of the New Age and who have tasted the sweet flavor and experienced the awesome potential that already grows within you, if you do not turn from your ways of persecution and intolerance, then you shall be the first to fall and feel the wrath of a planet that has grown beyond its willingness to submit. Those who seek to empower themselves by making Humankind slaves to their god have enslaved themselves already by their own choosing.

"Were they satisfied with enslaving only themselves it would be little threat to Humankind and might therefore be tolerated for a time. But that is not in their nature. Instead, their desire is to impose that slavery upon others. They are weak and primitive; they are totally alien to the present reality and do not belong to this millennium, much less to the New Age. They have no understanding of the present planetary situation. Their weakness must not be allowed to sap and corrupt the strength of those who are ready to proceed to the future. Under the leadership of John and Cohen, they have tried to do so by calling down every kind of disaster they could imagine. They have brutally and without sympathy brought about the deaths of untold millions of innocent people and they have caused unspeakable misery and suffering for those of us who survive. Yet still they have failed to break the human spirit! The human will stands unshaken before the ill winds of theistic persecution. We are defiant! We shall not bend the knee to any tyrant!"

Turning his attention from the KDP and again to his broader audience, Christopher declared, "It is not in your nature to be a servant to anyone!"

Because of the distance between the crowds and Christopher at the top of the pinnacle, and because of the way the wind blew his robes, no one had noticed the two objects at Christopher's feet. They were more evident to those who watched by television, but no one had really given them much thought during his electrifying address. Certainly, no one suspected that the items had been taken from the Ark of the Covenant.

"I have told you of an evil tyrant," Christopher continued, "a spiritual entity who has held the world in chains. For many who are listening and watching it will come as no surprise that the one of whom I speak—the one for whom John, Cohen, and the Koum Damah Patar have inflicted such ruin—is the same one who has demanded that his people offer him the blood of innocent animals as tribute."

Christopher paused to pick up the articles at his feet and raised them above his head. It was still not clear to the audience in Jerusalem, but it was now obvious on television that he held two stone tablets. On the tablets a strange script could clearly be seen as the cameras zoomed in. Christopher was holding the Ten Commandments. A sudden gasp swept through the multitude in Jerusalem.

"No longer," Christopher shouted, his voice now showing his full fury, "no longer shall the senseless dictates of spiritual tyrants have dominion over this planet!" With that declaration, Christopher hurled the two ancient tablets to the street, 180 feet below, where they shattered into pieces so small they could not be distinguished from the tiny bits of gravel. The mostly Jewish audience, which to this point had been largely favorable to Christopher, now stood stunned and motionless in shock. Christopher had just taken a national religious treasure and transformed it to dust. His address had been stirring, but no one expected it to result in this.

Christopher continued, aware that he must quickly re-capture the people's attention if he was going to win their support. "The things I have promised are real and they are within humanity's grasp. I say this from experience!

"Earth is not alone in the universe," Christopher explained. "Just as scientists have long suspected, there are thousands of other planets in the universe where life exists. One of those planets, an ancient and beautiful world circling a star beyond the Pleiades, is known as Theata. Life there evolved long before it did on earth. The people of Theata had already advanced to the beginnings of their space age four billion years before the first one-celled animals appeared on the earth. It is a planet where hunger and fear no longer exist, where death is unknown, where people have taken the final step of evolution and become one in spirit and flesh, a planet whose inhabitants have fully become the god that is within them! It is from this distant, highly advanced planet that life on earth came. The people of Theata are the parent race of human life here. I have come that all that is theirs may be yours!"

Christopher's account of the origin of human life on earth was interesting, but hardly sufficient to cause the people in Jerusalem to ignore what he had just done with the stone tablets brought down by Moses from Mount Sinai. Christopher sensed their unease and realized it was time to give the world a demonstration of his abilities.

"The future I offer you is a future of power," he proclaimed. "Including the power to control nature, as Robert Milner, who is Elijah, has shown you. But power, like the final steps of evolution, cannot be given. For it to be truly yours, it must be taken. Take and it will be given to you! I have ended the reign of terror brought on by John and Cohen; I have ended the plague of madness which threatened the whole earth; and now I shall begin the restoration of the earth!"

Christopher stretched out his right arm with his palm down. For a long moment there was no sound, and the throng began to murmur. Chaim Levin, the high priest, robes torn and covered with mud, saw his opportunity and began to try to draw their attention. But before he could speak, a stirring at the edges of the gathering distracted the attention of everyone.

From the recently rain-soaked ground along the road and around the buildings, anywhere with soil, there was a visible motion as, before the eyes of everyone, grass and flowers began to grow where before there had been none. As if watching time-lapse photography, the people witnessed in awe the earth release plant life of beautiful greens, reds, yellows, and purples. Flowering bushes sprouted from the barren ground and suddenly the air filled with the fragrance of spring.

But the miracle was not only in Jerusalem. Christopher remained silent and motionless for nearly five minutes as throughout the world plant life began to spring up and grow. Many of the smaller plants grew to full maturity in just moments, and in the fire-blackened areas, young trees grew to heights of six, eight, and ten feet. Finally Christopher dropped his arm and the amazing growth slowed again to normal speeds.

"I have come that power such as this may be yours," he shouted. There was evidence of exhaustion in his voice, suggesting that the proof of his powers had not come without a good deal of effort.

"As I have said," Christopher noted, making his point again, "I do not ask for or seek your worship. I ask instead for your allegiance." There was no hesitation now as the vast majority of the assembly, along with those around the world, clapped or cheered or shouted out his name.

Again Christopher raised his right hand, but this time it was to quiet the crowd.

"Some may ask," Christopher continued, "what of the billions who have died in Yahweh's disasters?" He paused to allow the thought to register with his listeners. He knew that while only a few might have that question in mind in the context of his speech, for many it undoubtedly would come to mind soon after. It was better to deal with it now instead of waiting for it to be asked.

Shaking his head sympathetically, he said, "It is not possible to restore their lives. But those of you who mourn the deaths of friends and family need not grieve. Instead, rejoice in the knowledge that they are not truly dead. They will feel the earth beneath their feet again, for gods cannot truly die. As Jesus told Nicodemus two thousand years ago, 'You must be born again.'[6] So it is for those who have died. Whether it is called reincarnation or being 'born again' or by some other name, the truth is that some who died over the past three and a half years have already been born again; though thankfully, few will remember their former lives. Nonetheless, as the Hindus and Buddhists teach, the suffering they underwent in their

[6] John 3:7.

previous lives serves as a stepping stone to higher, brighter futures. So do not weep or mourn. Dry your tears and rejoice that when they return, they will be born into the age to which Humankind has always aspired: the New Age, the Age of Ascension for all Humankind.

"People of the earth, people of Jerusalem, the time has come to put aside those things that separate us. The *destiny* of all Humankind awaits the *unity* of all Humankind. No longer let us consider such differences as skin color, gender, language, or place of birth. No longer let there be division between races or nationalities. And no longer let there be Gentile or Jew. All of these distinctions are now null and void," Christopher said. "All people are the chosen people!

"As such, let this building no longer be a temple to Yahweh, but a monument to the godhood of man. No more shall innocent animals be led here for brutal slaughter to a bloodthirsty god. From this day forward the killing must cease and the Temple shall be open to all!"

Toward the front of the assembly, Decker Hawthorne braced himself for what he knew was about to come.

"If any still doubt," Christopher said, preparing to conclude his oration, "I offer a final proof that I am who I say. Four billion years ago, it took twenty-three hundred years, traveling at nearly the speed of light, for the crude space vessels sent out by the people of Theata to reach the earth. Now that they have evolved to spirit form, that distance can be traveled in less than a second!

"All that is Theata's is yours for the taking. At this very moment there are millions of our brothers all around us. They have come to lead, to guide each person of earth in the way they must go to enter into oneness with the universe.

"Can you see them?" Christopher cried. "Can you see them?" Christopher raised his right hand in the air, held his head back majestically and shouted, "Behold the hosts of heaven!"

Suddenly the sky was filled with thousands or hundreds of thousands of beautiful lights, some hundreds of meters across, some as small as the head of a pin, some moving slowly, some darting about at incredible speed.

"Behold the hosts of heaven!" Christopher thundered and then leapt from the pinnacle.

A God Who Thrives on Fear

1

FOR MOST PEOPLE, the future Christopher described in his address from the Temple in Jerusalem was still far too ethereal to grasp. It was clear that he had great power— the whole world had seen his resurrection, his effortless dispatch of John and Cohen, and the amazing growth of plant life that he caused all over the planet. But, while Christopher's revelation of a coming period of dramatic world change and human evolution painted a much needed vision of hope, for most people just staying alive had become a full-time pursuit. It was difficult for them to imagine what tangible changes might actually result from what he said.

In the context of all that had happened—the asteroids, the locusts, Christopher's resurrection, and Milner's miracles—Christopher's account of the Theatans was not so difficult to accept. Most people already believed in extraterrestrial beings. The disclosure that Yahweh and Jesus were native to Theata was more the answer to an ancient riddle than it was a startling revelation. They were further persuaded by the appearance of the lights as they danced and moved about, passing over and around and even through many of the people in the crowd. (Those who experienced a "pass through," as the press called it, described it as exhilarating and energizing and perhaps even tickling a little.) And they had watched in amazement as Christopher suddenly leapt from the pinnacle of the Temple; but instead of falling to certain death, he had been "caught" and then suspended above the crowd by the strange lights, thus exhibiting the ability of the light creatures to take on a solid form and, more significantly, clearly demonstrating Christopher's authority over the strange beings. Later, on the flight back to New York, Christopher explained to Decker that the lights were what in earlier days had been called angels. They were, he noted, capable of taking on any form, including human.

Still, for most people the idea that they themselves would be part of humanity's evolution to some form of powerful spirit beings was more than they could readily accept. Evolution was an easy concept as long as it took place over tens of millions of years, but the idea that they would *personally* be witness to and a part of a great evolutionary leap, though enticing, was far more difficult to adjust to. Psychologists, discussing the subject on television, likened the anxiety and confusion people were experiencing to the emotions of people who had just found out they had won the lottery: They wanted to believe, but nothing this extraordinary had ever happened and they were not sure how to deal with it.

Additional confusion resulted from Christopher's allusion to people living for a thousand years, and he did little to clear this up later in his address—saying only that the path to this extended life "would be revealed soon, but not until the time was right." Decker, too, was unclear about this and later asked Christopher how he would give people thousand-year life-spans. Offering only slightly more clarification, Christopher answered that there would be a period of perhaps a year to allow people to adjust to the new realization of truth and the new paradigm of life, and then they would be given "the communion that gives eternal life."

But while there remained much that the world did not comprehend, what everyone *did* understand was that John and Cohen were dead and that the earth was miraculously being restored. Although the amazing plant growth that Christopher initiated had slowed to near normal when he lowered his hand, the earth's restoration was still obvious: Flowers bloomed, grass grew, leaves opened, and vines stretched forth. Even the most devastated areas of the earth were becoming green and lush again. After all the destruction and death the earth had experienced, most of those who survived were eager to believe in Christopher and all he had promised, even if they did not completely understand it. The world was alive, and once again there was hope.

Around the world great celebrations marked the death of Yahweh's prophets and the restoration of the planet. People sent gifts to each other to mark the end of John and Cohen's reign of terror. In Jerusalem—despite Christopher's warning that the bodies still possessed great residual power and should not be touched for at least four days—a crew of city workers had been dispatched to dispose of the corpses shortly after the crowds left. The results were disastrous. The three workers burst into flames the moment they touched the bodies. The

gruesome scene, captured live by cameramen and reporters, served to punctuate and confirm the earnestness
of all that Christopher had said.

And so the bodies were left where they had fallen,
with cameras poised nearby, should any other unexpected
event occur. In a way, the bodies became a sort of grisly
trophy, not just for Christopher, but for the people of the
earth—for Humankind—who had steadfastly refused to
bow to John and Cohen's teachings. The result was a
countdown until the remains of the two men could finally
be removed and buried. Thus, ironically, for the next
three days the celebration of joy and new life for the earth
and hope for Humankind revolved around the vigil of the
lifeless bodies of the two Jewish prophets that lay in the
streets of Jerusalem.

At the United Nations in New York, Christopher
Goodman officially took the office of secretary-general.
While many, including most of the members of the
Security Council, encouraged him to accept even greater
control over world government, Christopher declined, explaining that his purpose was not to establish a benevolent
planetary dictatorship but rather "to lead Humankind toward a place of complete individual self-governance." Any
other goal, he explained, would be anathema and contrary
to the design of the New Age. "Humankind must ultimately look within itself for the answers, not to me or to
any other savior," he stated emphatically. "In the days to
follow," Christopher vowed, "I will work together with
the Security Council and the rest of the United Nations to
lay the foundation for world recovery and the universal
advancement of the people of the earth toward the promise that lies ahead."

Nevertheless, because of the annihilation of the populations of the Middle East and East Africa, Christopher accepted caretaker authority over those regions while continuing in his role as primary for Europe on the Security Council.

As he promised in his Jerusalem address, one of his first acts as secretary-general was to recommend changing the international calendar to reflect the dawn of the New Age. The recommendation received unanimous backing from the UN, and thus, though the months and days remained the same, the year was officially changed to the first year of the New Age, notated as 1 N.A.; and March 11, Christopher's resurrection day, became New Year's day.

Not everyone welcomed Christopher's rise to power, however, and not all celebrated the death of the prophets. Certainly the members of the Koum Damah Patar and their followers did not, but neither did they mourn for their fallen leaders, nor did they retreat into seclusion. It seemed reasonable to assume that at least a few KDP would have accepted Christopher's offer to join him. His offer of amnesty and acceptance, thrice stated in his Jerusalem address and restated in his inaugural address to the United Nations, was certainly as generous as anyone could have expected. Instead, without exception, the KDP went about their customary activities with a new vengeance, declaring in contrast to Christopher's message of hope and peace, that the world was on the brink of even greater disaster. Of the 144,000 members of the Koum Damah Patar, approximately one-third were now in Israel, while the others continued their proselytizing throughout the rest of the world. In Israel the KDP ceased

their usual preaching and accusing and instead began to
tell the people of Israel to flee into the Jordanian wilderness east of Israel.

March 15, 1 N.A.
Jerusalem

It was the evening of the third day following the deaths of
John and Cohen. A light rain had been falling since before dawn and continued until about four o'clock, leaving
the formerly dry earth moist and alive. The air was filled
with the fresh smell of spring. The Jewish Temple,
though quiet since sunset, had been filled with activity
each day since Christopher's address from the Temple
summit. Attorneys representing High Priest Chaim Levin
had lodged formal protests against Christopher Goodman
with the United Nations, and Levin spewed an unceasing
fount of charges against both Christopher and Robert
Milner. As intended, the desecration of the altar and sanctuary by Milner and Christopher had brought to a halt the
daily animal sacrifices. Even more infuriating to the high
priest was the destruction of the stone tablets on which
the Ten Commandments were written. A massive effort
by a team of priests and Levites was underway to piece
the tablets back together, but there were so many
pieces—some little more than dust—and it appeared
that many of the recognizable pieces had been pocketed
by onlookers. There was little hope of actually completing the task.

The KDP were active as well. In addition to telling the
people to flee Israel, they were telling anyone who would

listen that the name Christopher Goodman, written phonetically in Hebrew (כרסטפר גדמן), has a numeric
value of 666—a number which, according to the book of
Revelation in the New Testament of the Bible, is the value
of the name of the Antichrist.[7]

Near the foot of the Temple steps lay the undisturbed
remains of John and Cohen. The bodies, still charged
with the strange power, lay unaffected by the passage of
time, untouched by insects, and with no sign of decay.
Though nothing had happened since the deaths of the city
sanitation workers three days earlier, a few cameras,
mounted on tripods, still remained trained on the two
bodies. The cameramen, who had the misfortune of being
assigned to what seemed to be the most boring assignment possible, were killing time playing cards while their
cameras continued to record the motionless scene.

Unnoticed by the men, three teenage boys taunted a
younger boy toward the corpses. Slowly moving closer,
one of the elder miscreants produced a stick and dared the
younger boy to use it to poke at the bodies. Quickly the
other two boys joined in, urging the younger onward.

One of the cameramen, who was having a less than
prosperous night of cards, looked up and saw the boys.
"Hey, look at that," he whispered to the other players.

One of the men started to get up to warn the boys to
stay away, but he was stopped by two others. "Let them
be," said one of them as he moved slowly and quietly
from his seat.

"Let them be," echoed the second as he moved with
equal stealth toward the tripod that held his camera.

[7] Revelation 13:18.

The fourth player, whose back was toward the dead prophets, turned to see what was so important as to interrupt him from his three eights. Almost immediately he understood and looked dumbfounded at the cameraman whose warning had been silenced. The latter offered only a shrug as he, too, got up to attend to his camera. Within seconds the cameramen had notified their respective networks of the situation. The boys were not yet close enough for the networks to decide to interrupt normal programming, but that decision would have to be made soon. If they went to live coverage and the boys chose to break off their mischief, the networks would appear foolish and would risk angering their regular program viewers. In a way the networks, like the boys, were playing a game of chicken; for while no one wanted to be too quick to commit to live coverage, neither did they want to be beaten to the story by their competition.

Soon enough the decision was made for them. Ten yards from the bodies, the boys suddenly froze in their steps as one by one they saw what had thus far eluded the cameramen. Following the boys' terrified stare, the cameramen quickly realized the reason for their distress. The bodies of the two men had begun to glow.

Immediately the networks went to live coverage and the boys ran in fear. The glow of the bodies continued to intensify, and soon the light was too bright for the cameramen to look at. One man reached into his jacket pocket to retrieve his sunglasses, but before he could, the light had grown too strong for them to be of any use. There was nothing to do but turn away.

As horrified millions watched on television, it became obvious they had seen this same drama played out just four days before at the United Nations. In mere seconds, the worst fears of the world were realized. There in the middle of the Jerusalem street stood the two prophets, John and Saul Cohen, restored to life.

In the stunned seconds that followed, the people of the world relived the personal suffering they had survived and the terror they had endured for the past three and a half years. When John and Cohen died, it had seemed that the worst was over. But now that they were back, no one dared imagine what savage horrors they and their god might bring with them.

Now unattended by the fleeing cameramen, the cameras, still on their tripods, continued to record the event as the two men dropped to their knees and appeared to be praying. It was an ominous sight. There could be no telling what curse the two were about to rain down upon the earth.

Then, with a voice that sounded like a mighty roll of thunder, and speaking in the same universal language used by Christopher when he addressed the world three days earlier, the sky itself seemed to speak. "Come up here," was the entire message. No sooner had the echo disappeared than those who had heard it began to wonder if it had not been a clap of thunder after all. That doubt quickly evaporated as the two men rose to their feet, and then looking to the stars above them, physically ascended into the night sky. One of the cameramen—perhaps more daring, perhaps more foolhardy than the rest—ran back to turn his camera to follow the prophets' ascent. The other cameramen quickly followed suit, pointing their cameras toward the steadily rising silhouettes.

Trembling from panic, it took a moment for the

cameramen to realize that it was not just their nerves that shook. As the live picture began to shift they soon realized that the earth itself was shaking. The tremors grew more quickly than they could react, throwing the cameras, tripods, and men to the ground.

March 18, 1 n.a.
New York

The meeting was not scheduled to start for another ten minutes, so Decker was in no hurry as he arrived at the auditorium in the UN's Secretariat building. His intent was to simply stroll in and find a place to sit where he wouldn't be noticed. Christopher had asked him to attend and so he would, but despite his closeness to Christopher, Decker had never been entirely comfortable around these people. Apparently the feeling was not mutual, however, for as he entered the room he was greeted with loud and sustained applause. His various positions in life had brought him close to many great men and women, and his position at the United Nations, one might argue, conferred upon him some modest level of greatness. But while occasionally his words had been applauded, he himself had never been accorded that honor—and certainly never for simply walking into a room. Decker nodded politely to acknowledge and thank the assembly.

"Come with me," a familiar voice said from behind him. It was Jackie Hansen, who, either by coincidence or design had been near the door where Decker entered. "Gaia wants you up front with her," she said, referring to

Gaia Love, the director of the Lucius Trust and sponsor of this gathering.

Attendance was high, and it took them several minutes to make their way to the front. Everyone they passed wanted to shake Decker's hand or pat him on the back. One woman in her mid-thirties, an adherent of Wicca—a nature religion aligned with the New Age— was a bit more expressive in her admiration for the man who had raised Christopher from a child. Unnoticed by Decker or Jackie, the woman slipped loose the knot of a cord wrapped around her waist, and when they were a few feet away she dropped the cord and opened wide the long robe she wore, revealing her totally nude and very well-endowed body. In a flash, she ran and wrapped her arms around Decker, swallowing him into the warm silken cocoon of her robe. Things had changed a lot in the world since Decker was young: Most of the old taboos had disappeared, except among a few conservative religious groups. Public nudity, or partial nudity with a few skimpy accessories that hid nothing, was common in most of the world, and it was not unusual to find couples or even groups having sex on the beaches or in the parks. Still, Decker was old-fashioned enough to be a little stunned by the Wiccan woman's attentions.

"Gaia is waiting for Mr. Hawthorne," Jackie said as she tugged Decker loose from the woman. Whether out of respect for Gaia Love or for Jackie's six-foot-two-inch stature, the woman grudgingly released her hold, allowing them to continue.

In this one room was nearly every major leader of the New Age movement. So many were there that it seemed to Decker that Christopher and Milner must have understated the extent to which the world had already been prepared for the arrival of the New Age. There were heads of state, members of the World Court, celebrities from television and movies, sports figures, labor leaders, the entire board of the World Council of Churches, several Roman Catholic and Orthodox bishops and cardinals, some high-profile Protestant ministers, and numerous other religious leaders.

Gaia Love's invitations for the meeting had stated its purpose as "a time of fellowship and celebration for the arrival of the New Age." But beyond the handshakes, greetings, and smiles, as Decker looked around him he saw the shadow of concern. Along his path he caught snippets of conversation about the events in Jerusalem, beginning with the resurrection of John and Cohen and the earthquake that followed. As he reached the front of the room, he even heard Gaia Love saying something about Israel, but he was unable to hear exactly what.

The quake had caused major damage throughout Jerusalem, with about 10 percent of the city utterly destroyed and a death toll of no less than seven thousand. Christopher spoke on television and radio immediately after the quake to assure the world that this was not the beginning of a new reign of terror. "John and Cohen will not return," he stated without reservation. "Their resurrection was intended to incite panic by a god who thrives on fear, but I appeal to you to remain calm. John and Cohen are gone and they will never return! It is those who serve Yahweh who should fear, for they know they are no match for the will of a united Humankind."

Insta-polls after the speech indicated that most believed Christopher. But in an ironic twist that defied logic, thousands of Israelis—many who had lost relatives in the quake—instead of seeing the death and destruction as proof of Yahweh's malevolent nature, actually worshiped him all the more, saying that this was evidence of his power, as though his power itself made him worthy of their worship. Even more absurd, however, was that the Jewish high priest and his followers were actually rejoicing in John and Cohen's resurrection. True, they had hated John and Cohen before their deaths; and true, they *still* hated John and Cohen's followers, the KDP, but a few things had changed. First, following the example of "my enemy's enemy is my friend," the resurrection of John and Cohen was seen as a direct challenge to Christopher's power. There was also the fact that John and Cohen, despite their strange ways and teachings, had, after all, been raised from the dead and apparently called by God into heaven. Additionally, throughout its history Israel had always looked more generously on its dead prophets than its live ones, and while John and Cohen were no longer dead, they were at least gone.

And there was one other factor: For while the proverb may be true that a prophet will not be honored in his own city, that same city will fight to defend even a local brigand if outsiders attack him. So it was that John and Cohen now enjoyed a significantly improved position in the hearts of those who had for years been their strongest opponents.

As Decker shared pleasantries with Gaia Love, the large auditorium fell silent, many previously noisy attendees stopping in mid-sentence. Secretary-General Christopher Goodman had entered the auditorium, followed by Robert Milner. To Decker, the mood in the room suddenly seemed far less like a meeting and much more like a spiritual conclave. It would take him a while to get used to the change in the way people responded to Christopher. The room remained silent as Christopher and Milner made their way to the dais, and then from somewhere in the huge auditorium a single clap was heard. When no one else joined in, the lone clapper quickly stopped, obviously embarrassed by the apparent faux pas. No one was quite sure, but it seemed somehow improper etiquette to applaud a god.

Sensing the tension in the room, Christopher quickly reached the microphone and in response to the lone clapper, dead-panned, "Thank you. It's nice to know I'm among friend." The humor had the desired effect as reflexive laughter broke the ice and resounding applause followed.

Christopher smiled and the large video screen behind him showed the look of appreciation on his face to everyone in the auditorium. "Friends, auspicious assembly, welcome," he began when the room finally quieted again. One of the things Decker had learned in his days as a speechwriter is that the more important a speaker is, the less he has to say to get applause. Now that it had been established that it was appropriate to clap for Christopher, that axiom once again held true.

When the applause for his greeting subsided, Christopher continued. "I have just come from a meeting of the Security Council. The main focus of that meeting was the situation in Israel. As all of you know, since the earthquake, the UN has made several offers to provide Israel with medical assistance and support troops to help restore order and rebuild the city. Each of our offers has been met by curt refusals from the Eckstein government," he said, referring to the Israeli prime minister. All things considered, this seemed to Decker a strange subject to lead off Christopher's address.

"Three things have made these refusals particularly troublesome. The first is the magnitude of the suffering, as we have all seen daily on news reports. The second is that while the Eckstein government fails to deal with the present human crisis, another crisis is looming as members of the Koum Damah Patar recklessly lead thousands of their naïve followers into the barren Jordanian desert. Third, based on Prime Minister Eckstein's own statements, there can be no doubt that his real objections to UN assistance are founded solely on his own stubborn religious prejudices and his loyalty to the ultra-orthodox religious groups within his party.

"Fortunately for the people of Israel, not all members of the Likud are as tied to the religious cords of Israel's high priest as is Mr. Eckstein. We have just learned that a few hours ago the Social Democrat Party under the leadership of Golda Reiner has formed a coalition with six other minority parties, thus forcing an election."

At this news, Gaia Love leaned over to Jackie Hansen and Decker and whispered excitedly, "Golda is a good friend. I'm sure we can count on her."

"In the meantime," Christopher continued, "because of the urgent nature of Israel's situation, Ms. Reiner has taken emergency control of the government and has officially issued a request that the Security Council immediately authorize assistance to Israel. I am pleased to announce that the Security Council has unanimously agreed to provide such aid."

With all the suffering that the world had experienced, it seemed strange to Decker that Christopher's announcement concerning Israel should elicit much interest or excitement, but suddenly the auditorium exploded into cheers and celebration. Obviously the news was far more significant to those gathered than he realized. His only explanation was that by asking for assistance, Israel—the only nation in the world that was not a member of the United Nations[8]—was at last recognizing its dependence on the rest of the world. While this was not the same as rejoining the UN, Decker could only assume that those around him believed that it was the logical next step. Still, the news hardly seemed worthy of mention, much less of such enthusiasm.

Christopher's speech continued for nearly an hour and a half, making it one of his longest ever. Leaving the subject of Israel, Christopher outlined his plans to repopulate the countries whose people had been wiped out by the madness. The UN would assist people who could trace their ancestry to the affected countries to move there and rebuild their society. Christopher acknowledged that it could take centuries to accomplish this goal, but he again pointed out that soon the human lifespan would no longer be limited to a scant few decades. To encourage migration to these countries, the Security Council had voted

[8] Israel resigned its membership in the United Nations after the realignment of the Security Council. See *In His Image, Book One of The Christ Clone Trilogy*, Chapter 17.

unanimously to offer land grants and substantial financial incentives to these immigrants.

"The Security Council has also voted," Christopher revealed, "to support my recommendation to build a major new United Nations headquarters complex at a site in the affected area which, if the General Assembly agrees, will ultimately serve as a replacement to the aging complex here in New York.

"I am particularly excited about this project," Christopher continued, "because of the location that has been selected. In a demonstration of the unyielding strength and defiance of the human spirit, the site for the new United Nations headquarters will be near the place where the madness began—in a place of tremendous historical significance to all Humankind—for it was near this site that the first Theatan ship landed over four billion years ago and life on earth began. It was near this spot, in what legend has called the Garden of Eden, that Humankind first established its independence from the rule of Yahweh and any other would-be god. Later, in this same general vicinity, Humankind first united to work together to build a great city and tower before being dispersed by the despotic Yahweh. And it is from this city that Nebuchadnezzar once ruled the world!" The auditorium filled with cheers, for it seemed that everyone there knew exactly what city Christopher was talking about, and they obviously approved: Babylon, already partially rebuilt by the Iraqi people over the last several decades. But again, the crowd's excitement and approval seemed to Decker to be inexplicably high for what to him was just a matter of real estate.

March 21, 1 N.A.
Jerusalem

"Our mission," said General Parks to the reporters assembled at 6:00 A.M. in the lobby of the King David
Hotel, which served as temporary headquarters of the
United Nations peacekeeping force, "is strictly humani-
tarian in nature. Thanks to the support and cooperation of
Prime Minister Golda Reiner, the arrival and deployment
of UN troops have been entirely successful, and UN
forces throughout Israel now number more than fifty
thousand. Food and medical supplies, which arrived last
night, will begin to be distributed within the hour. Only
one loose end remains.

"Preying upon fear and hysteria, the KDP has incited
many people in Israel, charging that the UN forces who are
here to assist in this time of crisis are actually an invasion
force. They have already led several hundred thousand
Israeli citizens—some estimates range as high as one-sixth
of the Israeli population—into the Jordanian wilderness as
though in some modern-day exodus from Pharaoh. Their
objective appears to be both to flee the supposed invading
forces of the UN and to take advantage of the recent deci-
mation of the Jordanian population to set up illegal settle-
ments deep in that country's territory.

"While I think we'd all like to see the KDP leave
Israel, in order to prevent this incursion into Jordan by
Israeli civilians, we have placed blockades at every road
leaving the country. However, we failed to anticipate the
level of hysteria. Faced with blocked roads, the KDP
and their followers have set out on foot across the desert

into Jordan. Because of the long drought, it was relatively easy for people to cross the shallow Jordan River undetected."

General Parks nodded to an aide who then displayed a satellite photo of the region.

"Those fleeing Israel are organized into seven major contingents with numerous smaller groups scattered up and down the length of Israel's border with Jordan." Parks pointed to an area on the display. "On foot, and left to their own devices," Parks continued, "we estimate that most of these people will not survive more than three to five days in the barren wilderness terrain.

"To prevent this tragedy, as we speak, six battalions of United Nations soldiers have moved to within three kilometers of a location west of the city of Ash-Shawbak, Jordan, where the largest contingent camped last night." Again Parks pointed to the satellite photo. "We have named the campaign Operation Roundup," he said with a self-amused grin. "Our objective is to encircle each of the camps, provide emergency food and water as needed, and then return the people to Israel. Members of the KDP who are captured will be held for questioning and possible criminal charges by the civilian authorities."

General Parks tucked his laser pointer into his shirt pocket. "I have time for three or four questions," he concluded. Several reporters shouted out their questions, but Parks ignored them and pointed to a reporter in the back.

"Do you anticipate resistance from the KDP and, if so, how will you respond?"

"Our reconnaissance indicates no organized defense, and we have found no evidence of weaponry. What we have here is a disorganized collection of frightened and confused civilians," he said authoritatively. "However, should we encounter resistance, our orders are first to defend ourselves and then to use all appropriate force to accomplish our mission."

"Is there any possibility that the KDP possess powers similar to those of John and Cohen?" asked the same reporter in follow-up to her first question.

"There is no record of any member of the KDP displaying any such ability. About the worst they've been able to do," he said with a chuckle, "is embarrass people."

"Did I understand you correctly, that as many as *one-sixth* of the Israeli population has followed the KDP into Jordan?" another reporter asked.

"Well, that's the high end on the estimates. It's probably closer to 10 or 12 percent," the general answered.

"Still, how can there be so many? No previous estimates indicated that the KDP had anywhere near that many followers."

"We believe that only about a third to a half are actually core supporters of the KDP, with the rest consisting primarily of ultra-conservative Jews who are upset about the decision to open the Temple to all races, religions, and nationalities. The remainder are just misguided civilians who believe the KDP's claims that United Nations forces have come here as an invading army."

"Is it true that former Prime Minister Eckstein and High Priest Chaim Levin are among those who have left Israel?" asked another reporter.

"I cannot answer any questions regarding specific individuals," General Parks said, pointing to another reporter.

"Why have you seized the Jewish Temple?" demanded a member of the Jewish press, who was obviously seething.

Parks immediately regretted having selected this particular questioner, but he knew better than to let that show on his face. "The order to secure the Temple," Parks said calmly, not responding to the tone of the questioner, "came directly from Secretary-General Goodman. With the complete cooperation of Prime Minister Reiner and in keeping with the promise he made when he was here nine days ago, the secretary-general has directed that the Temple be secured until order has been restored. Following the restoration of order, the Temple will be reopened to all people regardless of nationality or religion."

Parks ignored the questioner's bellowed follow-up about the unusual method by which Golda Reiner had seized control of the government and why no election had been held, and he quickly pointed to another reporter.

"Has Operation Roundup been approved by the secretary-general?" the next reporter asked.

"Operation Roundup is a tactical measure, not a strategic one. All tactical decisions are my call."

West of Ash-Shawbak, Jordan

As UN forces advanced cautiously in armored personnel carriers (APCs) to within a quarter mile of the Israeli encampment, a swarm of helicopters flew overhead and began to drop leaflets on the camp. The leaflets identified the UN's intent and instructed those in the camp to stay calm and surrender any weapons they might have. The leaflets promised that no one would be hurt as long as there was no resistance. Food and water would be provided for all, buses would be available for the elderly and handicapped, and an escort would lead the rest safely back to Israel.

The advancing APCs stopped, and the soldiers inside disembarked to go the remaining distance on foot. To avoid panic, they had been ordered to leave their rifles in the APCs and had been issued pistols, which they were told to keep holstered unless ordered otherwise.

As the soldiers moved closer, three men from the camp walked quickly toward them, apparently hoping to speak to those in charge. At once the commanding general, Harlan MacCoby, ordered the troops to halt in order to determine the intent of the three men. The soldiers obeyed and General MacCoby's jeep drove through the line toward the Israeli delegation.

Through binoculars the general was quickly able to verify his suspicions about the three men. The markings on their foreheads revealed that they were members of the KDP. The general held out little hope that talking would accomplish anything, but it was incumbent upon him to try.

"Tell your forces to go back and allow us to continue on our journey," one of the KDP stated firmly when the general's jeep stopped in front of them.

"I'm afraid I can't do that," the general responded.

"If even one of your men comes beyond where we now stand," said another of the KDP, "the Lord God will punish the whole of your command."

"We have no intention to harm anyone," General MacCoby countered, "but you must agree to return to Israel."

"Nor do we wish any harm to come to you or your army," one of the KDP responded, "but you must allow us to continue." With no further discussion the three KDP turned and headed back for their camp.

"Do not resist!" General MacCoby yelled after them in warning. He waited a moment for a response but when none came he gave the order for his troops to continue.

Within two minutes the first of the troops reached the point where the encounter with the KDP had occurred. For a moment the general held his breath, but as they crossed the imaginary line the KDP had drawn, nothing happened. Soon they were within a hundred yards of the camp. In front of them more than a hundred members of the KDP waited, forming a wall of flesh between the Israelis and the UN forces. Behind the KDP the entire camp waited anxiously, watching the advance. Then as if on cue—though no word was spoken and no sound made—every member of the KDP fell face down onto the ground and let out a wail to their god. With no more warning than that, as far as the eye could see, the ground beneath the soldiers' feet quivered briefly and became like quicksand, which swallowed the struggling and screaming soldiers and all of their equipment. In just seconds it was over. The ground became solid again, burying alive 7,200 men and women from twenty-seven nations. Not one soldier or piece of military equipment remained.

❑

For the second time in less than a week, Christopher was forced to go before the world to appeal for calm. Despite the fact that General Parks had ordered Operation

Roundup without consulting him, Christopher accepted sole responsibility for what had occurred. General Parks had acted in good faith in what he considered to be a tactical decision over which he had full authority. While it could have been argued that the operation was strategic and not tactical in nature—and therefore General Parks should have consulted his superiors—making such an argument now would not bring the dead back to life. All that Christopher could do, though belatedly, was to issue a directive that no United Nations forces were to engage members of the KDP unless he himself ordered them to do so. He pledged, however, that the day would come when such an order would be given and on that day those who had died would be remembered and justice would be delivered.

Undeterred by what had occurred, in fact encouraged and jubilant, the first large contingent of those who followed the KDP soon reached their destination. As satellite photography revealed, their objective was the ancient Moabite and Nabataean city of Petra in southwestern Jordan.

Decker struggled most of the night to remember why that name sounded familiar. It had been twenty-three years since he had overheard Petra discussed late one night in the Rosens' kitchen.

Signs and Wonders

```
October 2, 1 N.A.
The Albert Hall, London
```

TOMMY EDWARDS WATCHED CLOSELY as the magician lev-itated his hypnotized assistant above the stage. It was Tommy's fifteenth birthday, and he had come to the per-formance with his grandfather, who was himself an ama-teur magician of some note. Tommy had gotten into trouble recently, attempting to apply the sleight-of-hand techniques he had learned from his grandfather to shoplifting. He had seen the levitation trick performed on several occasions, but he was impressed with this magi-cian's technique. Then suddenly, strangely, as if hit by a gust of wind, a strange feeling of power swept over him. With no explanation, as if in a dream, he felt he had the power to do what the magician was doing, but not by some sort of trick. He felt—he knew, there was no doubt in his mind—that he could, by the sheer power of his will, cause the woman to levitate.

Looking toward the floating woman, he squinted slightly to aid his concentration. Then, with the power of his thought, he pulled her from her position above the stage and out over the audience, snapping the trick wires that had held her suspended. The audience at first thought this was part of the magician's illusion and were unaware of what was actually happening. The magician, of course, realized immediately that something was awry. So did his not-so-hypnotized assistant, who grasped wildly but vainly for the wires that she assumed still held her.

October 4, 1 N.A. Burgeo, Newfoundland

Peter Switzer took a deep breath of the salt air and opened the door to the small cottage that had been his home since he was born. His father, like his father before him, had fished these north Atlantic waters for his living, and had been killed in an accident twelve years earlier. His mother died shortly thereafter, leaving the family homestead and its responsibilities to Peter when he was eighteen. He was terribly lonely and would like to have married, but he was painfully shy around women. For ten years he lived alone until one day a lovely girl named Deborah whom he had known in school insisted he go out with her. Within two weeks they were married. It seemed to Peter a dream come true until a year and a half later when Deborah's father died. Her mother, taking advantage of Peter's mild nature, decided to move in with her daughter and son-in-law. Since then, Peter had not had one day of peace from her nagging and complaining. As he feared, she was waiting as if to pounce when he walked in the door.

"Why are you in so early?" she scolded. "There's still an hour of daylight left. What kind of fisherman are you, anyway? It's no wonder you can't provide better for my daughter if you're too lazy to work a full day."

Peter remembered the time before she had moved in with them. Then Deborah had greeted him each evening with a warm hug and a kiss. Now she was nowhere to be seen, intimidated by her mother's presence. On all previous nights Peter had simply tried to ignore his mother-in-law's sharp tongue, but on this night, for no apparent reason, he felt inexplicably determined to face her. Looking her straight in the eye and, surprised at his own nerve as he heard himself speak the words, he told her to shut her mouth and not to speak a word for a week. At this Deborah came into the room, shocked at her husband's raised voice and sure that a serious fight had begun. To her surprise, her mother did not respond. Even more surprised was her mother who, try as she might, could not make even the slightest sound. Deborah looked to her husband for an explanation, but Peter just smiled. He had no answer, but he was delighted with this strange development.

October 6, 1 N·A·
Snow Hill, Maryland

"Okay, now close your eyes and don't open them until I tell you," Dan Highland told his wife, Betty. It was their fifth anniversary and to make it special he had made reservations at a bed and breakfast on Maryland's Eastern

Shore. The only problem was that he was lousy with directions, so Betty waited with her eyes closed for about ten minutes as Dan drove up and down every street in the tiny town looking for the right address. He was just about to ask for Betty's help when he found it.

"Okay, you can open your eyes now," he said as he stopped in front of the old Victorian mansion that had been converted to a bed and breakfast. Betty didn't respond. "I said you can open your eyes now."

"Oh, I'm sorry. I guess I fell asleep," she joked as she pretended to yawn. Then, looking at the old house, her eyes opened wide and it seemed as though she had lost her breath as she stared in apparent disbelief at the house.

"You like it?" Dan asked. But he sensed something far more in her response.

"I've been here before . . . ," she started, and looking around, modified her statement. "I lived here! This was my house!"

This was not at all what Dan had expected. He had known Betty since they were teenagers and as far as he knew she had never even been to Snow Hill, Maryland. Nevertheless, he searched for some reasonable explanation for his wife's claim. "You mean you lived in a house that looked like this?" he asked.

"No! I mean I lived in this house!" she insisted, as she quickly got out of the car and began looking all around.

"But when?" Dan shouted, as he turned off the engine and followed her.

"I don't know, but I did!" Searching her memory she found what seemed proof of her claim. "One street over that way," she said, pointing, "is Washington Street. And two streets over is Collins Street where Uncle Jack and Aunt Olive lived." She was right.

"You must have seen the street names when I drove by them," Dan reasoned.

"But I had my eyes closed," she countered.

Dan didn't want to argue, but there was no other explanation. "Maybe they were opened just a little," he suggested, but Betty didn't reply. Instead she ran up the front steps to the porch and the front door. Without knocking, she went inside, leaving the door open for Dan to follow.

"It's been changed some, the furniture is different and there used to be a door there, but this is it. I'm sure it is!"

"Betty, you can't just run into a house, even if it is a bed and breakfast." But Betty ignored his pleadings. A thought had occurred to her and she intended to pursue it. Turning, she ran from the foyer down a narrow hall with Dan following close behind. Where the hallway widened they were met by a woman in her mid-sixties, dressed in homespun and wearing an apron.

"Hello," she said, wiping her hands on her apron, obviously surprised but not wanting to seem inhospitable.

Betty had already opened a small door off the hallway as Dan answered the woman. "We're the Highlands," he said, unable to offer any other explanation.

"Oh, good, I was *hoping* you were," she said cheerfully as she turned to see Betty Highland descending a rickety flight of stairs. "That's the cellar, dear," she said, and then taking her best guess at the reason for Betty's actions, she added, "the bathroom's right down this hall." But the Highlands were no longer there to hear her. Following them into the cellar, she reached for the light that neither Betty nor Dan had taken the time to locate.

"Betty, what on earth are you doing?" Dan pleaded.

"It's here! I know it is!" she answered as she felt her way along the stones in the foundation wall. And then she stopped. "This is it," she said in a hushed tone. Dan and the woman could only watch and wait as she wiggled the stone back and forth and pulled it from its place. Confidently at first, certain that she was about to be vindicated, she reached in, but did not find what she was looking for. Then in desperation she reached in with both hands, feeling her way over every square inch of the cavity. "It's not here!" she said with great distress.

Dan struggled for something to say but before he could speak, the woman asked haltingly, "What is it you were looking for, dear?"

"The locket," Betty Highland answered, almost crying. "The locket from Augustus."

"I'm very sorry about this," Dan told the woman.

"Augustus?" the woman asked with a strange tone of recognition.

"Yes," Betty answered, no longer holding back her tears, and still just as certain of her fantastic story. "They told me he had been lost at sea . . . ," she sobbed. "We thought he was dead. After a year, Papa insisted that I marry Micah Johnson." None of this made any sense to Dan Highland, who took his wife in his arms to comfort her. But Betty had not finished her story, and she continued to sob. "Just three days after Micah and I married, Augustus returned." Betty Highland looked up at her husband and then to the woman, her expression asking forgiveness for the things she was confessing, her voice filled with equal parts of guilt and desperation. "There was nothing I could do. I had to send him away . . . I was married. I never saw him again." Betty sniffled and wiped her eyes and tried to continue. "A few days later, Augustus' sister, my best friend, Regina, called on me and . . . and gave me the locket. I couldn't part with it, but I couldn't let Micah ever find it. So I hid it behind that loose stone."

"Honey, it's all right. It must have been a dream or maybe an old movie," Dan said consolingly. Betty knew it sounded crazy, but she was sure it was real.

"Come with me, child," the woman told Betty, and then turned and left the cellar. "My husband, Will," she said as Betty and Dan followed her up the narrow steps, "you'll meet him later, he's doing some repair work next door. He and I restored this entire house—spent six years getting it into this condition. We've been over every inch of this house. But it was just last year when he noticed that loose stone down there." The woman led them into the kitchen as she continued. "Will was going to put a little cement in to hold it, but Will—he never does anything halfway—he pulled the stone out to put cement in all around it. That's when he found *this*." The woman reached into a drawer of a period hutch and pulled out a dishcloth, which, when she unwrapped it, revealed an antique gold locket and chain.

"That's it!" Betty exclaimed, as she reached for the locket.

"After we found it, Will never did get around to cementing the stone, so I finally put it back in place."

Betty Highland carefully opened the locket. In it Dan could see the picture of a bearded man in his early twenties. On the other side was an inscription, which he could not help but read out loud: "I shall always love you." And below it was inscribed the name *Augustus*.

October 8, 1 N.A.
Cifuentes, Spain

Mercedes Xavier opened her eyes and immediately sat up. Something was wrong. She had fallen asleep only fifteen minutes before, after being up since three o'clock with her two-month-old son, Rauel. Finally, after nearly seven hours of crying, Rauel had fallen asleep. But now something was wrong. She did not stop to ask herself how she knew. Running as fast as she could to his room, Mercedes found her son, his blanket tangled around his throat and his face turning blue for lack of air.

"Rauel! Rauel!" she cried as she pulled the blanket away.

Rauel Xavier gasped and began to scream. Mercedes had reached him in time.

October 10, 1 N.A.
New Orleans, Louisiana

Brian Olson was having his usual run of luck shooting craps at the Rising Sun Casino, which is to say no luck at all. So far he had lost over two weeks pay in less than two hours. Holding the dice in his nervously perspiring hand and blowing on them for luck, he was about to throw them when the gnawing fear and anger about his misfortunes to this point suddenly left him and a cool rush of confidence swept over him. It was not a logical thing to do, but Brian Olson did very little based on logic. Reaching down to the table he increased his wager, betting everything he had left, $240, on his next roll of the dice.

With more confidence and certainty than he had ever had about anything, Brian closed his eyes and threw the ivory cubes, picturing in his mind a pair of dice with a four and a three showing.

"Seven, a winner," came the voice of the croupier.

"Let it ride," Brian said as he took the dice again. This time he pictured a five and a six.

"Eleven, another winner," came the voice.

"Let it ride," Brian said again, as he pictured a five and a two.

Within ten minutes, Brian Olson had won over $168,000. This, of course, attracted the attention of the casino management, who thanked him for his business and escorted him to the door with his winnings.

October 11, 1 N.A.
Lafayette, Tennessee

Esther Shrum had worked at Citizens Bank for two and a half years, but she had been working at trying to get Jack Colby, the bank's new vice president, to notice her since they were in fourth grade. Over the years she had tried everything, but nothing worked. He was cordial enough, but despite her best efforts he just never seemed to really notice her. Esther's interest in Jack Colby did not, however, go unnoticed by her coworkers, who found her attempts the source of considerable amusement. It was difficult enough for her to deal with her feelings for Jack and his lack of response, but the snickers of her coworkers, which she pretended not to notice, frequently caused her to cry herself to sleep at night.

Every morning Jack would greet those along his path as he walked from the bank's front door to his office, and Esther always managed to be along that path, even though she worked on the other side of the bank. Somehow, though, she felt today would be different. Today he would notice her. The strange confidence she felt was both invigorating and intoxicating. It wasn't the first time she had felt this way, but it had been a long time since . . . Suddenly a feeling of dread swept over her as she remembered the last time.

It was the night of the senior prom, nine years earlier. She knew that even though Jack could have his choice of girls, he hadn't asked anyone. Some other girls cruelly told her that he really wanted to ask her but was too shy. Acting only on this and her strange feeling of confidence, she convinced herself and told her friends that she was going to the prom with Jack. That confidence remained with her, and when the night of the prom arrived and he still hadn't asked her, she put on her prom dress and the corsage she bought for herself, drove to Jack's house, and went up to his door and knocked. When Jack came to the door, he acted as if he didn't even know who she was— a not-too-likely possibility in a town the size of Lafayette. Some unkind people had told her on occasion that she was "plain," and for Jack to act like he didn't even know her was a crushing reinforcement of that assessment.

Nonetheless, she boldly asked him to go to the prom with her. Jack politely thanked her but said he couldn't go because he was watching a ball game on television and, without a second thought, closed the door in her face. It was a week before she recovered enough nerve to go back to school.

The thought of that night caused a crippling pain that was every bit as real now as it had been all those years before as she stood on the front step of his house and heard Jack's mother ask who was at the door. "Oh, nobody," she heard him answer.

Esther looked around and saw that Jack Colby had arrived and was headed for his office, which would take him directly past her. The remembered humiliation was too much and she couldn't face him. Turning to get away, Esther somehow managed to trip over her own feet, dropping two rolls of quarters, which broke open, sending coins rolling everywhere. Flushed with embarrassment, she picked herself up off the floor and proceeded to collect the scattered quarters. Around her she could hear the laughter of her coworkers. She was about to burst into tears, only to find that Jack Colby had stopped to help. She bit her lips to keep from crying and hoped that he would just hand the coins to her, but then their eyes met.

In his eyes was a strange look of surprise; in hers was mortification, but she could not look away. The two of them stayed in this position for several seconds, squatting down a few feet apart, until finally Jack broke the silence.

"Esther?" he said, as though he wasn't sure.

"Yes?" she responded cautiously, preparing herself for the worst.

"Forgive me for staring," he said, without taking his eyes off her, "but as long as we've known each other, I don't think that I've ever noticed how beautiful you are."

All around them the bank was suddenly filled with the sound of jaws and additional rolls of coins dropping to the floor.

October 12, 1 N.A.
Sapporo, Japan

The noise of nail drivers and power saws filled the air around the site where new apartments were being built to replace those that had burnt to the ground only three weeks earlier. Because of its geography, Sapporo had been spared the damage of the tsunami two and a half years earlier and now was the fastest growing city in Japan. October was not the best time to start such a project, but every passing day represented hundreds of thousands of yen in lost rent. And so the crews worked in shifts, around the clock, seven days a week, in an attempt to meet the absurd schedule. If they *did* manage to meet the deadline, they would receive substantial bonuses.

The night shift replacement for Utura Nojo had fallen seriously ill and had not come in the previous night, with the result that Utura had been working more than twenty-four hours straight. Despite the raucous noise around him, despite even the sound of the circular saw in his own hands, Utura's eyelids slowly dropped shut. He awoke an instant later as he felt the saw rip a gaping path through his right thigh. Immediately he dropped the saw and fell to the ground, grasping the wound and screaming in intense pain as blood spilled out on the plywood floor.

The foreman called for an ambulance and those around him stopped their work to try to assist, but there was little they could do. One of the more resourceful men took off his T-shirt and fashioned it into a tourniquet. It was not easy to get Utura to hold still, but with the help of some of the others who held him steady, the man knelt down in the pool of blood to tie the fabric strip above the wound. As the man's hand brushed against Utura's leg near the wound, suddenly the screaming stopped. Startled by the unexpected calm, the man turned to see Utura's face reflecting not great pain, but great surprise. Looking back at the leg, he began to understand why, but at the same time he could not understand it at all. The bleeding had completely stopped.

Still kneeling in the pool of blood, he tore at the blood-soaked cloth of Utura's pant leg in disbelief. To the amazement of all, the wound was completely healed.

❑

Around the world, hundreds of other equally unusual events were occurring. People were remembering past life experiences. Many had premonitions of both major and minor events. A few experienced the ability to control physical objects by the power of their minds. Some acquired the ability to hold sway over other people's actions and decisions. Many others could read the thoughts of those around them. And some had the power to heal. The events appeared to be totally random and lasted for relatively short periods of time, usually leaving those who had experienced the power fatigued. Accounts of the events began appearing in tabloid newspapers, but when more than eight hundred people all picked the nine winning numbers in a national lottery, it was no longer just the scandal sheets that carried the stories. It didn't take a psychic to see what was happening. The changes in the human race predicted by Christopher had begun.

The Great City

③

A CROWD OF NEARLY HALF A MILLION PEOPLE listened, some swaying, some tapping their toes in time as the lilting music of Divination, a New Age band from Miami, poured from the speakers on a massive stage and drifted like falling leaves through the trees and fields of New York's Central Park. They had gathered there to celebrate the anniversary of the founding of the United Nations. The weather was perfect, with temperatures in the mid-seventies and just a few scattered white billowy clouds in the sky. It hardly seemed possible that only seven months earlier the human race had been threatened with the possibility of complete extinction. Now, not only was it apparent that the world would survive, there was undeniable evidence that Humankind was on the brink of both its biggest evolutionary step and its greatest adventure. The psychic occurrences that had begun a few weeks earlier grew more and more frequent, though at this early stage no one held onto their powers for more than about twenty-four hours. Among those in the park this afternoon, hundreds or perhaps thousands had been host to such abilities in the past few weeks, and scores were having similar experiences at this very moment.

Under a tree at the edge of the crowd, two women— strangers moments before—sat reminiscing of lives long past when they, as men, had fought and died side by side in the Second Battle of Bull Run. Elsewhere, a group of about thirty people listened intently as a fifteen-year-old girl told of the knowledge and wisdom she had gained in her previous life as a eunuch in the court of the ancient Babylonian king and law-giver Hammurabi. Not far away, a homeless man suddenly found himself very popular when it was discovered that, for the time being at least, he possessed the power to heal.

On the stage the band completed its set and the mayor of New York, who was serving as master of ceremonies, announced the arrival of United Nations Secretary-General Christopher Goodman. Christopher's United Nations Day address to the world would be his first major public appearance since the strange psychic powers began appearing, so the world was particularly interested in what he had to say.

At the very moment Christopher came to the microphone, the attention of the crowd was suddenly drawn to the sky above him. In the nearly cloudless heavens there appeared a small point of pulsating white light that grew so quickly it soon dwarfed the entire stage. News crews trained their television cameras on the spectacle as millions marveled at what new wonder Christopher was about to reveal. Had the cameras caught the pique on Christopher's face, they would have realized that this was none of his doing.

Somehow—no one was sure exactly when it happened—the shimmering light took on a familiar form. It was a man; that is, it had the appearance of a man, though it most definitely was not. It was far too large, as tall as any building in the city, and it appeared attired in a long flowing robe of purest white light. Later some swore that it had wings, though far more were certain that it did not, and the film of the event could neither confirm nor deny it.

Not wasting another moment, Christopher took the microphone. "People of the world, do not fear this apparition!" he declared. "It is a messenger of Yahweh, come to frighten and distract you from your rightful destiny."

It was all Christopher had time to say before the entity spoke.

"Fear God and give him glory," it began, "because the hour of his judgment has come." Its voice was like thunder and it spoke in the same universal language that Christopher himself had used in Jerusalem. "Worship him who made the heavens, the earth, the sea, and the springs of water."[9]

With that, the light vanished even more quickly than it had appeared. And though most of the world had seen it on television, the strange being apparently wanted to convey its message personally to the people of earth, with the full impact of its awesome size and voice. In the course of the day it appeared and repeated its message in nearly two thousand cities around the world.

In New York, Christopher reassured the world that there was nothing to fear. "In this act, Yahweh has revealed

[9] Revelation 14:7.

his desperation." he told them. "In his demand that we fear him and worship him, he has shown his true nature. We must not fear him for he is not our god. Humankind does not need a god, for we ourselves shall become as gods—bowing to and fearing no one. We must not yield to Yahweh's threats, whether they come from the mouth of an angel or the mouths of the Koum Damah Patar." This latter reference was to recently stepped-up efforts by the KDP. Though a few had remained in Petra, most KDP had returned to the outside world. And despite the best efforts of numerous police organizations, KDP members had become as elusive as their masters, John and Cohen.

"Yahweh makes his demands, but they are hollow," Christopher declared. "Test me and see if my words are not true: Wait a week, a month, a year, and you will see that Yahweh will do nothing to enforce his demand for worship. He will not, because he cannot! His demands are empty; his threats are hollow! Yahweh knows that his days are numbered," Christopher continued. "He has seen the evidence in your lives as you approach the beginning of your own self-realized godhood. Humankind does not need Yahweh or any other god. Our only god must be ourselves!"

March 11 (New Year's Day), 2 N·A· Jerusalem

As Christopher promised, Yahweh did nothing to enforce his demand for worship. For a while there was some anxiety as members of the KDP and their allies in a few fundamentalist Christian churches continued their entreaties for worship of Yahweh. If they had the power to do any more than that, they did not use it. Now, on the first New Year's Day of the New Age, nearly five months since the entity appeared in New York, the world was learning to trust what Christopher said.

Great celebrations were scheduled throughout the world to commemorate this first new year. More than simply offering an adequate replacement for the New Year's celebrations of the old era, this New Year's Day festivities were designed to underscore the reality of the New Age to those who were resistant to change. Television documentaries recounted everything that was known of Christopher's life and reminded the world of the terrible destruction and death that preceded his rise to power a year earlier.

Nowhere was the celebration larger or more enthusiastic than in Jerusalem, the incubator of so much of the world's history and the city from which Christopher had made his declaration of Humankind's independence from Yahweh. It was fitting then, that Jerusalem, and particularly the Temple, should be at the center of the New Year's Day celebration.

Many things had changed in the year that had passed. Despite pleas by Prime Minister Golda Reiner, the exodus of Jews to Petra in Jordan continued, and although none who went could be convinced to return, at least the flow had dwindled to a mere trickle. Reiner had noticed one rather ironic advantage to their departure in that she found it much less difficult to work with a Knesset void of militant religious partisans. With a more accommodating Israeli government, Jerusalem had become a truly international city, overseen in part by a United Nations administrator and open to all races and nationalities. The same was true of the Temple. No longer was access denied based on nationality or religion. All were now free to enter into all parts of the Temple, including the Holy of Holies. The Ark was preserved just as Christopher had left it, with its lid askew to remind the world that he had removed the tablets and replaced the laws of Yahweh with a new covenant—a decree that Humankind must pass from the age of adolescence into a New Age of maturity and self-reliance from which would come true justice and freedom for all peoples.

Christopher, Decker, and Robert Milner arrived in Jerusalem together by helicopter, reminding all of the events of one year before. But it was more than the celebration of the new year that had brought them to Jerusalem. They had come also to participate in the official dedication of a statue of Christopher, which had been commissioned by Robert Milner, paid for by the UN, and approved by the Israeli government. Although the statue had actually been erected just thirty days after Christopher's Jerusalem address, on the sixth day of the Passover week, Christopher had not been present, so in typical political style, an "official dedication" had been suggested to both mark the New Year's celebration in a symbolic way and to give a boost to Israel's flagging tourist trade.

The statue was a slightly larger-than-life re-creation of Christopher, appropriately placed on the spot where he delivered his Jerusalem address from the Temple's pinnacle, making it clearly visible to all. So that visitors could, in some small way, experience what it was like for those who had actually been in Jerusalem on that day, speakers near the statue broadcast Christopher's Jerusalem address three times daily, at sunrise, noon, and sunset.

October 24 (United Nations Day), 2 N.A. Babylon, Iraq

Little more than nineteen months had passed since the Security Council voted to build a new headquarters complex in Babylon. And yet, here on a site not far from the reconstruction of ancient King Nebuchadnezzar's palace, stood the structurally complete main building of the new headquarters. Much remained to be done inside, and the rest of the nine buildings were only shells. Still, United Nations Day came only once a year and it seemed the perfect occasion for dedicating the new complex. The first to move in would be the World Health Organization (WHO), a decision that had never been fully explained, since WHO's offices would ultimately be elsewhere in the city. It made little sense to have WHO move in now, just to relocate three months later, but for some reason the decision was important to Christopher, and no one felt it was really worth arguing about.

The city of Babylon, located on the Hilla branch of the Euphrates, just north of the modern town of Hilla, and 55 miles southwest of Baghdad, is one of the most famous cities of the ancient world. Depending upon whose account is believed, the size of the ancient city ranged from as much as 225 square miles to as little as 5 square miles. The earliest Greek writings in which Babylon is described are those of Herodotus, who represented Babylon as an exact square, 120 stadia (approximately 14 miles) on each side, located on a broad plain. Babylon's historic rise to regional importance came in the third millennium B.C., when the course of the Euphrates River shifted westward away from the ancient Sumerian city of Kish. Since that time there have been five well-defined periods of Babylonian history. Old Babylon, the capital city from which Hammurabi and his successors ruled, was almost entirely destroyed by the Assyrian king Sennacherib, circa 689 B.C. Within about a decade Sennacherib's son and successor, Esarhaddon, built a new city on the same site, but it too was destroyed by revolution and siege. Later, from 626 to 562 B.C., Nabopolassar and his son, Nebuchadnezzar, rebuilt Babylon and brought it to its greatest glory. It was during the reign of Nebuchadnezzar that the city's massive walls and the Hanging Gardens (two of the original Seven Wonders of the Ancient World) were constructed. In 275 B.C. the inhabitants of the city were moved to the new city of Seleucia on the Tigris River, thus bringing the ancient history of Babylon to a close.

Beginning in the 1980s, Iraqi President Saddam Hussein, who considered himself a twentieth-century version of Nebuchadnezzar, spent hundreds of millions of dollars from the sale of oil to rebuild the city as a monument—ostensibly to the Iraqi people but, more accurately, to himself. After the liberation of Iraq in 2003, interest in the reconstruction continued.

Now, a year and a half after the madness that decimated the region, the only Iraqis left to inhabit the city were immigrants returning home from abroad. There was no shortage of other inhabitants, however, as more than

38,800 engineers and construction workers poured into the city to work on the many building projects. Together with the workers' families and another 9,200 additional support personnel, the population of Babylon came to nearly 55,000 people, making it a bustling metropolis compared to the rest of Iraq and the surrounding countries, which, except for Israel, were all but uninhabited. Ironically, considering the history of hostility between the two countries, nearly a sixth of the people now in Iraq were Israelis. But this was the new Iraq, which, like the new Israel, was under United Nations control and open to all races and nationalities.

Christopher Goodman, together with an entourage of reporters, had begun the day with a tour of the city, followed by speeches by a host of dignitaries from around the world who praised Christopher's leadership and offered accolades for all who had been involved in the new UN headquarters project. Amid great cheers, Christopher himself praised the human spirit, which, by this project, "had proven itself supreme and unyielding to the whims of spiritual oppressors." As millions listened and watched around the world, he recalled the city's historical and spiritual significance.

Repeating what he had articulated to the gathering of New Age leaders at the UN, he noted, "It was near here that the first Theatan ship landed more than four billion years ago, and life on earth began. It was near this spot, in Eden, that Humankind first declared its independence from Yahweh. It was in this very place," he added, "that Humankind first came together in peace to work as one united people in the construction of a great city and the magnificent Tower of Babel, before being dispersed by the despotic Yahweh. And," Christopher said, completing his brief history lesson, "tragically, it was not far from here that Yahweh, in perhaps his cruelest act against Humankind, released the madness that led to the brutal slaughter of one-third of the planet's population." Christopher concluded by noting that the decision by the United Nations to build its new headquarters in Babylon had sealed for all time Humankind's emancipation from Yahweh's rule.

After his speech, Christopher held up an oversized pair of scissors and prepared to cut a wide red ribbon that had been stretched across the entrance to the new headquarters. It may have been the second year of the New Age, but some traditions would never change and Christopher had accepted the role of ribbon-cutter with good humor.

Aided by Robert Milner because of his crippled arm, Christopher reached out to cut the ribbon when suddenly someone in the midst of the crowd cried out, "Look!"

It took a moment for the rest of those gathered to understand, but then everyone saw. Directly above the new structure, a shimmering light was growing and taking shape, much like the one that appeared a year before over Central Park in New York.

"Fallen! Fallen is Babylon the Great, which made all the nations drink the maddening wine of her adulteries,"[10] it said. And then, after repeating its message, it vanished.

As before, the entire event was captured by television cameras and transmitted throughout the globe. And again, in order to convey its message to the people of

[10] Revelation 14:8.

earth personally, the angel appeared and repeated its message in nearly two thousand cities around the world.

In Babylon, all eyes and cameras shifted back to Christopher. For a brief moment there was silence and then, very much unlike his reaction to the first angel, he began to laugh. It was an infectious laugh and though they weren't sure why, many of those watching began to laugh as well.

Christopher stopped for a second but then laughed again heartily, shaking his head as if in disbelief over what he had just witnessed. "Well, one thing is for certain," he said, finally, "Yahweh really knows how to steal the spotlight!" Now everyone laughed.

"But his theatrics will not frighten us," he continued. Then, looking skyward and shaking his one good fist toward heaven, he shouted at Yahweh, "You will not succeed in frightening us! Humankind will not bend its knee to you or any other tyrant ever again!"

Several thousand fists now raised with Christopher's in defiance as a spontaneous roar of cheers resonated through the city.

"Yahweh knows," Christopher said, turning back to the crowd, "that by building a new UN headquarters here in Babylon, Humankind is delivering an unmistakable slap in his face. With each passing day he grows more and more desperate as he feels his grip on the earth slipping away." Again the people cheered. "In his desperation," Christopher continued, "he foolishly attempts to frighten us, even though by doing so he makes himself a laughingstock.

"Look around," he told them. "Babylon is not fallen as Yahweh's driveling minion has proclaimed so loudly:

Babylon stands! And it will continue to stand long after Yahweh is forced to abandon his fraudulent claim on this planet!"

Then, reaching out with the ceremonial scissors, Christopher and Milner cut the ribbon to thunderous applause, and the new headquarters building of the United Nations was officially opened.

4

**February 3, 2 N.A.
Babylon**

DECKER HAWTHORNE sat eating a late breakfast at a corner table in the new UN dining room. Looking up from the empty plate where once there had been a Belgian waffle and lots of bacon, he saw Christopher coming toward him, smiling. Decker waved and smiled back. "Have you had breakfast?" he asked.

"I had a donut in my office," Christopher answered and then got straight to the reason he was there. Still standing, he leaned down over the table and spoke quietly so that no one else could hear. "Would you like to see the secret of eternal life?" he whispered.

Decker raised his eyebrows. "The communion?" he asked, using Christopher's terminology from almost two years earlier.

Christopher nodded.

"I already know about it," Decker said, feigning disinterest.

"What? How?" Christopher gasped in surprise.

"I *was* once a reporter, you know."

Christopher pulled out a chair and sat down, looking a

little deflated. "I thought it was such a well-kept secret," he said, shaking his head. "We took every precaution." For a moment he stared at Decker, and then they both smiled. "So how much do you know?" he asked.

"Not that much, really," Decker admitted. "I know that there's some big hush-hush project going on at WHO," he said, referring to the World Health Organization. "I also know that you've said this 'communion' is supposed to dramatically extend the human lifespan. My guess," he said, studying Christopher's face for a response that might confirm his suspicion, "is that WHO has been working on something similar to what your Uncle Harry was doing before he died."

"You're pretty close," Christopher said, "but that's not exactly it. What Uncle Harry was working on was actually far more complicated. What he didn't realize was that there is a much easier way to accomplish what he was after."

"What do you mean?" Decker asked, leaning forward and finally showing how interested he really was.

"Decker, I know it's been a long time, but do you remember when we were at the refugee camp in Sāhiwāi, Pakistan, about five years ago?" Decker nodded. "On our last day there, I was in my tent and you came looking for me. When you found me, I told you that I had seen the death of one who sought to avoid death's grip."

Decker nodded as he recalled the events. "That was the day Secretary-General Hansen was killed in the plane crash."

"But there was also someone else in my vision," Christopher continued, "one who sought to accept death's release." Christopher shrugged and shook his head as he spoke. "I really didn't understand it then. If you had asked me about it at the time, I'm not sure what I would have said, but I understand it now. It was John." Decker knew immediately that Christopher referred to Yochanan bar Zebadee, the Apostle John.

"I told you once that when I was crucified, John was the only one of the apostles who came to see me. At first I thought he came to ask forgiveness for betraying me, but of course he had not. But he hadn't come just to mock me, either," Christopher explained. "Do you remember the legend of the Holy Grail?"

"Sure," Decker answered. "It was supposed to be the cup that you used at the Last Supper. I remember reading stories when I was a kid about the Knights of the Round Table going on quests to find the Grail. Of course they never found it."

"One of the legends about the Grail," Christopher continued, "says that when John came to the cross, he brought the Grail with him."

Decker thought for a second. "I do remember something about that," he said slowly, trying to awaken any additional recollection of the matter. "The legend was that John collected some of your blood by letting it drip into the cup." A long forgotten memory began to make its way into Decker's consciousness. He started to speak but then paused to be sure his memory was correct. "According to the legend," he continued tentatively; and then suddenly he was struck by the connection to the current conversation. Had he not already been sitting down, he would have done so now. Could Christopher really be implying that . . . "According to the legend," Decker began again, "if anyone drank of the blood from the Grail, he would have eternal life!"

Christopher nodded, and it was clear that he was doing more than just confirming Decker's accurate recollection of the legend. He was also implicitly confirming Decker's realization of the larger point: There was no need for anything nearly so complex as the genetic engineering on which Professor Goodman had been working. Total immunity from all disease and the power of rapid healing—the secret of eternal life that Harry Goodman had sought—was attainable by simply ingesting the blood.

"Somehow John knew that by drinking the blood, he would gain eternal life," Christopher concluded. "I suppose it was part of his bargain with Yahweh."

"But in Pakistan you said John 'sought death's release.' That makes it sound as though he *wanted* to die."

"I believe that he did; I'm not sure why. I doubt it was because he felt guilty for betraying Humankind into Yahweh's hands. I suppose that after two thousand years, he was simply tired of living."

Decker considered what Christopher said and then returned to the more pressing topic. "So if the benefits of the blood are gained by drinking it, what about Milner?" Robert Milner was now in his mid-nineties but appeared younger than Decker, who was seventy-one.

"Apparently it can either be ingested or transfused," Christopher answered, referencing the time fourteen years earlier when Robert Milner, then on his deathbed, had received a transfusion of Christopher's blood. "It's rather puzzling why it works at all, but with what we knew about what the blood did for Robert Milner, we had to pursue it. Originally, it was believed that injections would be more effective, thus requiring far smaller dosages than with oral administration. But by adding a new genetically designed absorption agent to the blood, WHO found that two average-sized capsules taken orally were as effective as a 50cc transfusion."

"Sort of a 'take two capsules and you'll never need to call me in the morning again' approach," Decker said, unable to resist the joke.

"I guess you could say that," Christopher laughed. "We're not entirely sure why, but a week after taking the capsules, the human immune system grows incredibly robust and resilient. Within a month, the body is entirely immune to all bacteriological and viral disorders. Preexisting illnesses wane and then disappear altogether. And though it's too soon to tell with the volunteers in the test group, if what we saw with Bob Milner holds true, it may even reverse the effects of old age."

"You've already begun human testing?" Decker stammered.

Christopher nodded. "Of course, the communion can't prevent injuries," he said, continuing his train of thought. "It won't keep you from breaking your leg or cutting yourself, but the healing of such injuries is vastly accelerated. It also won't prevent death from an injury, but barring that, it will allow people to live long enough for the evolution of Humankind to the spirit form to be completed. Then not even an injury will be able to kill."

"This all sounds fantastic," Decker interjected, "but isn't it going to be a little hard on you to be draining out all this blood?"

"The blood won't be coming directly from me," Christopher said. "WHO is cloning the blood from a sample."

"Of course," Decker said, acknowledging his oversight of the obvious. Then, bringing the discussion around to a facet of the subject to which he had been giving a great deal of thought prior to this conversation, he asked, "Is it your intention that the communion be given to everyone?"

"Of course," Christopher responded, his tone indicating surprise at the question.

Decker thought for a moment, choosing his words and tone carefully. "Why should we provide the communion to our enemies?" he asked, "to the KDP and the fundamentalists who oppose everything you say and do?"

Christopher thought for a second and then started to speak, but before he had gotten out the first syllable he stopped again, apparently unable to find a convincing response.

Decker answered his own question. "You know that ultimately they'll die without it."

Christopher didn't speak but his expression indicated that Decker's assumption was correct.

"Christopher, I think I understand how you feel about this. You hate the thought of leaving anyone behind. It has cost so much: so many lives uselessly lost over the centuries because of Yahweh's oppression. You hate to allow more suffering because of him. But if you allow the KDP and their fundamentalist Christian supporters to take part in the communion, you'll be giving Yahweh a foothold, not only in this century but in all the centuries to come.

"You've given the KDP every opportunity to turn from their ways and join you in the battle for Humankind's independence," Decker said, a little surprised at how much he was sounding like Robert Milner. "You've bent over backward to accommodate them, but not a single one of them has joined us. What hope is there that they'll ever change? I think the time has come to let them suffer the consequences of their own choices.

"Besides, you told me yourself, when people die they're reincarnated to live again. Those who oppose you are remnants of the old age. Why not allow them to go their own way? When they die they'll be reborn with no memory of what they were or how the world once was. They'll be born anew, leaving behind all of their prejudices and their learned ignorance.

"If you look at it that way," Decker continued, "it becomes obvious that you're not helping anyone by giving eternal life to people who are not ready for the New Age from which that life comes." He took a breath, and then concluded his argument, "Let those who are *bound* to the old age *die* with the old age, so that in their next life they may truly *live*."

Christopher thought for a moment. Decker's logic was indisputable and he would not deny it. "You've been reading too many of your own speeches," he said finally.

Decker smiled, but that was not the response he wanted.

"Okay," Christopher added finally. "I suppose that the clinics *could* be directed to not give the communion to members of the KDP—that should be easy enough: They're pretty hard to miss with the writing on their foreheads. But how could you prevent the fundamentalists from receiving communion? Unfortunately, they're not so easy to spot; they look pretty much like everyone else when they're not beating you over the head with a Bible."

"But that's the answer," Decker declared. "We can use

their fundamentalism to make them *not want* to take the communion."

"I'm sorry, Decker. I don't follow you," Christopher replied.

"I've been thinking about this," Decker said.

"Yes, I noticed."

Decker brushed aside Christopher's comment and continued. "The book of Revelation in the Bible says that those who follow the Antichrist will be required to take a mark on their forehead or on the back of their hand."[11]

"I'm familiar with the passage," Christopher said.

"Well, it seems to me we can use that to our own benefit. If we require anyone who takes the communion to also take some kind of a mark on either the back of their hand or on their forehead—though I doubt that anyone would really want to have something tattooed on their forehead—then the fundamentalists won't dare do it for fear of angering Yahweh."

Christopher appeared to be giving the proposition some serious thought, but Decker wanted to drive home his point even more. "Again, it's just my opinion, but it seems to me that the communion should be given only to those who have pledged their loyalty to you and what you stand for. Taking the communion should, therefore, be done only in full recognition and agreement with what it represents—a declaration of independence from the demands of a dictatorial god, a statement of belief in individual self-worth and the collective value of Humankind, a statement of self-determination, a resolution to make one's own decisions and to live with the consequences,

[11] Revelation 13:16.

and a commitment to leave the nest and to declare that Humankind has come of age and has outgrown the need for a guardian."

"I hope you've written all this down somewhere," Christopher said. Decker nodded, a little embarrassed by his speechmaking. "So, how exactly do you propose that we apply this mark?" Christopher asked.

"Well, I don't think we want anything too conspicuous or no one will want to get it. It should be as small and unobtrusive as possible on the back of the right hand. As I said, I don't think anyone is going to want to have it on their forehead, but we should offer the option so it will match the prophecy and keep the fundamentalists away. It should be something permanent, but it also should to be as painless as possible. I've been doing some research on the subject and it turns out that very few tattoos are done using needles anymore; most are done with permanent dyes that soak deep into the flesh so they don't wear off."

"And I suppose to have the desired effect of keeping the fundamentalists away, the mark will have to depict either my name or the number 666?" Christopher asked, cringing a bit.

"Well, the KDP *have* made a big deal of the fact that when your name is written phonetically in Hebrew the sum of the letters equals 666, so I guess that makes it the natural choice," Decker remarked, and then added, "It's a lot shorter than writing out your whole name."

Christopher took a breath and let out a deep sigh. "Well, let me give it some thought," he said.

"Great, that's all I'm asking," Decker answered, confident he had presented his argument with undeniable logic.

"Now," Decker said, as he pushed his chair back from the table, "when you came in here you asked if I wanted to *see* the secret of eternal life. Is there something you were going to show me?"

"Yes, there is," Christopher answered, apparently ready to move on and let Decker's proposal settle in for a while. "Come with me," he said.

Decker followed Christopher from the dining room and down the hall to the elevator. He quickly guessed that they were headed for the World Health Organization.

Inside the WHO facilities they passed two armed guards and approached a secure door. Christopher placed his hand on the print reader, spoke his name, and the door opened. Decker expected to find a laboratory with dozens of WHO personnel busily running tests or engaged in discussions on the best methods for cloning Christopher's blood. What he saw instead was immeasurably more striking. Beyond the door in the secured area was a simple warehouse full of pallets stacked high with boxes.

Christopher tore back the top of a box and held it open for Decker to see. Inside were thousands of blister packs, each bearing two capsules filled with a thick red liquid. The entire warehouse was filled with Christopher's blood.

Communion

5

JULY 4 WAS CHOSEN as the day for the communion to begin. The selection was largely symbolic, being the day that was best recognized by the world as representing a day of independence. Centuries earlier it had marked the declaration of America's independence from the tyranny of Britain's monarchy; now it would mark the independence of Humankind from the tyranny of Yahweh. The date was also chosen as a matter of coincidence—it being the approximate date by which adequate supplies of the communion blood could be distributed to the nearly twelve thousand clinics around the world.

The decision to limit distribution to those who swore allegiance to Christopher and the advancement of Humankind necessitated significant security measures. Doctors, nurses, and medical technicians having access to the blood supply first had to be cleared of any connection with the KDP and the fundamentalists, and then had to be trained to apply the mark. They also had to swear their own allegiance to Christopher and receive both the communion and the mark themselves.

The entire project was financed through heavy taxes upon the wealthy and near-wealthy throughout the world, including William Bragford, the heir to David Bragford's estate. As noted by Robert Milner, who in years past had frequently gone to David Bragford with hat in hand, "In the New Age all is to be evenly shared. Soon enough there will be no need of money at all." The formerly rich took little comfort in that prediction, but it seemed fair to almost everyone else.

❏

People began lining up at the clinics three full days before they were to open. By July 2 the lines stretched for over two miles at some clinics. In part, the long lines resulted from stories in the media about some of the doctors, nurses, and medical technicians who had already received the communion. Most had nothing unusual to report beyond a general feeling of good health and well-being, but among more than 80,000 health care workers, it was inevitable that a few would experience more dramatic benefits. In one such case, a few days after receiving the communion, a medical technician had been severely injured in a car accident. Three days later, he was out of the hospital, his injuries completely healed. In another example, a nurse who suffered from advanced osteoporosis was able to stand fully erect just weeks after receiving the communion, her bone structure entirely restored. There were also a score of others who were healed of diabetes, hypertension, and other non-debilitating maladies.

The lines at the clinics were also due in part to the

psychic powers and abilities that had begun more than a year and a half earlier. By now nearly everyone had experienced some type of psychic episode in their lives, many more than once, but in every case these powers were short-lived. Most people longed to extend the experience, and the communion offered the hope that they could possess those powers forever. The promise of eternal life involved far more than just avoiding death: It offered the opportunity to grow and to evolve to a future of limitless possibilities.

July 2, 3 N.A.
Philadelphia, Pennsylvania,
near Independence Hall

Still two days before the clinic was scheduled to open, 4,000 people waited in line. Many brought lawn chairs or blankets to sit on to make the long wait as pleasant as possible. Some brought magazines and books to read. Others had radios, portable televisions, or computer games. A few played cards. Others tried to sleep. The street vendors very gladly accepted the challenge of keeping up with the demand for food and drink, and the city brought in portable restrooms. Most who came respected the queue, falling in at the end of the line, but there were a few fights. All in all, despite the Philadelphia summer heat, things were pretty calm.

Then, as had happened on two previous occasions, a small pulsating white light appeared above the crowd. Everyone knew what it was, and even though neither of the two previous angels had done more than make their pronouncements, it was an awesome and unnerving sight, and many left their place in line to seek cover.

"If anyone worships the beast and his image," the angel's voice boomed, "and receives his mark on the forehead or on the hand, he, too, will drink of the wine of God's fury, which has been poured full strength into the cup of his wrath. He will be tormented with burning sulfur in the presence of the holy angels and of the Lamb. And the smoke of their torment rises for ever and ever. There is no rest day or night for those who worship the beast and his image, or for anyone who receives the mark of his name."[12]

As with the first two angels, the third delivered its message, vanished, and then appeared and repeated its missive around the world.

Also, as with the previous appearances, Christopher responded quickly. The anger in his voice was unmistakable. "Twice before," he began, as his message was beamed to the world, "Yahweh has used his messengers to make his infantile threats, and each time the calamity he promised has failed to come to pass. The KDP and the fundamentalists warn that these things will yet befall us. But it is with their dire predictions of the future that they hope to draw us back into our past, a past in which there is only death for the spirit of Humankind.

"Now, as Humankind is poised to take its first step into the realm of immortality," he continued, "Yahweh has reverted to cries of hellfire and damnation! Well, he may frighten a few—the KDP and the fundamentalists

[12] Revelation 14:9–11.

who would wish us into this mythical hellfire rather than allowing us the freedom to choose for ourselves and our children which road we will take—but he cannot frighten the rest of us! Our hearts are steady and strong and bound for the future!

"We *will not,* we *cannot,* indeed *we must not* capitulate to the demands of those who would drag us with them to worship a failed deity! We must forge our own course onward to the future!"

It was very quickly apparent that Christopher's words had had the desired effect, as the lines at the clinics grew at an even faster rate.

July 4, 3 N·A·
Babylon

"Protests by fundamentalists turn violent, marking the first day of the communion."

"Snooze," Decker Hawthorne mumbled.

"Good morning, I'm Amelia Witherspoon and this is *World News This Morning.* "

"Snooze," he said again, a little louder.

"What started out this morning as peaceful protests—"

"I said, snooze!" he growled as he covered his head with the pillow. This time the clarity and volume were sufficient for the voice monitor to register his command and to shut off the television. Some people liked to wake up to music, others to a bell or buzzer, others to recorded sounds of nature. Decker found television news to be the most effective.

"No, wait," he said a second later, as the news commentator's words finally sank in. "I mean, TV on!" he shouted, as he quickly sat up to see the screen. The television immediately came back to life.

"In scenes reminiscent of the sit-ins of the 1960s or the fundamentalist blockades of women's clinics in the 1990s, fundamentalists started the day in dozens of cities from Sydney to Beijing by attempting to block the entrance to communion clinics as they opened this morning." As the commentator spoke, the image on the screen showed a clip from Sydney, Australia, where twenty to thirty people were lying on the ground in front of a communion clinic, singing hymns.

"The protests quickly turned violent, however, when fundamentalists refused to clear the way for those who had been waiting in line for as long as three or four days. Police were called in and arrests quickly followed." The screen showed a jumble of shoving, kicking, and flying night sticks. Police handcuffed protestors and carried them to vans. To slow the arrests as police tried to carry them away, the protestors went limp and continued singing their religious songs.

"In much of the world it is still night," the commentator noted. "As morning dawns and the communion begins in other cities, no one knows if these scenes of protest by fundamentalists will be repeated. Authorities, however, are not taking any chances. Reports from cities in other time zones indicate that police are being dispatched just in case."

❑

Such reports continued as Christian fundamentalists suddenly seemed to be coming from nowhere, attempting to block clinic doors and taking advantage of the captive audiences to preach to those waiting in line. Those arrested for obstructing access were given jail terms of up to two years. Those who merely preached were allowed to continue as long as they did not come within 100 feet of the clinics. To drown them out, those in line chanted the words of the pledge that was required of everyone before taking the communion:

> By taking the blood, I pledge my allegiance to him who is its source and to the advancement of all of Humankind. By accepting the mark, I declare my emancipation from any person or power that would seek to subjugate me or the family of Humankind.

Certainly the fundamentalists were in the minority, but they were vocal and undaunted in the delivery of their message. And occasionally they were even successful in their efforts as one or two of those waiting in line dropped out, apparently to reconsider.

One unexpected response to the protests and the third angel's threats was that many who received communion defiantly chose the option of taking the mark on their foreheads. At first there were only a few, but it quickly became a matter of great pride to have the mark emblazoned on one's forehead for all to see. Many who had earlier taken the mark on the back of their hand got back in line, hoping that they could take the mark on their forehead as well. Clearly the mark had become what Decker intended that it be—an emblem of Humankind's emancipation, a symbol of solidarity with Christopher, and a sign of resolute defiance against Yahweh and those who served him.

❑

And so it continued for nearly a week, as 12,000 clinics processed an average of a thousand people per clinic per day. Then during the night of July 11 the situation changed dramatically as, one after another, seven communion clinics were firebombed. The next night there were twelve, and the next night forty. Seven, twelve, forty—all were numbers favored in biblical text, a fact not missed by the authorities. The fundamentalists denied responsibility, but no one else had motive.

Because the bombings took place at night when most clinics were attended only by security guards, there were very few serious injuries inside the clinics. Outside, however, it was another story. Dozens of people waiting for the clinics to open suffered burns and serious cuts from flying glass, and three individuals were struck by terrorists' cars as they sped by the clinics and threw their Molotov cocktails. So far no one had been killed.

While the terrorists were successful in completely shutting down only a very few clinics, by the third morning, it was obvious they were having an effect. Even though most of the clinics continued to operate at full capacity, the length of the lines began to dwindle. So far, only 145 million, or about 5 percent of the world's 2.9 billion people, had received the communion. Interviews with people who had not yet taken communion revealed that fear of the terrorists was the number one reason for not going to the clinics. "What good is the communion going to do me," asked one interviewee, "if I get killed on my way in the door?"

The problem was further exacerbated on the afternoon following the third night of bombings when two armored vehicles bringing new supplies of the communion blood to clinics were hijacked and set ablaze. An eyewitness captured one of the hijackings on video, which was shown on television around the world. The video started just as the truck's guard was shot when he tried to resist the assailants. Two of the five terrorists then pulled the driver from the truck and violently threw him to the pavement and forced him to kneel on the street. Holding a gun to the driver's head, one of the terrorists told him to pray and ask God's forgiveness for his sins. Terrified, the driver did as he was told, shaking and stuttering in fear as he repeated every word. When he had finished, the terrorists all said, "amen." The man who held the gun then shouted, "Hallelujah! Thank you, Jesus!" and pulled the trigger, blowing the man's brains out on the street. Despite all that the world had suffered over the past few years, the inhumanity of this scene, shown repeatedly on television, struck viewers with a very personal sense of outrage.

Local authorities attempted to stem the terrorism by providing escorts for the armored trucks and additional security at the clinics, but these efforts met with only limited success. Despite their efforts, ultimately the responsibility for dealing with the problem belonged to the United Nations. Secretary-General Christopher Goodman officially asked the Security Council to provide UN forces to protect the citizens, the clinics, and the communion supply.

In an address designed to calm fears and to let the people of the world know what was being done, Christopher took verbal aim at the terrorists. "No one is being forced to take the communion or to accept the mark. It is entirely voluntary. Those who do not want it are free to refuse it. Neither have we made any attempt to stop those who oppose the communion from expressing their opinions, as long as they are peaceful. But this is not enough for them—instead they have turned to violence and bloodshed. We cannot, as a civilized people, allow terrorists to operate with impunity. The rights of individuals to make their own choices must be protected!"

The Security Council quickly granted Christopher's request to deploy UN forces, but it was not soon enough. That night thirty-three more clinics were bombed.

August 2, 3 N.A.
Babylon

"I am tempted," said Robert Milner, "to use such euphemisms as 'eliminate' or 'nullify,' but, while such terms may play more favorably with the public, it is important that we in this room face squarely the reality of this proposal." His honest appraisal was like a splash of cold water in the face of one in the penumbra of consciousness: It was unwelcome in its jarring impact but appreciated in that it brought the reality of the situation into clear focus. "What we are faced with is sanctioning the reinstitution of capital punishment—the death penalty."

With him in the room were Decker, Christopher, and the ten members of the Security Council. Christopher had surrendered his position as primary for Europe and caretaker for the Middle East and East Africa in January so that there were again ten primary members. The meeting, informal and very strictly off the record, had been requested by Christopher to assess what options existed for dealing with the fundamentalists' continuing reign of terrorism. The response to his question kept coming back the same.

For three weeks the terrorist onslaughts had continued. The use of UN security forces had reduced the number of bombings and drive-by shootings at communion clinics, and only three more hijackings had taken place. Yet somehow the fundamentalists always seemed to know beforehand where the weakest point in security lay and how to use that weakness to their advantage. While on rare occasions this might have been attributable to security leaks within the UN forces, more often than not the UN forces were unaware of the particular weaknesses until they were so skillfully exploited by the terrorists. What the terrorists knew went beyond inside information and demonstrated a knowledge of details no one else knew. Neither did coincidence or dumb luck provide a sufficient explanation for the success of their attacks. The only reasonable explanation was that members of the

KDP were employing their psychic abilities to aid the fundamentalists.

Surprisingly, however, the fundamentalists seemed sloppy in covering their tracks. Despite the precise planning of their offensives, they left behind a trail of eyewitnesses who were only too eager to point out the culprits. Equally surprising was that after committing their crimes, the fundamentalists apparently went right back to their homes and jobs, making their capture almost too easy. It was as though they wanted to be arrested, as though they sought the martyr's role.

Around the world, UN security forces and local authorities had taken hundreds of fundamentalists into custody for terrorist activities. While this should have provided some encouragement, there was little to celebrate, for it seemed that no sooner was an enclave of fundamentalists identified and taken into custody than another stepped in to fill its shoes.

Despite the testimony of eyewitnesses, those arrested claimed innocence or simply refused to answer the charges at all. Some just prayed while others did their best to disrupt the proceedings by singing or shouting praises to their god. Most tried to turn the hearings into an opportunity to preach to the court and their accusers.

Outside the courts, they were having an impact. Because of the relentless strikes against the clinics, the number of people receiving the communion had dropped to a mere trickle. Clinics set up to handle thousands of people a day served only a few hundred.

"What is most frustrating to me," Christopher said to those in the meeting, "is that we are not opposed to them or their religion as such. They could keep their religion, or at least much of what they believe, and still be welcome in the New Age. We have not restricted other beliefs, nor do we wish to. Soon all of Humankind will grow beyond the need for religion and it will make no difference if, in the past, a person was a Buddhist or a Taoist or a Christian. All that we ask is that the fundamentalists accept the fact that the truth, as others see it, is equally as valid as the truth they believe they see."

"There, indeed, lies the problem," Milner lamented. "After all, the very nature of religious zealots is that they believe that they alone know the right way. They are unwilling to concede that anyone outside of their particular orthodoxy may possess a small portion of the truth. Their exclusivity is a source of great pride. They see Humankind as primitive and regressive. They view the world as evil and unfit and Humankind as deserving of annihilation and eternal torment in hell. They define their value, not in being fully human, but in becoming the slaves of Yahweh. For them, only those who are willing to sacrifice their own humanity on the altar of subservience to an angry god are worthy of salvation from such a torturous end. Were it in their power, they would call down a flood such as they believe Yahweh sent in the days of Noah to drown out the rest of humanity. And is it any wonder, with such examples of wrath and destruction as are found in the Bible, that these people will justify any behavior, any crime, to stop us? They believe that they not only have a right, but indeed they have a duty to eliminate any other way of thinking.

"We have the support we need to punish those responsible," Milner continued, "and I, for one, am convinced there is no other way to stop them."

"The people demand justice," Ambassador Tanaka said resolutely.

As others continued to voice their feelings, Christopher listened without additional comment for more than an hour. Decker could see that he was uncomfortable with what he was hearing.

"I began," Robert Milner said in closing, "by saying that euphemisms were out of place in an honest discussion of the alternatives available. Let me now conclude by noting that in light of what we now understand about the nature of the human animal, as that light has been given to us by Christopher, we are not truly condemning anyone to death, for death is but a fleeting passage in the eternal circle of life. The seed is buried in the ground, but it returns anew to life. So it is also with the human seed. What we are talking about is not execution, but liberation. What we accomplish is not termination, but rebirth."

❑

The meeting ended without a decision in order to give everyone a chance to consider what had been said. In truth, all except Christopher seemed resolved to a course of action. "What are you going to do?" Decker asked after everyone else had left.

Christopher leaned back in his chair and exhaled in pained exasperation. Decker waited for his answer.

"I'd like to just quit," Christopher answered to Decker's amazement. "A part of me would like to just say, 'Okay, Yahweh, you win. You can have the planet.'

But, of course, I can't simply surrender the future of Humankind just because I'm faced with having to do something I don't want to do. And yet capital punishment seems so contrary to our overall goals. I have the greatest respect for the men and women who were just here," he said of the Security Council and Robert Milner. "It is clear that they have approached this problem with a great deal of serious thought."

Christopher sat silently for nearly three minutes, occasionally allowing the pen he was holding to slip through his fingers and tap the table. Decker waited without interrupting. The opinions had all been aired; all that Decker could do now was offer moral support. Finally Christopher spoke. "I suppose that tough decisions are the bane of everyone in government. Who am I to think that it should be different for me?

"You know, Decker," he continued, "I guess I've never really faced a dilemma like this before. I've been able to discover some way around nearly every problem."

Decker's mind flashed back to his own youth—he had been much the same. And then he came to that one moment when he, too, had faced a true dilemma, a situation from which there was no way out: the deaths of Elizabeth, Hope, and Louisa. The memory was old, but his pain was still as real as the day they died.

Christopher's voice pulled Decker's thoughts back to the present. "I've always found some way to accomplish what was necessary without having to do something I found to be morally compromising," he continued. "I'm afraid this is one part of being human that I had not counted on."

Christopher stopped and thought for another moment before finally answering Decker's question about what he was going to do. "As unpleasant as it is, I suppose I'll do what I have to do," he said. "I guess Thomas Jefferson was right: 'The tree of Liberty must be refreshed from time to time with the blood of patriots and tyrants.' "[13]

[13] A letter from Thomas Jefferson to William S. Smith, dated Nov. 13, 1787.

Hope

6

June 2, 4 N.A.
Babylon

DECKER WAITED OUTSIDE Christopher's office, talking with Jackie Hansen. He marveled at how young she looked. He knew her age: Though she had forbidden anyone to give her a party, she had just turned fifty. And yet every day it seemed she grew younger and more beautiful. The small mark on the back of her right hand explained why. She had been among the very first to receive the communion, and after fourteen months its beneficial effects were unmistakable.

Decker would have liked to talk with Jackie for a while longer, but Christopher returned to his office, and it was Christopher he had come to see. Or more precisely, it was Christopher who had asked to see him.

Inside the office, Decker could not help but comment to Christopher on Jackie's appearance. In doing so he unintentionally provided the opening for what Christopher wanted to see him about.

"Decker," Christopher began, and then paused. It was clear that something was bothering him. Somehow

Decker sensed that this was not a matter of state but something far more personal.

"What is it?" Decker asked, urging him on.

"I don't want this to sound like . . . well, like I'm calling you on the carpet. I hope that I would never be so presumptuous; you know how I feel about you. It's just that, well, I don't understand."

Decker didn't speak, but his expression made it clear that he had no idea what Christopher was getting at.

"The communion," Christopher said finally.

The comment was cryptic: He might have meant anything by it. But Decker was sure he now understood what this meeting was about.

"I've been meaning to talk with you about that," Decker said a little sheepishly. It had been more than a year since the communion had begun. The strict penalties against terrorist activities at clinics had had the desired effect, and now nearly everyone had received the communion and bore the mark. Many clinics had all but suspended operations because everyone in the population who wanted the communion had received it. There was, however, one notable exception: Decker himself.

"Decker, certainly you of all people are free to make your own choice on the matter. I just don't understand."

"Christopher, you know that I love you."

"And I love you," Christopher responded.

"And you must know that I consider myself fortunate above all men to have been a part of what you have begun. But I'm seventy-three years old. I'm an old man."

"But, Decker, the communion will make you young again!"

"Christopher," he said, shaking his head regretfully, "I

know. I know. And this may be hard for you to understand, but I don't want to live forever. I've had a full life, but—"

"But what?" Christopher prodded.

"There is one thing missing from my life. It was taken from me twenty-three years ago."

"Your family?" Christopher asked.

Decker nodded. "After all these years," he said haltingly, "I still miss them." Tears began to form in his eyes. "I still ache for them. I still find myself thinking I hear Hope or Louisa's voice when I hear children playing." Decker wiped his eyes and shrugged. "I still sleep on one side of the bed," he said. "Now don't start thinking I'm getting suicidal or anything," he added quickly. "I'm in no hurry to die or anything. It's just that when my time comes, it comes. I shall welcome death as rest."

"Decker, I had no idea you still hurt so much," Christopher said softly.

"It's okay," Decker answered. "On a day-to-day basis I'm fine. It's just that when I look at the long run, I don't think I could live forever with this emptiness I feel."

"I'm so sorry, Decker. I wish I had known."

"There's nothing anyone could have done."

"But, don't you see? There *is!*" Christopher let slip an ironic laugh that left Decker struggling to understand what he meant. "Don't you see?" he said again. "Haven't you been listening to your own speeches? For more than three years you have overseen the creation and administration of training and indoctrination for those unfamiliar with New Age concepts. You've lectured on dozens of college campuses, been interviewed by hundreds of reporters, written who-knows-how-many articles, and yet you still don't realize that what you've been saying applies to you, too? No one really dies, Decker; not forever! Life goes on long after the body dies. We're reborn time and again. It's no different with Hope or Louisa . . . or Elizabeth!"

Decker felt as though his heart had stopped. He wasn't sure what Christopher meant, but it seemed he was saying there was hope that he might see his family again.

"Decker, there's no reason for you to accept death! You haven't lost Elizabeth forever! She's alive! She has *already* been born again!"

"What are you saying?" Decker asked, his voice trembling as he choked back tears.

"Elizabeth is *alive*. Can't you feel it? She was born again just months after you lost her."

"But where is she? Can I see her?"

"Not yet," Christopher answered apologetically. "But you will. I can tell you a little about her, though. She's twenty-one years old and lives in New Brunswick."

"How long have you known? Why didn't you tell me? Why can't I see her?"

"Decker, it's not time yet. She wouldn't know you."

Decker was confused. "Will she remember me?" he asked slowly, a wave of dread telling him Christopher's answer would be no.

"Yes, Decker. She will. Even now she knows there is something missing from her life. In a few years—it's impossible to say exactly when—she will go through past life therapy and will remember who she was in her previous life. Then she will remember you."

"And . . ."

"Yes, Decker," Christopher said, smiling. "She will

come to you. How could you believe otherwise? Decker, there are some things that are stronger than death. Yours will be a love story for the New Age."

"But . . . you said she's twenty-one? I'm old enough to be her grandfather."

Christopher started to laugh, but this time he didn't hold back. It was a joyous laugh. "Decker, when you're going to live forever, you don't let a little thing like fifty years get in your way!"

"No, I guess not," Decker acknowledged, starting to laugh along, though his eyes were still filled with tears. "Besides, I guess I'll seem a lot younger by then."

"Then you'll take the communion?" Christopher asked.

"Of course! I'll go right now!"

"Well, I don't think you'll find a clinic open this late. You'll have to wait at least until morning."

Decker looked at his watch and nodded. "What about Hope and Louisa?" he asked.

"One day they will remember you, too," Christopher smiled. "Soon, Decker, in perhaps a hundred years, *all* the veils will be lifted and all of Humankind will remember who they were in *all* of their past lives. And they shall understand just how really connected all of us are to one another. Many will find that their enemies in one life were their dearest friends in another. And in that day, when they know who they *were*, they shall begin to understand who they truly *are*."

"Can you tell me about . . ." Decker hesitated to ask. He wanted to ask about his old friend, Tom Donafin, but he was not sure how Christopher would feel about his continued interest in the man who had shot him.

"It's all right, Decker. Who do you want to know about?"

"Can you tell me about Tom Donafin?"

Christopher smiled, not at all upset that Decker would ask. "He was reborn last year to a family in Paraguay."

Decker shed another tear and tried to thank Christopher, but words failed him.

"It's all right, Decker. Why don't you go home now and get some rest?"

Decker nodded.

As he was about to close the door behind him, Christopher went after him to give him a hug. With tears in his eyes, Christopher said, "I'm sorry I didn't understand before how you felt. I'm just glad we've got this worked out now and that you're going to take the communion. I need you, Decker. I don't know how I could get along without you."

❏

Decker left the building in a euphoric daze. Suddenly his whole life . . . his whole eternity had changed. He had something worth living for . . . something worth living *forever* for.

❏

"That's him in the gray suit," whispered one of the two men who stood waiting in the shadows.

Decker walked along, totally lost in joyous thought and unaware of their presence.

They emerged from the alley as Decker passed, the

red Hebrew lettering of the Koum Damah Patar now clearly visible on their foreheads.

Decker struggled to get away, but the two men overpowered him. The chloroformed rag, though old-fashioned, was effective.

7

Petra

```
June 3, 4 N.A.
The wilderness of Jordan
```

DECKER SAT QUIETLY in the back seat of a dirty, rapidly moving, four-wheel-drive vehicle, his hands and feet firmly tethered, bouncing with each bump in the road. As the two men in the front seat spoke to each other in Hebrew, Decker observed everything, trying to memorize each characteristic of the Jordanian wilderness. After eighteen hours in their custody he was exhausted, but if an opportunity presented itself, he would need to know every feature of the terrain to make good an escape.

The early afternoon rays of the sun beat down with blistering heat and Decker thought back to his escape from Lebanon twenty-three years earlier. While it was true that when he fled Lebanon he was badly malnourished, he wondered which was worse, being malnourished or being old. Of course, he lamented, attempting flight by foot over this wasteland at his age would cause rapid dehydration and starvation to accompany his advanced years. It was hard not to be pessimistic, even though he knew discouragement was probably the worst impediment to his chances of getting out alive.

It seemed bitter irony that his life should be placed in jeopardy at this particular time. Had he been kidnapped an hour earlier he would have considered his life of little consequence. Only moments before his abduction, he had told Christopher that when his time came, he would welcome death as rest. But that was before he really understood, before he learned that Elizabeth was alive. Now more than anything —more than ever before in his life— he wanted to live.

Passing the ruins of the ancient stepped village of Elji and the more recent but no less deserted village of Wadi Mousa, Decker scanned the horizon for any sign of their ultimate destination. In the distance the desolate jagged slopes of Seir, a rocky chain of mountains stretching from the Dead Sea to Akaba, rose above the gray stony wilderness floor. Looming above the rest of the range was the mountain Gebel Haroun, said to be the burial place of Moses' brother, Aaron. It was another twenty minutes before they reached the mountains, and it became evident that this was the end of their journey.

"We'll have to walk from here, Mr. Hawthorne," the taller of the two KDP said as the other pulled the jeep to a stop.

Decker looked around for what it was they were going to be walking *to* but found nothing but barren cliffs. Could they have brought him to these rocky crags just to kill him in some ritualistic execution? The KDP who had been driving pulled his seat forward so Decker could get out of the jeep. This was not an easy task with both his feet and hands bound.

"Where is it?" asked the other KDP, who was behind the jeep rummaging through a small metal bin.

"It's in there," answered the other. "Just keep looking . . ."

"Oh, here it is," said the first. Coming around to the other side of the vehicle, Decker could see what had been the object of his search. Now standing directly in front of him, the KDP revealed the knife he held in his hand. It was not very frightening in appearance, but it was sufficient to do the job. Decker braced himself as the man dropped to one knee and raised the blade with a quick thrust and cut the cords that held his feet.

"Let's go," said the other KDP as he took Decker by the arm to lead him. But still there was nowhere *to* go and no explanation that did not smell like death. Furiously Decker surveyed his surroundings for any avenue of escape. If he was going to make an attempt, this might be his one and only opportunity.

They walked a short distance and Decker heard voices: They were not alone. Coming around a bend he saw them: scores of other people, nearly all KDP. They were all walking toward the mountain. There was no chance to flee—Decker's captors never left his side and, except for the path before and behind them, there was nowhere to go but up the rocky slopes. All those around him spoke in Hebrew, making it impossible for Decker to understand. Their path now brought them along the bank of a small stream—the Wadi Mousa, or river of Moses— which they followed toward the mountain.

Looking to his right, Decker was startled by the unexpected form of three square stone pillars, each about four feet wide, the tallest of which rose twenty feet above its base. They had not been erected there, but were cut from the solid stone, carved right out of the mountain. This clearly was not the work of nature but rather of some ancient craftsmen.

Rounding another bend, they came upon a scene even more unexpected than the pillars. Carved into the white stone face of the mountain were two large facades that looked like buildings—weathered by thousands of years, one above the other like layers of a cake. The upper was dominated by four stone obelisks with a door in the middle. The lower was far more ornately designed, perhaps Roman or Hellenistic in style. In addition to a door, it appeared to have a rectangular window near the facade's leftmost corner.

The stream and the path they followed now looked to be heading for a dead end. Instead, the wadi made a sharp right turn and ran along the base of the sheer rock cliff. On the left was a dam of relatively recent construction, built across a wide fissure in the rock wall. Decker guessed its purpose was to prevent flash floods from rushing into the passage at the base of the mountain. It was into this fissure that the flow of people now carried him. On his right, opposite the dam, Decker caught a quick glance at several small obelisks carved into the rock in low relief.

The rock walls on either side of the gorge were about twenty feet high. Just beyond the entrance were faint remnants of what could only have been a man-made arch, though it had long since collapsed. A small channel had been cut into the rock along the foot of the left wall of the gorge, and a stream of water from the wadi had been diverted through it. A little farther in, the gorge opened up, but this was not the end of their journey. Instead, along the path, which sloped slowly but constantly downward as the rock walls rose steadily higher, the flow of people entered into another smaller cleft.

The path went on and on, passing down long straight stretches and then winding through narrow turns, with the rock palisades rising to as much as four hundred feet. From time to time they passed stone monuments, wall carvings, and niches cut into the stone, as well as steps leading up and away from the path. The color of the rock, which had been bleached-white before they entered the gorge, now ranged from pearly white to yellow gold to red to grayish pink.

At places, the narrowing path opened up wide enough for bushes and even a few trees to grow, but each time led into a narrower opening. Along a few short stretches the path was marked by paving stones from some ancient civilization.

Decker was beginning to tire. They had gone on for over a mile through the narrow chasm, and it seemed the journey would never end. Then finally, around a turn, at the narrowest and darkest point through the passage, Decker saw the most curious of sights: a large baroque Greek temple-styled building cut out of, or more precisely, cut right into the side of the mountain. As they exited the fissure—which Decker would soon learn was called the *Siq*—they entered into a deep wide canyon. Decker's captors allowed him to rest there a moment and take in the magnificence of the monument. It was beautifully preserved, cut deep into the mountain's face with perfectly formed columns, ornately carved capitals and pediment, and towering 120 feet from its base to its pinnacle. The color of the rock appeared a beautiful rosy red as it reflected the sun.

Turning right, they continued past numerous additional ancient facades cut into the canyon's walls. The most ornate were tombs, but many others seemed to have been carved as primitive homes—a purpose that they now served to a new set of residents. A little farther on they came upon a Roman-style amphitheater large enough to seat four or five thousand people. It, too, was carved entirely out of the stone. The canyon grew slowly wider and soon it emptied into an immense valley spreading out for several miles—a huge basin, surrounded on all sides by jagged-topped mountains. The massive cliffs were predominantly red but with alternating patches of black and white and yellow stone, and everywhere the sheer slopes were dotted by magnificent stone facades.

On the floor of the basin were tens of thousands, probably even hundreds of thousands of tents, housing a whole city of people. And there was one other thing: Between the tents and on nearly every patch of ground there were fruit trees and well-tended vegetable gardens, all lush with produce waiting to be picked.

"Welcome to Petra, Mr. Hawthorne," one of the KDP said, as Decker took in the sight.

Ahead he saw a single wooden building about fifteen feet wide by twenty-five feet long, which could best be described as a cabin with a small porch off the front. That being the only structure in sight with walls of anything more substantial than canvas, Decker assumed it to be his destination, the place where he would be imprisoned pending whatever action the KDP had in mind. This assumption was reinforced by the six large men who stood around the periphery of the building—obviously the guards who would terminate his exodus should he attempt to flee. The two KDP brought him to the front door.

The inside of the cabin was not at all what he had expected: It looked more like a rustic vacation home than a jail. Upon entering and looking around, Decker half expected to see fishing rods or deer antlers on the wall. The first room was a combination kitchen and sitting room that ran the full width of the building and about ten feet deep. The sitting room had two old but recently recovered chairs, a coffee table, and a couch. The kitchen, which was separated from the sitting room only by the placement of the furniture, was furnished with a gas stove and a small refrigerator.

Decker scanned the area for knives or any other kitchen implement that might make a good weapon, but he saw nothing more intimidating than a spatula and a large wooden spoon. In the center of the kitchen area was an empty space bordered by two straight-backed wooden chairs with padded seats, where it looked as if there had recently been a table. Slumped over in one of the wooden chairs with his feet propped up on the seat of the other sat a man with reddish blond hair. He was asleep. On his lap was a decades-old copy of *Mad* magazine in Hebrew. Decker noticed that he did not have the mark of the KDP.

"Charlie, wake up!" one of the KDP said. "Your guest is here."

The man sprang from his chair, though it was clear he was not yet fully awake.

"We'll let the appropriate people know he's here," the other KDP said. Then, cutting the bonds from Decker's hands, he added, "I know you won't believe this, Mr.

Hawthorne, but I sincerely regret having to bring you here under these circumstances."

Decker glared and after a moment the two KDP left.

"Welcome to Petra," the other man said as though he really meant it.

"So, are you my jailer?" Decker asked.

The question caught the man off guard. "I'd, uh, prefer not to be described that way, but I guess I can't blame you for thinking so." Decker would not so easily be charmed from his indignation by the man's disarming disposition. "Well," the jailer said uncomfortably, "your room's right over here." He pointed to a door behind them. "It's not the King David," he said, referring to the hotel in Jerusalem, "but it's better than most in Petra."

The jailer opened the door and motioned for Decker to follow. With six guards outside and hundreds of miles of wilderness all around, resistance seemed rather futile. Besides, from the looks of it, this was not the most uncomfortable dungeon he had ever been sentenced to. Inside the room was a metal-framed bed, a table (which looked to be the size of the empty spot in the kitchen), two chairs that matched the two in the kitchen, and a dresser. The room was light and pleasant, with windows facing east and west. The curtains were made of colorful Israeli cloth that matched the chair seats and bedspread. Off the back of the room was a bathroom and a closet, in which hung two pairs of pants and four or five shirts that Decker guessed would be his size. They obviously planned to keep him there for a while.

"This is where you'll be staying," the jailer said. And then turning to leave he paused to add, "I'm sure you must be hungry. If I had known when you'd arrive, I'd have had a meal waiting. I'll be back just as soon as I can put something together for you."

❑

True to his word, the jailer soon returned with a tray that included a few slices of baked apple and small portions of beans and squash. The main course of the meal was a bowl of some type of porridge made of a sweet white flour. In his years at the UN Decker had eaten foods from every country in the world, but he had never tasted anything quite like this.

After lunch, Decker lay on the bed, and despite his concern about his situation, slipped off to sleep. He was awakened around 7:00 P.M. by a knock at the door. In protest Decker did not respond, and after a moment, the knock was repeated. When he still did not respond, the visitor came in uninvited.

"Good evening, Mr. Hawthorne." The speaker was a large man, over six feet tall, and strong, though in his mid-sixties. His thick curly hair, now gray with age, still held a trace of color, revealing that it had once been jet black. On his forehead beneath the curls was the blood-red insignia of the KDP. "I apologize for keeping you waiting," he said.

"Why have you brought me here?" Decker demanded.

"Only to talk with you," the man answered calmly.

"You mean to brainwash me, don't you? The way you did to Tom Donafin!" Decker watched for any reaction by his captor, and though there was none he continued. "That's right! I know what you did to Tom!" Tom Donafin had told Decker that he had been with the KDP:

It was only logical to conclude that it was the KDP who had convinced him to assassinate Christopher. "Well, it's not going to work. Not this time!" Decker continued to study his captor's face closely for any reaction or hint of a weakness he might use to his advantage.

"Mr. Hawthorne, I assure you, no one brainwashed Tom Donafin." Decker was a little surprised that the man so freely admitted his familiarity with Tom.

"Oh . . . well," Decker sputtered in feigned contrition, and then very firmly added, "you'll forgive me if I think you're a liar!"

"If you wish. But liar or not, this is my stated intention for bringing you here: It is not to brainwash you, but only to talk with you. Whether you believe this to be a lie or the truth is up to you."

"So I'm supposed to believe that kidnapping me has nothing to do with my relationship with Christopher Goodman? Your thugs just picked me at random for a free trip to Petra."

"I apologize for my methods, Mr. Hawthorne, but there didn't seem to be any other way to get you here."

"If you think you're going to use me to get at Christopher, you can just forget it. And if you think that by holding me you can manipulate Christopher, you're not only mistaken, you're stupid. Or maybe you're just hoping to make him mad. Well, you might just succeed at that!"

The man shook his head at each of Decker's conjectures. "I only want to talk with you," he repeated.

"You don't really believe that the UN Security Forces are just going to *overlook* the fact that you've kidnapped the Director of Public Affairs, do you?"

"You travel frequently in your job, Mr. Hawthorne. I suspect it may be several days before anyone is sure you're actually missing."

He was probably right, but Decker had no time to consider it. As he studied the man's face, suddenly something seemed vaguely familiar. Decker cocked his head and looked closely at him, trying to remember. He strained his memory but to no avail. "Do I know you?" he asked, finally. "I *do* know you!" he said, not giving the man a chance to answer. In part at least, Decker was bluffing: He wasn't really sure that he had ever seen the man before, but still there was something undeniably familiar about him.

"Yes, Mr. Hawthorne. We know each other," the man admitted. "My name is Scott Rosen."

Decker shrugged. The name meant nothing to him. It had been many years since he had last heard it.

"My parents were Joshua and Ilana Rosen."

Decker remembered Joshua and Ilana well, but could not immediately recall very much about their son, other than the fact that they had one. The family resemblance was obvious, however. In fact, as Decker considered the man's face, he realized that it was only this resemblance that had made him think he recognized the man. Then he remembered.

"Oh, yeah!" he said. "I know you! You betrayed your parents to keep them from getting their Israeli citizenship." The reference appeared to sting a little, and Decker looked for some way to exploit it. "So I see you're still an obnoxious bully," he said, shaking his head in disgust. He wanted to do everything he could to belittle his captor. It was not just to strike back at him for the kidnapping, however: It was the beginning of a plan. Decker knew from intelligence summaries and news reports that the fundamentalists did not kill their hostages before getting them to "convert." He assumed the KDP probably did the same. It was a long shot and he knew it, but Decker hoped that if he could quickly convince his captor that it was hopeless to try to convert him, perhaps he might still get out of this alive.

It was not that easy.

"Mr. Hawthorne," Scott Rosen answered, "I have come to realize that I was wrong, but not only for the way I treated my parents. I was also wrong about their beliefs. I know now they were right. Yeshua—Jesus—*is* the Jewish Messiah."

"So this is all an attempt to make up for what you did to your parents," Decker said, without missing a beat. "Well, if you have any respect at all for the memory of your parents, you'll release me immediately!"

"Mr. Hawthorne," Scott Rosen said again, "all I want to do is talk to you."

"Well, I don't want to talk to you!"

Rosen ran his fingers through his long thick beard. "As you wish, Mr. Hawthorne," he said as he got up to leave.

Decker felt a rush of success: He had gotten a reaction. He was still the prisoner, but he was in control, even if it was only control of the conversation. Though he would have liked to continue lecturing Rosen on the impropriety of his actions, he decided to hold his tongue. For now he would wait and see what came next.

As Scott Rosen reached the doorway, he turned in

apparent afterthought with one question: "Mr. Hawthorne, why have you not taken the communion?"

"I was on my way to get it when your people kidnapped me," Decker answered quickly, hoping to negate any significance that Rosen might attach to the fact.

"My friends—the ones who brought you here," Rosen said, "had specific orders not to take you if you had the mark. If you had, it would have been too late."

Decker glared at this kidnapper who would presume to judge him.

"It's not an accident that you haven't taken the mark," Rosen continued. "It's the grace of God."

Decker laughed mockingly. "You people interpret whatever suits you as a sign from God. Well, you're wrong, Rosen. The whole idea of the mark was mine. I'm the one who originally suggested requiring the mark, and I would have taken the communion myself and had the mark by now if your thugs hadn't grabbed me!"

"Going to get the mark and having the mark are not the same thing, Mr. Hawthorne. God—I have learned— is never too early and never too late, but always right on time."

❑

Decker's supper was much the same as lunch with the exception that it included a small mutton chop, and the sweet meal used earlier to make the porridge had been used as flour to make a sort of pancake, which was fried in olive oil. After eating, Decker lay down and tried to go to sleep. It was only 9:30 P.M., but he was certainly tired enough. Besides, he knew if he was to survive whatever

Rosen and the KDP had in mind for him, he would need all the rest he could get. The mountains that formed the walls of Petra did their part by shutting out the sun well before it grew dark outside this city hidden in the hollow of the mountains. Still, despite his best efforts, or perhaps because of them, he just couldn't fall asleep. No amount of sheep-counting seemed to help; there was simply too much on his mind. It felt as though he had been lying there all night. In truth, it was only about 11:30 when he finally dozed off.

June 4, 4 N·A·
Petra

Rising early, Decker crept silently toward the window and looked out, hoping his guards might be asleep. They weren't. That, however, was not what caught Decker's attention. Shaking his head to clear his mind and his vision, he looked again at what seemed an impossible sight, for as far as he could see, everything lay blanketed with a covering of what looked for all the world like snow. It wasn't snow—it couldn't be—it was a hot morning in June. But despite all his attempts over the next several minutes, he could come up with no other explanation. A hundred yards away, a woman and a young boy came out of one of the thousands of tents that speckled the ancient tableau and began scooping up the white material and putting it into a tub. Soon others came out of their shelters, carrying in their arms pots and pans and baskets, and they too began collecting the snowy material.

Decker heard the door open and looked over to see the

jailer bringing in breakfast. "What is *that?*" he asked, pointing out the window.

"Exactly," the man answered.

"No," Decker said, trying again. "Is that *snow?*"

"No," the jailer laughed.

"Well, then, what is it?"

"Exactly," the jailer repeated.

This was getting nowhere, and Decker was not going to ask again.

"I'm sorry," the jailer laughed when he saw he could press it no further. "I always hoped somebody would ask me that."

Decker was not amused.

"That's what it is: 'what is it,' " the jailer said as if that was supposed to be the answer. "The white stuff outside is called 'what is it.' At least that's the English translation. In Hebrew, it's called *manna*. Here, look," he said, motioning toward the tray he had brought in. On it was a bowl filled with the white substance. "Try it," the jailer said.

Decker took a pinch from the bowl and tasted it. It was crunchy and white like coriander seed and it tasted like wafers made with honey. He recognized the taste immediately as the grain from which the porridge and fritters had been made the day before.

"We use it for everything," the jailer said. "There must be a thousand different recipes. We've got manna bread, manna donuts, manna cookies, manna pasta, manna spaghetti, manna waffles; we've got fried manna, boiled manna, broiled manna, toasted manna, and even raw manna; we've even got manna manicotti. And this morning we've got manna muffins and manna cereal."

"But what is it?"

"Exactly," the jailer said again. Decker wondered if he was ever going to get a complete answer.

"When Moses led the people out of Egypt," the jailer explained, "God provided manna for them to eat.[14] He has done the same here in Petra. Each morning, except on the Sabbath, a dew sets in and when it lifts, it leaves behind the manna. Later, as the sun gets hot, the manna melts away, leaving no trace that it was ever there."

It was a preposterous story, but there it was, outside the window and in his bowl.

❑

After breakfast the jailer returned for the tray and brought two cups and a plastic pitcher filled with cold water. Shortly after, Scott Rosen returned.

"When are you going to release me?" Decker grizzled as soon as Rosen walked through the door.

"I prayed about our conversation last night," Rosen said, as though he had not heard the question.

Decker chuckled and then laughed out loud. His laughter mocked Rosen but it was the most sincere form of mockery: He truly found Rosen's pitiful piety funny.

Rosen was forced to wait until Decker stopped before he continued. "I realized I didn't entirely answer your question about why I brought you here. You asked me if I was trying to make up for what I did to my parents. The answer to your question is still no. In a way, however, my parents do have something to do with your being here."

[14] Exodus 16.

"I'm really not interested," Decker said, but to no effect.

"You see, I'm sure they would have wanted us to talk."

"So now you not only know the will of God, you also know the will of your dead parents."

"What I want to tell you is no different than what they would say to you if they were alive."

"They would not have kidnapped me and forced me to listen," Decker shot back. "I am quite certain that your variety of Christianity—if that's what you call it—differs markedly from the Christianity practiced by your parents."

"It is not our beliefs that differ, Mr. Hawthorne, but our times and circumstances."

"Your circumstances are of your own making!"

Rosen caught himself. He was letting Decker get control of the conversation again, and he had not yet finished his explanation. "We can discuss my methods later," he said. "For right now I'd like to finish explaining why I brought you here."

At every point in the conversation Decker looked for opportunities to keep Rosen off balance, which meant weighing whether he should try to frustrate Rosen's agenda by interrupting or listen for information he might later be able to use to his benefit. Sometimes the decision was based on his assessment of what Rosen was getting at, sometimes it was sheer intuition. For the moment, he decided to listen.

"Besides bringing you here because I think it's what my parents would have wanted, there are two other reasons. The first is that for a long time, almost since the day of my own conversion to follow Yeshua, I have felt drawn to talk to you. This isn't the first time I've made the attempt, either. Six years ago, you and Christopher came to Israel before the war between India, Pakistan, and China." Decker remembered the trip well: It was just before Christopher went into the Israeli wilderness for forty days. It was also the first time Decker had heard of the KDP.

"I don't remember seeing you then," Decker said, not to inform but to challenge Rosen's assertion.

"You didn't," countered Rosen. "I backed down."

Decker made a quick mental note of this piece of information. It showed weakness on Rosen's part—something had scared him, made him "back down."

Rosen continued, "I felt that God had directed me to talk with you, but you were so close to Christopher, it seemed impossible to me that you would listen." Even though many people referred to Christopher by his first name, Decker found he bristled at Scott Rosen's familiar use.

"You *mean,*" Decker answered, "it seemed impossible that I would *betray* him." The response had been intended only as a polemic jab, but as Decker heard the words he spoke, he suddenly believed he understood why it was so important to Rosen that they talk. On the plane to Israel after his resurrection, Christopher had said that in a past life Decker had been Judas Iscariot, the apostle who, according to history, had betrayed Jesus. Two thousand years ago, Christopher said, it had been the Apostle John who had convinced Judas to betray Jesus. Now Scott Rosen was attempting to play John's role. Yahweh had indeed directed Rosen to talk to him, Decker realized. Christopher had said that Yahweh would become more and more desperate as he saw the planet slipping from his grip. This must be a sign of that desperation. *Well,* Decker promised himself steadfastly, *it's not going to work this time.* He had never been able to recall any part of his past life as Judas, so he had no remembered experience to draw upon for guidance, but one way or another he was determined that he would *not* make the same mistake twice. He would rather die than betray Christopher.

"There will be no reason for you to die, Mr. Hawthorne," Scott Rosen said, unexpectedly.

Decker was infuriated. Rosen had read his thoughts. The one thing Decker had assumed he could count upon—the privacy of his own thoughts—was shattered in a single instant.

Decker stared at Rosen in disgust. "You know," he shot back, "I admit that it was crazy, but somehow I had held on to this ridiculous notion that even though you were a kidnapper and who knows what else, there might be some small shred of decency in you, some little something that would compel you to play fair. You pathetic hypocrite, you've been reading my mind!"

"Not entirely, Mr. Hawthorne," Rosen responded, apparently unaffected by Decker's tone or terminology. "I only know what I am able to perceive from your behavior and by a few glimpses that God gives me of your thoughts."

Decker glared.

"And, though I'm sure you won't believe this either, those things that Christopher told you about John and Judas were lies . . . all of them."

Decker clenched his teeth in rage.

"We can deal with that later, however," Rosen continued, oblivious to Decker's reaction. It was as though suddenly Rosen had lost not only his ability to read Decker's mind, he was also blind to the fury on his face. It was clear that Rosen's tactic was to ignore whatever Decker said or did that did not further his cause. "Right now," he went on, "I am determined to finish my explanation of why I brought you to Petra."

"I wasn't just *brought* here!" Decker screamed. "I was kidnapped! Can't you even be honest enough to admit *that?*"

"If when we are through, you still believe as you do now, then my crime will indeed be kidnapping. If, however, I am able to show you that you've been wrong about the KDP and that you're wrong about Christopher, then I will not be guilty of kidnapping, but rather, of rescuing you."

"That's pure drivel," Decker growled.

"As I was saying," Rosen continued, "after I backed down from talking to you in Tel Aviv . . ."

Decker's mind raced. For a second time, Rosen had admitted backing down. Did he not care that this exposed a weakness? Did he think that since Decker had caught the point the first time he said it that there was no harm in saying it again? *The man's not only a lunatic, he's stupid,* Decker thought. Or did Rosen think that by bringing it up again it might make it appear that he either no longer held or cared about that particular fear? . . . Or did he *really* have only a limited ability to read Decker's mind, so that he didn't realize the importance Decker assigned to the statement about backing down?

Decker decided to test the theory. *I'm going to slug this guy,* he thought. *I'm going to slug him,* he thought again, almost trying to send his thought to his captor. *I'm going to slug him . . . now!* And then, lunging across the small table and knocking over the pitcher of water, Decker planted his right fist on the left side of Rosen's face.

Scott Rosen spun around and fell from his chair with the force of Decker's punch.

Sprawled across the table and struggling to keep his balance, Decker watched with great satisfaction as the big man tumbled to the floor. Now the question was: Had Rosen been unable to read his thoughts or had he taken the blow just to make Decker believe that? He had watched Rosen's eyes as he hit him, and there was no sign of an early flinch that would have indicated he knew the blow was coming. Returning to his chair, Decker realized the test was not really conclusive. Either way, it had felt good to hit him.

Rosen winced in pain on the floor, his clothing wet as he lay in the puddle of water from the pitcher, his head spinning. Then looking at Decker, he got up slowly and relocated himself in his chair. "I suppose you expect me to turn the other cheek now?" he asked.

"If you'd like," Decker said with triumph in his voice that disguised the throbbing pain he felt in his hand.

Rosen rubbed his cheek, but refused to be distracted, and amazingly went back to his story as though nothing had happened. His persistence was getting a little unnerving. "I continued to struggle with the feeling that I needed to talk with you," he said. "Then Saul Cohen, on the day before he was killed in Jerusalem, came to me and, without explanation, told me that when the time was right I was to do as God instructed me. I knew immediately he was talking about you."

"So far you've blamed my abduction on God, your parents, and now Saul Cohen—none of whom, I notice, are here to defend themselves."

"And finally," Rosen continued, ignoring Decker's comment, "there's one other reason I brought you here: I believe that in some part I am responsible for the fact that you didn't accept Yeshua as your savior long ago."

Decker rolled his eyes. "Oh, brother," he sighed.

"You see," Rosen said before Decker could go on, "I once interrupted a conversation between you and your wife, that if I hadn't, might have dramatically changed your life."

Decker's eyes flared red, though he tried to hide it. He wanted to shout, "You leave my wife out of this!" but he knew if he did, Rosen would realize he had hit a nerve. As long as there was any chance that he did *not* always know what Decker was thinking, it was better not to react. "I don't know what you're talking about," Decker muttered through clenched teeth.

"It was in the hospital in Tel Aviv," Rosen said. "You and Tom Donafin had just returned to Israel after your escape from Lebanon. When I heard that you had actually been abducted on Israeli soil, I was outraged that the Hizballah had dared to take hostages from inside Israel. I insisted that you and Tom report the details to the authorities immediately, but everyone else said it could wait until later, so I stormed off to call the police myself. When I got back with the police, you and your family and my parents were talking."

Decker remembered the event, but he had no immediate recollection of what they had been talking about.

"You are aware, I believe, that while you were a hostage, your family spent a lot of time with my parents."

Decker *did* remember that. Elizabeth and the girls had talked about Joshua and Ilana a lot before the Disaster. Apparently they had gotten pretty close.

"Well, that night after the event with the police in the hospital lobby, I overheard my parents talking. Apparently, I had walked in and interrupted your wife just as she was about to tell you that she and your daughters had accepted Yeshua as lord and savior and become Christians while you were in Lebanon. If I hadn't interrupted, they were planning to tell you that and to explain the Gospel to you."

"You needn't have troubled yourself, Rosen," Decker said mockingly. "If my wife—" Decker chose not to defile Elizabeth's name by saying it in Scott Rosen's presence, "—had wanted to *explain the Gospel* to me, she had ample opportunity after that night."

"True," Rosen replied, "no doubt, she did. And for that I bear no responsibility. However, your wife was certainly not the first Christian to make the mistake of thinking she had plenty of time to get around to sharing her faith with those she cared about. But then the Rapture came, and there *was* no more time."

Decker gaped blankly at Rosen, his expression unintentionally revealing that he had no idea what Rosen was talking about.

"Your wife and children didn't die," Rosen explained. "Nor did my parents or the millions of others who the world believes died in what they call the Disaster." Decker's expression made it obvious that he was incredulous at such a preposterous claim. Was Rosen insane?

"There was no Disaster," Rosen continued, unabated. "Your family, my parents, and all the others—except of course, some who died in resulting accidents—didn't die. They were 'raptured,' caught away by Yeshua to remove their influence from the world and to spare them the horrors of the times in which we now live. What the world knows as the Disaster, Mr. Hawthorne, was really the Rapture, just as was described prophetically by the Apostle Paul when he wrote:

> . . . the dead in Christ will rise first. After that, we who are still alive and are left will be caught up together with them in the clouds to meet the Lord in the air. And so we will be with the Lord forever."[15]

Decker shook his head several times in disbelief. "You fanatics have an amazing ability to ignore the most obvious flaws in your theology," he said. "What about the bodies? My wife and children didn't 'go up in the clouds to be with Jesus'; they died, just as your parents did! And their bodies are the proof!"

"The bodies of the people who were raptured were corruptible—the decaying remains of the family of our fallen ancestor, Adam," Rosen propounded. "Those bodies never would have been permitted in heaven and so were simply sloughed off, or shed like old clothes. When they were raptured, they were given new bodies: perfect, incorruptible, and without flaw. Again, I refer you to the words of the Apostle Paul:

[15] 1 Thessalonians 4:16–17.

> *. . . flesh and blood cannot inherit the kingdom of God,*
> *nor does the perishable inherit the imperishable. Listen,*
> *I tell you a mystery: We will not all sleep, but we will all*
> *be changed—in a flash, in the twinkling of an*
> *eye . . . the dead will be raised imperishable, and we will*
> *be changed. For the perishable must clothe itself with*
> *the imperishable, and the mortal with immortality.*[16]

"The Greek word[17] in the passage that is translated as *changed*, is elsewhere[18] translated as *exchanged*. Indeed, *exchanged* is probably a more exact translation because it is the term used when discussing changing clothes,[19] which in reality, of course, is *exchanging* one garment for another. In another Scripture, the change that took place at the Rapture is described in terms of exchanging a tent for a house.[20] The tent does not become the house. Its materials are not used to build the house. It is discarded in exchange for the house. And concerning Christians who died before the Rapture, Paul said that the resurrected bodies would not be the same as the bodies that were buried.[21] Thus, as I said, the old bodies of those who appeared to die in the Disaster were actually exchanged for *new* ones, and the old ones were left behind."

[16] 1 Corinthians 15:50–53.

[17] ἀλλάσσω (allasso).

[18] Romans 1:23.

[19] See for example here (1 Corinthians 15:53) and in Hebrews 1:12.

[20] 2 Corinthians 5:1–4.

[21] 1 Corinthians 15:35–44.

Decker shook his head again, amazed that Rosen could believe what he was proposing. "And how do you explain all the Christians who were not 'raptured'? I don't recall hearing that all the churches were emptied by the Disaster," he noted sarcastically. "And what about the churches today? What about the fundamentalists?"

"Not everyone who claims to be a Christian *is* one, Mr. Hawthorne. Going to church doesn't make you a Christian any more than going to a football game makes you an athlete. As for those you call the fundamentalists, these are non-Jewish people who accepted Jesus after the Rapture."

"So you're saying that you and your fundamentalist allies are the only *real* Christians?" Decker challenged.

"For the most part, yes, that is true," Rosen answered without excuse.

"Do you guys just sit around making up this stuff, or what?"

Rosen didn't answer, but Decker was not through with him. "Explain this to me," he chided. "If God wanted to have people 'accept Jesus as lord and savior,' it seems rather odd that he would decide to 'rapture' all the Christians out of the world and replace them with lunatic fanatics whose tactics drive away everyone except *other* lunatic fanatics."

"As I already said, in part the Rapture was to spare those who were already Christians from the suffering, just as God spared Noah and his family before the flood[22] and just as he spared Lot and his family before the destruction of Sodom and Gomorrah.[23] But by far the most

[22] Genesis 6:8–7:7.

[23] Genesis 19:15–25.

important reason for the Rapture was to remove from the world what was good so that the world would sink to its lowest levels. God wanted to show just how corrupt the world would become without his influence.

"Christopher and the New Age teach that 'Humankind' is on the verge of a great evolutionary advancement. But where is the evidence? Have people stopped hating each other? Have jealousy and envy ceased? I won't even ask if crime has been reduced because there is so little that is considered a crime anymore. All but the worst offenses have been legalized or are now considered matters of 'personal choice.' The parks of your great cities are filled with nudity and nameless, faceless sex. There are no limits—sex with children, even bestiality is commonplace and considered normal. And what passes as 'performance art' is intentionally aimed at turning even the strongest stomachs.

"Those who do not participate have turned a blind eye, ignoring what is all around them, until they have become numb to the depravity. What used to be limited to raunchy X-rated movies is now standard fare on daytime television. Abortion is looked upon as nothing more than birth control. Drugs, now legal and easily available, are used on a regular basis by more than 30 percent of the population. People have become gluttons, indulging their every appetite.

"Tell me, Mr. Hawthorne, have pride and greed and selfishness been eliminated as Humankind stands ready to enter the New Age? Have the number of murders dropped so dramatically or the cases of violence been so reduced? Is that why such things are so seldom reported by the news media? Or is it that they have become so commonplace that they are no longer considered newsworthy? And the psychic powers that Christopher has told us are the signs of the coming New Age—are they used to help others, or are they used almost exclusively for the benefit of the individuals who possess such powers?"

Rosen shook his head. "Left to their own devices, without God's influence, it is absolutely stupefying just how truly debased and vicious the world has become. Are these things the evidence that should convince us that mankind is ready for godhood, or are they proof that all of us are hopelessly lost without a forgiving and loving God?" Rosen didn't wait for an answer. "God knew," he continued, "that only when things are at their worst will some people realize their need and turn to him. Those who have are the ones you call fundamentalists.

"But I think there may have been one other reason for the Rapture," Rosen added. "I admit I did not know many Christians before the Rapture, but from all the division that existed among them, I suspect that if God had left them here, many of them would be too busy arguing over church rules and trivial doctrines to have been of any use in reaching the lost.

"And as for our tactics, which you believe make us 'lunatic fanatics,' I would submit that confronting people with the sin in their lives and calling them to repent is no different than what Jesus did in the story of the woman at the well."[24]

"This is all very amusing," Decker interrupted with a forced laugh. "But I know what happened to my family

[24] John 4:16–18.

and it has nothing to do with your religious fantasies." Then, even though he was sure it was a waste of time, Decker tried to reason with Rosen. "Can't you see what you've done?" he pressed. "You feel guilty for what you did to your parents and you've bought into this whole crazy story to convince yourself that your parents didn't really die so you won't have to deal with your guilt."

Scott Rosen apparently was not in the mood to be reasoned with. "We'll talk later," he said, and got up to leave without explanation.

"You're a sick man!" Decker yelled as Rosen closed the door behind him.

Matters of Fact and Faith

8

SHORTLY AFTER ROSEN LEFT, the jailer returned carrying a mop. Surveying the spilled water, he shook his head. "If you felt you had to hit Scott, that was one thing, but did you have to dump water all over the place?" he asked.

"Sorry," Decker said, and he was, a little. He wasn't sure whether it was the afterglow of having hit Rosen or the jailer's pleasant demeanor and sense of humor, but he found that he was actually beginning to like him. He thought back to their conversation that morning about manna and smiled. "Manna manicotti?" he laughed.

The jailer stopped mopping. "So you liked that?"

Decker smiled and nodded. "Do you really have a recipe for that?"

The jailer shook his head. Then, thinking about it for a moment as he leaned on his mop, he added, "I suppose there's no reason I can't come up with one, though. In fact, I'll get to work on it right after your lunch. I may even be able to have it for you for dinner." The jailer smiled to himself at the idea. "I bet it'll be a big hit around here."

❑

After lunch, Decker pulled one of the chairs over to the window to watch the comings and goings around the cabin. There was little else to do, and though he could have called the jailer in to talk, he resisted, thinking it best not to grow too attached to anyone. If he had a chance to escape, there was no way of knowing who might get hurt. He could not allow caring about his jailer to interfere with his judgment.

He wondered if there *was* any way to escape. Assuming that Rosen did not simply want to talk to him, as he claimed, there appeared to be only two other possibilities: Either Rosen hoped to convert him—after which Decker would be killed so that he couldn't later change his mind—or else Rosen hoped to use him somehow to sabotage Christopher's plans. Truly, Decker was caught on the horns of a dilemma. Would pretending to be convinced—acting as though he believed what Rosen said—be his ticket out or his death sentence? The whole matter was probably moot, however. While it might be possible to fool Rosen long enough to get himself killed, it was unlikely he could be fooled long enough to let Decker go.

As he watched from the window, he slowly became aware of something: There seemed to be far more KDP now than there had been the day before. It was impossible to be sure—the observed area was much too small. It might just be that there were more KDP at this side of the camp than there had been the day before, or it might mean something more.

❑

It was 2:30 when Rosen returned. Decker smiled to himself with zealous satisfaction as he saw that Rosen had a black eye and bruised check. Over his shoulder he carried a small leather satchel, which he sat by the door.

"Have you ever taken a class in comparative religions, Mr. Hawthorne?" Rosen asked.

Decker didn't give an answer, but Rosen didn't really need one.

"If you had, at the end of the class you'd probably have a basic knowledge of the teachings, ceremonies, and traditions of each religion and maybe some familiarity with the cultures that spawned them. But you'd have no way of knowing which, if any, of the religions were correct and which were incorrect. In fact, you would probably come away from the class with the 'enlightened' conclusion that while none of the religions are completely true, all have some value in that they provide comfort and moral guidance to their adherents. And as long as those adherents didn't try to impose their belief system on you, everything would be fine.

"If you did try to judge the correctness of one religion over another, your only measure would be whether the teachings of a particular religion seemed appropriate for *your* life."

"What else would you expect?" Decker asked sardonically.

"What else indeed?" Rosen answered. "Certainly, you

would *never* expect to find proof that one of the religions was true and the others false."

"Oh, boy. Here we go," Decker groaned.

"But comparing religions," Rosen continued, "usually involves only looking at what the religions have in common and ignoring where they are truly different. It would be like comparing a bicycle, a car, a truck, a train, and an airplane. You might look at the number of wheels on each, the different navigational controls, the means of propulsion, the number of passengers each can carry, their maximum speed . . . In fact, as you continued to consider the similarities you might never get around to the fact that there is something that makes one of the vehicles completely different from all the others: The airplane flies."

Decker intentionally yawned to show disinterest, but Rosen was undistracted.

"The same is true when comparing religions. We compare everything about them, but we never get around to looking at whether any of the religions can be proven true. I can prove that what I believe is true!"

"You know, that's your whole problem, Rosen. You have this chauvinistic idea that you're right and everybody else is wrong. You can't admit that someone else might have some piece of the truth. You think you've got it all to yourself, and that's the way you like it. If people don't agree with you, then as far as you're concerned, they're damned to hell!"

"Fine," Rosen replied, apparently changing his tactic. "Let's not talk about what I believe. Let's talk about Islam." Decker was taken aback by Rosen's sudden shift and did not respond.

"You've probably heard or read that at one point Mohammed—who claimed that the truth had been revealed to him by the angel Gabriel—decided to demonstrate that he was God's messenger by moving a mountain by the power of his faith. According to the story, after three days of trying without success, Mohammed gave up and said, 'If the mountain will not come to Mohammed, Mohammed will go to the mountain.' Now, no one knows if that really happened or is just a legend, but my point is that if Mohammed *had* moved a mountain, and if geologists today could confirm that the mountain had been, or even appeared to have been moved, then we'd have tangible evidence of Mohammed's claim to be God's prophet. And based on that, we would want to seriously consider the things he taught.

"Or let's look at Joseph Smith, the founder of Mormonism. In 1827, Smith said that an angel named Moroni gave him golden tablets inscribed in elaborate detail with the history of the ancient inhabitants of the Americas. This history, Smith claimed, included the complete and true Gospel of Jesus, who, Smith said, had gone to the Americas after his death and resurrection in Jerusalem.

"Unfortunately for our search for proof, there has never been any shred of archaeological evidence to support Smith's account of the history of the Americas. Not one non-Mormon archaeologist or scholar has ever found anything to lend even the slightest credence to Smith's claims. And as for the golden tablets, Smith said that after he translated them, an angel took them into heaven, so we don't have any physical evidence that there even *were* any tablets. There *were* eleven other people who said Smith had shown them the tablets, but all were either close friends or members of Smith's family, and the stories these witnesses told did not match in many of their important details.

"Fortunately though, the golden tablets were not the only documents that Joseph Smith claimed to have translated. In 1835, after starting his religion, Smith acquired some ancient Egyptian papyri that he said were the lost books of Abraham and Joseph. At the time very few had been able to decipher Egyptian hieroglyphics and so, just as with the golden tablets, Smith again relied upon God to give him the translation. Incidentally, Smith discovered a number of very interesting things from the papyri, including, he said, that black people were supposed to be servants and slaves to whites and Asians.

"Unlike the golden tablets, however, the Egyptian papyri were *not* taken to heaven by an angel, but were placed in a museum. Thanks to the discovery of the Rosetta stone,[25] Egyptologists were later able to translate Smith's papyri and determined that, far from being the books of Abraham and Joseph, they are actually copies of the *Egyptian Book of the Dead* and another book called *The Breathing Permit of Hôr*.[26] While not nearly so sensational as promising to move a mountain, Smith's

[25] Discovered in 1799 by Boussard and used by Jean Francois Champollion beginning in 1821 to decipher Egyptian hieroglyphics, the Rosetta stone is inscribed in hieroglyphic, demotic, and Greek.

[26] Translated by Egyptologists John S. Wilson and Klaus Baer of the University of Chicago Oriental Institute and Richard A. Parker of Brown University. See Fawn M. Brodie, *No Man Knows My History, The Life of Joseph Smith,* second edition, revised and enlarged (New York: Alfred A. Knopf, 1977), pp. 168–175 and 421–423.

demonstration of his authority obviously met with no more success than Mohammed's.

"Of course, most religious leaders have not been so willing to go out on a limb to prove themselves or validate their teachings. Their claims to authority are generally based on the visions or experiences of their founders. Siddhartha Gautama, the father of Buddhism, based his authority on having achieved *nirvana* and *bodhi*. Nanak, the founder of Sikhism, said that he had a mystical experience in which he visited heaven and spoke with a god named Sat Nam. Lao Tzu, the father of Taoism, and Confucius, the father of Confucianism, simply claimed to know the truth based on their own acquired wisdom. Thousands of New Age groups throughout the world today purport to have the truth as it has been revealed by such entities as angels, space aliens, inner selves, ascended masters with names like Ray-O-Light,[27] and even a 35,000-year-old warrior from Atlantis.[28] The founders of Hinduism and Shinto are unknown, leaving those religions to stand entirely on the merits of their teachings. We have, therefore, nothing on which to base our decision about the truth of any of these religions except what the founder of the religion said and whether the teachings seem to work in our own lives. Whether we reject one religion or accept another is simply a matter of blind faith."

"And now you're going to tell me that your religion is different, right?" Decker was careful to ensure that his voice had not lost any of its sarcasm, yet Rosen still seemed unaffected.

---

[27] Elizabeth Claire Prophet, Church Universal and Triumphant.

[28] Ramtha, who is channeled by JZ Knight.

"I never cared for blind faith, Mr. Hawthorne. I want something that can prove itself worthy *before* I put my trust in it."

"And you think your religion gives you that?" Decker asked dryly.

"Absolutely! You see, there's the key difference. All the other religions stand or fall on something that no one can prove or disprove. No one can prove whether angels appeared to Mohammed or Joseph Smith. No one can tell if Siddhartha Guatama achieved *nirvana* or whether Nanak visited heaven. No one can tell if a New Age channeler is just putting on an act or is really channeling a spirit, or for that matter, if it *is* a real spirit, is it a benevolent one or a malevolent one? It's left entirely up to the faith of the follower.

"But Christianity isn't based on what Jesus said an angel told him. It's not even based on spiritual truth that he himself revealed. It's based on who he said he was— the prophesied Jewish Messiah—and what he did to prove it—specifically, rising from the dead. Jesus staked his whole claim to authority on his resurrection. Everything else he said and did stands or falls on that. If he wasn't the Messiah and he didn't demonstrate it by rising from the dead, then you might as well take everything else he said and use it to stuff fortune cookies.

"Since the very beginning, belief in Jesus' resurrection formed the core of Christian teachings.[29] And remember, Jesus' followers weren't telling people about what had happened in some heavenly realm. They didn't talk about what had happened on Mount Olympus or in some far-off

[29] 1 Corinthians 15:14.

land. There's no 'once upon a time' in their story. They talked about what had happened right there, in the very same city where they lived. If Jesus' resurrection had not happened, if the body of Jesus were not, in fact, missing from the grave, then all anyone had to do to disprove it and discredit the apostles was simply go to the tomb. All that the Jewish or Roman authorities had to do to crush Christianity was produce the body. But they couldn't. And since there was no body, the only thing they could do to try to stop Christianity was persecute and then finally kill its leaders."

"So maybe the apostles just removed the body," Decker said with a bored groan.

"If they had, do you really think they would have willingly died as martyrs for something that they *knew* was a lie? And remember, I'm not talking about those who came later—those Christians who died because they believed what they had been told or because of some religious experience. Every major religion has those. I'm talking about people who, if the resurrection were a lie, would have known it! These people said they had seen Jesus resurrected from the dead and chose to die rather than change their story! Some people may be willing to die for what they believe to be true, but no one gives up his life for what he *knows* to be a lie."

"You're forgetting one thing, Rosen," Decker said, sounding very much like a teacher correcting a presumptuous student. "I don't question whether Jesus rose from the dead. Remember, I've seen a resurrection myself, firsthand. It's not the resurrection that's the problem. It's the twisted meaning you give to it."

"I haven't forgotten, Mr. Hawthorne," Rosen replied.

"In fact, you've hit the nail right on the head. As much as the resurrection itself, the real issue is its meaning. I believe that Jesus' death and resurrection provided the way for man's reconciliation to God and proved that Jesus is the Messiah."

"I really don't care what you believe!" Decker snorted.

"No, but you should. Because if I can prove Jesus is the prophesied Jewish Messiah, it will prove Christopher is a liar!"

"It makes no difference whether Jesus was the Jewish Messiah or not," Decker countered. "And as for what that has to do with Christopher, the answer is obvious: nothing! You're grasping at straws!"

Rosen got up from his chair and began to pace. "Consider this, Mr. Hawthorne," he said. "If a man testified that he was innocent of some crime—that he had been somewhere else at the time—it would prove nothing. He might really be innocent, or he might simply be lying. If the man's friends substantiated his alibi, you would still have some doubts. But if the man's *enemies* also supported his alibi . . . well, then you could reasonably conclude that he was innocent.

"In the same way, if I show you in the New Testament where Jesus said that he was the Messiah, I will have proven nothing. And if I then show you where Jesus' followers said that he was the Messiah, I still will have proven nothing. But if I could show you that Jesus was the Messiah based on the *Old* Testament—a book that has been preserved through the centuries by people who have rejected and even hated Jesus—then I might just have something."

"The Bible is thousands of years old," Decker retorted. "It could have been changed hundreds of times by hundreds of different people."

"The discovery of the Dead Sea Scrolls showed that in over two thousand years, those who copied the Old Testament were so meticulous that not one significant change has been made. And surely you're not suggesting that the Jews changed or added material to their Bible that would aid the Christians!"

Decker struggled to not let the embarrassment of his error show on his face. He would have to be more careful. Rosen had scored his point and the best Decker could do was let it pass and cover his chagrin with a dirty look.

Rosen did not dwell on it but continued his onslaught. "Of course, since the Old Testament was completed four hundred years before Jesus was born, anything I could find there to prove Jesus was who he said he was would have to be prophetic."

Decker saw his chance to regain some ground and shook his head. "I knew you'd have to resort to religious mumbo jumbo sooner or later. You said you'd prove Christianity with historic evidence, but you can't, so you start talking about prophecy. That's not historic evidence; that's strictly a matter of faith and opinion."

"Like most skeptics, Mr. Hawthorne, you're missing the whole point of prophecy. Prophecy is inherently historical. It stands or falls based only on whether it *does* or *does not* accurately predict future historical events. God used prophecy to prove the authenticity of the Bible as his Word. Of all the religious documents in the world, the Bible is the only one that deals with events of the future with the same certainty that it deals with events of the past and present. No other book, religious or otherwise, includes the minute details and the grand scale of prophecies as does the Bible; whether discussing the rise and fall of empires and kingdoms that had not even been created when the prophecy was written, or prophecies of individuals who would not be born for hundreds of years afterward. One of these individuals—the most important one—is the Messiah.

"The Messiah has always been central to Judaism, Mr. Hawthorne, and the Old Testament includes scores of prophecies about him. The prophet Isaiah said that he would be born to the linage of Jesse.[30] Jeremiah narrowed it down further to the descendants of Jesse's eighth son, David.[31] Isaiah said that the Messiah would be born to a virgin.[32] The prophet Micah said he would be born in the province of Judah, in the small village of Bethlehem.[33]

"Isaiah went on to say the Messiah would be called 'Mighty God,' the 'Everlasting Father,' and the 'Prince of Peace;'[34] that his ministry would begin in Galilee;[35] and that he would perform numerous healings and other miracles.[36]

"But to make it even more exact, the prophecies of Zechariah and Daniel even specified *when* and *how* the

[30] Isaiah 11:1–2, 10.

[31] Jeremiah 23:5.

[32] Isaiah 7:14.

[33] Micah 5:2.

[34] Isaiah 9:6.

[35] Isaiah 9:1–7.

[36] Isaiah 35:3–6.

Messiah would arrive in Jerusalem, so that no one who was willing to see the truth could miss it. According to these prophecies, the Messiah would come into Jerusalem riding on a donkey[37] 483 years after the decree to rebuild Jerusalem,[38] which had been destroyed by the Babylonians. That decree was issued by the Persian emperor Artaxerxes in 457 B.C.[39] When you account for the fact that there was no year zero, that means the Messiah was to come in the year 27 A.D. From the Gospel of Luke, we know that Jesus was born during the first tax taken while Quirinius was governor of Syria,[40] or about the year 7 B.C.,[41] so in the year 27 he would have been thirty-three or thirty-four when he rode into Jerusalem and a week later was crucified. In brief, he exactly fulfilled Zechariah's and Daniel's prophecies.

"But if that's not precise enough for you, Zechariah said that the Messiah would be betrayed by a friend for thirty pieces of silver, that the money would be thrown on the floor of the Temple, and that it would be used to buy a potters' field."[42]

For the moment, at least, Decker was interested enough in what Rosen was saying that he did not take

[37] Zechariah 9:9.

[38] Daniel 9:25–26.

[39] Artaxerxes I served as emperor from 464 to 424 B.C. According to Ezra 7, Artaxerxes issued this decree in the seventh year of his reign, i.e., 457 B.C.

[40] Luke 2:2.

[41] John Elder, *Prophets, Idols and Diggers* (Indianapolis: Bobbs–Merrill, 1960), p. 160.

[42] Zechariah 11:12–13.

note of the fact that the "friend" the prophet Zechariah referred to was obviously Judas . . . or as Christopher had
revealed, Decker himself in a past life.

"And Isaiah said," Rosen continued, "that at his trial,
the Messiah would not defend himself, but would be led
as a lamb, silent to the slaughter.[43]

"Writing more than a thousand years before anyone
had even heard of crucifixion, King David prophetically
described the Messiah's death in painful detail down to
the piercing of his hands and feet, the taunting of the
crowds, and the casting of lots for his clothing.[44] Isaiah
gave additional details of the crucifixion of the Messiah[45]
and said that though he would be innocent of any wrong-
doing, the Messiah would be executed with criminals,
and then buried in a rich man's grave.[46]

"But the prophets said Messiah's death would not be
in vain. In fact, Isaiah explains that the Messiah would intentionally give his own life as a sacrifice to save each of
us, that he was pierced for our sins and crushed for our
iniquities.[47]

"The prophecies also reveal that Messiah would be
resurrected.[48] And though he had been killed, what he had
done and said would be told throughout the world[49] for

[43] Isaiah 53:7.

[44] Psalms 22:7–8; 16–18.

[45] Isaiah 52:13–53:12.

[46] Isaiah 53:9, 12.

[47] Isaiah 53:4–6, 8, 11–12.

[48] Isaiah 53:10–11; Psalms 16:10; 30:3.

[49] Isaiah 49:6.

generation after generation, forever, and that ultimately, all people of all nations would bow down to him.[50] It doesn't take a Bible scholar, Mr. Hawthorne, to see that all of these prophecies are describing Jesus. In fact, the only way you could miss it is if you wanted to."

"That's swell, Rosen. But tell me what that's got to do with anything or else just pass the collection plate and let me go," Decker mocked.

"Christopher told you that Jesus came to earth to settle an argument between Lucifer and Yahweh, and that while Jesus originally sided with Yahweh, after living thirty years among the people of earth, he began to change sides. Christopher claimed that *that* was why Yahweh had him killed. He said that Yahweh made a deal with the Apostle John, who in turn tricked Judas—who Christopher said was actually you in an earlier life—to betray Jesus. But the prophecies prove that *can't* be true because all the major details and even many minor details of Jesus' life, death, and resurrection were written down hundreds of years before he was even born. What Christopher told you, what he has told the whole world, is a lie."

Decker knew that Rosen must have used his telepathic abilities to have such a detailed knowledge of what Christopher told him on the plane to Jerusalem. He had not given that much detail to the news media, and he certainly had not told them the part about him being Judas. Right now that didn't matter, though. Rosen's arguments were becoming much more convincing than Decker had expected. And if Rosen's references to Jewish prophecy

[50] Psalm 22:27–31.

were accurate, then his conclusion that Christopher had lied would be hard to argue.

He tried to find the flaw in Rosen's logic. He wondered if there might be something that was overlooked, some way perhaps that Christopher and Rosen could both be right. Maybe there was something Christopher had missed, something that occurred after the resurrection of Jesus that he would not have known about because he was cloned from cells left on the Shroud only seconds after the resurrection occurred.

Then he thought of the one thing that proved Rosen was wrong.

"Well, Rosen," Decker said with renewed confidence, "I have to admit you tell a pretty good story. I can even see why many people, including Tom Donafin, would believe as you do. I could almost believe it myself. There's just one little problem. Unlike Tom and the KDP and the fundamentalists, I have known Christopher Goodman almost all of his life, and he has never once told me a lie or done anything that was the least bit self-serving. Your logic may seem sound now, but I'm sure there's another side to the story. And assuming you really do intend to let me go, when I get back to Babylon I'll ask Christopher about it. And frankly, when it comes down to who I believe, I can guarantee you that I'll give more credence to what Christopher says than to what a kidnapper has told me."

"I can live with that," Rosen said, to Decker's great surprise. "And I realize there's no way to argue conclusions based upon your experience, so I won't even try. But regarding what I've told you, I know that I rushed through it and later you may want to check to see if all the things I told you are actually in the Bible. I've made a list of the key prophecies, and I'll leave you a Bible so you can look them up if you like." Rosen retrieved the satchel he had brought with him and pulled out a sheet of paper and a white leather-covered Bible. The paper contained handwritten notes listing the references for the prophecies Rosen had used.

"And just supposing I did decide to check your references," Decker said, "how do I know it's not just the KDP's version of the Bible?"

Rosen didn't answer directly but handed him the book. "I think you'll recognize the handwriting," he said.

Decker hesitantly took the Bible and opened it. There, scattered throughout the pages were handwritten notes and yellow-highlighted text. The lettering of the notes was small and precise, and despite the years, there was no doubt in Decker's mind who had written it. Turning to the front page, he found confirmation, a note that read: "To Elizabeth Hawthorne, with love from Joshua and Ilana Rosen."

For a moment Decker could not speak, a fact he disguised by blindly flipping the pages. "Where did you get this?" he asked quietly after a moment, avoiding eye contact with Rosen. His whispered tone failed to hide the emotion in his voice. The book itself was unimportant, but the notes, which contained his wife's thoughts, made it unspeakably precious to him.

"I found it in my parents' house after the Rapture. There was a note with it from my mother to your wife, but I'm afraid that's been lost. Your wife apparently left the Bible at my parents' house when she came to Israel to get you. They were going to mail it back to her. When I found it I intended to send it to you, but it mistakenly got put in a box for storage when I packed up my parents' belongings. I forgot all about it until I was going through my things a few weeks before I left Israel to come to Petra."

Decker could feel that his defenses were down. He just wanted this session to be over so he could gather his thoughts and deal with his emotions in private.

9

Necessary Risk

June 5, 4 N.A.

THE NEXT DAY Decker awoke much later than the previous morning. His back and shoulders ached from the gymnastics of having thrown himself across the table to hit Rosen. Just as before, he found Petra covered in white. There were far fewer people out gathering, and the many bare spots revealed that most had already gathered the manna for the day. Also as before, it seemed to Decker that the number of KDP had significantly increased.

❑

Rosen did not return until after lunch.

"Good afternoon, Mr. Hawthorne," Rosen said as he came in. His black eye looked every bit as bad as it had the night before, a fact that Decker found quite satisfying.

Decker folded his hands over his stomach and leaned back on the bed, electing not to respond to Rosen's greeting. As always, his response or lack of one did not deter Rosen from saying what he had come to say.

"Yeshua told a story about a farmer who had two

sons,"[51] Rosen began immediately on his sermonette. "The younger of the two sons decided that he wanted to be on his own, so he went to his father and asked for his inheritance. Reluctantly the father agreed, and the son took his money and left. On his own, the younger son fell in with people who were only too happy to help him spend his money. And, of course, before very long his money and his 'friends' were both gone. He found himself with nothing, far from home and working on a pig farm—which, incidentally, is not a good place for a nice Jewish boy to be. Looking at the mess he had made of his life, he remembered that his father was much more generous to his servants than was his current employer. It occurred to him that it would be better to admit his failure, go home, and ask his father for a job rather than stay where he was. Along the way, as he neared the farm that had been his home, his father saw him coming. To his surprise, his father ran to meet him on the road, 'and received him, not as a servant but as a son, and celebrated his return.

"But though he was welcomed back by his father, remember I said he had already taken his part of the inheritance. Everything that remained belonged to the older brother. The father couldn't change that. He couldn't just take what was left and split it in half again—that wouldn't be fair to the son who had stayed with him. And I think it's safe to say that, human nature being what it is, if the father had done that, the younger brother would not have learned much from his experience.

"Your friend, Tom Donafin, had an interesting way of

[51] Luke 15:11–32.

putting it. He said it was like in the movie *The Wizard of Oz*,[52] where the good witch of the north, Glinda, tells Dorothy that all she has to do to go home is click her heels together and say 'There's no place like home.'"

Decker smiled despite himself as he recalled Tom Donafin's penchant for describing everything in terms of a movie. "When Dorothy asked Glinda why she hadn't just told her that to begin with, Glinda answered that she wouldn't have believed it. I saw that movie a dozen times when I was a kid and several times as an adult, but I never did understand what she meant. The point was that until Dorothy had experienced life away from home, she couldn't truly understand and believe that there *really* is no place like home. The way Tom Donafin put it was that in order for Dorothy to *learn* her lesson, she had to *earn* her lesson so that she could appreciate how true it really was.

"The same was true for the farmer's younger son. Like almost everything else in life, Mr. Hawthorne, wisdom has a price. Lessons bought too cheaply seldom stay learned. If there is no price, there is no value, and consequently nothing is learned. Of course, some lessons cost more than others."

Decker could not deny the truth in what Rosen said, nor could he tell where he was going with it, so he stayed silent.

"When God created the earth," Rosen said, "he gave Adam and Eve a perfect paradise to live in and nearly total freedom to do as they wished. The only thing he told them *not* to do was eat from a particular tree—the tree of

[52] 1939, MGM.

the knowledge of good and evil. But of course, as soon as you tell someone not to do something, that's exactly what they want to do: It's human nature. So sure enough, before long Adam and Eve were checking out the tree, where they met Lucifer in the form of a snake. Lucifer told them that the reason God didn't want them to eat from the tree was because it would make them like God. Now when you think about it," Rosen said, "that's got to be the greatest temptation in the world. Everyone wants to be in charge, to make their own rules, to be their own god. It's certainly proven to be a successful drawing card for Christopher and the New Age movement."

"Twice now you've blamed human nature for the way people act," Decker interrupted, "and I don't really disagree with you on that. But explain to me, *if you can,* why this god of yours, who you think is all-powerful and all-knowing and all-loving, made human nature so imperfect to begin with. And, while we're on the subject, what kind of an idiot is this god of yours to put the tree in the garden, within easy reach of Adam and Eve, if he didn't want them to eat from it? Unless, of course . . . ," Decker said, pausing to drive home his point, "he *wanted* them to fail. And if that was his intention, then surely you have to admit that he's every bit as evil as Christopher says he is." Decker hoped that his questions might catch Rosen off guard, but as always, Rosen had a ready answer.

"People have struggled with that question and questions like it for thousands of years, Mr. Hawthorne. But the answer is really pretty simple."

"Oh brother," Decker moaned, already regretting that he had asked the question.

"But to understand it," Rosen began, despite Decker's protests, "you need to look at what it was that Adam and Eve actually did. It wasn't the fruit itself that was the problem. The real problem was their defiance. They defied God and his law because they wanted to be like God. That's really not so unusual, though. We all want to have our own way, to be in effect, our own lawgiver, our own god."

"So far all you've done is to restate the problem. You still haven't answered why."

"I'm getting to it," Rosen said. "Because we are made in God's image, it's our nature to want to be God."

"Oh, I see! You're saying Yahweh made a design error!"

"Not a design error," Rosen countered, "for now let's just call it a necessary risk. It's the same risk every parent takes when they have children. Just as a child is created in the image of its parents, God created us in *his* image to be his family. Anything less and we would not be his children—we'd be his pets or slaves. Now it's up to us to decide whether we want to be his children or not, just as the decision was up to the farmer's two sons and just as it was up to Adam and Eve. And though, like Adam and Eve, we all may want to be gods, there can be only *one* God. A wheel with two centers will not turn. A universe with two gods cannot function."

"There comes a time when children need to leave the nest, to go out on their own," Decker countered. "And whether the parents like it or not, they have to be willing to let go."

"That is true, Mr. Hawthorne. The child must be given more and more responsibility for himself as he grows.

But we should clarify our terms. The term 'child of God' does not speak of immaturity on *our* part, but of unceasing love for us on God's part. A child will cease to be a youth, but a parent never ceases to be a parent. The relationship goes beyond the ages of the individuals involved. Being a child of God denotes a relationship of love, trust, and respect—not of oppression."

"Yeah, sure," Decker said, "just as long as we're willing to obey *his* laws and follow *his* orders."

"I know Christopher says that Yahweh's laws are designed to oppress people, to keep them forever unable to reason for themselves. But God himself said to mankind, 'Come now, let us reason together.'[53] If you really take the time to consider God's laws, you'll find that they are as reasonable, beneficial, and necessary to our survival as are gravity and the other laws of nature. God's laws are designed not to oppress, but to protect and sustain.

"Jesus was asked by one of the religious leaders what God's greatest commandment is. He answered, 'Love the Lord your God with all your heart and with all your soul and with all your mind.'[54] And he said the second greatest commandment is like the first: 'Love your neighbor as yourself.'[55] Not only are those the two greatest commandments, Jesus said that every other law in the Bible is wrapped up in those two commands."[56]

---

[53] Isaiah 1:18.

[54] Matthew 22:37; Deuteronomy 6:5.

[55] Matthew 22:39; Leviticus 19:18.

[56] Matthew 22:40.

"Yeah, but those aren't the only things Yahweh said we had to do," Decker argued. "The Bible includes a lot more laws than just the Ten Commandments."

"But all of those laws, every one of them, has as its foundation the two laws Jesus talked about," Rosen replied.

"So why didn't Yahweh just give us two laws and leave it at that?"

"And just leave everything to individual judgment?" Rosen asked rhetorically. "That would be fine if you could be certain you knew everything about a given situation and you were always sure of your own motives. But can you *really* know all of the consequences of your actions? Can you look into the future to determine every outcome of your decisions? You'd be a liar or a fool to say you could. Very little in life turns out as we expect it to. It's Murphy's Law: *If something can go wrong, it will.* And of course, something almost always *can* go wrong. At best, those who depend on their own judgment to determine right and wrong end up guessing based on the known data and the range of anticipated possible outcomes. At worst, they ignore the obvious consequences of their actions—telling themselves everything will work itself out—just so they can do what they wanted to do in the first place. And somewhere between the best and worst cases are the decisions that, despite our intentions, find their origins in judgments unavoidably clouded by self-interest. God's laws are the standard established by the only one who knows everything—past, present, and future—so that we're not limited to our own knowledge of situations."

"So we're just supposed to put our brains on hold and

follow blindly along the path that God has set for us!" Decker sneered.

"Not at all, Mr. Hawthorne. Remember, Jesus said that the greatest commandment is to love God with all your heart, and with all your soul, and with all your *mind*. He included your mind. He doesn't want us to blindly accept what somebody tells us; he wants us to consider the evidence, to use our mind as well as our heart in coming to him and in following him. Blind faith is an alien concept to Christianity. It's the New Age religions that tell their adherents to put their minds on hold and let some spirit guide or unknown force direct them. It's the New Age religions that tell us that our future is determined by such things as the location of certain stars on the day we were born."

Rosen had hit upon two things that had always made Decker a little uncomfortable about the New Agers. He had never had any difficulty with anything Christopher said and only occasional problems with most of what Milner said, but some of those who followed Christopher and Milner held what seemed to be very bizarre and unscientific beliefs and practices that he would rather not try to defend. Spirit guides and astrology were two of them. And since he preferred not to dwell on these things, he did not mind at all when Rosen went on to what appeared to be another subject.

"When Jesus was crucified," Rosen continued, "there were thieves crucified on either side of him. One of the thieves, even though he was dying on a cross, taunted and insulted Jesus. But the other thief realized that while he deserved punishment for the crimes he had committed, he knew that Jesus was innocent.

"You might think that a condemned man doesn't have much to lose, but even *then* a person may still cling to his pride. Even as he hung there on the cross, the first thief wanted to be accepted by the crowd. I suppose he thought he could make himself appear better by tearing down someone else. The other thief, though, was willing to give up his pride and dignity, admit his guilt and, there in front of everyone, turn his fate over to the Messiah, saying, 'Jesus, remember me when you come into your kingdom.'[57]

"Jesus' response to the thief's request was very unusual. He didn't give him a list of things to do so that he could be accepted by God. He didn't tell him he had to be baptized, or sanctified, or take communion, or do good works, or walk across burning coals, or make a pilgrimage, or chant, or anything. He simply said; 'I tell you the truth, today you will be with me in paradise.'[58]

"It may seem like the thief didn't do anything except ask, but we should not miss the point of what he *did* do. Just like the farmer's younger son, who admitted his failure and returned humbly to his father, so the thief recognized his guilt and turned humbly to Jesus.

"You see, Mr. Hawthorne, just like the farmer's son and the thief on the cross, people don't become Christians because they're good people; they become Christians because they realize that they've failed. They know that they've broken God's laws and that they are sinners.

"When you get right down to it, Christianity is like bankruptcy. To accept Yeshua is to admit defeat and

[57] Luke 23:42.

[58] Luke 23:43.

throw yourself on the mercy of the court because you realize that justice demands more than you can possibly pay. The down payment alone would cost you your life. And what good is *learning* the lesson if the cost of *earning* the lesson leaves you dead?

"I remember reading in school about a bizarre practice used by European royalty to punish a prince. Instead of punishing the prince himself when he was bad, a boy of the prince's same age—called a whipping boy—would bear the punishment for the prince. It always seemed both incredibly unfair and incredibly stupid to me—unfair because a boy who had done nothing was punished for what someone else did, and stupid because the prince had no motivation for changing his behavior. More recently, though, it occurred to me that it was *not* so stupid as I had assumed. Properly administered, it could be a very effective deterrent against bad behavior by the prince."

Decker shook his head. "You've lost me on that one, Rosen."

"If the prince did not know the whipping boy or did not have to watch the boy being punished for what *he* had done," Rosen explained, "then of course it meant little or nothing to the prince and the punishment did no good. But if the prince knew the boy—if they were friends and playmates—then even though the prince did not bear the physical marks of the lashing, he would feel the pain of knowing the suffering he had caused to his friend. Do you have any brothers or sisters, Mr. Hawthorne?"

"One older brother, Nathan. He died in the Disaster," Decker answered, though after he had, he could not understand why he had been so forthcoming.

Rosen raised an eyebrow in surprise at this revelation,

but did not allow it to distract him. "Then you can probably understand that, if your parents punished your brother whenever *you* did something wrong, you might think it was a pretty nice arrangement for a while. Soon, though, if you cared for your brother at all, you would start to feel bad about it. So that even though it was your brother who had been punished, you would suffer, too, and pretty soon your behavior would change.

"The practice of sacrificing animals is similar to the concept of the whipping boy. Christopher has said that the animal sacrifices required by Yahweh prove that he is a bloodthirsty god. But God didn't tell us to sacrifice animals because he's bloodthirsty. God doesn't like to see suffering; he doesn't like to see animals die. According to the Bible, originally animals didn't even kill each other.[59] They were all vegetarians, and they will be again after Jesus returns.[60] The reason God told us to offer animal sacrifices was so that we would realize just how terrible our sin is. As bad as you would have felt about your brother being punished in your place, imagine how much worse you would have felt if your parents made *you* administer the punishment. That is what God intended with animal sacrifices. He wanted us to understand in no uncertain terms how destructive sin is and that the price of sin is death.

"In the story Jesus told about the farmer and his two sons, in the end there was no inheritance left for the younger son. Everything the father had left was the inheritance of the older brother. There *was* one way, however,

[59] Genesis 1:29–30.

[60] Isaiah 11:7; 65:25.

that the younger son could have gotten an inheritance and yet still have *earned* his lesson: that is, if his brother died and left no heir. If that happened, he would receive the older brother's inheritance because there was no one else for it to go to. But he would still have *learned* and *earned* his lesson because he would know that what he received came at the price of his brother's life."

Rosen paused a moment to make his point. "Well, *our* brother *did* die," Rosen continued, finally, "not because Yahweh is a bloodthirsty God, but because the only way for us to understand the seriousness of our sin without paying the price for that sin ourselves is to understand the magnitude of the price that Jesus paid by dying for us.

"I said earlier that when God created us in his own image he took a 'necessary risk' because only by being created in his image could we truly be his children. Actually, since God knew in advance that Adam and Eve would sin, it would be more accurate to call it *not* a 'necessary risk' but an 'accepted cost.' God knew we would sin and he knew that he himself, in the person of his son Jesus, would have to be tortured and die to pay the penalty for that sin. Yet despite all this, he did it anyway. His own death was a price he was willing to pay because he loves us so much that he would rather *die* than live without us.

"The inheritance is ours, Mr. Hawthorne. To claim it, all we have to do is what the farmer's younger son did: Admit we've made a mess of our lives without God, swallow our pride, and ask him to forgive us and take us back. Like the younger son, we must be willing to come back as a servant, but like the father in the story, God waits anxiously to accept us as sons.

"Jesus told the thief on the cross that he would be in paradise. And, interestingly, that thief was the only person Jesus ever directly made that promise to. I believe Jesus used that situation, where the one he was talking to could not possibly do anything to earn God's forgiveness, so that in the centuries to come no one could ever read that story and honestly believe that being forgiven and accepted by God was something that could be earned.

"It's up to us to decide which role we will play in life: the proud, mocking thief or the humble, repentant thief. That's just how simple it was then, and it's just as simple now. All that you need to do to be forgiven and accepted by God is to recognize that you need to be forgiven and then ask. Come humbly to God just as the farmer's son returned humbly to his father and he will accept you with open arms."

"That's quite a story, Rosen," Decker said. "But you haven't changed anything. As I said last night, no matter how convincing a story you might tell, there's no way I'm going to trust the word of a kidnapper over Christopher."

"And I told you last night that I would not try to convince you otherwise. What I have attempted to do is make clear to you what we believe, since I doubt you've ever taken the time to adequately investigate it for yourself.

"Now, there's just one other item we need to cover before you leave. I told you earlier that God had taken his people from the earth so that they wouldn't have to suffer through the times in which we now find ourselves. The Bible calls these times the 'Tribulation,' a period that would begin with the signing of a treaty with Israel and last for seven years. That treaty was the one between the United Nations and Israel arranged by Christopher

Goodman when he returned the Ark of the Covenant. Of the seven years, less than four months remain."

"As far as I can tell," Decker interrupted, "things have been going pretty well since Christopher got rid of John and Cohen three years ago—no asteroids, no plagues of locusts, no homicidal madness, not even any wars. The whole world has been at peace. The only 'tribulation' that I'm aware of is the killings and violence by the fundamentalists at the communion clinics. I guess you could also throw in the appearances of the three angels," he added, "but they just made empty threats."

"Nevertheless," Rosen said, "over the next four months things are going to get much worse fast. Of course, Christopher will blame Yahweh, the KDP, and the fundamentalists."

"And you just can't imagine why he'd do that, can you?" Decker shot back sarcastically. "Are you trying to say that Yahweh is *not* responsible for the death and destruction that plagued the earth before Christopher killed John and Cohen?"

"What God has done to this point," Rosen answered, apparently denying nothing, "has been designed, for the most part, to get our attention. The plagues that befell Egypt in the days of Moses were designed to demonstrate God's supremacy over the false gods of Egypt. The Egyptians worshiped the Nile River, so God turned it to blood; they worshiped flies and frogs, and so he gave them plagues of flies and frogs; they worshiped the sun, and so he blacked out the sun. In the same way, God has selectively struck the earth with plagues that demonstrate his supremacy over the false gods of this age. People worship the heavens and look to the stars to guide their futures, so God used asteroids—falling stars—to plague the earth. People worship nature, so God used nature to afflict mankind with storms, volcanoes, and locusts. People seek the guidance of spirits, so God allowed spirits to bring madness and death upon the earth. But what is coming in the next three months is designed *not* to get our attention, but to punish and to show 'Humankind' that it is unable to stand against a righteous God.

"To strike back at Yahweh, Christopher will order the arrest of all who oppose him, and ultimately the execution of all who refuse to take the communion and the mark. When the plagues continue, he will call for the people of all nations to gather and march on Petra to destroy those who still pledge their allegiance to Yahweh. He will justify his actions by saying that it is necessary to destroy the opponents of the New Age just as you would destroy a disease or cancer—so that the rest of the world can break the final hold that Yahweh has on the earth. And, of course, it will be argued that killing us is really for our own good since in a few years or so we'll all be reincarnated, free of our past 'prejudices' and 'bigotries.'

"Do you understand why we are called *Koum Damah Patar*, Mr. Hawthorne?"

"Yeah," Decker answered. "Because there's supposed to be 144,000 of you kooks, and the Hebrew characters used to write 144,000 are the same characters used to write *Koum Damah Patar*."

"There is an additional reason—a prophetic reason," Rosen said. "In English, *Koum Damah Patar* means 'Arise, shed tears, and be free.' In the book of Zechariah, speaking through the prophet, God said:

I will pour out on the house of David and the inhabi-
tants of Jerusalem a spirit of grace and supplication.
They will look on me, the one they have pierced, and
they will mourn for him as one mourns for an only
child, and grieve bitterly for him as one grieves for a
firstborn son.[61]

"The time is coming soon when these words will come to pass, when all Israel will *arise* as one and *shed tears* for the one they have pierced. As Christopher marches on Petra, the people of Israel will understand that Yeshua, whom they rejected and their ancestors pierced, is indeed their king and Messiah. When that happens, Messiah will return to save them from Christopher, just as Moses, whom they also rejected, returned to rescue their forefathers from Pharaoh, and they will at last *be free.*"

"And then you'll all live happily ever after, right?" Decker said dryly.

"Something like that," Rosen answered without embarrassment. "The Bible says that God will establish his kingdom on the earth and Yeshua will reign as king on the throne of David. The earth will be restored to the paradise that it was in its Edenic state. As it was in the Garden of Eden, the Bible says:

The wolf will live with the lamb, the leopard will lie
down with the goat, the calf and the lion and the year-
ling together; and a little child will lead them. The cow

[61] Zechariah 12:10.

*will feed with the bear, their young will lie down to-
gether, and the lion will eat straw like the ox. The infant
will play near the hole of the cobra, and the young child
put his hand into the viper's nest. They will neither
harm nor destroy on all my holy mountain, for the
earth will be full of the knowledge of the Lord as the waters cover the sea."*[62]

Decker groaned and shook his head.

"I've done all I can. I've rolled away the stone—the
rest is up to God," Rosen concluded, drawing an analogy
to the biblical story of the events preceding the resurrection of Lazarus.[63] "I assume you'll want to leave as soon
as possible," he added without ceremony.

Decker was momentarily taken aback, unsure he had
heard correctly. "Just like that?" he asked after a moment,
wondering if this ordeal could really be ending so simply.

"Just like that," Rosen repeated. "You see, God has not
instructed me to be successful, only to make the effort. It's
not my responsibility to change your mind, only to present
you with the truth. What you do with it is up to you."

Decker wished that for just one moment he could read
Rosen's mind. Was he serious or was this just a trick?

"I've made arrangements for you to leave the day after
tomorrow."

That did not sound promising. "Why not right now?"
Decker asked, suspicious of any delay. He knew that if
the KDP intended to kill him it would probably happen

[62] Isaiah 11:6–9.

[63] John 11:38–41.

soon. Or this might just be a transition into a second phase of a longer brainwashing program. Would they now lock him in solitary confinement for a few weeks or months to "consider" what Rosen had told him over the past three days? He could only guess which it would be. Whatever happened, Decker determined that he would endure it with dignity. He would not let them break him. He reminded himself of his nearly three years as a hostage in Lebanon. So far, this was a cakewalk by comparison.

Of course, there was also the possibility that Rosen really intended to let him go, but he didn't put much hope in that prospect.

"You'll be taken to Israel and released," Rosen continued. "I'm sure that from there you can get back to Babylon on your own."

"Why can't I leave right now?" Decker asked again, more forcefully.

"It's after 4:00 on Friday afternoon," Rosen answered. "There is not enough time for anyone to take you to Israel before sundown when the Sabbath begins."

Of course, devout Jews would not travel on a Sabbath. Rosen's answer was just plausible enough to be either the real reason or a well-considered lie. "And so I'm just supposed to sit and wait?" Decker grumbled.

"You're free to go wherever you like in Petra."

"And if I choose to go farther?" Decker asked reflexively and then cringed that he had asked such a stupid question. Petra was in the middle of the wilderness. Where else could he possibly go?

Whether it was the look of embarrassment on Decker's face or Rosen's ability to read his mind, he didn't answer. "There's just one last thing," he said instead. "Somehow, Mr. Hawthorne, you have avoided the communion and the mark this long. I don't know if you can continue to do so, but if you can, and if you believe that there is even the smallest, most outside chance that I might be telling you the truth, then I urge you to do everything in your power not to take the communion or the mark."

"I'll keep that in mind," Decker answered with obvious insincerity. He found possible encouragement in what Rosen had said, though. It might have been an indication that he really did intend to let him go. Why else would he take the time to urge him not to take the communion and the mark?

"I must leave now," Rosen said. "I pray that you will consider what I've said and what the Spirit of God is saying to you even now, and that our next meeting will be as brothers and fellow heirs in Messiah's kingdom."

"Yeah, sure," Decker harrumphed. The fact that Rosen had once again referred to something that would necessitate his living for a while longer, however, did not escape Decker's attention.

Rosen sighed and left the room, leaving the door open behind him.

10

Donafin

DECKER SAT QUIETLY for a few minutes, unsure of what might come next. When nothing happened, he got up to look out the window. The guards that had been posted outside were gone. For a while, he just watched and waited. There was no place to go except out into Petra, so what was the point? After all, though it was larger than the cage he had been in for the previous three days, Petra was still a cage. Whether he stayed in the cabin or not, the risk was the same. Whatever the KDP had in mind for him, they were going to do it whether he stayed or left. He decided to leave. Better to die in the sunshine, he thought, though he could not give a reason why that should be so.

Stepping carefully from the room and taking only what he was wearing and the leather satchel that held Elizabeth's Bible, Decker was surprised to see that not even the jailer was anywhere to be found. His mind flashed back to his escape from captivity in Lebanon when his guards had all mysteriously disappeared. This was not quite so mysterious; Rosen had said he was free to leave. Still, the feeling of déjà vu was strong.

At first, Decker stayed near the cabin, but the inclination to do so quickly faded and he decided the safest thing was to get lost in the people and the surroundings. He knew that trying to avoid Rosen and the KDP would ultimately be hopeless: There was no escape from this island in the desert. And what if Rosen had been telling the truth and he really did intend to have someone take Decker to Israel on Sunday? If so, then he needed to stay where Rosen could find him. Still, he found it hard to convince his feet of any of that. For nearly forty-five minutes he bobbed and weaved his way erratically through the rows of tents and their crowded inhabitants. Everyone he passed greeted him with a traditional *Shabbat shalom*, meaning "Sabbath peace." But for Decker there was no peace: He just wanted to lose anyone who might be following him.

Finally, he slowed down. He had to—he was too tired to continue. Only now did he begin to allow his mind to focus on the beauty of the natural and man-made wonders around him. Stopping to rest, he sat down on the excavated stones of a two-millennia-old structure and surveyed his surroundings. From his location at what archaeologists called the Roman House, he could see most of Petra. In the west the sun hung just above the jagged red-faced mountain that surrounded the city. Under other circumstances, he might have lost himself in the study of the archaeology and architecture of this ancient but now thriving metropolis. Then he noticed something else: a young boy, perhaps ten or eleven years old. He had seen him before. The first time had been right after leaving the cabin. Thinking back, it seemed that he may have seen him again some time later. Both times it had appeared as though the boy had just been out walking, but here he was again. Decker had made too many turns along the way for this to be a coincidence. The boy must be following him. A wave of disgust passed over him at the thought that Rosen would recruit one so young as a spy.

Pretending not to notice the boy, Decker looked around for the best avenue of escape to slip away from his unwanted attendant. It would be impossible to simply outrun the boy; Decker was just too old to win such a race. But now that he knew who his pursuer was, he thought he could probably lose him amongst the people and tents and stone structures. He was about to leave his perch when he heard a woman's voice. He wasn't sure, but it sounded like she was calling his name. There were scores of people within earshot, all crowded into this self-imposed exile, and many voices competed for the ear's attention. Still, it truly had sounded as though a woman's voice had called his name.

"Decker!" he now heard distinctly. He did not recognize the voice.

"Decker!" it called again. Finally the woman came around a row of tents and into view. He was certain he did not recognize her. Stranger still, she headed not toward him, but for the boy who had been following him.

The woman and the boy obviously knew each other and they talked for a moment, and then both looked at Decker, who was very conspicuously watching them. The eye contact was undeniable and the woman, apparently believing some explanation was required, came over with the boy in tow to where Decker sat.

"Are you Decker Hawthorne?" the woman asked.

He could find no good reason to deny it. "Yes," he answered.

"I'm terribly sorry, Mr. Hawthorne," the woman said. "I'm afraid my son has been following you. He didn't mean any harm."

Decker wanted to ask her why her son had been following him, but there was something even more perplexing he wanted to know. "Did I hear you call the boy Decker?"

"Yes," the woman answered. "I guess I should introduce myself. I'm Rhoda Donafin. Tom Donafin was my husband." Decker was stunned, unable to respond. But there was more. "And this is my youngest son, Decker. Tom named him after you."

Decker felt as though he had been hit by a blast of cold water, thrusting him into an unexplored reality. Here was evidence of a past of which he had obviously been a part—hence a child named in his honor—and yet it was totally unknown to him beyond the fact that Tom had told him before he died that he was married and had children.

"Decker has been asking about you since we found out that you were in Petra," Rhoda said of her son. "He really wanted to meet you."

"How did you know I was here?" Decker managed to ask.

"My brother, Joel Felsberg, and Scott Rosen are good friends," she answered. "Besides," she added, "I'm a doctor: Scott came to see me the other day. Seems he walked into a door or something with his eye," she said.

Decker couldn't tell if she was making a joke or, because of the boy, she was avoiding acknowledgment that Scott Rosen's injury had come as the result of a meeting with Decker's fist.

Rhoda Donafin looked toward the western rim of the city at the sun that would soon be setting. "It's almost Shabbat," she said. "My children and I would be honored if you would join us for dinner."

"I . . . uh," Decker stammered. This was all happening so fast. He felt a little uncomfortable imposing on the hospitality of someone he had just met, and yet he had so much to ask this woman. "Thank you," he said finally. "I'd like that."

Rhoda Donafin smiled, but not half so big a smile as that of young Decker Donafin.

❑

The Donafins' tent was only a quarter mile from where they met and there was little time to talk, but once the initial surprise of meeting Tom Donafin's wife and son had settled in, Decker noticed how young Rhoda looked. "You're uh—" Decker hesitated, for despite all the social mores that had changed in his lifetime, one taboo that still stood was talking about a woman's age, "—quite a bit younger than Tom," he said, finally.

"I'm fifty-five," she answered, showing no timidity about telling her age. "He was seventeen years older than me. Tom was sixty-one and I was forty-four when Decker was born. He was a surprise to both of us." Rhoda affectionately ran her hand through her son's hair.

Decker sorted through questions in his mind. It seemed that the ones he most wanted to ask would require too long a response to be given fair treatment before they reached the tent—which Rhoda assured him was just a little farther on—and everything else he might ask would seem like small talk and terribly inappropriate to the circumstances. With little choice then, Decker maintained an uneasy silence, hoping somehow that Rhoda might volunteer answers for his unspoken questions. Rhoda, however, did not oblige.

❑

The Donafins' tent looked like so many others—plain, gray, something less than fifteen feet square, with a canopy extending from the front under which the family did its cooking and had its meals. Busily working there to prepare the Sabbath dinner was a young woman who smiled as they approached.

"Mr. Hawthorne, this is Rachael," Rhoda said, giving her daughter a little hug. Rachael was a handsome girl, not what anyone would have considered a great beauty, but with strong features that were a blend of the best from both her parents.

"Rachael, this is an old friend of your father's, Mr. Decker Hawthorne." The girl was very polite and greeted Decker with great interest, though some of that interest could have simply been eagerness to find some distraction from her chores and the pot of boiling manna on the gas camp stove, which seemed to be standard issue for the city's residents.

"Rachael is our middle child," Rhoda continued. "She's sixteen."

"And this is Tom Jr.," Rhoda said, as her eldest came out of the tent carrying a pair of silver candlesticks. Tom Donafin Jr. looked very much like his father had when Decker first met him, with the notable exception of the

protruding forehead that Tom Sr. bore as a result of the
childhood automobile accident that killed the rest of his
family.

"Tom, this is Mr. Decker Hawthorne."

Tom nodded recognition of the name as he reached to
shake Decker's hand. "So Scott Rosen finally let you go,"
he said.

"Well, that remains to be seen," Decker answered.
"I'm still here."

"I wouldn't worry about that. If you're out, I'd say you
were out for good."

The comment sounded as though Tom might have
some experience in the subject. Decker wanted to find
out. "So does Rosen do this often?" he asked.

"No, you're the only one," Tom answered with a
strange tone that seemed to imply that Decker should
consider the exception as some kind of honor.

"Tom is eighteen," Rhoda said, rounding off the
introductions.

❑

Dinner was soon ready and they shared a traditional
Sabbath meal, with Tom filling the role of his father at
the table. Finally, Decker felt he had the proper setting
to ask his questions. He wanted to know what had happened during the missing twenty-one years between the
time Tom was presumed dead and the day he
reemerged. In the presence of Tom's children, Decker
was careful to omit any mention of Tom's death or any
questions that might necessitate such a reference. Those
questions could be saved for Rhoda alone. His interest

was in uncovering all that he could about who Tom Donafin had become during those years.

As it turned out, however, it was not Decker Hawthorne who asked most of the questions, but Decker Donafin, so that without realizing it the elder Decker spent most of the meal telling stories. Whether the events he recounted had, in truth, been as interesting and amusing as they now seemed to be, or whether it was simply the old reporter's ability to weave a tale, even Decker did not know. What he did know was that it was delightful fun to remember and even more so to see the interest in the faces of Tom's wife and children as he told the tales.

After dinner they were joined by neighbors who had overheard Decker's stories and the Donafins' laughter and wanted to hear more. It started with just a few children but continued to grow as the children's parents dropped by to meet the unusual guest. As he spoke to what had become a group of more than twenty people, Decker was struck by the incredible irony that he, the closest friend of Christopher Goodman—the man these people considered their worst enemy—would be telling them funny stories about his experiences with the man who had been Christopher's assassin.

As the evening wore on and it got to be past Decker Donafin's bedtime, the elder Decker and the Donafins went in the tent, but the conversation continued for another hour and a half. Tom and Rachael Donafin drifted off to sleep a little before ten. Young Decker held on for another half hour, though it was doubtful he was really catching much of the conversation. Finally, with all but Rhoda sound asleep and her looking droopy-eyed, Decker suggested they go back outside. There were a few things he still wanted to talk about, and he felt it best that their conversation be away from the children.

"I don't know if you can answer this," he began once they were outside. He kept his voice down so as not to be overheard by those in the neighboring tents. "I've always wondered," he asked, "why, during all those years that I thought he was dead, Tom never tried to contact me."

Rhoda nodded, understanding why Decker would want to know the answer to that question. "I can't really give you a full explanation," she said. "I wish I could. I know that he tried during and just after the war, but he was never able to reach you. After that, he never tried again. I asked him about it because he frequently talked about you and he always watched when you had a news conference, but he said that he and Rabbi Cohen had discussed it and agreed it would be best to wait. I do know that he wanted to let you know he was all right, but he said he just couldn't.' "

It was more of an answer than Rhoda realized, for it confirmed Decker's assessment that Tom had somehow become a puppet of Cohen and the KDP.

"There's something . . ." Rhoda hesitated. "There's something I'd like to ask you."

"Yes?" Decker prodded. He could sense her discomfort.

"You were with Tom when he died," she said finally. "Did he suffer?"

Decker shook his head reassuringly. "No. I don't think he did."

She bit her lip to hold back the tears as she nodded both understanding and appreciation.

"I only spent a brief time with him, but I know that he loved you very much," he added. In reality, Tom had said very little about Rhoda or his children, but this was not the time for strict adherence to the facts; for Rhoda's sake a little supposition seemed in order. "I have some wonderful news for you, though," Decker added. "Just before Scott Rosen had me kidnapped, Christopher told me that Tom has been born again—reincarnated—to a family in Paraguay. If you'd like, you and the children can come with me when I leave—assuming, of course, that Scott Rosen really does intend to let me go. I'll talk to Christopher for you; I'm sure I can convince him to tell you where Tom is. He may not tell you all the specifics until Tom is older, but with patience, and if you're willing to take the communion, you and Tom could be reunited."

Rhoda shook her head politely. "I appreciate your concern, Mr. Hawthorne, but the Bible clearly teaches against reincarnation. It says, '. . . man is destined to die once, and after that to face judgment.'[64] When Yeshua talked about being 'born again,' he wasn't talking about reincarnation. He was talking about a spiritual change that is so complete it's as though we've been reborn as new people."

"But what about all the people who say they were reincarnated and who remember their past lives? Some of them remember things that they couldn't possibly know without having lived before," Decker replied.

"I think that in most cases what they think they remember is really just something from a dream or their imagination or perhaps something similar that happened in their own life. Or maybe it was something that they

[64] Hebrews 9:27.

heard or read about or saw on television. There are all sorts of possibilities. But in those cases where they really do know something that no one could know without having been there, I think that someone *was* there in that other life. But it's not the people themselves. To use the vernacular of the New Age, I would say that an 'ascended master' or 'spirit guide' was the one who really remembered the event and that the guide shared the memory with the person. Of course, the Bible would call that ascended master or spirit guide a demon."

"You don't really believe in demons, do you?" Decker gently chided.

"You don't really believe in ascended masters and spirit guides, do you?" Rhoda responded.

Decker smiled. He had left himself wide open for that. "Okay," he said, "so you don't believe in reincarnation. Are you so sure you're right that you're unwilling even to ask Christopher?"

"I would not ask Christopher even if he was standing here with us," Rhoda answered. "I know where Tom is and I'm quite certain it's not Paraguay."

Decker sighed in defeat. He could see there was no use arguing.

"Mr. Hawthorne," Rhoda said, "I knew when Tom left that I would not see him again in this world."

"You knew where Tom was going? He told you?"

"I wasn't sure exactly where he was going. But I knew he would be killed."

"And you let him go? You didn't try to stop him?"

"I know you won't understand this, Mr. Hawthorne, but I had no choice. I knew from the day I first saw Tom that he would die a violent death."

"How did you know that?"

"Right after the Rapture, God gave Rabbi Cohen a prophecy about the Avenger of Blood, a man who the prophecy said 'must bring death and die that the end and the beginning may come.' When Rabbi Cohen brought Tom to me on the night the war started, he appeared so badly injured that I didn't think I could help him. But Rabbi Cohen insisted. He said that Tom would recover— he had to—he was the Avenger of Blood."

Decker shuddered. That was what Tom had written on the note he slipped into Decker's pocket just before he died.

"I don't understand," he said. "What does that mean?"

"There's an ancient law, older even than the Ten Commandments. Its validity was recognized by Moses[65] and by Joshua[66] and by King David.[67] It allowed, within certain limitations, for a relative of a murdered person to avenge the murder by killing the murderer. It sounds rather barbaric, I suppose, by some standards, but it did keep down the number of murders and it prevented full-fledged blood feuds between families."

"But what does that have to do with Tom?"

"Before the children were born, Tom was the last of his line, Mr. Hawthorne. He didn't even know it for most of his life, but Tom was the direct descendant of James, the brother of Jesus."

Decker's first inclination was to ask how Tom could possibly have "discovered" such a heritage, but there was

[65] Numbers 35:19–27; Deuteronomy 19:6, 12.

[66] Joshua 20:3–9.

[67] 2 Samuel 14:11.

something else that needed to be cleared up first. "I didn't think Jesus had any brothers."

"Actually, the Bible specifically mentions that Jesus had at least four brothers—James, Joseph, Simon, and Jude—and at least two sisters.[68] Actually, I should say half-brothers and half-sisters because, of course, while they had the same mother, Jesus had no earthly father."

Decker found the information interesting but went back to the other question. "And just how was it that Tom *discovered* he was related to Jesus?" he asked. "I suppose it was probably Saul Cohen who told Tom that he was the Avenger of Blood."

"I don't know how he found out," replied Rhoda. "He never told me. I think he probably realized it over a period of years."

"Okay, so even if we assume Tom *was* related to Jesus, what does that have to do with him deciding to assassinate Christopher?" Decker asked, getting back to the original issue. To his surprise, the emotion evoked by his memory of the assassination charged his voice with anger. He hoped Rhoda would not assume it was directed at her.

Rhoda apparently did not take offense. "The very first prophecy about Jesus, in the third chapter of Genesis,[69] says that Satan would strike the heel of the offspring of God, and the offspring of God would crush the head of Satan. The offspring of God is Jesus. The striking of Jesus' heel took place at the crucifixion when nails were driven

---

[68] Matthew 13:55–56.

[69] Genesis 3:15.

into his wrists and feet. And then, adding insult to the injury, it was the cells from the wound to his heel that were used to create Christopher."

The expression on Decker's face asked how she could have known that bit of information.

"You mentioned in an interview after Christopher's resurrection that Professor Goodman had found the cells on a slide from the heel," Rhoda answered in response to his unspoken question.

"And why do you say that added insult to injury?" he asked.

"Well, think about it. Satan used cells from the wounds that paid the price for the sins of the world to give life to the Antichrist."

Decker sighed. "I suppose if I believed that story, I'd find it rather ironic, yes. But how can you call Christopher the Anti-christ? I know that when John wrote about Christopher in the book of Revelation, he called him that. But can't you see that Christopher and Jesus are the same person? Christopher *is* Jesus, an exact duplicate of Jesus with all his memories, all his powers, and all his love for Humankind!"

Rhoda laughed. It was not an unfriendly laugh, but it was clear she did not agree. "Hearing you say that, I can't help but be amazed at just how detailed and exact the prophecies about the Antichrist really were. At one point in the book of Revelation," she explained, "John was talking to an angel who told him that one of the reasons the world would follow the Antichrist is 'because he once was, now is not, and yet will come.' "[70]

---

[70] Revelation 17:8–11.

"Meaning what?" Decker asked.

"Meaning just what you were saying. You say Christopher is Jesus—that he came to earth, he was gone for two thousand years, and now he's back in the form of Christopher. Or from the perspective of John and the angel in about 90 A.D., *he once was,* but at the time they were talking *he was not,* and yet *he was to come* in the future. And because of this, the world trusts Christopher and follows him, even while rejecting everything the real Jesus ever said or did."

Decker let Rhoda's musings go unanswered and tried another tack. "If you believe Jesus is God and that God is good, then how could anything evil be made from the cells of Jesus?"

"Nothing in the universe was evil when God made it. But Satan takes what God meant for good and uses it for evil. Even Lucifer was good when God created him. But by his free will he chose to rebel. In the same way, Satan used the cells of Jesus' own body for evil. It's the ultimate evil irony, but it's entirely in keeping with Satan's standard operating procedure."

Decker shook his head and sighed again.

Rhoda continued. "Somewhere—it was probably in the same interview after Christopher's resurrection—you said that Professor Goodman had named Christopher not after Christ, but after Christopher Columbus. You said that Goodman believed Jesus was an alien observer from a highly advanced planet and he hoped that by cloning Jesus he would be able to learn about and maybe even contact these aliens. You said Professor Goodman named him Christopher because he hoped that like Columbus, Christopher would lead us to a new world."

Decker nodded affirmation to Rhoda's recitation of the facts.

"You say that Jesus and Christopher are the same, but the story of how Christopher was named illustrates that there is an important difference. Jesus was God who became a man to provide a way for us to be reunited with God. But Christopher was created by a man who denied the existence of God and who hoped to further separate man from God by replacing belief in God with belief in super-advanced aliens.

"But Christopher has taken what Professor Goodman intended one step further. He makes God out to be the enemy of mankind—the one force that stands in man's way, preventing him from achieving godhood.

"In short," Rhoda concluded, "Jesus was God made in the image of man, sent to reconcile man to God; Christopher is a man-made god created to separate man from the true God. So you see, when Tom shot Christopher, he was acting as Jesus' Avenger of Blood, striking the head of Satan in accordance with the prophecy in Genesis."

Decker paused for a moment as he shook his head at Rhoda's explanation, then he spoke. "I just wish you could meet Christopher and get to know him. If you did, you'd realize what you're saying about him could not possibly be true."

"I just wish you could have met John and Cohen," Rhoda responded.

"I *did* meet them," Decker replied, "on the streets of Jerusalem."

"That's not what I meant. If you could have really gotten to know them, then you'd know that they were kind, generous men." It was obvious to Rhoda she was failing miserably to make her point. Quickly she turned to an example to strengthen her case. "You knew that Tom was blind for several months before God instructed Rabbi Cohen to heal him?" she asked.

"Tom mentioned that," Decker answered.

"But you didn't believe him?"

"I had no reason to *disbelieve* him. Cohen was a very powerful man, but I'm not so sure that he did it for Tom's benefit. I think he used Tom for his own purposes—that he convinced him of this Avenger of Blood story in order to get him to kill Christopher. After all, if Tom had remained blind, he would not have been able to shoot Christopher, and Tom would still be alive today."

Rhoda looked at Decker and Decker at Rhoda. Both could see that neither was going to convince the other. Even though they disagreed, however, Decker found Rhoda not at all disagreeable. She was, in fact, quite pleasant to be with. He could easily see how Tom could love her. Ultimately, they each resolved to let the matter pass. As for Decker, at least he had gotten an answer to what Tom's note had meant. There was one other thing he hoped Rhoda might be able to explain.

"Just before he died," Decker said, "Tom's last words to me were, 'He was going to leave me.' Does that mean anything to you?"

Rhoda shook her head. "I'm sorry," she said. "I don't know."

❑

When Decker arrived back at the cabin he was greeted at the door.

"Welcome back, Mr. Hawthorne."

"Jailer, I thought you were gone," Decker responded.

The jailer shook his head. "Nah," he said. "I can't leave. I run this place. Besides, I still haven't perfected my manna manicotti recipe for you, but I'm working on it. I hope to have it done before you leave."

Decker was still far from certain that Rosen was really going to let him go, but it was beginning to seem as if everyone else believed it. "I'd like that," he said.

"There's just one thing, Mr. Hawthorne," the jailer said. "Now that you're free to come and go as you like, would it be all right if you didn't call me 'jailer' anymore? My name is Charlie."

"Sure, Charlie," Decker said.

11

Rescue

June 6, 4 n.a.

FOR THE FIRST NIGHT since he had arrived in Petra, Decker really slept well. In the morning he was greeted by a knock on the door, followed by the friendly voice of his young namesake.

"Mr. Hawthorne," came Decker Donafin's voice from the other side of the door.

"Wake up, Mr. Hawthorne. My mom says breakfast will be ready soon. If we're late, Tom will eat everything."

"Well, we can't have that," Decker answered as he sat up. "Run back to the tent to protect our share and I'll be there as quick as I can."

"My mom said I could wait here for you."

"Oh . . . well, okay. I'll be just a few minutes."

Decker quickly brushed his teeth, ran a washcloth over his face and got dressed. There was little choice of what to wear; all he had was what he had been wearing the night he was kidnapped and some well-worn but clean clothes that had been provided by the KDP. Soon he and Decker Donafin were on their way. It was about three quarters of a mile to the tent and they had gone nearly half that distance before Decker realized that something was missing.

"Decker," he asked the younger, "why is there no manna this morning?"

Decker Donafin looked at the elder in surprise that he should have to ask. "It's the Sabbath, Mr. Hawthorne. The manna doesn't fall on the Sabbath; that's why we gather twice as much on Friday. It will be back tomorrow."

Rhoda and Rachael had prepared a breakfast of fruit and manna pancakes. The manna was becoming a little monotonous, but the company more than made up for it. After breakfast Rhoda and the children went to a worship service at one edge of the camp. Decker was invited to attend but he declined, opting to wander about on his own until later, when Rhoda and young Decker had offered to give him a proper tour of Petra's ancient ruins.

When the Donafins returned, Rhoda packed a picnic lunch and her doctor's bag and they headed out. Their plan was to start with the Broken Pediment Tomb, the Renaissance Tomb, the Triclinium, and the Roman Soldier Tomb. From there they would visit the facades of the Wadi Farasa and work their way around the rest of the southern end of the city. Along the way, Rhoda explained, she would be making a few stops to visit some patients. Decker and Decker could continue on whenever she stopped and she would catch up with them.

Rhoda's plan brought up a question that had not previously occurred to Decker. "There's something I don't understand," he said. "Why do you need doctors here? I thought the KDP had the power to heal. Why don't people just go to the KDP when they're sick or injured?"

"It is God who has the power to heal, not the KDP,"

Rhoda answered. "Sometimes God chooses to have a member of the KDP act as his agent to heal someone, but it's not up to us to decide when that will be."

"So if you're sick you just have to hope Yahweh's in a good mood. And if he's not, then you call a doctor." Decker was not looking for an argument, but he couldn't help himself.

"No," Rhoda smiled, taking Decker's remarks more as a joke than as a challenge to her beliefs. "It's not a question of God's mood. It's what his will is for the life of the individual. God never intended to do everything for us. He has given us feet to walk and a brain to think and hands to work. Yahweh is a creative god, and as his children, it is in our nature to create. When we work, whether it is as a farmer or a builder or as a doctor, we are participating in God's creation. A farmer takes the land and the seed and the rain that God has created and produces a harvest to feed his family. A builder takes the resources God has created and builds a home. As a doctor, I study the workings of the human body that God has created, and when an injury occurs or when the body is invaded by some disease, then I do what I can to repair it. Work has always been a part of God's plan," she said. "Adam and Eve were told to tend the Garden of Eden, and we will continue to work even after Jesus returns and sets up his kingdom."

They stopped to rest for a moment on the ledge in front of the Broken Pediment Tomb. Before them on the plain of Petra tents stretched for mile after mile, broken only by groves of fruit trees, small play areas for the children, meeting areas, latrines, etc.

"Tell me about Petra," Decker asked as he took in the sight.

"I guess you know," Rhoda replied after a moment, "that the name Petra comes from the Greek word *petros,* which means rock. The origin of that name for this place is obvious enough." Decker nodded and Rhoda continued. "Originally, Petra and the area around it were inhabited by the Edomites, the descendants of Abraham's grandson Esau, who was also called Edom. Later, sometime around the third or fourth century B.C., Petra was settled by the Nabataeans, who were wealthy nomadic Bedouins who traded between Arabia and the Mediterranean. The city served as their capitol for four hundred years. At one point more than 250,000 Nabataeans lived here. Petra provided them with security and an abundant water supply and became the crossroads of the trade routes linking Syria to the Red Sea and India to the Gulf and the Mediterranean.

"In the first century, Petra became a part of the Roman province of Syria. Over time the Roman influence brought the decline of Nabataean culture, and as the trade routes changed to favor Rome, Petra went into gradual decline. By the time of the Crusades, the city was an uninhabited ruin. If you can make the climb, you can see the remains of three forts the Crusaders built when they occupied Petra in the twelfth and thirteenth centuries. After they left, the city was totally uninhabited. Soon its location was entirely forgotten and it survived only as legend— a sort of Arabian version of Troy," she said, referring to the legendary city of Homer's *Iliad.*

"Then in 1812 a Swiss explorer, who had disguised himself as an Arab Muslim on pilgrimage in order to be allowed into Mecca, came across Petra on his journey and reported his discovery to the world. After that, literally hundreds of archaeological expeditions and tens of thousands of tourists poured into Petra."

"What about now?" Decker said, making a sweeping motion across the panorama with his hand. "Tell me about Petra today."

"Oh," she said, adjusting her temporal perspective. "Well, the Bible says in the book of Revelation that God would prepare a place in the wilderness for Israel to escape from Satan in the last half of the Tribulation.[71] Before the Rapture, many believed that the place would be Petra. A few, including Rabbi Cohen and Scott Rosen's parents, even began to raise money to purchase defensive weaponry for the city. After a while, though, they realized that God intended to defend Petra himself and that their efforts would not be needed, so they spent the money they had raised for seeds, fertilizer, and farm tools. God promised to provide a refuge in the wilderness for us, and he said he would provide us with an ample supply of water—" Rhoda paused and pointed out the *Ain Musa,* the waterway that provided most of the water to Petra "—and trees.[72] And of course you've seen the manna every morning. But God never promised to give us variety; that part we've provided for ourselves with our gardens. Of course, it's God who makes the seeds grow. We do our part and he does the rest. The gardens give us something to do, too," she added. "It can get a little monotonous around here after a while."

"You said God intended to defend Petra himself. Defend it from what?" Decker asked.

[71] Revelation 12:6.

[72] Isaiah 41:17–20.

"From Christopher, of course."

Decker shook his head in disbelief. "And why should Yahweh need to defend Petra from Christopher? Has Christopher ever done anything to threaten Petra?"

"Not yet, but he will. And he would have long ago were it not for the angels of God that surround this place."

"The KDP really has you convinced that Christopher is going to send troops against you?" Decker said, both in amazement and disgust.

"It's not just what the KDP says," Rhoda answered. "It's what the Bible says."

Decker sighed and continued looking over the camp. "Are all the people here Christians, followers of the KDP?" he asked.

"No, *most* of the people here are *not* believers in Yeshua, though they will be soon. They are Jews who have come here because they found the KDP to be a not-so-evil ally and because Petra offers refuge from the greater enemy: Christopher and the United Nations."

"So just exactly how long do you and they plan on staying here?"

"Not much longer. In September Christopher will bring the armies of the world against us here. Then Yeshua will return to destroy him."

"I assure you," Decker said, no longer willing to just let the matter pass, "that Christopher has no intention of sending troops to Petra."

"That will change soon."

"And what if it doesn't?" Decker asked as an idea suddenly occurred to him.

"It will," Rhoda said confidently.

"But what if it doesn't?" Decker insisted.

"But it will. There's no question about it."

No words left his mouth, but it was clear he was unwilling to settle for Rhoda's answer.

"Well, then I guess," Rhoda said reluctantly, "and this is *just* being hypothetical: If Christopher does not march on Petra, then we will have been wrong."

"And then you'll leave Petra?"

"It won't happen, but yes. I suppose many would leave Petra," Rhoda conceded grudgingly.

"Well, then, I hope you'll come see me in Babylon in October," Decker chimed.

"If we see each other in October, it won't be in Babylon," Rhoda replied. "It will be in Jerusalem."

"Why Jerusalem?"

"Where else would you expect Yeshua to establish his kingdom?"

"Oh, you mean if I convert."

"Of course."

"So you think there's still hope for me?" Decker laughed.

"There's always hope, Mr. Hawthorne. Scott Rosen says that you're a pretty tough customer, but then so was Tom. Of course, Tom never slugged anybody."

"I will admit Rosen tells a convincing story," Decker said. "He knows his subject. But there are two things that neither he nor you, nor anyone else can explain away or justify, no matter how you might try. The first is the death and destruction caused by John and Cohen, and the second is the murder of innocent men and women by the fundamentalists at the communion clinics."

"I can assure you, those responsible for what happened at the clinics are *not* the fundamentalists," Rhoda responded. "Yes, originally Christians did try to peacefully block the entrances and try to talk people out of receiving the mark, but they certainly have not been responsible for the violence and the killings."

"How else do you explain it?"

"Christopher and the UN are doing it to create hysteria and hatred of Christians and of Yahweh," Rhoda answered emphatically. "Of course, you probably think that because you're a man of the world and I'm secluded out here in Petra, you must be right and I must be wrong."

"The thought had occurred to me," Decker responded. The admission was not a confession but an attempt to drive home the obvious truth in the observation. After all, how much could anyone in Rhoda's position, living in the middle of the desert, know about what was really happening in the rest of the world? "And then of course, there are the eyewitnesses," he added.

"True," she acknowledged. "But if Christopher can find people to do the bombings and killings, then surely he can also come up with witnesses."

"I suppose," Decker said, his words granting the hypothetical possibility but his voice making it clear that he did not for one moment believe the proposition.

"And even if the witnesses are not *officially* being put up to it by the UN, then certainly they are *unofficially,*" she asserted.

"What do you mean?"

"Have you listened to what the news media says about the fundamentalists? They make it sound like they're subhuman. Some of the people who claim to be eyewitnesses probably feel like they're doing the world a big favor to help get rid of the Christians. It's a regular witch hunt out there."

"I admit that some have let their emotions get away from them," Decker granted.

"What they say about the fundamentalists sounds remarkably like what the Nazis said about the Jews in World War II," Rhoda responded.

"You can't blame Christopher or the United Nations for what the media says," Decker answered.

"No, but I would think that anyone as caring as you claim Christopher is would make some attempt to dispute the impression that the media is giving about the fundamentalists. He wouldn't stand for charges like that against any other minority, would he? Why should he ignore it when it's the fundamentalists?"

Decker wanted to respond but he wasn't sure he had an answer. Perhaps Rhoda had a point. Perhaps some of the fault was his own.

"Judaism and Christianity are the only two religions that can be proved based on material evidence, yet they are the only ones whose followers are being persecuted."

"Yeah, well, I've heard all this from Rosen. But how can you really prove anything?" he asked, diverting the conversation away from Rhoda's point. "How can you be 100 percent certain we're even having this conversation? Maybe you're just dreaming."

"The real question is not whether I can be 100 percent sure of something," Rhoda answered. "The real question is this: Is the evidence sufficient to make it absurd to believe anything else? There is enough evidence that Jesus was the Messiah to convince even the most hardened skeptic if he would take the time to examine it and not discount it out of hand. With Christianity, the question is not 'can you believe?' but 'will you believe?' "

Decker shook his head in frustration. "Rhoda, there's just no need for any of this. Christopher offered to accept the KDP, and I'm sure he would be willing to reissue that offer if they would just give up their narrow-minded claim to exclusive truth and stop saying that everybody who disagrees with them is going to hell. You can even venerate Jesus if you want. Christopher is very open-minded to different beliefs; he doesn't care if someone is Buddhist or Hindu or Sikh or Muslim or any other religion. Millions of people from the mainstream Christian denominations have taken the communion."

"No Christian can take the communion or the mark. Anyone who has is a Christian in name only and is eternally lost."

"Rhoda," Decker said, exasperated, "that's exactly the narrow-minded attitude that's the cause of the whole problem. Why can't you just acknowledge that someone else might have some piece of the truth that you and the KDP don't have?"

"I know that our beliefs must sound narrow-minded, Mr. Hawthorne, but it's really just the opposite, because the *one* truth, the *one* way to God that we believe in is entirely unrestricted, completely free, totally accessible and available to everyone. God is no farther from any of us than our willingness to call upon him. I ask you," she said, drawing on the words Saul Cohen once used when speaking to her husband, "would it be narrow-minded to say that there is only one thing that everyone must breathe in order to live? I know you'll say, 'Air is available to everyone.' But, Mr. Hawthorne, so is God. The Bible says that God has placed knowledge of himself inside each of us.[73] That includes Jews and Gentiles, Hindus and Buddhists, Muslims, Christians, atheists, agnostics, and pagans. This isn't some kind of a treasure hunt, where the prize goes only to the lucky or the shrewd, or a game show where you're forced to choose blindly between the god behind door number one, door number two, or door number three. Inside each of us, we already know which is the right door. God calls to us and tells us what he is like, who he is, and where to find him. We may not know his name, but we know his nature, we know his call, and we can witness his power throughout the universe. But it's up to each of us individually to decide whether we will answer God's call.

"If a person loves God and loves his neighbor as he loves himself, then in his own time God will reveal himself more and more to that person until finally he will realize that the God he serves is in fact the God of the Bible, and the one who has paid the price for the forgiveness of his sins is God's son, Jesus.

"As for who goes to hell, in the final analysis no one *has* to go to hell. In fact, the only ones who do are those who refuse to go to heaven. Damnation is a sentence we impose upon ourselves. If anyone truly seeks God, then God will provide that person with sufficient knowledge to be saved. The bottom line, Mr. Hawthorne, is this: God is, God loves, and God can be found." Rhoda was obviously finished but Decker remained silent, not wanting to argue the subject further.

"I have some other patients I need to visit," Rhoda said when it became apparent that Decker was not going

---

[73] Romans 1:18–25.

to respond. "If you'd like, you and Decker can continue to explore. We'll be having dinner just after sunset."

"Sure," Decker responded. "We'll be fine."

"Okay," she said, and then addressing the younger Decker: "Take it easy. Don't wear Mr. Hawthorne out."

"Yes, ma'am," Decker Donafin answered politely as his mother gave him a kiss and then turned to leave.

❑

"So, it's just you and me," Decker said after Rhoda had gone. "Where do you want to go first?"

"Can we go to the Lion Monument?" the younger asked.

"You bet!" he responded enthusiastically, unaware of the climb that awaited them.

❑

The two Deckers walked and climbed and explored for the rest of the afternoon. Inside one of the carved-out tunnels that connected two adjacent facades, they had to feel their way along through nearly pitch black. The elder Decker felt the younger take his hand. It was now so dark it was impossible to see at all. "Are you afraid of the dark?" the elder asked as he felt the younger's hand tighten.

"My mom says there's no reason to be afraid because Yeshua is always with me," the younger answered. "Are you afraid?"

"A little," the elder answered.

"Yeah, me too," Decker Donafin admitted. "A little."

"Let's go somewhere else, then."

Decker Donafin nodded, but of course Decker Hawthorne could not see it.

After visiting a few more sites, the elder Decker finally insisted that they stop to take a break. Half sitting, half leaning, they rested against an outcropping of stone below *Ad Dier* (the Monastery). For a few moments neither spoke—the elder because he was catching his breath, the younger because he had something on his mind—and then Decker Donafin broke the silence.

"I think I remember my dad pretty well," he said. "But sometimes my mom or Tom or Rachael will talk about him and it will be about something I don't remember at all." At last it had come to the surface—the one thing that had never left either of their minds throughout their time together: their memories of Tom Donafin. In everything they had done that day the memories had floated and wafted through their thoughts. And yet, neither had mentioned him. Everything the younger Decker did or said had either reminded the elder of his old friend or caused him to note how the father and son differed. With equal attention the younger had observed the elder and wondered how much this man for whom he had been named was like the father he now struggled to remember.

"I miss him a lot."

"I miss him, too," the elder said.

"My mom says he was a good man and that he loved God. She says we'll see him again soon when Yeshua returns."

Decker wasn't sure how to respond. "He was a good friend," he managed after a moment.

"Mom said you were with my dad when he died."

"Yes," Decker answered. It was a gruesome memory and he hoped the boy would not ask him more about it. He need not have worried; Decker Donafin had no intention of asking for the details. After a moment's silence, Decker looked down to see tears in the boy's eyes. He hesitated and then leaned down to hug him. Decker Donafin put his arms around him as the tears flowed.

❑

That evening after supper, Decker again entertained the Donafin children with old stories of nearly forgotten adventures and misadventures he had with Tom. A few of the stories Rhoda had heard before from Tom, but Decker's slightly different telling made her wonder if either man remembered the events as they had actually occurred. Decker told them how he and Tom had been captured and taken to Lebanon, though he left out details of the torture they had endured. The Donafin children knew that their father had once been a hostage, but they had not realized that his captivity had lasted almost three years.

The stories did not go on nearly so long this night, as first young Decker and then Tom and Rachael fell off to sleep. Once again, Rhoda and Decker left the tent to talk a while longer.

"You'll be leaving tomorrow?" Rhoda asked.

"First thing in the morning," he answered, surprised at the confidence in his voice.

"You're welcome to stay here with us," Rhoda said. "All that waits for you outside of Petra is death."

Decker shook his head. "Tell Decker good-bye for me."

"You'll probably have an opportunity to do that yourself. He's an early riser. I expect he'll want to see you before you leave."

Decker nodded. "I'd like that."

❑

That night Decker lay awake thinking about the events of the past few days. He no longer thought much about whether he would ever get out of Petra and back to Babylon alive. Somehow he felt certain now that he would. Now his thoughts centered on young Decker and Rhoda and the rest of the Donafin family. He thought also of the others in Petra who lay crammed together, huddled in confused, misguided fear of what was happening in the outside world. As long as he had thought of them as simply followers of the KDP, he could ignore the fact that they were people. Now he knew better: He had seen them face to face, had talked with them, and felt he was beginning to understand them. He was ashamed that it had taken being kidnapped for him to realize it. Even Scott Rosen, for all his faults, was only doing what he thought best. Decker wasn't sure how, but he was determined that he would find a way to reach these people, to let them know that Christopher was not their enemy, and that what Christopher promised the world was not to be feared, but welcomed.

On the plane to Jerusalem after his resurrection, Christopher had said that Decker's role would be to communicate his message to those unfamiliar with the concepts of the New Age, and to this point Decker had served him well. But that was more than three years ago and the job was nearly complete. Christopher's message of the evolution of Humankind was known throughout the world. Most people had experienced some clairvoyant, telepathic, telekinetic, or healing power, and 87 percent of the population had already received the communion and the mark. It had not occurred to him before, but as Decker considered it now he realized that he had in effect nearly worked himself out of a job.

But now there was a new mission, a new job to do: to persuade even those who were Christopher's opponents. And, ironically, it was Scott Rosen who had given Decker the means to effect that conversion. Rosen had told him of the calamities that were soon to be visited upon the earth, and both Rosen and Rhoda had stated their belief that Christopher would respond by assembling an army to march on Petra. In large part it was a self-fulfilling prophecy. Faced with renewed devastation, Christopher would be forced to strike at the agents of Yahweh who precipitated the devastation. If Decker could somehow alter the events predicted by the KDP so that Christopher did not march on Petra, then the KDP and their followers would have to admit they had made a mistake. And if they had made a mistake about this, then they could be wrong about other things as well. The KDP's claim to inerrancy made their hold on the people both very tight *and* very brittle. Like a house of cards, it was necessary only to re- move one card—to cause one of their prophecies to fail—and the whole structure would collapse.

Even if all else was true, even if all the calamities did strike the earth, it was still possible to turn this around. Instead of assembling an army to march on Petra for war, Christopher could send a peace envoy or simply do noth- ing at all. In this way he could short-circuit the prophecy, prevent it from coming true, and show his true face as peacemaker and benevolent leader instead of the demonic beast the KDP made him out to be.

Perhaps, also, knowing what the KDP planned would allow Christopher to initiate countermeasures to limit the effects of the plagues they predicted.

Scott Rosen had kidnapped Decker and brought him to Petra to convince him that Christopher was evil and that Yahweh was good. As Decker nodded off to sleep, he realized that Rosen's actions were only a ploy of fate, which, as it had so many times before, was again putting Decker in the right place at the right time. There could be no doubt that the real reason he had been brought to Petra was so that he would come to know and understand these people so that he could find a way to convince them of the truth about Yahweh and Christopher.

❑

"Mr. Hawthorne."

"Mr. Hawthorne."

"Wake up, Mr. Hawthorne, it's time to go."

Decker opened his eyes and looked around the room. As he twisted his body and shifted his weight to sit up, the ropes that bound his hands and feet slipped off like oversized gloves and shoes.

"It's time to go, Mr. Hawthorne," the voice of a young boy said again.

Decker rubbed his eyes and looked toward the voice. He was no longer in Petra; he was back in Lebanon, a hostage of the Hizballah. There in the open doorway of his room stood fourteen-year-old Christopher Goodman.

"Christopher?" Decker asked, puzzled at this obviously unexpected turn of events.

"Yes, Mr. Hawthorne," Christopher answered.

"What are you doing here?" Decker asked in confused disbelief.

"It's time to go, Mr. Hawthorne. I've come to get you," Christopher said, making no attempt to explain.

Christopher walked from the room and signaled for him to follow. Decker lifted the 115 pounds that remained of his body and followed Christopher out of the room and toward the front door. Halfway there, he hesitated. There was something he was trying to remember, something too important to forget, something he could not leave behind.

"Tom!" he said suddenly. "Where's Tom?" he asked of the friend he had not seen since they were brought to Lebanon.

Christopher hesitated and then raised his arm slowly and pointed toward another door. Silently, Decker opened it, looking for any sign of his captors. There was none. Inside, Tom lay on a mat identical to the one Decker had now spent nearly three years sleeping on, sitting on, eating on . . . living on. Tom was lying with his face to the wall. Decker entered and began untying the bonds that held his friend's feet.

"Tom, wake up. We're getting out of here," he whispered.

Tom sat up and looked at his rescuer. For a moment they just stared at each other's faces. Finally, Decker forced his eyes away and began untying Tom's hands. He had not looked in a mirror at any time during his captivity, and though he knew his body was emaciated, he had not seen his face, where the most dramatic effects of his

captivity were evident. Seeing Tom's face, he was struck
with such grief and sympathy for his friend's similar condition that he had to look away to hold back tears.

Outside the apartment, Decker and Tom walked
stealthily down the hall, hoping to avoid detection.
Christopher, on the other hand, walked on ahead of them,
showing absolutely no sign of concern about the seriousness of the situation. They went down three flights of
stairs, cluttered with trash and broken bits of plaster and
glass. Still there was no sign of their captors. As they
emerged into the open air, Decker closed his eyes as the
bright sunlight struck him in the face with its warmth and
glow.

"Mr. Hawthorne."

"Mr. Hawthorne."

Decker opened his eyes and looked around, struggling
to remember where he was. Standing at the door was
Decker Donafin. He was still in Petra.

"Wake up, Mr. Hawthorne, it's time to go."

Horror filled Decker's eyes as he suddenly understood
what Tom Donafin's final words had meant.

12

Judas

```
Sunday, June 7, 4 N.A.
The wilderness of Jordan,
north of Petra
```

THE DUSTY GRAY four-wheel-drive truck sped across the off-road terrain north from Petra, negotiating its way around rocks and ruts. Having long since given up on the notion of conversing with her passenger—he had not said ten words since he got in the vehicle outside the *Siq* of Petra an hour before—the driver thought about plans for her upcoming wedding. When she received her assignment to drive Decker to Jerusalem, she had expected a hostile passenger, still enraged about his abduction. Instead he seemed almost in a trance, so preoccupied with his thoughts that he acted as though she wasn't even there. Time and again he ran his right hand up the side of his face and over his head, pulling at his thinning gray hair as it passed between his fingers. Alternating between nervous twitching, tapping his foot on the floorboard, and a frozen tableau, Decker tried to understand, tried to think if there was something that he had missed. But there seemed no doubt what Tom had meant.

Christopher was going to leave Tom in Lebanon.

It must have been, Decker thought, his eyes squinting

in reflection, that all the similarities between his current situation and what happened in Lebanon all those years ago had caused him to have the dream again. That part was simple enough. Still, that did not negate the larger meaning. How could he have missed it for so long? All these years and it had not sunk in until now. Could it have been just an accident? Decker's mind was filled with the single thought and its awful implications. It didn't make sense; it couldn't have been an accident. Decker knew that if he was right, he had discovered the single slip in an otherwise flawless plan. Christopher's hesitation when Decker asked about Tom had seemed so insignificant at the time, but if he was right . . .

Another hour passed before the truck finally came to a real road, bounced onto the blistering hot blacktop, and turned west. Decker's mind flashed back to the road in Lebanon where he and Tom Donafin had been rescued by the convoy carrying Ambassador Jon Hansen. Had that really happened just by chance? he wondered.

About three miles down the highway, the driver pulled to the side of the road and stopped behind a Japanese-built station wagon. "The key is in the glove box," she said as she handed him a canteen full of water. "Just keep heading west for about thirty kilometers and you'll come to Jericho."

"Thanks," Decker said reflexively as he took the canteen and the leather satchel that held Elizabeth's Bible, and got out of the truck. The temperature was well over 100 degrees Fahrenheit with the sun beating down through perfectly clear skies, but he was oblivious to such details. Going to the car, he mindlessly opened the door, got in, and closed the door behind him. The driver who had brought him from Petra sat in the air-conditioned comfort of her own vehicle waiting for him to start the car, but despite the heat Decker just sat there, absorbed in thought. Finally, when she was about to go and check on him, he remembered something about the key being in the glove box and reached over to find it.

Without looking back at the driver, Decker started the car and drove off. Only the intense heat of the steering wheel in his bare hands broke his concentration, and he used his shirttail to hold the wheel as he tried to determine how to turn on the car's air-conditioning. It was fortunate that the car was pointed toward Jericho, for he had no recollection of the woman's directions and no thought of where he was going.

□

Decker got past the UN border guards in Israel without incident, though they were a bit unnerved to have a high official of the UN arriving unexpectedly. Their response gave no indication that he had been reported missing. Apparently, Rosen was right: Decker traveled so frequently that after being gone for only four days, no one was seriously concerned about where he was. This was a point of some relief, as he had no desire to explain where he had been or what had happened to him until he first had some time to think.

He found a small restaurant off the beaten path where he thought it unlikely that anyone would recognize him. As he ate, he agonized over what to do next. Certainly he should call someone to let them know where he was and that he was all right—*all right,* he thought in pained irony, now *there* was a relative term. He decided the best course of action would be to call Debbie Sanchez, his second in command, tell her that he had taken some time off and would be gone for another week or so. She could tell anyone else who needed to know. That *should* work, he thought; Debbie would probably be irritated that he hadn't told her of his plans ahead of time, but she was too new in her job to question him or demand an explanation. When she got over being mad, she'd probably welcome the opportunity to be in charge for a while.

Decker crossed his fingers and hoped the video on the telephone might be broken—it was going to be hard enough to sound like nothing was wrong without trying to look the part as well. He could turn the video off, but that would just raise questions; and he couldn't lie and say the equipment was broken because the monitor at the other end would indicate that it was turned off.

Putting on the best face he could manage, he dialed the phone. Debbie Sanchez had worked for him for less than a year, and although she was a very intelligent woman, he hoped she might not be able to see through his performance.

"Ms. Sanchez' office," a woman said. Decker looked at the face on the screen. It was Kwalindia Oshala, Debbie Sanchez' administrative assistant.

"Mr. Hawthorne!" she said. The inflection in her voice and the look on her face made it clear she was surprised to see him. This was not a good sign: Obviously there was some concern about his unplanned absence, even if they hadn't begun an all-out search.

"Yes," Decker answered, as if everything was fine and he had not noticed her surprise. "Let me talk to Ms. Sanchez."

"Sir," she responded, "she's out. She's covering for you at a meeting of the World Press Club." Decker had forgotten about being scheduled to speak, and for an instant he felt guilty about missing the appointment.

"What about Martin?" he asked, referring to Debbie Sanchez' aide.

"He's covering for Ms. Sanchez at a meeting in Beijing," she answered.

Decker really didn't want to leave a message with a secretary. That would hardly seem like appropriate behavior from someone who had been missing for the past four days. He quickly discovered that the option was not really open to him anyway.

"Mr. Hawthorne," Kwalindia said, "Jackie Hansen left orders for me to contact her immediately if you called. She said not to let you off the phone until she talked with you."

Decker thought fast but came up with nothing. This was not working out as he had planned. If Jackie was so insistent on talking to him, it probably meant that Christopher wanted to talk to him, and he was not at all prepared to do that just yet—not until he had time to think this whole thing through. But he couldn't refuse to talk to her. There was nothing to do but hope he could talk to Jackie briefly and try to appear as if nothing was wrong. "Put me through to her," he said reluctantly, with a pasted-on smile.

"Jackie Hansen," came the answer a second later, followed by, "Decker! Where have you been?"

Decker was about to try to answer when he heard another voice from out of camera range. "Decker?" the voice said. It was Robert Milner. "Let me talk to him!" A second later Milner came into view on the screen. "Decker, where have you been? Are you all right? We were about to send out search teams!"

Mentally Decker groaned, but his face maintained its smiling innocence. "I'm fine," he answered. "I just decided I needed a little vacation."

Milner was dumbstruck for a moment that Decker would so trivialize their concern by not even offering an explanation. "I'm sure you deserve it," he said, finally, "but it's customary to let someone . . . at least someone on your staff, know where you're going and when you'll be back."

"I'm really sorry," he said, trying to come up with some believable lie. "I mentioned it to Debbie Sanchez before I left. I guess I didn't make a big deal of it. I should have been clearer. I certainly didn't mean to worry anybody."

"Just so you're okay," Jackie interjected.

"Yeah, I'm fine. I hope that Christopher—"

"No," Jackie responded, anticipating Decker's question. "I asked him about you yesterday, thinking that he might have sent you on some mission somewhere; but I didn't tell him why I was asking or mention that nobody else knew where you were. I didn't want to worry him before I knew if something was really wrong. He's got enough on his mind right now."

"Good, good," Decker said. The look of relief on his face was in earnest.

"When can we expect you back, then?" Milner asked.

"I'm not sure," he replied. He wished he could just leave it open-ended but he knew he had to give them some kind of answer. "Maybe a week," he said finally.

"Where will you be?" Jackie asked. Decker didn't want to answer. He needed uninterrupted time to think, and once this conversation was over he didn't want to have to talk to anyone close to Christopher for a while. Worse still would be receiving a call from Christopher himself; Decker was certain that Christopher would be able to see through his act and know something was wrong. Still, he needed to give an answer.

"I'll be at my house in Maryland," he said finally. "I'll see you when I get back," he added, hoping to bring the conversation to a close.

"Okay," Jackie said, instinctively complying with his intention. "Well, I'm glad you're all right."

"Thanks," Decker responded.

"Enjoy yourself," Milner said halfheartedly. "And next time you decide to take off, make sure you have your phone with you."

"Yeah, I'm sorry," Decker said. "I guess I left it in my office."

And with that, Decker ended the call. *Milner knows something's wrong,* he thought. *He didn't believe me.* Quickly he ran over in his mind everything he had said for anything that might have given him away. Then he remembered: Debbie Sanchez had not been in the office the day before he left. If Milner followed up on it, that mistake would surely fuel his suspicions that something was indeed wrong.

Before he left the restaurant, Decker made two more calls: one to arrange for passage on the next UN flight to the U.S. and the other to have Bert Tolinson, the man at the agency that took care of his house, get the place ready for an extended visit.

❑

That evening Decker caught a United Nations troop transport in Tel Aviv bound for New York. The accommodations were less than those to which he was normally accustomed, but there was no one else on the plane except the crew, so he had plenty of privacy. Though he tried, he could not sleep. From New York he took a commuter flight to Reagan National Airport in Washington, D.C. It was on this second leg of the flight, and on the way to his house in Derwood, that he first began to notice something that he would soon realize had far greater meaning than he could have imagined.

Having raced the sun across seven time zones, Decker arrived at his house in Maryland. Now, despite all that was on his mind, after visiting the grave of his family in the backyard, he went inside and quickly fell asleep.

Monday, June 8, 4 N.A. Derwood, Maryland

Decker rolled over on his back and allowed his eyes to open slightly. Closing them again, he groaned and fell back to sleep. It was seven minutes after noon before he was finally really awake. He awoke with one thought so clear that it had doubtless been deliberated for hours by his unconscious mind. Rested and in the brilliant light of day, with the sound of birds outside, it seemed inconceivable to him that he ever could have imagined such an awful thing about Christopher. Yes, there were some things that needed to be explained, but he must have been out of his mind to have thought . . . He didn't even want to think about what he had thought. It was all so ridiculous. He shook his head in disbelief and more than a little embarrassment.

Of course, there were extenuating circumstances that had facilitated Decker's lapse of lucidity. After all, he had been kidnapped; and while the KDP apparently had not intended to harm him, he did not know that at the time. It was a traumatic experience and he realized now that it was foolish of him to think that he was immune to its ill effects. One of those effects, no doubt, was being open to suggestion: the suggestions of Scott Rosen and of the dream.

The clock beside his bed said it was 12:30 P.M. Adding eight hours to that meant that it was 8:30 P.M. in Babylon. He toyed with the idea of whether he should call or just get on a plane and go back. He opted for the latter. Right now, he was going to get out of bed, go downstairs, and fix himself some breakfast. Then he would call and find out when the next plane was leaving for Babylon.

Decker opened the refrigerator and freezer in unison. Bert Tolinson had done his job well—all his favorites were there. For a fleeting moment he thought maybe he wouldn't go back right away after all. He really could use a vacation. As he fixed breakfast, with the smell of bacon and waffles and coffee in the air, it was hard not to think back to better days: days of getting up early and having breakfast with Hope and Louisa before they headed off to school, days of driving to the "kiss-and-ride" at the Metro with Elizabeth. He would never have that back.

But he would have Elizabeth.

Christopher had promised him that. The joy of that thought made him all the more sickened that he could have doubted Christopher.

Decker carried his breakfast into the living room and turned on the television. It wasn't the same as having breakfast with a real live person, but it was better than eating alone.

The picture came on immediately and he was greeted by a very unusual sight: the newscaster on the screen had bandages on her forehead, cheek, chin, and two on her neck. She was obviously in some discomfort. His first thought was that she had been in an accident or mugged but it was not just the one reporter. The camera pulled back to reveal another reporter who was wearing multiple bandages as well. The picture then went to a newsman on a nearly abandoned street, interviewing whomever could be found of the local citizenry. Had Decker looked more closely at the background, he would have recognized the location as DuPont Circle in Washington, D.C., not far from the headquarters for *NewsWorld* magazine, for which he and Tom Donafin had both worked, and usually one of the busiest areas of Washington. But Decker was not interested in where they were. What had captured his attention was that almost everyone in the picture was bandaged. The few who were not revealed by their lack of gauze and tape what the rest had hidden: ugly, red, ulcerous lesions.

"TV stop," he said, and the picture froze. "Restart at beginning of this program." Instantly, the program started again at the top of the hour. Decker had always found this to be one of the most useful features of interactive television. Without missing a thing, it was possible to have any program in the past two months replayed. It was even possible, as the current example demonstrated, to restart a program that was in progress by accessing a delayed video feed.

Replaying from the beginning revealed that the whole program was focused on an unexplained worldwide outbreak of lesions that affected nearly the entire population. According to the news anchor, the epidemic had begun with a reddening of the skin and mild itching, which continued to worsen until lesions began to form and finally erupt. Suddenly Decker recalled something he had noticed that had been too insignificant to pay much attention to before: people scratching—nothing ominous, just minor but repeated scratching. It had been most obvious on the shuttle from New York and on the Metro ride from the airport. But as he thought back, he remembered seeing some of the crew on the UN troop transport scratching, as were people at the restaurant where he had eaten in Jerusalem. Then, as he recalled his phone conversation with Jackie Hansen, he remembered that she had scratched a spot on her arm.

Decker flipped through the channels. On most of the general interest networks the story was the same, with pain-racked, bandaged reporters interviewing bandaged health officials or bandaged politicians or bandaged people on the street. Nearly all business had come to a halt. Only the hardiest ventured out at all. Most governments around the world had shut down except for essential services. Later, there were public service advisories on how to treat the lesions to prevent infection and reports of long lines of people waiting to buy gauze, tape, and pain relievers at the few drug stores that remained open.

"As for the cause of the lesions," one of the reporters said, "while most scientists tell us it is still too early for any scientific evidence to have been collected and analyzed, one scientist at the Centers for Disease Control and

Prevention, speaking off the record, told me that there is clearly one distinguishing factor between those who have the sores and those who do not. As far as has been determined, only individuals who have taken the communion have the sores . . . a bitter irony that while so many have taken the communion because of the promise of good health, it now appears the communion itself may be the cause of this mysterious plague."

It's happening already, Decker thought. This is what Rosen was talking about when he said that things were going to get much worse fast. There must be some connection between this and why he had seen so many KDP arriving in Petra. But though he recognized the connection, he had no idea what the KDP were planning next.

❑

Decker did not call that day to make arrangements for passage back to Babylon, nor did he do so the next. He told himself that there was no hurry and that if he went out in public and was recognized, it would not be well received that someone so close to Christopher did not have the mark and the sores. At the same time, it made no sense to Decker to go out and get the communion when that would cause him to get the sores. He had enough food to last for a while, and anything else he needed, Bert Tolinson would get for him. It was far more reasonable, he thought, just to wait. In reality, however, Decker was again beginning to wonder if he had not been right about the dream after all. What had changed his mind? he wondered, though he could not yet admit to himself that a change had occurred. Why had the certainty of a few hours before so quickly evaporated? Was he now thinking more clearly or was he once again falling into the role he had played two thousand years earlier—a part he performed so well that after two millennia the role still bore his name: Judas.

13

Red Tide

Wednesday, June 10, 4 N.A.
Derwood, Maryland

WEDNESDAY MORNING, two days after it began, Christopher addressed the world to discuss the frightening outbreak of the lesions. Decker watched on television.

"People of the world," Christopher began in a somber but defiant tone. "People of the New Age of Humankind," he paused, "nothing worth having comes without cost . . . even in this New Age.

"I shall waste no time today on platitudes. In simplest terms, Humankind is under attack. For more than three years the world has been at peace—with no war, no famine, and with disease nearly eradicated. The future of Humankind, *our* future, rose like a brilliant light before the eyes of all the universe—a future that welcomed all people with open arms.

"No one has been forced to join our cause, to see our vision, to take up our enterprise. All people have been free to live out their lives in peace. Never, in fact, throughout all history has change come more peacefully than it has to the entire planet in this, the New Age of Humankind.

"But for some, it seems, choice is too great a burden, even when it is being made by someone else. Like their spiritual predecessors—those who opposed women's legal, sexual, and reproductive freedoms, those who imposed unrealistic and puritanical drug laws, and those who opposed an individual's right to choose their own time to die—our opponents are opponents of choice. They are unwilling to allow others to make their own decisions.

"And yet, even when those who oppose us reverted to heinous acts of violence to shut down the communion clinics, we responded with only enough force to prevent them from interfering with the rights of others.

"Today, all who love Humankind and freedom know and feel the anguish and grief that Yahweh inflicts in his obsession to obstruct us. You know it by the wounds you bear. And yet our enemies continue to absurdly claim that Yahweh is a god of love.

"I know your pain. Though I do not bear the sores, I, too, have suffered and even died to bring about the New Age for all of Humankind. I beg of you, do not allow this temporary discomfort to the physical body, these vile attacks to the flesh, to divert you from your spiritual goal. Do not allow the KDP, or the fundamentalists, or the demon god they serve to stay us from our course. Our goal is too noble, our purpose too great, our ambition too high to yield to anyone, whether man or god.

"Instead, wear your wounds as badges of honor and defiance and take heart in this: The evil that Yahweh and his followers do will not go unanswered. Yahweh's only hold upon this planet is in the grip of his confederates— the KDP and the fundamentalists. If their resolve is broken, so too will the last vestiges of Yahweh's power upon earth be broken.

"To break this grip, the Security Council has authorized the following actions. First, anyone who has not taken the communion and the mark shall no longer be permitted to buy or sell, under penalty of arrest. Second, warrants have been issued for the immediate arrest of fundamentalist and KDP leaders.

"Prohibiting the right to buy and sell is an altogether appropriate restriction for those who by their own actions have demonstrated their desire to separate themselves from the rest of Humankind. If they insist upon separation, then separation they shall have. Let us see how well they make out without the rest of society. As for the fundamentalist leaders, they will be treated with respect, and any who swear to cease their efforts against Humankind will be released on their own recognizance.

"There are many who will say that these measures are not strong enough or who fear that the fundamentalists and the KDP will respond by calling down even worse plagues—but it is not our desire to punish preemptively. We wish only to make the point that actions against Humankind will not go unanswered. It is our hope that from this, those who wish us ill will learn not only that Humankind cannot be assailed with impunity, but also that we are just and merciful, not meting out punishment beyond what the offense demands.

"Nevertheless, to our foes—to the KDP and the fundamentalists—despite the suffering that you have brought on the earth because of your blind obedience to Yahweh, *still* we offer you the olive branch of peace. Renounce your allegiance to your god of pain and suffering and we will welcome you as brothers and sisters!

"But if this plague continues, or if others follow, know this with all certainty: Humankind will not continue to suffer your malevolence forever." Lightly pounding his fist to accentuate his words, he concluded, "We will not allow you or anyone to change our course, to deter or deny our destiny!"

Decker wanted to cheer. It was a moving speech. Christopher had shown both decisiveness and great restraint in not striking out more harshly at his opponents. Somehow it eluded Decker for the moment that, because he had not taken the communion, the restrictions on buying and selling applied to him as well.

Based on the World Health Organization's records, 87 percent of the total world population, or just under 2.5 billion people, had received the communion and the mark, leaving approximately 375 million who had not. After Christopher's speech the insta-polls found that of those who had taken the communion, 64 percent agreed that the action of the Security Council in restricting the right to buy and sell was appropriate; 36 percent felt that the action was not strong enough; and virtually no one said they felt the restrictions were too severe. Among those who did not have the mark, the numbers were much different: 93 percent disapproved, and of the 7 percent who approved, nearly all indicated they would take the communion within the next week. Those who disapproved of the Security Council's restrictions gave several reasons for doing so: about 0.5 percent said they considered it a violation of their civil rights; 3 percent—presumably fundamentalists—said they would not take the communion or the mark for religious reasons. The remaining 96.5 percent said they didn't want the communion because they didn't want to risk getting the lesions. Not surprisingly, Christopher's approval rating, which had dropped from 97 to 85 percent after the lesions appeared, rose 5 points, back to 90 percent.

Sunday, June 14, 4 N.A. Seaside, California

Amos Hill heaved the second of two metal tubs into his wooden-hulled boat and went to start his truck. In the tubs were 500-foot trot lines, each with 250 leaders and hooks baited with salted squid. Ordinarily he would have had twice as many lines, but the sores on both of his hands and arms made working with the salty bait very difficult. Despite his best efforts, he had repeatedly felt the sting of salt in the lesions. He would have preferred not to work at all under the circumstances—he cringed to think about the salt spray on his face—but it had been a full week since he last fished and he had bills to pay.

As he drove toward the Monterey harbor he noted how little had changed since his last time out. This area of California was growing fast, and Monterey itself was a literal boomtown since the fish had started to come back. It had been five years since the tsunami and earthquakes had destroyed most of the West Coast and filled the Pacific with the murky red cloud of rust that had killed the phytoplankton and destroyed all sea life from the Americas to China. Now, not only were there fish in the bay, but signs of progress were everywhere, especially in the construction trade. Until last week Amos Hill had been able to track the progress of building projects on a daily basis as new foundations were laid or walls went up. Since the lesions had appeared, however, almost no one was working and progress had become imperceptible. Amos Hill was not, however, the only one who had decided that, sores or not, he had to make a living. Around the city, crews were once again loading up trucks and preparing to get back on the job. Others, while they were not up this early in the morning, had set their alarms and would be getting up soon. No one really felt well enough to work, but after a week most had no choice but to try to get back to their jobs. The same was true throughout most of the world.

❑

Amos Hill launched his boat, started the engine, and headed out into the bay, traveling much slower than usual in order to minimize the spray. He was forty-five minutes off his usual schedule when he reached the approximate area where he would set his lines. Looking to the stern and starboard of the boat, he located the outcroppings of rock on shore that he used to determine his position and moved his boat directly above the underwater rock ledge where Monterey Bay drops off into the much deeper water of the Pacific. It was here he knew that he'd have the best catch of rock and ling cod. Most fishermen would have used a depth finder to find the ledge and they would *never* have used a trot line, opting instead for nets. Amos Hill fished the way he did because that is how he was taught by his father and because his primary customers were restaurants and fish markets that would pay a premium price for fish that had not been marred by nets.

Dropping the anchor and buoy that would mark the beginning of his first set, Amos moved the boat slowly northward, tossing out the line as he went. The winds and the tide were favorable and, based on experience, he sensed the line was falling just right for a good catch. Finishing the first set, he started the second almost where the first had ended. Ordinarily he would have moved a hundred yards farther before casting the second line to play the odds on how the fish might be running, but fishing had always been, in large part, a matter of feelings and intuition, and today this felt like the right thing to do.

Twenty minutes later, he moved the boat back to the first buoy. It was important not to leave the hooks down too long or the fish that had been caught would become easy prey for predators.

From the weight, Amos Hill could tell immediately that this was going to be a good catch. His first three hooks each had ling cod over eight pounds. From there on it was mostly rock cod, bright golden orange with bloated air sacks protruding from their mouths from being pulled so quickly from the bottom. The fish would be beautiful on display, lying on a bed of ice in some market. Nearly every other hook had something on it, most of them edible, though there was the occasional ratfish, a brilliantly colored creature that is as poisonous as it is frightening in appearance. It was by far the best catch Amos Hill had had since before the tsunami.

He was nearly finished with the second line when

something caught his eye and he looked up toward the waters of the Pacific in the west. Wrapping the cord around a deck cleat, he paused to wipe his brow and looked again toward the west. Something was wrong. A half mile away and moving quickly in his direction was an ominous expanse of dark water. Quickly he unhooked the line from the cleat and began pulling in fish as fast as he could.

He had only about fifty hooks left when it reached him. The sea was a blackish red and carried with it the smell of death. It did not progress like a normal tide but spread with astonishing speed that did not seem affected by the waves. Like a great cloud of blood, the redness passed beneath him, headed for the shore. From that point on, everything he pulled up was dead. Nearly retching from the smell, Amos Hill cut the nylon cord and let the remainder of it drop into the sea.

As he started his engine he realized one other attribute of the red sea: It was much thicker than regular seawater, so much so that it clogged the cooling ports of his engine, forcing him to shut it off or risk burning it up.

With his holds full of fish, he pulled out an oar and reluctantly began paddling, hoping to get his catch the two and a half miles to the dock before it spoiled.

❑

Unlike five years earlier, when the second asteroid had struck and turned the Pacific red with rusting iron particles, this time the bloody sea was not confined to one ocean but filled all the oceans of the world. Within twenty-four hours every salt sea on the planet had turned crimson, and in that single day, every creature, *every creature,* in the sea was killed. This time Christopher did not wait so long to respond.

"I cannot express," Christopher said, addressing the United Nations and the world, "the utter grief I feel—that I know we all feel—at this unthinkable atrocity." The pace of his words was slow and measured; shock and disbelief showed on his face. In the corner of the screen, the television network showed scenes of dead sea creatures floating on a rolling sea of blood. "In a single blow," Christopher continued, "Yahweh has destroyed tens of thousands of species. Fish of unbelievable variety—shell creatures, the great whales, porpoises, manatees, otters and seals: All have been cruelly exterminated to satisfy Yahweh's wretched desire to terrorize and dominate the earth. A few species survive in aquariums, but most have been lost forever.

"No longer can there be any doubt that Yahweh and those who support him are at war with this planet and its inhabitants. And what Yahweh has done to the seas, he would most certainly do also to the rest of the planet were it not for Humankind's sheer strength of will. Yahweh knows that he cannot defeat us as long as we are united, and so he seeks to demoralize and dishearten us by striking at the defenseless creatures in our seas.

"Seeing this wanton destruction and death, one would think that surely those who have sworn their allegiance to this self-proclaimed god would now be able to see him for what he truly is. And yet, based on their own confessions, the fundamentalist leaders who have been arrested continue to pray to their god for the destruction of Humankind; for the deaths of friends, neighbors, and even their own relatives who do not agree with them; and for the establishment of a theocratic dictatorship on earth, a dictatorship where Yahweh would crush like grapes all who oppose him.

"As I have said before, Yahweh's only hold on this planet is in the grip of his confederates. That hold must be broken and it must be broken soon, before even more destruction occurs, before even more die at his hand.

"The profound urgency of this matter and the severity of the offense require an immediate and appropriate response—a response that neither I nor the members of the Security Council desire, and which all of us would prefer to avoid if there were any alternative. However, we cannot simply allow Humankind to remain targets for Yahweh's aggression. The fundamentalists are a gun in Yahweh's hand, cocked and ready to fire into the heart of all Humankind. We cannot ignore that threat or simply wish it away. The Security Council has, therefore, voted unanimously to instate capital punishment for anyone found guilty of leading activities intended to subvert Humankind's advancement and providing aid and support to Yahweh's attempts to reestablish control of the planet. However, because even now we are merciful and wish no one to perish, this penalty shall be limited only to the leaders; and even among them, any who pledge to cease their activities will be granted a full pardon and released on their own recognizance.

"To the rest of the fundamentalists, I say, there is still time to turn from your allegiance to the god of death. All of Humankind will welcome you and cheer your decision. But know, too, that if you continue to align yourself with Yahweh, you will pay the price.

"As an added measure, effective twenty-four hours from now, in addition to the prohibition on buying and selling, any who have not taken the communion are also prohibited from owning property. The destruction of the world's seas is a crime against the planet. It is only fitting that you shall not be allowed to own that which you have shown, by your worship of Yahweh, you do not respect."

❑

The Security Council acted quickly to put muscle into the new restrictions. Governments around the world were directed to seize all property of anyone who had not taken the communion and the mark. Property ownership could be restored only if they took the mark. All who refused were to be evicted from the property within a week.

Wednesday, June 17, 4 N.A. Derwood, Maryland

Sgt. Joseph Runningdeer stepped up onto the porch and rang the doorbell. His partner, Officer Amanda Smith, stayed behind about ten feet to observe and act as backup. A moment later a woman came to the door.

"Yes?" she said, with the level of surprise one typically displays when receiving an unexpected visit from the police.

"I'm Sgt. Runningdeer with the Montgomery County Police. This property is registered to Mark Cleary. Is Mr. Cleary in?"

"Yes," she answered, obligingly. "He's asleep, but I'll get him."

As the woman ran to rouse Cleary, Sgt. Runningdeer turned without thinking to look back at his partner. Keeping an eye on one's partner was a constant imperative in police work. But as he turned to look, the crusted drainage from the lesions on his back clung to the gauze bandages, tearing at the raw skin and causing him to wince in pain.

Mark Cleary reached the door a moment later, wearing only a pair of boxer shorts and a confused sleepy expression on his face. It was immediately obvious that his body bore no sores.

"What is it, officer?" Cleary asked.

"Mark Cleary?" Sgt. Runningdeer asked for confirmation.

"Yes," came the reply.

"Are you the owner of this property?"

"Yes."

"Sir, it's my duty to inform you that your property is hereby confiscated by the County of Montgomery, State of Maryland. Should you desire to reclaim your property, you may do so anytime within the next three days by presenting proof of your participation in the communion."

"But, I took care of that yesterday," Cleary protested. "See," he said, extending his right hand and showing Runningdeer the mark.

Sgt. Runningdeer looked at Cleary's hand. "Okay," he said, though something in his voice said it really didn't change anything. "Let us run a check."

Officer Amanda Smith groaned and took the hand-held data link from her belt and initiated a query.

This was not the first time this had happened today. In fact, it was happening more often than not.

"I don't understand this," Cleary complained. "Don't your computers talk to each other? I took care of this yesterday. I work nights or I would have gotten the mark months ago."

"I'm sorry, Mr. Cleary. Our systems have been running a little slow. My partner is checking on it right now."

"We're still getting a negative on it," Officer Smith reported.

"This is ridiculous. You can see the mark for yourself."

"I'm sorry, sir," Sgt. Runningdeer said again. "We'll indicate in our records that you have shown us the mark, but I'm afraid you're still going to have to go to the courthouse. You'll need to clear this up within seven days to avoid eviction."

"I just told you, I work nights," Cleary protested. "It's bad enough that I should have to get this thing, knowing I'll probably get sores all over me. Why should I have to lose sleep or miss work to go to the courthouse just because your computers are slow?"

"There's nothing we can do about it, sir. That's the law. Oh, and sir, I wouldn't worry about missing work," Runningdeer added. "Without the mark it's illegal for you to take part in *any* commerce. That isn't limited to buying and selling of products; it includes employment for pay or barter. Your employer will be notified if he hasn't been already."

"But I've got the stupid mark," he said through clenched teeth, trying hard not to explode in anger, and showing the mark to Sgt. Runningdeer again.

"You still need to go to the courthouse," Runningdeer affirmed. It wasn't that he *wanted* to be difficult; he was just doing his job, and sometimes that meant being irritating.

"Can someone else go for me?" Cleary asked, trying his best to regain his calm.

"No, sir. The law requires that you appear in person."

Cleary shook his head in disgust. There was nothing more to be done.

"I'm sure it will only take a few minutes," Runningdeer offered, though he knew better. Nothing took only a few minutes at the courthouse. "We're sorry to bother you," he concluded and turned to walk back to the squad car.

Sgt. Runningdeer carefully climbed into the vehicle, doing his best not to tug at the gauze on his sores. "Who's next?" he asked.

Officer Smith checked the assignment sheet for the next name on the list. "Decker Hawthorne on Millcrest Drive," she said.

Sgt. Runningdeer looked surprised. "Let me see that," he said as he checked the list to confirm what Officer Smith had read.

"What's wrong?" Smith asked.

"Don't you know who this is?"

Amanda Smith thought for a second and then realized where she had heard the name before. "You mean that's *the* Decker Hawthorne?"

"How many Decker Hawthornes do you think there are?"

"I don't know," she said, embarrassed at her lapse. "I didn't even know he lived here."

"He doesn't. But he used to, and he still has a house here." Sgt. Runningdeer scratched his head in thought, being careful to avoid a lesion just above the hair line. "This is probably just another screw up," he said, as he reached for the call switch on the police radio. "I'm going to check it out."

"Dispatch, this is two Baker thirteen," Runningdeer said into the microphone.

"Two Baker thirteen, go ahead," a voice replied.

"Request Captain Martin verify assignment: Hawthorne, Decker."

There was a pause for about ten seconds. "Two Baker thirteen, please repeat," dispatch replied finally.

"That's right, Ed," Sgt. Runningdeer said, recognizing the voice of the dispatch officer. "We've got Decker Hawthorne on our assignment sheet."

"Somebody must be playing a joke," the dispatch officer said.

"Well, joke or not, he's on our list."

"I'll get the captain for you," dispatch replied.

Sgt. Runningdeer and Officer Smith waited.

"Two Baker thirteen, this is Captain Martin," the radio squawked after a moment.

"Sir, can this be right?"

"We're checking that right now," Martin answered.

At headquarters Captain Martin watched over the shoulder of Officer Ed Cook as he checked first to see if Decker's name was on the list of those who had taken the communion, and then checked on his whereabouts. In a moment they had their answers.

"Joe," he said, calling Sgt. Runningdeer by his first name, "we're showing that as a good assignment.

Hawthorne shows negative on the communion and his last known location was June 7 at Reagan National Airport. The assumption is that he's at his home in Derwood."

For a moment there was silence, then Sgt. Runningdeer replied. "Sir, request permission to ignore this assignment. That last known location is ten days old; he's probably not even there. But even if he is, we have plenty to do without annoying Decker Hawthorne."

Captain Martin thought for a second. It *was* about the most bizarre assignment he could imagine: charging the person closest to the secretary-general of the United Nations with not adhering to United Nations law. On the other hand, he did not want to be responsible for ignoring an assignment. In the end, common sense won out.

"Permission granted," he said. "We don't need the United Nations coming down on us for invading Mr. Hawthorne's privacy. Disregard assignment Hawthorne and proceed to the next name on your sheet."

Thursday, June 18, 4 N.A.

Decker looked at his watch. It was just after four o'clock—which meant midnight in Babylon. Another day had passed without a call or e-mail from Christopher or Milner. He had now been gone from Babylon for fifteen days. In his last contact with Milner eleven days earlier he had said he'd only be gone a week. Either Milner or Christopher, or at least Jackie was certain to call soon. He still had no idea how he would explain his continued absence.

Decker watched live television coverage of a fundamentalist family being evicted for refusing to take the
communion and the mark. There was no brutality on the
part of the police, and, in fact, they provided protection
for the family from a few hot-headed neighbors whose
suffering from the lesions had caused them to let their
emotions overrule their reason. Decker wondered why
the police hadn't come to *his* door yet. There was no
doubt the World Health Organization's database showed
that he hadn't taken the communion, and though he limited his activities so that no one would realize he was in
the house, he was certain the police would be able to locate him. The only explanation he could find was that
they were too overworked and would get to him later.
When they did, he would be ready. He had prepared half
a dozen bandages which he could slip on, including one
that conveniently covered the back of his right hand
where the mark should have been. If the police showed
up, he would quickly don the bandages, answer the door,
flash his UN identification—just in case they didn't realize who he was—and act outraged that they had bothered
him. With any luck, he thought, he could probably intim-
idate the police enough to leave him alone for a while, regardless of what WHO's database said.

Friday, June 19, 4 N.A.
Tel Aviv, Israel

Along the beach of the Mediterranean, nearly fifteen thousand people had gathered to witness a miracle. Because of
the smell, most wore gas masks, millions of which had

been left over from some long-forgotten war. Robert Milner, dressed in the same robes he had worn at Christopher's resurrection, sat cross-legged on the sand in a lotus position in deep meditation, waiting for the proper moment. In each hand he held three highly polished spherical quartz crystals given to him by Christopher. Behind him, a hundred reporters waited in silence. Before him, waves of blood washed over the reddened sand in black coagulated chunks.

For the occasion the beach had been cleared of the carcasses of countless dead fish and sea birds. Except near the shorelines, most of the surface of the oceans and seas had become a huge scab, which heaved and ebbed with the motion of the sea of blood beneath it, and now crawled with maggots as far as the eye could see.

As the sun began to set, Robert Milner, eyes still closed, rose to his feet. Holding his hands straight out from his sides, he began to walk toward the sea. Television cameras transmitted the scene around the world. Just short of the waves, he stopped. Frozen in that position, he waited for the first full moment of twilight, then shouting as loudly as he could, he proclaimed his purpose and his commission.

"In the name of the Light Bearer, and of his son, Christopher, and in the name of myself and those with me, and all of Humankind, I declare my independence and my defiance of Yahweh, the god of sickness and disease and oppression! We will not yield to you! We will not submit to you! We will not bow to you! We declare our freedom from you! We spit upon you and upon your name!"

Then reaching back with both his hands, he hurled the

six quartz crystals he held as far out into the sea as he could, where they landed on the floating congealed mass with a dull thud. As the sea rolled, it was possible to catch the glint from the spheres as they lay scattered on the huge scab and it seemed as though nothing had happened. But quickly it became clear that the light that came from the crystals was not a reflection of the camera spotlights but rather was radiating from the orbs themselves, and the light was growing.

Excitement filled the crowd as slowly the spheres melted into the sickening mass of maggots and blood and sank out of sight. Suddenly, beneath the orbs, the sea began to churn and glow until the area around it shone like a full moon. Then in all directions at once, radiating out at unbelievable speed, the light transformed the bloody sea back into water. In just seconds, the transformation traveled the length of the occupied beach and, as the waves washed the shore, the hardened lumps melted away and blended in with the waves.

On the beach with Milner, the crowd erupted in thunderous applause and a triumphant cheer filled the evening sky and rose defiantly to heaven, as the cleansing swell continued to spread. Traveling at a speed of nearly a thousand miles per hour, the purifying wave stayed just within the twilight of the setting sun as it rolled over the seas of the earth like a gentle blanket. Robert Milner turned and raised his hands in triumph and after a moment, though bearing at least a dozen lesions, he pulled his robes up over his head, revealing his nude body, and turned and ran naked into the sea. Many followed, shedding their clothing where they stood, though all but a handful of the most hardy quickly turned back as the salty waves washed over their lesions, causing unbearable pain.

Within twenty-four hours the transformation traveled around the world and the seas returned to normal, though nothing could restore the sea life that had perished.

14

Steadfast

Sunday, June 21, 4 N.A.
Derwood, Maryland

DECKER OPENED HIS EYES and looked at the clock beside his bed: 9:34 A.M. Another night had passed in the eastern United States, and the greater part of the day had passed in Babylon, and yet still there was no call from Christopher. Two full weeks had passed since the call to Jackie and Milner, and except for a call to Debbie Sanchez to say he'd be gone "longer than expected," he'd had no contact with anyone from the UN. Sooner or later, Decker knew Christopher would contact him and he would have to give some explanation for his absence, not to mention explaining why he had not yet taken the communion. He still didn't know what he would say. It had been one thing to lie to Milner, though he still wondered if Milner really believed him. It would be quite another to try to hide the truth from Christopher.

What *was* the truth, though? Decker still had not decided. He could not ignore the dream in Petra. It wasn't just that Christopher had hesitated when Decker asked about Tom. It was the look of indifference on his face— as though he truly didn't care whether Tom got out of there or not. It was as though he only told Decker where Tom was because he knew Decker wouldn't leave without him. The image haunted and tormented him. But though he could not ignore the dream, neither could he ignore more than twenty years of knowing Christopher as intimately as anyone could have. He struggled to find an explanation.

Perhaps, he thought, perhaps the dream in Petra was *not* identical to the dream in Lebanon after all! He tried to compare the two dreams in his memory and they seemed identical, but how could he be sure? Perhaps in the second dream his imagination had added the expression of indifference to Christopher's face, and now, as he looked back through the years, his mind had transposed the image to the events of the first dream as well.

Then a new possibility occurred to him: Maybe it wasn't his imagination at all! Maybe Rosen had used his telepathic abilities to plant the image in his head! Almost as quickly it hit him: Maybe Rosen or some other member of the KDP had done the same sort of thing to Tom, planting the idea in Tom's mind to kill Christopher! Could that be what this was all about? Could Rosen have altered Decker's memory and let him leave Petra only to betray Christopher? Maybe that was why they kidnapped him in the first place, and the indoctrination from Rosen was either to soften him up or it was a front to hide the KDP's real purpose. Maybe at the proper moment some other latent image would be recalled that would compel him to believe that he had to kill Christopher! Would history repeat itself? Was he destined to again play the role of Judas the betrayer?

But what could Rosen hope to gain? If Christopher

were killed again, then surely he would once again be resurrected. Or perhaps he wouldn't. There was no way to know how many times Christopher could die and come back. Maybe it only worked once. Or possibly Rosen and the KDP were simply trying to get Christopher out of the way temporarily so they could launch some larger plan like the murderous madness that had struck while Christopher lay dead for three days. Perhaps this time they were devising a scheme to kill *everyone*.

The real question, Decker realized, was *who* was the monster?

If the dream was accurate and Christopher was simply going to let Tom remain a hostage in Lebanon because he was insignificant to his plans, then Christopher was indeed the monster that the KDP made him out to be and Decker had found the one flaw in Christopher's otherwise perfect performance. On the other hand, if the dream had been altered by Rosen and the KDP, then it was Decker himself who was the monster—a time bomb waiting to explode and hurl the planet back into a dark age of subservience to a tyrannical despot who would reduce humans to the level of cattle.

He held his head in his hands and let out a low moan. He wished there *was* a benevolent God that he could pray to for wisdom and then trust the answer. The only thing that seemed relatively certain was that until he could straighten this all out, the best thing to do for both himself and for Christopher was to stay where he was.

Decker rubbed his eyes and realized that his mental distraction had obscured a rather significant headache. Going into the bathroom to take some aspirin, he turned on the faucet to allow the water to cool while he attended to another pressing bodily need. His mind momentarily drifted back to the silent telephone, but from the corner of his eye he caught a glimpse of unexpected color, which drew his attention. Looking over at the sink, he saw that the water flowing from the faucet had taken on a definite pink hue that grew quickly darker as he watched. By the time he finished relieving his bladder, the water was bright red. "Oh, no!" he said out loud, as he grasped its likely meaning. Out of habit, he reached to flush, but then jerked his hand back as if the toilet handle had become a venomous snake.

Decker turned off the faucet and ran to the television in his bedroom. It took only a moment to confirm his fears. As the picture changed to show scenes from numerous locations, the anchorman summarized the story. Throughout the world, all fresh water supplies, all rivers and springs, all lakes and ponds and reservoirs fed by rivers or springs, had turned to blood. The only sources of fresh water that had not turned to blood were those that were detached or sealed off, such as water towers, swimming pools, and holding tanks at water treatment plants.

Decker ran back to the bathroom and removed the cover from the back of the toilet. As he expected, the water inside was still clear. By not flushing, he had given himself a three-gallon supply of clean water. With the toilet downstairs, that gave him six gallons. Going next to the refrigerator and pantry, he quickly inventoried everything suitable for drinking. In the refrigerator, there was about a half gallon of milk and three one-liter bottles of soda. In the freezer, the ice-maker was full of ice that Decker estimated could be melted down to a little more than a gallon of water. In the pantry he found only a bottle of tequila. In all, he estimated that he had about eight gallons of liquid suitable for drinking. Then, realizing that the next time the ice-maker took in water it would instead get blood, Decker ran to the laundry room to turn off the water main.

When he returned to the television, the scene had changed to the parking lot of a supermarket in Virginia. A woman's body lay on the pavement in a pool of blood, surrounded by police tape to keep back onlookers. Assuming that the report was of a simple homicide, Decker was at first surprised that the media's attention had so quickly shifted to this from the more important story of the fresh water turning to blood. The reporter explained the connection. The water had changed during the early morning, and most grocery stores had sold out of all bottled water, milk, and other drinks within a half hour of opening. Even canned vegetables like green beans and corn were bought up for the water in the cans. Some who arrived late at the stores panicked, and fights had broken out over what little was left. At this supermarket in Virginia, two women had fought in the store over the last gallon of milk. The woman who lost the battle left the store, went to her car, and retrieved a gun. Waiting for the other woman to leave the store, she followed her to her car, shot her three times in the back of the head and then fled. A few feet from the lifeless body lay the remains of the plastic milk bottle, which had broken open when it hit the ground.

❑

Keeping or obtaining water quickly became the full-time occupation of everyone, for though fresh blood can be drunk,[74] even this became impossible as bacteria quickly filled the rivers and springs, turning them into open cesspools of disease and stench. Those who in desperation broke through the scabbed-over surface to the blood flowing below either turned away in revulsion or, if they did drink, quickly vomited it up, thus losing additional body fluid and worsening their dehydration.

Resourceful people devised numerous ways to collect water. Where rain fell, people put out pots, pans, and bowls to catch whatever they could. Others rigged sheets of plastic or bed sheets, gathering the rain into the middle, then into a pan.

Public service television programs told where and how to find water. In addition to toilet tanks, small amounts of fresh water could be found in recently used garden hoses. The programs also told how to collect water condensed by air conditioners or from drip pans in refrigerators. By leaving the refrigerator door ajar, it was possible to condense as much as two quarts a day, except in areas of low humidity. In coastal areas warnings were repeated every half hour not to drink seawater because the salt would actually absorb more body fluids than the water would replenish. Instead, seawater could be boiled and then condensed on a cold surface and collected. One very productive method was to place an electric skillet or Crockpot in the refrigerator and boil the seawater. The steam then condensed on the refrigerator's wall and ran down into the drip pan. Literally gallons could be collected by this method in a single day and many near the coasts set up business, charging incredible prices to eager

---

[74] The Masai natives in Kenya frequently drink a mixture of milk and cow's blood.

buyers. It was also possible to distill the water from the blood by the same means, but few had the stomach for it.

Christopher and Milner promised relief within the week. Television cameras captured pictures of Milner deep in meditation atop the United Nations building in Babylon, and it was said that he was neither eating nor drinking in order to prepare himself for a miracle of similar magnitude to the one he had performed with the world's oceans. Even so, few were taking any chances. Those who had water guarded it by whatever means available, while those without it used whatever force was necessary to get it. Wealthy neighborhoods where swimming pools were common became war zones as those less fortunate tried to relieve the residents of their liquid assets.

There were, of course, many areas of the world where things like swimming pools and refrigerators and Crockpots and flush toilets were unknown—the lesser developed areas of Asia, South America, Africa, and India. In those areas people and animals withered from dehydration after only a few days. Those who had taken the communion lasted longer than those who had not, but ultimately the lack of water took its toll and tens of millions died. As much as possible, the UN attempted to send water to such places, but the supply was extremely limited and distribution unreliable.

Thursday, June 25, 4 N.A.

George Rollins dug through rakes, shovels, saws, hedge trimmers, and various and sundry other tools and gadgets in his shed looking for something he could use to pry open a door. But George Rollins had never been much for keeping his tools in order, nor did he have the patience to keep looking, so when he found a combination hatchet and hammer, he altered his plan of entry and decided the hatchet was just what he needed. Climbing back over his old lawnmower, which hadn't worked in three years but which he planned to get around to working on someday, he called to his son, George Jr. "Take these two buckets," he said, handing his son two plastic pails with dried paint in the bottom.

"Are you going to chop the door down?" George Jr. asked, looking at the hatchet in his father's hand.

"Not if I can help it," his father answered. "Let's see if we can find a window that's not locked. If not, then we'll either break a window or try to break the door open at the lock."

"What if somebody's home?" the younger asked. It was a silly question; everybody in the neighborhood knew that no one lived there. Still, the idea of breaking into someone's house was a bit unnerving to a ten-year-old.

"We've lived here three years and no one has ever been in that house. We'll just go in and, if the water is okay in the toilet tanks, then we'll bail it into the buckets and bring it back home. It's probably been in there for years so we'll want to boil it before we can drink it."

"What if the police come?"

"George, as busy as the police are, they're not going to bother us," the father answered reassuringly. "All we're doing is trying to get a little water. No one can blame us for that. Besides, if we don't take it somebody else will. We just thought of it first." Arriving at the house, George Sr. added, "Let's start in the back. We don't want anybody knowing what we're up to or they'll want some of the water for themselves."

They tried the sliding glass door to the dining room first but without success. Next they tried the windows, but they were all locked. Though the curtains were all pulled, George Rollins knew the floor plan of the house well; it was the exact reverse of his own house. There was only one more place to try in the back of the house and that was the door that led into what in the Rollins home was the media room.

"Look, Dad," George Jr. said, as he pointed to a set of three gravestones.

"Yeah," his father replied. "They probably died in the Disaster."

George Jr. responded with a puzzled look, having never heard of the event.

"I'll tell you about it sometime," the elder said. "It happened before you were born."

George Jr. got to the door before his father and tried it. To his surprise it slid open about an inch, but then stopped. "Let me try," George Sr. said, as he stepped in front of his son and tried to jiggle it loose. It wouldn't budge. "Ah, here's the problem," he said, pointing through the glass. "There's a cut-off broomstick laid in the track to keep the door from opening, but it's in there crooked. I think if I can just shove it hard enough, that it will . . . ugh!" he said as the door slid open.

"Yay!" the son cheered at his father's success.

Suddenly the curtains that hung across the doorway were thrown open, revealing an old man in his seventies. He was holding a shotgun. "What do you want?" he demanded, pointing the gun in George Rollins' face.

Bandages hung loose about him. George Jr. had not yet reached twelve years old, the age of majority, and therefore did not have the mark and the resultant sores, but he was certainly accustomed to seeing grown-ups and teenagers with bandages over their sores. Somehow though, almost as much as the gun, the bandages seemed to add terror to the old man's appearance.

Instinctively throwing his hands skyward in a sign of surrender, George Sr. tried to answer. "I'm sorry! We . . . we didn't think anybody lived here!"

"Well, somebody does!" the man growled. "Now, get off my property!"

"Yes, sir!" George Sr. said and then ran to catch up with his son who was already headed for the gate.

Decker Hawthorne closed the door quickly and locked it, placing the cut-off broomstick properly into the track. Pulling the curtains closed again, he slumped into a chair, still holding the barrel of the shotgun in one hand. In the other hand was the shotgun shell that he had not had time to load. It was a close call. He had barely gotten his phony bandages on before they opened the door. If they had gotten in and seen him without any bandages or sores, they surely would have called the police and turned him in as a fundamentalist, if for no other reason than to get his water. From then on he determined that, uncomfortable as they might be, he would wear the bandages day and night.

It baffled him why the police had not yet come. And why had Christopher or Milner still not called? None of it made sense.

❑

A half mile away Montgomery County Police Officer Amanda Smith waited for her partner, Sgt. Joseph Runningdeer, to get back in the car. "You want some?" he asked, offering her a can of water collected in a reservoir under the car that was attached to the condensation line from the air conditioner.

Smith didn't answer, but took the can eagerly, drinking it down as Sgt. Runningdeer picked tiny pieces of gravel from a sore on his arm.

"Who's next?" he asked as he readjusted the bandage.

Officer Smith looked at the assignment sheet. "Take a look," she said, handing him the clipboard.

Runningdeer found the next name, shook his head, and pulled a pen from his pocket. Scratching out the name Decker Hawthorne without excuse or explanation or authorization, he looked down the list to the next name. "Okay," he said. "Carter, off of Needwood Road."

"We evicted them last week," Officer Smith said, questioning the accuracy of the assignment.

"According to the neighbors, they're back in the house."

"They're making this too easy for us," she said as she started the car and headed toward the former Carter residence in South Riding, an established upper middle-class neighborhood. Driving slowly past the address, looking for any sign of activity outside the house, Smith rolled the car to a stop to allow Sgt. Runningdeer to get out. "Give me about sixty seconds," he said, and then got out and ran around behind the house next door to the Carters'.

Amanda Smith waited a moment and then put the car in reverse and backed it in front of the Carters' house and turned on the flashing bar lights. This made it obvious to anyone inside that the police were there, but in many cases the element of fear proved even more effective than the element of surprise. Though the fundamentalists were not known for violence when being arrested, Smith took her service revolver from the holster in accordance with standard operating procedures for these arrests. Going to the front door, she checked the police security lock to see if it had been tampered with. It had not, and so she punched in the six-digit code and slowly opened the door. When she did she heard a voice.

"They're in here," Sgt. Runningdeer called to her.

Officer Smith found the Carter family, Sid and Joan Carter and their two sons, sitting around the table in the dining room. Alerted to their imminent arrest by the flashing police lights, they sat with their hands joined and heads bowed. Sgt. Runningdeer stood in the door to the kitchen. "Mr. and Mrs. Carter," he said, "you and your family are under arrest for crimes against Humankind and for trespassing on government property."

Acting on the most recent directive from the United Nations, the Carters were taken into custody and booked. After receiving counseling, any member of the family who still refused to cease their anti-human activities and to take the communion and the mark would be held for transfer to a correctional facility.

It was swift and inexorable punishment, but in light of the incredible suffering and untold deaths that had resulted from the corruption of the fresh water supply, it seemed to most people to be a very mild escalation in the penalty. This conclusion was further reinforced by the frequently televised scenes of fundamentalists in prison praying to Yahweh to punish the people of the earth with even greater and more violent afflictions. In a related action, the United Nations ruled that anyone caught selling goods to a fundamentalist would also be jailed, though the term of the sentencing was left up to the local authorities, depending on the circumstances.

Friday, June 26, 4 N.A.

Decker poured himself a cup of coffee and went back into the bedroom to watch television. Many would have killed for the liquid in that cup, but Decker had carefully rationed his water and still had about half of what he had started with on Sunday. Most of his water came from condensation from the refrigerator and he had to depend very little on his reserves. He felt bad that others were dying while he had plenty, but there was no way of telling how long this would last. He chose not to think about the fact that by hoarding his water "just in case" he was demonstrating a lack of faith in Christopher and Milner who said they would resolve the crisis in less than a week. It was just best to play it safe, he thought.

"Welcome back," said Suzanne Wright, the television program's host, when Decker turned on the TV. "Joining us in the studio today is my very special guest, Reverend Timothy Dowd." Her voice revealed sincere respect for the man. "Reverend Dowd is here to talk about the charge that the recent cataclysms—the sores, followed by the oceans and now the fresh water turning to blood—are the result of collusion between the fundamentalists and Yahweh."

"I don't think you can really call it just a charge anymore," Reverend Dowd responded. "Based on the confessions and the scenes of fundamentalists praying in prison for Yahweh to punish the earth, I'd say there's no question that the charge is supported by the evidence."

"I'm sure we've all seen the videos and heard the confessions," Suzanne Wright said. She could make that assumption with some confidence: For days the video recordings had been shown, analyzed, reviewed, considered, discussed, and shown again on nearly every network and independent broadcast station in the world. "But," she continued, "here's my real question: Does Yahweh really need the prayers and support of the KDP and the fundamentalists to do what he's doing? Can't he just do it on his own? He *is* God, after all."

"Well, one would certainly think so," Reverend Dowd answered. "If Yahweh is really an all-powerful god, one would think he would be capable of doing whatever he wanted, regardless of what anybody else thinks. But in the sixth chapter of Mark in the New Testament, we find that he is not quite as all-powerful as he would like for us to believe. In that account we read that Jesus was in a certain town and because so few people were willing to believe in him, he was unable to do anything more spectacular than a few minor healings.[75]

"The point is that we humans have tremendous power to use our mental and spiritual energy to determine what happens on this planet. Christopher is absolutely correct when he says that Yahweh's hold on the earth is in the grip of his confederates. Without the KDP and the fundamentalists—I call them the 'Cult of Yahweh'—without

[75] Mark 6:1–5.

their prayers and support, without their focused mental and spiritual energies, Yahweh really could do very little. In fact—and this is key—what has happened to the earth over the last few weeks is not the result of Yahweh's superior powers. Rather it is the result of the fact that the KDP and fundamentalists are more focused on their vision of keeping Humankind subservient to Yahweh than those who follow Christopher are on the vision of freeing the planet of Yahweh's rule."

"That's amazing. I never realized that."

"In the same way, Suzanne, we must understand that as powerful as Christopher is, he cannot defeat Yahweh and the KDP and fundamentalists on his own. Christopher needs us, all of us, to support him with every ounce of positive mental and spiritual energy we can muster. We need to put off any dissension and disagreements among ourselves and focus instead on supporting Christopher and Robert Milner."

"You've been a minister for over fifty years," Suzanne Wright said. "You're probably the best known preacher since Billy Graham. You've served for years on the World Council of Churches. And yet, from what you say, it sounds as if you . . . well, almost as if you've lost all faith in Yahweh."

"Well, with all that has happened, I'd be less than honest to tell you that I haven't struggled with that issue. But I still hold out hope. I pray to God every day that he will repent and turn from his wrath, that he will realize that we have grown beyond the need for an autocratic god, and that he will allow the people of this planet to advance to the next stage in their evolution so that one day we can join him as equals."

Suzanne Wright smiled thoughtfully and nodded, inspired by Reverend Dowd's hopeful vision, then continued. "It should be obvious to our viewers from all that you've just said, as well as from the bandage on your cheek, that even though you're a Christian—" She paused for clarification. "You do refer to yourself as a Christian?" she asked.

"Yes, of course, though I certainly don't beat anyone over the head with it and tell them my way is the only way."

"Okay, then . . . even though you're a Christian, you are not a fundamentalist."

"God forbid," Dowd said with a slight laugh. Then pointing to the bandage on his cheek, he added, "I didn't get this shaving."

"And I know from talking with you earlier in your dressing room that the lesion on your cheek is not the only one you have."

"No," Dowd said. "I've taken the communion and the mark and I've got the sores to prove it." As he spoke, one of the cameras got a close up of the mark on the back of his right hand to further validate his statement.

"You seem proud of that fact," Suzanne Wright said.

"I am, Suzanne. Christopher said we should wear our sores as badges of honor, and I do."

"If I recall, his exact words were to wear our wounds as 'badges of honor and *defiance.*' How do you feel about that term 'defiance'?"

"I prefer to think of it as steadfastness," Dowd answered.

Wright nodded both her understanding and approval. "What do you say to those who say that the communion is a violation of the command not to drink blood and that the mark is the 'mark of the beast' referred to in the Bible?"

Timothy Dowd shook his head in complete disagreement. "That is such a tired old excuse that I hesitate to even address it again. The fundamentalists and the KDP began making these arguments as soon as the communion was announced. Nevertheless, to the first charge I would say you have to really stretch your definitions to equate taking a couple of capsules with drinking blood. The command not to drink blood is such an obscure law in the Bible that it's hard to believe Christopher's opponents would rely on such a feeble excuse. It's a sign of just how desperate they are."

"But the 'mark of the beast' is far less obscure, isn't it?" Suzanne Wright countered.

"You're right," Dowd acknowledged. "Over the past fifty years or so, reference to the mark of the beast has been one of the most frequently mentioned passages in Scripture. And for that very reason, it is one of the least understood. It has been so twisted by radicals and kooks, so abused by rock music groups and pulp novelists to sell recordings and books, and so frequently cited by right-wing fundamentalist preachers to engender fear that almost no one knows what it really means. I'm sure you remember several years ago when the current bank credit system began to replace the cash systems of the world. The outcry then from various lunatic fringe groups was that the imbedded bio-chip was itself the mark of the beast. Instead of a curse, it has proven to be not only tremendously convenient, but the biggest single deterrent to organized crime. I doubt if anyone today wants to go back to carrying around pockets full of coins and paper money, not to mention credit cards, driver's licenses, medical records, and assorted other personal ID. My particular denomination has always held the position that the events described in the book of Revelation occurred in the first century with the fall of Jerusalem and that the 'beast' and the number 666 referred to Nero Caesar."

"You've just begun a major crusade to bring your message around the world," Suzanne Wright said, interrupting the natural flow of the conversation, as so many reporters do in order to fit in all the pre-scripted questions. "Tell us a little about that."

"Actually, Suzanne, this is a continuation of the work I've been doing for the last several years. During that time, I've been working through the World Council of Churches with the leaders of all the major Protestant denominations as well as the Pope and leaders from many other world religions."

"I take it that doesn't include any fundamentalists," Suzanne Wright interjected in jest.

"No," Dowd grimaced. "The people I'm working with are all intelligent, reasonable, open-minded people, many of whom recognize the tremendous power for good that the communion offers for Humankind and were among the first in line to take the communion in order to calm any misgivings among the members of their denominations.

"So," Dowd continued, "as I was saying, I've been at this for some time. It's just that now with the sores and the waters turning to blood, people are beginning to listen. I've never believed in forcing my beliefs on anyone: I've always held that a person's religious beliefs are a private matter. For me, what the Bible has to say about what happened two thousand years ago is far less important than what we do to help our fellow human beings and other living creatures to have a better life today."

"Well put," the interviewer said as she nodded agreement.

"But there is a reason for renewing my efforts right now"—with this, his tone became deathly serious—"and that, quite frankly, is that the suffering and death must stop." His expression revealed both fervor and distress. His eyes seemed to hold a flood of tears in check only by his determination to deliver his message. "The suffering and death must stop," he repeated. "And we must do everything in our power to stop it."

"Which brings up the current crisis," Suzanne Wright said. "Reportedly millions have died already from lack of water, and millions more are at death's door. From what you've said, can we take it that you feel the Security Council was justified in reinstating capital punishment for leaders of the fundamentalists?"

"I'm a man of peace. In general I am absolutely opposed to capital punishment. However, as you said, millions of people have already died and millions more are close to death. Seldom are things so black and white as they are now. Without support from the Cult of Yahweh, this crisis simply would not be occurring. The people we're talking about, the fundamentalist leaders, are no different than the Nazis of World War II except that they leave the actual slaughter to Yahweh. If the involuntary life completion of a few fundamentalist leaders will result in breaking Yahweh's hold on the planet and thereby save the lives of innocent millions, then as unpleasant as it is for all of us, we must not shirk our responsibility to ourselves and our children to do what is necessary. The life completion procedure should not be carried out in anger or malice or out of a desire to get even; but for the sake of all Humankind, it *must* be carried out."

"Right now only the leaders face involuntary life completion," Wright said. "I think the question all of us are wondering about is, will that be enough? Will it be necessary to extend punishment to include other members of the 'Cult of Yahweh,' as you have called them?"

"I don't know," Dowd answered. "Let us hope that it *is* enough, because if it's not, I fear that even worse plagues will follow."

"That's a horrible thought." Suzanne Wright winced.

"Which is why we must give our total support to Christopher and the Security Council. I'm not a soldier, but as I understand it, in time of war it is the responsibility of the troops to support their commanding officer. The more desperate the situation, the more important it is that his orders are followed to the letter. As Christopher has pointed out, we are at war. Yahweh has declared war against the planet earth and, like it or not, we are either the soldiers or we are the victims. Even if we disagree on how some things are being handled by the UN, we should acknowledge that those making the decisions are more aware of the overall situation than any of us are. Unless we know different, we should wholeheartedly support the decisions of Christopher and the Security Council."

"Do you think that the decision to use involuntary life completion was influenced by the recent discoveries concerning reincarnation; that is, that no one ever really dies—that after a time they are born again?"

Reverend Dowd nodded thoughtfully. "Absolutely," he said. "Let me give you an analogy, Suzanne, that might make their decision more clear. When a woman terminates a pregnancy, the fundamentalists call that sin. But, of course, we know that's ridiculous. How could it be wrong? All she is doing is controlling her own body, her own life. She makes the decision for the good of herself, for the good of her family, and for the good of society. For many women, carrying the pregnancy to term would lock them into a cycle of poverty—if not financial poverty, then emotional and spiritual poverty—because they would never discover their true selves: They'd be too busy taking care of the children to do anything else. And quite often, perhaps more often than not, the unwanted child would become a burden not only for the mother and family but for society. How many thieves and murderers were unwanted children? Psychologists say many. It would have been better for those people and their victims if they had never been born. Love—self-love—is the greatest and most important love. That is the foundation upon which the New Age is built. A child cannot learn to love himself if he is not loved and wanted by the one who bore him. It is better for those children that their spirits return to the 'collective unconscious'—to use Carl Jung's terminology—before they are even born.

"The elimination of regressive people groups is really the same thing. Their inability to achieve self-love is evidenced by the fact that they rely on someone else, in this case Yahweh, to give their life meaning. They place a burden on society so great that their very existence prevents Humankind from advancing to the next stage in its evolution. Like the unwanted pregnancy, the regressives must be removed so that the rest of Humankind may advance. And just as the termination of an unwanted pregnancy is best for all concerned, so it is for the best of everyone that radical fundamentalism be erased.

"Of course, this should be accomplished in the most humane manner possible. Certainly the desire to limit the suffering of the condemned prisoner must be taken into account, and—I would think—that is why the Security Council chose the method of life completion that it did."

"I was wondering about that," Wright cringed. "It seems rather . . . well, gruesome to me."

"As I understand it," Dowd counseled, "despite appearances, doctors consider decapitation to be both painless and very quick. And I think when it comes to a choice between what is least upsetting to us and what is least painful and quickest for the condemned, we are obliged to think first of those who must undergo the procedure. Despite the suffering they have caused Humankind, we must not lower ourselves to their level; there is no reason to cause them to suffer.

"But there is another factor that should not be overlooked in our evaluation of the method, and it is that because beheading does *appear* brutal, hopefully it will deter other fundamentalists and help them realize the foolishness and futility of their intolerance."

Suzanne Wright nodded in agreement, though it was obvious that the thought of it still made her squeamish.

"But I think all of us and, in fact, even those who are to undergo involuntary life completion, should take consolation in the knowledge that death is temporary."

"We're almost out of time," Wright said, "but can you tell us very briefly what it will be like for those who die?"

"Well, not from personal experience," he answered dryly. "Our reliable data is limited to information gathered from people who have undergone detailed analysis of their past life experiences. What I *can* say is that there is strong evidence that when we die we do not remain dead long. Many are born again within just a very few years; for some, it's just a few days. Seldom do we find anyone who went more than twenty years between lifetimes. And, of course, when a person dies and is reborn, they almost never remember events of their past lives without undergoing past life therapy. What that means—and I'm thinking now primarily of those who undergo involuntary life completion, though in truth this applies to those who have died in the plagues as well—is that those who die leave behind all the regressive tendencies they have learned in their former life. They return, stripped of the vestiges of the old paradigm, to a world in which the New Age is not just beginning, but is in full bloom. When they return, they will be able to accept the truth because the lies of Yahweh will be so obvious to them."

"So there is hope, even for the most fanatical of the fundamentalists?" Suzanne Wright asked, making no attempt to hide the wonder in her voice.

"There is hope," Reverend Dowd concurred with certainty.

"Our guest today has been Reverend Timothy Dowd," Suzanne Wright concluded with an optimistic smile for her audience. "We'll be back after this."

Allāhābād, India

As cameras watched, hundreds of thousands of pilgrims waited anxiously upon the banks of the tongue of land at

Allāhābād, where the Yamuna, Sarasvati, and Ganga (Ganges) Rivers join. Few had enough strength to stand, many were near death from dehydration, and tens of thousands more had died before making it this far. To this, the site of the "true *Prayag,*" or place of pilgrimage, where annually millions of devout Hindus come to wash away their sins in the sacred river and where also is held the great festival called the *Maghmela,* had come the prophet of Babylon, Robert Milner. Wearing the same robes as he had the week before in Tel Aviv, and again waiting until twilight to begin his work, Milner walked barefoot to the point where the rivers unite and where the flow of blood was sufficient to prevent any scabbing over.

This time he bore no crystal spheres. Also, unlike before, he did not stop at land's edge, but continued into the river until the blood washed around him up to his knees. The fabric of his robe reacted like a straw and drew the blood through it up toward his waist. Reaching into a pocket hidden by the robe's many folds, Milner retrieved a large knife, made of ivory and bearing unusual markings. A few in the crowd recognized it as the ceremonial knife of the *Khond* sacrifice of the *Meriah,* a ritual not openly practiced in India for at least a hundred and fifty years, where a human sacrifice was put to death by strangulation and his body dismembered and spread over the fields to entreat the gods for a good harvest.

Standing there, Milner raised his eyes to the heavens. His right hand formed a defiant fist and was bent at the wrist so that the mark he bore there faced the skies. In his left hand he held the knife, point up, as if ready to stab at the heart of God. Then, as he had in Tel Aviv, again he shouted, "In the name of the Light Bearer, and of his son,

Christopher, and in the name of myself and those with me, and all of Humankind, I declare my defiance of Yahweh, the god of sickness and disease and oppression! We will not yield to you! We will not submit to you! We will not bow to you! We declare our freedom from you! We spit upon you and upon your name!"

Then, with his arms still upraised and all the world watching, he held the point of the knife to his right wrist. Placing the blade against his flesh, he pulled down sharply, cutting a deep gash that cleanly severed the ulnar artery. Immediately blood began spurting from the wound with each heartbeat and ran down his arm.

Those watching nearby and on television gasped in surprise, and though Milner already stood knee-deep in blood, some still turned their heads in revulsion. For a few seconds the cameras focused on Milner, who stood unflinching with blood pouring from his arm, the knife still raised high. Then someone noticed that as his blood mingled with the blood in which he stood, a change began to occur. Then everyone saw it. Rapidly, the river around Milner lightened and then turned crystal clear, clearer than anyone had ever seen it. With great speed, the reformation rushed up and down stream in all three rivers. In three minutes it had spread as far as the Bay of Bengal at the mouth of the Ganges, south of Calcutta. From there the cleansing began to occur in other rivers and springs, traveling around the world just behind the setting sun.

In Allāhābād there was no great cheer as there had been in Tel Aviv. Instead, all who had strength to move walked or crawled to the water to drink.

With a sigh drowned out by the rushing waters, Robert

Milner dropped his arms and walked back to shore. Staggering past cameras and reporters who cleared a path, he turned and collapsed onto the ground in exhaustion. There was an initial flurry of concern, but as he lay there still conscious and assuring those around him that he was fine, the cameras revealed an amazing image: His arm was entirely healed.

The Fourth Angel

(15)

IT DIDN'T TAKE A GENIUS to see the pattern. Each of the recent plagues had begun on a Sunday of the past three consecutive weeks. If another plague was coming, it was only logical to assume that the same pattern would be continued. That meant that whatever the next affliction was, it would probably start within the next twenty-four to forty-eight hours. There was no way to know *exactly* when, for though the turning of the salt and fresh water had occurred relatively quickly, the lesions had originally appeared only as dry itchy skin and had grown worse throughout the day. Perhaps the next plague would also start as something minor and grow worse over a period of a day or two. There was, however, a way to know *what* the next plague would be.

Decker sat on the couch in his living room and took Elizabeth's Bible from the leather satchel on the coffee table where it had been sitting since he arrived from Israel three weeks before. When Scott Rosen had given it to him in Petra, Decker had thought of it as simply a remembrance of Elizabeth. He had read her handwritten notes and the sections she marked by yellow highlighter only to see into her thoughts during the time he had been held in Lebanon. To read it now, though—after having the dream again, after entertaining doubts about Christopher— seemed like collusion with the enemy or tacit admission that there was value in its words. He did not need that additional guilt added to what he felt already. There he was, hiding like a hermit in a cave while the world suffered around him—hiding, in truth, from Christopher, who except for that cursed dream, had never done anything to cause Decker to doubt him. And so the satchel had remained unopened since he left Petra.

Now, however, he told himself that there was a good reason to read it: to understand the adversary. For that same reason a year and a half earlier Decker had read another copy of the Bible and found the verse that gave him the idea to use the mark to prevent the fundamentalists and the KDP from taking the communion.

On the plane to Jerusalem after his resurrection, Christopher had said that the plagues brought on by John and Cohen had occurred exactly as they were predicted in the book of Revelation. But that was before John (the author of Revelation) and Cohen had died. Decker assumed their deaths had put an end to such catastrophic events; the past three weeks offered convincing evidence to the contrary. So, if by reading Elizabeth's Bible he could determine what Yahweh was going to do next, Decker reasoned, it would not be disloyal to Christopher for him to do so; rather it would be insane for him *not* to. Still, the discomfort did not pass.

Finally Decker opened it and turned to the back to the book of Revelation. He quickly found what he was looking for: There was the plague of sores,[76] and the seas turning to blood,[77] and the fresh water turning to blood.[78] And there was the description of the next plague, which would be the fourth in the recent series:

> The fourth angel poured out his bowl on the sun, and the sun was given power to scorch people with fire. They were seared by the intense heat. [79]

How hot would it get? How much heat was "intense heat"? More important, Decker wondered, how could he prepare for it? Presumably, it would be significantly hotter than the normal summer heat. How would his air conditioner handle it? The subject of air-conditioning had been a major concern when plans for housing were being made for Babylon, where temperatures can reach 120 degrees Fahrenheit. He remembered hearing that standard air conditioners could cool a house only about 15 to 20 degrees below the outside temperature. The air conditioner in his house was as old as the house itself, which meant it would not be nearly as efficient as the newer models and thus would not cool nearly as well. There was not enough time to do anything about that, though. Nor did he have time to better insulate the exterior walls. Whatever preparations he could make had to be made in the next twelve to twenty-four hours.

[76] Revelation 16:2.

[77] Revelation 16:3.

[78] Revelation 16:4–6.

[79] Revelation 16:8–9.

After some consideration, Decker decided his best course of action was to limit his efforts to a single room. The house didn't have a basement, which would be naturally cooled by the earth around it, so the obvious choice was the laundry room. It was on the ground floor and the concrete slab had never been covered, and thus it was the coolest room in the house. It had water and a floor drain down which he could flush wastes. It was also small enough that he could quickly add insulation to the walls and ceiling.

Decker prepared a list of materials and got on the phone to Bert Tolinson, the caretaker. So far Tolinson had been willing to get Decker whatever he asked for, never realizing that by making such purchases he was in violation of United Nations law and could have been jailed. He just assumed Decker had the mark and drew the money for the purchases directly out of the account that had been established for upkeep of the house. Although the account was well funded in case of emergency, Decker's shopping list did raise some questions.

Decker had tried to get by without running the air conditioner in order to keep anyone from realizing the house was occupied. Now the neighbor, George Rollins, and his son knew and it didn't matter anymore. So even though it was a pleasant day, Decker closed all the windows and turned the air conditioner on full blast to cool the house in preparation for what was coming. If it got too cold, he would put on a coat. Next, he found his hand tools—a handsaw, a drill, a hammer, and a pair of pliers—and then moved everything he could out of the laundry room. He would turn off the gas to the hot water heater after he had finished his preparations and showered.

When Bert Tolinson arrived with the items that Decker had said he needed right away, Decker was ready, all bandaged up, including his right hand. Tolinson might well think he was crazy because of the shopping list, but he would certainly not leave thinking that Decker did not have the mark.

❏

It took Tolinson fifteen minutes to get everything into the house. Looking over the items, which except for some groceries, Decker had him leave in the foyer and living room, Tolinson removed the Washington Senators baseball cap he always wore, wiped the sweat from his brow, and scratched the back of his head where he still had hair. "If you don't mind me asking," Tolinson said, "what's all this stuff for?"

Decker looked at the items stacked and displayed before them—ten rolls of fiberglass insulation, a staple gun, twelve rolls of duct tape, two battery-powered lamps, two flashlights, two dozen assorted long-life batteries, a large plastic tub, two boxes of twelve-penny nails, eight large picnic coolers filled with twenty-two bags of ice (all that Tolinson could get because of the recent water problems), half a dozen eight-foot two-by-fours, three window air conditioners, and three heavy-duty hundred-foot electrical extension cords.

He wanted to answer Tolinson's question. If he could help it, there was no reason to let Tolinson and his family suffer through what was to come. But how could he explain how he knew that the next plague would be heat? He sure couldn't say he read it in the Bible. Not that the

Bible was outlawed or restricted or anything, but only the fundamentalists actually read it or believed what it had to say. Then an idea occurred to him.

"There's going to be another plague," he said. "Starting tomorrow, I think. It's going to get terribly hot."

"How do you know?" Tolinson asked, his voice registering his concern. "Did Secretary Goodman tell you?"

That was an explanation he hadn't considered and he paused for a second, thinking it might be a better answer than the one he had planned. Ultimately, though, he saw the flaw and rejected it. If Bert Tolinson warned anyone else, he would have to explain how he knew and, even though he was pretty good at keeping a secret, it might come out that he had gotten the information from Decker. That, of course, would draw attention to the fact that Decker was in Derwood. He needed to give an answer that was of a source common enough that if Tolinson repeated it, no one would question its origins.

"No," Decker answered. "A psychic I know warned me about it."

Somehow, the explanation had seemed far more believable before he actually said it. Now he wondered if there was any chance Bert Tolinson would buy it. Perhaps it would have been better if he'd said nothing. To Decker's surprise, Tolinson accepted his answer without question.

"So what do you plan to do?" Tolinson asked anxiously.

"First you've got to promise me that if you tell anyone else about this you'll say *you* heard it from a psychic. Don't mention my name at all."

"Of course not," Tolinson assured him, a little offended that Decker felt it necessary to even say it. In the fifteen years he had been responsible for upkeep of the Hawthorne house, he had never told anyone of Decker's comings and goings, and he didn't need to be reminded now of his responsibility for discretion.

Decker sensed his offense but launched into his explanation without apology. He would use the insulation, he told Tolinson, to cover the walls and ceiling and door of the laundry room two layers thick. The tape and staple gun were to hang the insulation. One air conditioner he would put in the laundry room window and the other two he would mount in holes he would cut in the laundry room door. The two-by-fours would serve as braces to help support the weight. These two would draw the pre-cooled air from the rest of the house and cool it further. He would use the extension cords for the two air conditioners in the door so that he wouldn't overburden the circuit in the laundry room. The third cord was an emergency backup. The plastic tub would catch the condensation from the two units mounted in the door. The ice and the coolers were just in case everything else failed. Decker admitted that it was probably overkill, but after everything else that had happened, he didn't want to take any chances.

"What about food?" Tolinson asked.

"With what you brought me, I have enough for about two weeks," Decker answered. "I'll keep a couple days' supply with me in the ice chests. I figure that no matter how hot it gets during the day it's got to cool down at night, so I can get more food and ice from the refrigerator in the kitchen then."

"What about the lamps and flashlights and all those batteries you had me get?" Tolinson asked.

"Oh, well," Decker said, trying to hide the fact that he didn't have a good answer for that question. "The . . . uh, well, I just thought it might be a good idea to have some flashlights around. And you can never have too many batteries."

To Decker's relicf, Tolinson simply nodded agreement. Then looking around the room again at the inventory, apparently running mental calculations of his own requirements, Tolinson thanked Decker for telling him and then quickly left to buy what he needed for his own house.

Sunday, June 28, 4 N.A.
UN Research Station, Mount
Erebus, Ross Island, Antarctica

Though it was the middle of summer in the north, in the Southern Hemisphere it was the dead of winter. The temperature on Ross Island, seven hundred milcs below the Antarctic Circle, should have been well below zero, but it wasn't. Instead, Brad Mulholland, the lone scientist assigned to the UN research station, sat on top of a table, dressed in just his first layer of long underwear trying to radio the UN World Meteorological Organization to report his situation. There was no response. Outside his shelter, the stars of the four-month-long night sparkled down and were reflected by a large and growing lake of water that had been ice only twenty-four hours before. Inside the shelter, the water had seeped in around the door and was now four inches deep.

Setting the radio down on the table, Mulholland again faced the question that had thus far eluded answering: what to do next? He checked the outside temperature again. It was 47 degrees Fahrenheit, up another three degrees in the last hour. In the starlight, except for the outlines of Mount Erebus, which was eighteen miles away, and Mount Terror, which was even farther, all he could see was water. There was no way of knowing how deep it was, but he assumed that for the most part it was not much deeper than the water in his cabin. Whatever the current depth though, it was getting deeper and would continue to do so as long as the heat persisted.

Beneath the station was about nine and a half feet of ice between him and the true surface of the island . . . that is, there *had* been when the station was erected. He could try to make it to McMurdo, the permanent U.S. base camp— at least there were other people there. But he had radioed them earlier and they were having the same problems staying dry that he was. Mount Erebus in the distance offered higher ground—or rather higher ice—where he might wait out the thaw, but that would mean wading through eighteen miles of ice water with everything he could carry and no way of telling how long he'd be without shelter before he was rescued or could return to the station. Still, he knew he couldn't just stay there and wait while the building slowly sank into the melting ice.

Queenstown, New Zealand

Two thousand, two hundred and seventy miles almost due north, nestled in a valley east of the Richardson

Mountains near Lake Wakatipu on the South Island of New Zealand, the people of Queenstown awoke to the shrill wail of police sirens. Like Ross Island, New Zealand was in the middle of winter, and though the warm oceanic winds generally made for mild weather, Queenstown's location on the eastern side of the Southern Alps made it one of the coldest spots on the island. It had been colder than usual this winter. Frequent and heavy snows blanketed the mountains with a thick coat of white, and the cold temperatures had frozen Lake Wakatipu with ice fourteen inches thick. Yet, overnight the temperature had risen dramatically and was now 68 degrees. The sudden heat was melting the snowfall on the mountain, resulting in growing torrents of water cascading down the mountain in flash floods, threatening the city.

North of Monrovia, Liberia

Thirty-five hundred miles still farther north and halfway around the world, on the west coast of northern Africa, warm weather was the norm. Located just seven degrees north of the equator, winter was little more than a story told by tourists.

In a small nameless community on the northern outskirts of Monrovia, Elizabeth Lincoln, an elderly woman of eighty years, removed the white cloth from the kitchen table and draped it over her head for protection from the sun. Under her arm she held a half dozen old bed sheets and assorted rags. The temperature was over a hundred degrees inside her small but immaculately kept home.

Outside it was worse. Still she knew she had to leave her
house and go outside to tend her garden. If she didn't
water the plants and cover them with the bed sheets to
protect them from the intense rays of the sun, many
would wither and die and she would have nothing to eat.
She had refused to take the communion, so she could not
apply for assistance from either the government of
Liberia or from any of the United Nations agencies.

She did not actually own the small plot of land or the
house in which she lived. She had at one time. In fact, the
property had belonged to her family for nearly two centuries. Her ancestors had been among the first of the freed
slaves from the United States who had come here to build
a new life. Because she had refused the communion, she
had been officially evicted and the property now belonged to the government. But because her nephew was
the local constable, he had thus far turned a blind eye to
her being there.

After giving the garden a thorough soaking, she covered the lettuce, peas, potatoes, and other plants she
thought were least likely to survive the intense sunlight.
Sweating profusely and panting for breath, she returned
to the house, sat down in a rocking chair that had belonged to her great-great-grandmother, and passed out
from heat exhaustion. She never opened her eyes again.

Derwood, Maryland

In Derwood, Maryland, the temperature was 128 degrees.
The streets and highways around Washington were virtually empty. No one ventured outside, and even in air-

conditioned buildings and homes temperatures were as high as 115 degrees with almost none below the century mark. Decker, however, was relatively comfortable with the two door-mounted units running, drawing the pre-cooled air from the rest of the house. To replace the moisture being pulled out by the air conditioners, Decker kept a steady stream of water running onto a splash pan in the utility sink.

Though he was glad to have avoided the heat, he took minimal pleasure in his foresight. Instead, his thoughts were tormented by the ubiquitous spectacle of suffering and death that he saw on television. There were none of the usual man-on-the-street interviews: The few reporters and cameramen who were working outside would not leave their air-conditioned vehicles. This gave the reports a rather cold, inhuman quality, as cameras captured the silent anguish of homeless people—some shaking and gasping for breath as they lay in pools of sweat under whatever shade they could find, others already dead. Studio newscasts were shot with the least possible lighting to avoid making the studios any hotter than they already were. And there was really only one story to cover. Everything that happened was either the result of, or an attempt to deal with, the oppressive heat.

Decker flipped through the channels.

"I pray every day for the death of Christopher and for the destruction of all 'Humankind,'" the man sneered through the bars of his cell. "Yahweh is a righteous and holy God. He demands payment for your evil ways," he ranted as sweat dripped from his chin. "Humans were not made to rule but to serve. Repent!" he screamed, though he gave no indication what he wanted his listeners to repent of.

Decker paused from his channel surfing long enough to watch for a few moments as the incarcerated man railed at the interviewer. It seemed that no matter what the interviewer asked, the man's answer was the same: fear God and repent. How different the man seemed, Decker thought, from the people he had met in Petra. But this was not the only fundamentalist leader who made such comments. At least half a dozen others who were interviewed made similar pronouncements, and the news media said that there were hundreds of others as well.

Sunday, June 28, 4 N.A. Babylon

As evening set in Babylon, Christopher again addressed the world as he had with each of the previous tribulations.

"Thousands of innocent men, women, and children are dying," Christopher said, "and there can be no doubt it is the Cult of Yahweh—the KDP and fundamentalists—who bear the guilt for this atrocity. This cannot go unanswered.

"The time has come to employ more forceful measures to separate from society those who by their own actions and words have proven their inability and unwillingness to take part or even coexist with the rest of Humankind! For our own survival and for the survival of our children, indeed for the survival of the planet itself, we must have the courage of our convictions. Humankind must be free!

"We must separate from the rest of society those who

insist upon such regressive tenets. We must reject those whose karma it is to be rejected, to free them from their own blindness so that the slate may be wiped clean and through rebirth they may once again join Humankind on its bold evolutionary journey.

"As it has been with their leaders, so *their* sentence shall be. It is my hope that this form of correction will be dramatic enough to bring many to their senses and that the death of a few will spare many more who will realize the futility of their ways and will cease their crimes against Humankind.

"Ultimately, however, their fate rests entirely with each one of them. No one will undergo involuntary life completion who does not choose it of their own accord. Each will be asked a simple question: 'Are you willing to relinquish your belief that your way is the only way; that your truth is the only truth; and to acknowledge that the beliefs of others may be equally as valid for them as your beliefs are for you?'

"If they will answer yes to that question and demonstrate their willingness to peacefully coexist by denouncing their allegiance to Yahweh, they will be allowed to go free and will be welcomed back into society.

"If, however, even this simple and reasonable requirement is too much for them, then we will have no choice. We must deal with regressives or we doom ourselves and our children to a life of subservience to Yahweh.

"Now, as to our current situation—this wretched curse of heat that has been heaped on us by the one who claims to be a god of love and mercy. The true measure of Humankind's fitness for the New Age is our ability to rise above our situation, to take that which seems to be a weakness and to transform it by the sheer force of our own will, into strength. The trials that face us today are a test of that fitness, and I am confident that from our current suffering shall spring our strength—a strength so steadfast that even Yahweh must yield before it.

"We must turn our suffering not into sorrow but into anger, not into surrender but into defiance, not into acquiescence but into hatred of the one who has caused our pain: Yahweh himself!

"We must make it clear that we will never go back. We, as individuals, must free ourselves from any residual love or respect we might feel for the one we used to call God. We must rid ourselves of any quaint myths of Yahweh that may have been implanted by well-intending parents or grandparents. For we have seen the real Yahweh: We have heard his hatred and invectives; we have tasted his indiscriminate cruelties; we have felt the suffering that comes from his sadistic temper.

"We must make it known by our scorn that we are no longer his slaves. I urge you, I plead with you! For your own sake, for the sake of all Humankind, for the sake of this planet. The universe itself awaits your decision. We must go forward; we cannot go back. Raise your voice in anger and outrage at Yahweh! Curse him and curse his name! Rid yourself of the final vestiges of respect and fear of this sinister menace."

❑

After Christopher's speech and the standard banter from the network commentators, Decker switched channels to a public affairs report advising viewers of how they could stay cooler. Most of it was just common-sense things like staying inside, out of the direct rays of the sun; moving into a basement; drinking lots of water; taking cold baths; wearing clothes that were lightweight and light in color. "One other item," said the young female reporter—chosen as much for the fact that her face was free of the sores as for her abilities in front of a camera— "as we reported earlier, most life completion clinics are closed because of the heat." The screen shifted to a scene of half a dozen bodies, killed by the heat and baking in the sun as they lay outside a life completion clinic. "Officials say that even if you have an appointment, you should call ahead to be sure the clinic is open."

"Well, I can certainly see why the completion clinics would be very busy right now," said a male reporter, commenting on the scene of crumpled bodies still on the screen.

"Yes, Bill," the woman reporter responded, "especially when you realize that they will come back to a world that is much better than the one they left. Still," she pointed out, "as the pictures we just saw indicate, a trip to a life completion clinic right now may end your life, but it might be in a manner far less pleasant than you had intended."

Tuesday, June 30, 4 N.A.
Derwood, Maryland

Decker slept fitfully and awoke to find himself in a sweat. The air conditioners were not running. He checked the light switch. Nothing. He checked the circuit breakers in the fuse box. Everything seemed okay and yet nothing was running. The power to the house was out. The thermometer read 92 degrees. He turned on the portable television, which had a battery backup. The answer came quickly: The primary power company that provided electricity to Decker's house was using a "rolling blackout" to cope with the tremendous power drain caused by the heat. Ordinarily, other suppliers on the power grid would have stepped in to cover the demand—that was supposed to have been one of the benefits of the break-up and deregulation of the power companies. The other companies, however, were experiencing the same problems and were themselves using rolling blackouts. The bottom line was that the electricity would be off for another two hours. By then, even with all the extra insulation, the room was likely to get pretty uncomfortable. Decker opened a cooler, scooped up a few pieces of ice, and put them in his mouth.

❑

The blade of the guillotine sliced quickly through the air and with similar ease cut through the neck of the fundamentalist, severing his head from his body and dropping it into a large plastic barrel.

"Oooh gross!" mewled Bert Tolinson's youngest daughter, Betty, who was watching the involuntary life completions on television with her two older sisters.

Without pause, the body was removed and another fundamentalist was brought up to take the place of the one before. "Will you disavow your allegiance to Yahweh, take the communion, and save your own life?" an officer of the UN Department of World Justice asked.

"I will not," the man answered.

"Then you leave us no choice," the official said, as he pointed toward the guillotine. "In your next life, you will thank us."

"I told you not to watch that," Martha Tolinson said to her daughters, and then paused long enough to watch the next blade fall. "Now change the channel."

"Oh, Mom. It's not as bad as watching people die from the heat," the middle daughter, Jan, said as she amused her sisters by pretending to collapse in a manner imitating a homeless person they had watched die on television.

"Besides," Megan, the eldest, added, "it's so boring being stuck here in the basement with nothing to do."

"Just be glad your father had the foresight to prepare the basement so we wouldn't be out in the heat with everyone else."

"But you said the fundamentalists deserve to die," the youngest chimed in.

"That doesn't mean you have to watch it. Now, isn't there something else on?"

North of Lexington, Kentucky

It was a miserable night. The cloud cover, which would have been welcome during the day to block the sun, had waited until evening to roll in. This made the night all the hotter by blocking the release of the heat absorbed by the earth during the day. North of the city, against the blackened background of night, occasional whispers divulged the presence of creatures alien to this dark world where rats and roaches ruled. The lure of fresh garbage had brought them—the men, the rats, and the roaches—for all had empty bellies. A veritable mountain of waste—old tires, bed springs, broken appliances, and other household debris—hid secret caches of nourishment: table scraps, rotting fruit, and vegetables.

Quietly, to avoid detection, the men gathered all they could find, tearing open bags of garbage and scraping bits of food from discarded cans. It was unlikely that anyone else would be out in the heat, but they could not take chances.

Suddenly, the unexpected snarl of a gasoline engine broke the silence. An instant later, the night evaporated as a ten-thousand-candlepower flash ignited the sky, revealing a tableau of a score of men seemingly frozen by the light. None of them bore the lesions or the mark.

"Police!" came an amplified voice.

Instantly men and mice scattered, but for the men, their attempts at escape were futile. They were entirely surrounded. One by one they were captured, handcuffed, and put in a truck for transport. It took only minutes for the police to finish their work and then they were gone, leaving the dump silent and dark, restored to its previous occupants.

Soon the rats were out of hiding again, foraging for whatever they could find. One of the rats, had he the intelligence to reflect on what he saw as he emerged from under a pile of rags, would have considered this his lucky night, for there before him lay a hill, ten times his size and weight, of the choicest garbage he had ever seen. The humans were good gatherers; there was no doubt about that. Instinctively he sniffed the air for danger as he approached. The strong scent of man still lingered, but this was no time for timidity: Soon a dozen other rats would be here, after his spoils.

Running to the heap of victuals, he began to eat as quickly as he could. But no sooner had he taken his second bite of baked apple than, without warning, he was heaved upward by the garbage beneath his feet. Tumbling over, he scurried for cover back under the mound of rags. Turning to see what had happened, he saw a man emerging from beneath the garbage.

Jason Baker shook the filth from his clothes and out of his hair and beard and looked around, hoping that he had not been the only one to escape. Softly, he called out to his comrades, but there was no answer. He called again, a little louder, but with the same result. The only thing to do was to gather up as much food as he could carry in his pack and head back.

Ten minutes later, he stepped through the hole they had cut in the fence around the dump and headed for the abandoned farm where the others, including his parents and wife, waited. It was a long walk—he guessed about seven miles. He prayed that some of the other men had escaped, and he struggled with each step to try to find the words he would need to tell the others that their husbands and fathers and brothers had been captured. In his despair, he hardly noticed the heat. Maybe he would catch up with some of them on the way, or maybe they would catch up with him. Maybe one of the other men would reach the farm before him and the responsibility for sharing the bad news would not fall to him alone.

It was two and a half torturous hours of walking, sweating, and panting in the heat before he reached the farm. The clouds had finally lifted, giving way to a beautiful starry night. Without the starlight, he might have missed the farm completely. Soon he would wish he had.

There was no sign of life at the farm, but that was exactly as it should be. Except for his band of friends, no one had lived here since the Disaster—twenty-three years before—and now forest, thicket, and weeds encircled and hid the small sanctuary from any who did not know it was there. Altogether there were nearly a hundred in the camp. For the most part they lived on wild berries, roots, vegetables, fruit from a nearby orchard, trapped game, and a few items they had purchased before they lost the right to buy and sell. They had a few shotguns, but did not dare use them for fear of alerting someone to their presence. With the heat, the game had disappeared and the berries quickly shriveled, leaving only a few wild beets and onions. That was why the men had decided to risk going closer to town to find food.

Quietly Jason Baker approached the enclave and the old barn where many of his number slept. They would not be asleep tonight, though. They would all be awake, waiting for the men to return. As he approached, he listened closely, still hoping that one of the other men had gotten there before him. He heard nothing.

He dared come no farther without announcing his arrival with the appropriate password, lest they think he was an intruder. "He will return," he said clearly but not loudly.

With this the encampment came visibly, but barely audibly, to life.

"Who is it?" a single voice called out in a loud whisper.

"It's Jason," he answered.

"How'd you make out?" said a man in his sixties as he emerged from the shadow.

This was the logical first question, but not the one Jason Baker had expected and he did not have an immediate answer. Obviously they did not suspect the gravity of the news he brought.

"Thank God you're okay," Baker's wife, Judy, said as she ran to him.

"Are the others behind you?" another woman asked expectantly, as now nearly the whole camp came to meet him. His silence revealed the weight that was on his heart.

"The police," he managed. "I don't know how many others got away."

Even in the dark he could see the distress on everyone's face. In all his life, Jason Baker could not remember anything more difficult than having to deliver this news.

Then something even worse happened. It was imperceptible at first, but the sound grew quickly as a multitude of armed state police came from nowhere and encircled the camp.

Jason Baker suddenly realized that his escape had not been by providence at all, but was a cold and calculated maneuver to find the encampment.

Wednesday, July 1, 4 N.A.
Derwood, Maryland

It was 137 degrees outside and not much less than that inside. Decker lay naked, flat on his back, panting for breath and dripping with sweat, drawing every bit of relief he could from the comparative coolness of the bare cement floor. His skin and eyes burned from the salt of his sweat. The power had been off for six hours. This time it was no rolling blackout; it was a full-fledged power failure. No one was sure how long it would last.

Decker longed for the next plague, which ironically offered hope of relief from the current one. He had read what was coming and he knew that with the next plague would come the end of this accursed heat. In fact, after the heat, the next two events described in Revelation seemed rather innocuous by comparison. Decker considered the words he had read:

> The fifth angel poured out his bowl on the throne of the beast, and his kingdom was plunged into darkness. Men gnawed their tongues in agony and cursed the God of heaven because of their pains and their sores, but they refused to repent of what they had done.
> The sixth angel poured out his bowl on the great river Euphrates, and its water was dried up to prepare the way for the kings from the East.[80]

Right now darkness sounded like soothing balm to relieve the heat. After all, how much harm could be done by darkness? While it might be considered a curse in a few primitive countries, in most of the world it would be a mere inconvenience. Even if the electricity didn't come back on, most people would be able to make do. And Decker was ready for it: He didn't have the sores,

[80] Revelation 16:10–12.

so he didn't have to worry about "gnawing his tongue in agony because of the pain of the sores." And as for the darkness, that was why he had Bert Tolinson buy the lanterns and extra batteries. Of course he didn't tell Tolinson about that at the time. It was one thing to know about one plague before it happened. It would be quite another to know about the next two, as well. Compared to all the other plagues, the sixth one about the Euphrates River drying up sounded like a joke. At most it would harm the crops in the region (if any crops remained after this heat) and it would halt shipping in and out of Babylon. But so far each of the plagues except the sores had lasted only six days, so it hardly seemed significant if the river dried up for a week or so.

❑

Decker turned on the television for some distraction from the heat. It provided none. It was not that there was nothing else on—a few stations were still in operation—but Decker was drawn by the habits of a lifetime to turn to the news channels where the stories all focused on the current adversity.

He came to rest on a "talking heads" program, a format where a handful of reporters sit around a table and talk about the news and predict how current events will play out in the short and long term. In his work as director of public affairs for the United Nations, Decker had found these programs a convenient window into the mind of the media. In many ways the programs served as the fountainhead of self-fulfilling prophecy: A reporter who opined that a recent event would have a particular impact could be counted upon to be watching very closely for that impact to occur, thus validating his prognosticating abilities.

Part of Decker's job had always been a mix of communicating the news and of shaping how the news was reported. Monitoring these programs and knowing what the press expected to happen sometimes gave him a real advantage. He had found that the quickest way to win a reporter's favor was to tell him that he had seen him on a program and agreed with his comments and, what's more, he had an exclusive tip for the reporter that proved the point. It was not unusual for Decker to orchestrate events on occasion or modify the words of a speech to fit a reporter's expectations in order to get favorable coverage. On the other hand, if he felt a reporter's interpretations of an event or a policy needed "adjustment," he or someone from his office might call and offer to discuss the matter with the reporter over lunch. The methodology wasn't foolproof by any means, but it sometimes made a world of difference.

As it was everywhere else, the discussion on the current program centered on the heat. There was a new twist, however, something that caught Decker by surprise.

The host began, speaking in sentence fragments—a style that, strangely, had endured for decades in this genre of program: "The American president, Jane Todd-Sinclair: Quoted by sources inside the White House as complaining about Christopher Goodman's handling of the current crises. Comments."

"She hasn't denied it," responded one of the reporters.

"I don't think she's alone," said another. "From what I hear, President Todd-Sinclair was simply saying out loud what a lot of other world leaders have been thinking since this recent set of plagues began."

"I think we all believed that after Goodman's resurrection and the declaration of the New Age, that the hard times were past. Certainly I don't think anyone expected anything like what has happened over the past four weeks."

"Exactly," the first reporter said.

"Something I think we all need to think about," another reporter suggested, "is how much did Secretary Goodman know about all of this before he took the United Nations and the world in the direction he has?"

Decker shook his head. This did not bode well. These reporters were not traditional antagonists of Christopher. All of them bore the mark and the sores. He had known all of them professionally and personally for years. Instinctively he began considering strategies to deal with the situation.

"More important," another reporter said, "is what *can* he, and what *does* he plan to do to deal with the problem?"

"My sources say *that* is the real question. Since the leak from President Todd-Sinclair's office, there are rumors that a number of governments are beginning to question Secretary Goodman's tactics to end these plagues. I think they're growing impatient with Goodman's persistent attempts to persuade the fundamentalists and KDP. They feel the United Nations should be responding more forcefully. While Goodman is holding out the olive branch of peace, the fundamentalists and KDP are offering back poison ivy and cattle prods."

"A colorful way of putting it," laughed the host.

"Well, that's why you keep inviting me back," the reporter answered.

"And Robert Milner?" the host asked.

"He'll make another dramatic appearance somewhere on Friday, I suppose—I hope!—and end the heat. But I don't think anyone is convinced that will be the end of it. If the pattern continues, we'll have a couple days' respite and then some even worse plague will hit us on Sunday."

"Not to mention these infernal lesions," added the host.

Decker had to do something. For the moment it seemed that all his apprehensions about Christopher took a back seat to his instinct to defend him. He would at least call one of the people from the program after it was over and try to . . . well, he'd play it by ear. Then an idea hit him. He could say that although other plagues might follow, he was certain that they had seen the worst of it and that Christopher's policies would be proven effective because any future plagues would be very minor by comparison. His explanation fit perfectly with what he knew the next plagues would be, and the reporter would just assume that he had been given the information from Christopher. He grinned slightly in a sort of self-congratulatory way for his quick thinking despite the heat. For a moment, he forgot about everything else; his purpose was clear, and for just a moment it seemed that life was back to the way it had been before Petra, before the dream.

When the program ended, Decker waited a few minutes for the host to get back to his dressing room. As he reached for the phone, he watched a report on the arrest of a group of fundamentalists on a farm in a southern state of the U.S. Halfway through dialing, a recorded female voice came on: "Due to noncompliance with United Nations regulations, long distance services have been disconnected for the number from which you are calling. If you need assistance, please hang up and dial the operator."

Decker's position at the UN had thus far kept the police from his door, but it had failed to impress his long distance service provider's computer.

Thursday, July 2, 4 N.A.
Petra

"Chaim, it's nearly midnight. Come to bed," Rose Levin, wife of Israel's high priest, pleaded with her husband.

"Soon," Chaim Levin answered.

"When?" his wife pressed.

"Soon," he answered again.

The weather was warm but not at all like the unbearable heat that scorched the rest of the earth. A soft breeze wafted the canvas sides of the tent that had been the Levins' home for the past three years. It was one of the largest tents in Petra, as befitted his position, but even here a raised voice would be heard clearly by neighbors, so Rose spoke firmly but softly. "You shouldn't be watching that," she said, referring to the executions her husband had been watching for more than an hour on television. Rose could not look at the set herself; she had no stomach for executions.

"Have you seen how they die?"

"What?" she asked, surprised by the question.

"How they die," he repeated.

A sickened look came across her face.

"No," he said, realizing that she misunderstood the intent of his question. "I don't mean how they are killed. I mean the way they *die*—with resolve and confidence. I have been watching for hours and I have not seen a coward among them."

Rose Levin did not answer. After forty-seven years of marriage to the scrawny Jewish kid from Brooklyn, she knew when he really wanted an answer and when he was just making an observation.

"Even the children seem at peace," he added.

"It's not healthy to watch so much of that," she said.

"It's not healthy to watch *any* of it," he corrected.

"So why don't you turn it off and save your batteries?" she urged. "You know how hard it is to get batteries."

"For this television?" he asked rhetorically. "It's impossible. I know. I've tried to get some for when these wear out. Nobody has them."

"Well, that's all the more reason to turn it off and come to bed."

"Do you know how long these batteries have been in this television set?" he asked.

Rose Levin was beginning to regret bringing up the subject.

"More than three years," he said, not waiting for her response. "I put them in before we left Jerusalem. I've never had the batteries in this set last for more than a few months . . . but these are still like brand new." His attention, never entirely off the picture on the television as he talked with his wife, was now drawn back by the frightened but determined expression on the face of a young girl. Her time had come and she was next in line for life completion.

Friday, July 3, 4 N.A.
Vilcas Plateau, Peru

There was the distinct feeling that this should have been getting monotonous. It was the third time—a time between piqued interest and repetitious boredom when, according to international traditions in comic timing, the punch line should have been delivered. Still, with the extreme unlikelihood that anyone would ever see humor in what had been suffered in recent weeks, this replay of Robert Milner taking on and exorcising the latest vexation of Yahweh should have been received more with tedium than with any sense of engrossed enthusiasm. And yet, with a flair for the theatrical that overwhelmed any feeling of ennui, the television cameras and all eyes of the world watched with intemperate passion as the solitary figure of Robert Milner, dripping with sweat and dressed again in his long, white linen robe, climbed the jagged Peruvian mountain to the Vilcas-Huamán, the ancient temple of the sun from which the Incan man-god Sinchi Roca had presided over countless human sacrifices.

Milner's arrival here was no surprise to the news media. An official press notice had been issued the day before. Television crews had positioned remote cameras along the path and at the mountain's summit the night before to capture the event. That Milner would be doing something like this somewhere was not only expected, in an unspoken yet nonetheless real way, it was demanded by a world wearied to indignation by the physical manifestations of the spiritual battle in which it was now engaged.

Reaching the plateau 11,000 feet above sea level, which overlooks the Vischongo River, Milner came at last to the stone entryway and climbed the thirty-three steps to the truncated apex of the pyramid-style temple. Dropping to his knees, he prostrated himself in the direction of the setting sun. There were no eager crowds looking on. Only a few photographers, willing to brave the heat for the sake of the story, had been dropped on the plateau by helicopters and now climbed the stone steps to capture Milner's words and actions for the anxious audience.

Lying there flat on his face, Milner remained motionless until the sun began to drop behind the horizon. Rising then to his feet, he thrust out his open hands and called out to the sun.

"Oh great Sol, giver of light and life to this planet, I stand before you in your ancient temple and call upon you to break free and resist the will of the villain, Yahweh, who torments us by your rays." Closing his eyes, Milner seemed to wait for a response. Apparently he received the answer he wanted, for a smile slowly creased his face. Spinning around to the east, he clenched his open hands into defiant fists and again shouted as loudly as he could, proclaiming his purpose and his commission. "In the name of the Light Bearer, and of his son, Christopher, and in the name of myself and all of Humankind, I declare my independence and my defiance of Yahweh, the god of sickness and disease and oppression! We will not yield to you! We will not submit to you! We will not bow to you! We declare our freedom from you! We spit upon you and upon your name!"

Immediately a cool breeze radiated outward from where Milner stood.

Darkness

16

Saturday, July 4, 4 N.A.
Derwood, Maryland

BY SATURDAY MORNING, the heat was gone and soon the electricity was back on. Decker took a long-needed shower and moved back into his bedroom. He had a few things to do to prepare for the next plague—the darkness—but for the most part, Decker planned to just take it easy and recuperate from the heat. He'd worry later about the disorder in the laundry room and put everything back in its proper place.

He wondered again why no one from the UN had contacted him. He assumed that even though he couldn't make a long distance call out, they could probably still call him as long as he had local service. And certainly, they could e-mail him. For the first time he began to wonder if a call would ever come. As for the police, he had decided that they must not know he was there. But just in case his attempt to call out a few days earlier had been logged and passed on to the police, he decided to continue to wear his bandages at all times except when bathing, just to be safe.

Sunday, July 5, 4 N.A.

Decker opened his eyes halfway and saw the morning. It seemed like any other summer morning: The air was clear and the first rays of dawn began to illuminate his room. Perhaps the darkness would not begin today. He rolled over to look at the night table beside the bed. There were the flashlights and extra batteries, just where he'd left them. He closed his eyes again. For right now he just wanted to sleep.

❏

Hours passed and Decker slept soundly, peacefully, dreaming of nothing in particular. Then suddenly he realized something was wrong. Something was very wrong, and it wasn't just in his dream. Even in his sleep he could sense it.

He opened his eyes and looked around his bedroom. A cold sweat began to form on his brow. Everything seemed all right, but the dread that filled him did not go away.

Outside his window the sun shone brightly, casting warm beams of light into his room. Still he could not shake the feeling that something was terribly amiss.

Drawn by the light, Decker rose from his bed to open the window. But as he looked out from his second-floor bedroom, the faceless terror that had awakened him took on a loathsome and ghastly form. Seeping upward out of the ground below his window and everywhere he could see, a hideous evil oozed like black pus, obscuring everything it covered. In only seconds it grew from simple puddling in the low-lying areas to a depth that obscured the ground completely. Decker's curiosity, normally one of his strongest drives, was utterly silenced by the stark panic that consumed him. He did not want to know what the darkness was; he did not need to know. He knew already. It was evil—the sum total of all the evil that had been done upon the earth—every murder, every lie, every rape, every torture, every act of cannibalism, every beating of an innocent, every human sacrifice, every brutal mutilation of a child, every gulag, every pogrom, every death camp of every war, every slaughter of the blameless, every cruelty to a helpless animal, every destructive act upon the earth itself. All of it had been absorbed and held in by the earth until it could be held no longer, and now it gushed forth like nefarious vomit.

Neither did Decker wonder how high it would rise. There was no question: It would cover and consume everything. Already it had covered the gravestones of Elizabeth, Hope, and Louisa. Only at this did another emotion—rage at the indignity to his family's grave— briefly exceed his trepidation.

Decker pulled the window shut.

It didn't matter. He knew it didn't matter.

He ran out of the room to the landing at the top of the stairs. The darkness was in his house. It had filled most of the bottom floor of the split-level and was two or three feet deep in the second level, rising quickly up the stairs toward him.

Hurrying back to his bedroom, he slammed the door shut and tore the sheets from his bed and shoved them into the gap at the base of the door. With strength born of fright, he effortlessly pulled the dresser away from the opposite wall and thrust it against the door.

It was hopeless.

Somehow he knew it, even as he did all that he could to prevent the malevolent shadow from entering the room. Nothing on earth could stop it. Still, he had to try.

Soon the bedroom floor was covered, and Decker screamed like a frightened child as he pranced atop his bed, trying hopelessly to climb the wall.

All reason had left him. There was only fear.

In scant seconds the ooze rose to the level of the bed and rolled over onto the mattress, running quickly into the depression at his feet. From the second it touched his bare skin, he was paralyzed with more terror than he had ever before imagined.

❏

Throughout the world, everywhere, everyone, the entire planet, was covered with the evil darkness—everywhere except Petra . . . and a single office in the United Nations' Secretariat Building in Babylon.

There would be no news coverage of *this* plague.

No speeches.

Only terror.

❏

Decker stood, unable to help himself, as the blackness crawled up his legs, his undefined fear so great he dared not even blink. The darkness was not just around him, it was on him—all over him, like a cold, dark, wet blanket of gaseous slime that no light could penetrate. He feared for his life, and yet he wanted nothing so much as to yield and die, to be done with it.

The darkness was filled with razors and acid and sharp venomous teeth; Decker was sure of it. And yet there was no pain, not yet anyway, only the certainty that those injurious things and even worse were poised only inches away, ready to cut and burn and rip his flesh from his bones at his slightest move.

The blackness now reached his genitals and despite his fear of movement, involuntarily his eyes closed and his jaw locked tight in clenched anguish. With every centimeter more that it swallowed him, the terror grew. Finally, it reached his chin and the last bit of light was about to be eclipsed.

Years before, after finding his wife and children dead, Decker had teetered on the brink of insanity and chosen to come back; he realized now that had been a mistake. He had many times taken risks that taunted death and had survived; now he wished he hadn't. It was not death that he feared. Had he been offered poison at this moment, he would have drunk it eagerly. Had he a gun, he would not have hesitated to take the barrel into his mouth and quickly fire a bullet into his brain. Had he a knife, he would have joyously thrust it into his chest.

It was not death he feared, but the life that would allow him to feel the torment he knew would begin before his next breath. Finally, he could bear it no more. With his head tilted back and every vertebra in his neck stretched to keep his mouth and nose above the darkness as it rose above his chin, he collapsed into unconsciousness in a heap on the bed.

The veil of stupor provided no relief, for even in his

unconscious state his mind filled with the images of what he could not see. It was only moments before his eyes opened, though he quickly shut them again. On either side of his head, two huge crows perched, waiting anxiously for him to open them again so they could pluck his eyes from their sockets. He could not see them in the blackness but he knew they were there, just as he knew also that the floor beside his bed crawled with snakes. Even closer, on the bed all around him, teemed rats, starving for their next meal. And though his body had fallen in a crumpled contorted mass when he passed out, he dared not move an inch, for any motion at all was sure to rouse the rats and make them aware of his location.

There was something else in the room, too. He could not see it but he knew it was there. Perhaps there were many of them: bloodthirsty creatures that defied description and would no doubt tear the living flesh from his frail human form as they devoured him. His only hope— though he certainly would not have used so positive a word as hope—was that the darkness was equally as impenetrable to the eyes of the beasts as it was to him.

Decker became aware of his nervous perspiration as it formed and pooled before running off his body. Could they smell his sweat? If so—and he felt certain that they could—their claws were already extended, ready to sink deep into his flesh to hold him still as they drove their fangs into his squirming body.

He wanted to scream. He needed to scream, but he dared not. Even as they sank their teeth into him and slurped up his blood and tore the raw meat from his bones, he was determined that he would not cry out, for by his scream he would only draw others to the feeding frenzy.

He longed to sink into his bed, the one direction from which nothing seemed to threaten, but then saw the folly of his desire, as he realized that only inches below a pool of bloodthirsty piranha waited anxiously.

As all the horrors filled his mind, and spiders and scorpions scurried across his flesh, suddenly it became clear that he had been a fool, for it was not a bed below him at all. All that he had dreaded—the crows, the rats, the snakes, the spiders, the razor sharp knives, the claws, and fangs, the teeth—all were supremely preferable compared to his true fate. For what he had believed to be his own sweat was in fact saliva dripping down upon him, and that which he had thought was his bed was in fact the tongue of some hideous leviathan, which even now savored the salty pre-chewed flavor of its meal and would, with Decker's first twitch, begin to slowly crush and chew, perhaps sucking the blood from his body, allowing a warm pool to collect in its mouth before swallowing.

Decker listened closely and thought he could hear the grinding of the beast's teeth. It was half an hour before the pain in his jaw brought him to realize that it was his own teeth, clenched in terror, that he had heard grinding. He tried to stop, fearing that the sound would alert the predators to his location, but no sooner had he resolved himself to this intent than his attention was diverted by some new apprehension and he again began grinding and gnashing his teeth.

❏

The terror went on, unceasing. With time it actually grew worse, as Decker weakened and became susceptible to sensory delusions that fed and were fed by his hysteria. With muscles reflexively tightened, his body lay stiff and motionless, barely yielding even to the demands of his lungs and heart for air. He lost all perception of time. Had he been there days or years? Had he ever been anywhere else? He had no memory of anything before this. Indeed, even to call himself Decker served merely as a convenience, for in his state of mind, a name—even his own name—was a meaningless concept. He was simply the prey, shaking with fear, and about to meet his grisly doom.

❑

For three days and nights Decker endured this condition, barely moving, imagining ever-worsening scenarios of his situation and environment, fearing even the sound and movement of his own breathing lest it should betray him. Parts of his body, dead numb from the endless hours of cramping—he believed these to have been somehow cut away like Shylock's pound of flesh, leaving what remained still alive only to endure further savagery. Sleep, real sleep, was impossible, and though there were periods of unconsciousness, they were filled with apparitions no less horrible than when he was fully awake. The only way he knew he had slept at all was that from time to time he became aware that he had changed position, and he was certain he had not moved intentionally. He wondered why the predators had not seized the opportunity to strike. He was certain of only one thing: Death would come, and any delay would only extend his suffering.

Wednesday, July 8, 4 N·A·

When the darkness subsided after three days, its black murkiness seeping back into the earth just as it had arrived, Decker found himself lying on his bed unharmed. Dried feces lay smeared on the bed around him and caked on his hips and back. The room stank from the feces, urine, and sweat, but having been in the room with it for so long, he did not smell it.

There was no thought of getting up to wash. Now that he no longer feared to move, he did not have the strength to do so. His jaws and teeth and head ached so badly from three days and nights of clenching and grinding that he was not certain he would survive the pain. Gently he moved his tongue along the inside of his cheeks trying to assess the damage. Loose flaps of flesh and deep ulcers revealed the pieces he had unknowingly bitten off in his torment. His tongue, too, was badly gnawed, and he could only assume the missing bits of flesh lay scattered around him on the bed or had been swallowed, washed down by the warm blood that still seeped from the wounds.

Thursday, July 9, 4 N·A·

Decker opened his eyes and saw black. His heart raced in panic that the darkness had returned, until a point of light, a star outside his window, caught his eye. It was night. He had no idea how long he had been asleep, but his thirst was unbearable and the simple disgust he had felt earlier at his condition had now turned to burning discomfort: For four and a half days he had lain in his own excrement and its saline and acidic qualities had eaten away at his flesh, leaving raw sores on his buttocks, thighs, and back. His head and jaws still hurt, but he managed to get to the bathroom to clean up.

After a long warm shower, he found some gauze and antibiotic cream to tend his wounds. Returning to his room, he determined his mattress to be a total loss. He'd have to do something with it later, but for now he decided to sleep the rest of the night in the guest room.

Friday, July 10, 4 N·A·

When Decker awoke the next morning, having slept most of the forty-eight hours since the darkness ceased, he got up and slowly made his way to the kitchen. He was weak, not only from surviving the darkness, but from hunger and thirst as well. He didn't know how long it had been since he'd eaten, but he was not surprised to find mold growing on the bread and the milk soured in the refrigerator. He hadn't restocked after the heat, which was just as well since most of the perishable items were turning bad. Apparently the power had gone out again.

After looking around the kitchen, he finally settled on scraping the mold from the bread and heating up a years-old can of cream of chicken soup. He had eaten worse, far worse. Besides, his jaws and teeth still ached, and his tongue and the inside of his cheeks felt like raw hamburger. For the next few days, at least, soup and soft bread were as close to solid food as he wanted to get. Still, he would need to call Tolinson soon to restock . . . if indeed, Tolinson had survived this last plague.

As he ate, Decker turned on the television to determine the effect the darkness had on the rest of the world. He got an immediate sense of the impact as he flipped through channel after channel of dead air. Two days after the darkness, only a few stations had resumed broadcasting. Only now did he learn that, unlike the previous plagues, the plague of darkness had lasted just three days, half as long as the others. Living through it, it had felt to Decker like an eternity. He was certain that if it *had* lasted six days, no one on earth would have survived.

Even so, many had not fared so well as he. No one was certain of the count, but the most conservative estimates of the dead were in the tens of millions. Most of the deaths resulted from heart failure. The toll was especially hard on the elderly. Many others had been killed in motor vehicle accidents. Forty-eight hours after the darkness had lifted, the streets and highways were still littered with bodies. Some had died instantly, others bled to death over the three days of darkness. Babies died in their cribs. Hospitals had become morgues. Planes, trains, subways, and buses—all means of mass transit—had become mass sepulchers. No aircraft in the air at the onset of the darkness had landed safely.

For more than three full days every human activity on the planet had come to a complete halt. Even now, two days after the darkness, most of those who survived were just beginning to recover enough to start to move about. Decker supposed that this plague, like the others, had somehow been ended by Milner, but from what little news there was so far, no one really seemed to care.

❑

After eating, Decker fell asleep on the couch for several more hours. When he awoke, he had another bowl of soup and turned the news back on. With all that had happened, the media could not ignore the political impact. It was no surprise that the insta-polls found a significant drop in Christopher's approval rating. What *was* surprising was just how big the drop was.

"The lead story this half hour," the anchor said, "is Secretary-General Christopher Goodman's meteoric fall in the polls. With a special report on our poll and the impact it will have on the secretary-general," the anchor continued, "here's Ree Anthony."

"Betty," the reporter began, addressing the news anchor, "according to our exclusive *CTN Worldwide Insta-Poll,* taken within the last twenty minutes, the secretary-general's approval rating has fallen to a new low— only 11 percent overall—with even lower ratings among some segments of the population." Decker listened in disbelief. An insta-poll graphic appeared on the screen showing Christopher's continuous dramatic decline in approval from 97 to 85 percent in the first week after the onset of the sores, to 71 percent after the second plague, to 55 percent after the fresh water turned to blood, to 35 percent after the heat, and now to his current rating of only 11 percent. As the reporter pointed out, the graph showed valleys and peaks corresponding to each of the plagues and their conclusions. But with each additional plague there came an overall trend that moved steadily and rapidly downward. That the polling company could count on sufficient audience response despite what the world had just been through was sad testimony to the power of interactive media.

No less disconcerting than the polls was the growing number of world leaders who were calling for Christopher to step down as secretary-general.

"The secretary-general has scheduled an address to the world on Sunday evening at 8:00 P.M. local time," the reporter said. Decker quickly ran the computation in his mind: That would be noon his time. "Until then, we are told that neither Secretary-General Goodman nor Robert Milner will be granting any interviews or making any comments. No one seems to know why Goodman is waiting until Sunday evening before addressing the world, but some insiders expressed concern that the delay just feeds the fear that another plague, perhaps one even more deadly than the ones before, is coming. With that kind of concern, we could see Goodman's approval rating drop even lower."

The picture switched back to the anchor. "One important note on the findings of that poll," the anchor said as she concluded the segment, "is that while the poll does show a significant loss of support for Secretary-General Goodman, there is no evidence of any corresponding switch in allegiance toward the KDP or Yahweh. Our poll shows that it is not that people are turning to Yahweh. Instead, many are cursing Yahweh and Goodman in the same breath."

The story of Christopher's drop in approval led the news for another hour and was replaced by a story that for the first time revealed the true extent of the loss of life from the last plague. One of the polling experts at the network had thought to apply features of the methodology used in insta-polling to the process of estimating the number of deaths. By having viewers enter the number of

deaths in each viewing household and then estimating the
approximate number of deaths represented by the reduc-
tion in the total number of poll respondents in areas that
had not lost service for that day-part as compared to the
previous weeks, a conservative death toll of well over 130
million was projected. The actual number would reach
240 million.

❏

News abhors a vacuum, and in the absence of an explanation from Christopher or Milner, rumors began to cir-
culate that Christopher was planning to resign and that he
was waiting until Sunday to allow the Security Council to
determine how to proceed.

Saturday, July 11, 4 N.A.

Decker dragged the mattress down the steps and out the
back door and dropped it on the patio. It was not a permanent solution to the problem, but the smell was so offensive that he had to get it out of the house. Closing the
door behind him, he collapsed in the first chair he came
to. As he sat trying to catch his breath, he was startled by
the sound of the phone. Despite his exhaustion, he ran
past two other phones to get to the one in the kitchen,
which had the caller ID feature.

Decker exhaled in relief; it was Bert Tolinson.

"Hello, Bert," Decker panted.

"Mr. Hawthorne, I'm afraid we've got a problem. I
got a call from a Ms. Liston at the bank today about the

transfer of funds from your account. She said no funds can be withdrawn. I asked her why, and she said that the computer said that you hadn't taken the communion. Can you believe that? I started to argue with her, but she insisted the computer was right. She said that all your funds had been frozen and she'd be surprised if you hadn't already been arrested. I didn't want to push it any further because I know how important your privacy is, but you're going to have to get this straightened out."

"This is crazy," Decker said with a little laugh, trying to sound convincing.

"That's what I told her. I guess she didn't realize who you were or she would have figured that out for herself."

"Okay, Bert. I'll take care of it," he said confidently. "You did the right thing, though. Thanks for handling it with such discretion."

"That's part of what you pay me for," Tolinson said. "You want the number for the bank?"

"Yeah," Decker answered, though he had no intention of actually making the call. Tolinson gave him the number and Decker recited it back as though he was writing it down. "I'll give you a call when I get this taken care of," he concluded.

He put down the phone. This presented a serious problem. There was probably enough food to last for about a week if he rationed it carefully. After that, he would be forced to leave the house to scavenge or steal what he could, which would greatly increase the chances that he'd be discovered and arrested. There was the additional problem that in a few days, Bert Tolinson would begin to wonder why he hadn't gotten things straightened out at the bank. At the least, it would mean that Decker would have to admit he could no longer pay him and, therefore, he could no longer depend on Tolinson's assistance. At the worst, Tolinson might notify the police. There was now a substantial reward for turning in people who had not taken the mark.

Sunday, July 12, 4 N.A.

Decker sat straight-backed on the couch in front of the television set. Christopher was about to make what everyone acknowledged was a make-or-break speech, not only for his own position as secretary-general, but for the very life or death of the New Age. Leaders of governments around the world were openly calling for Christopher to resign his position, though no one had offered a plan of how to go forward from here. Decker was torn. With his heart he hoped the speech would be everything Christopher needed it to be. But there was a strong nagging doubt that had kept him here on the other side of the world from Christopher, fearing the very thing for which his heart hoped.

For Decker, however, the importance of this speech was not primarily what Christopher would say. What he was looking for would not be spoken; it was the look in Christopher's eye.

Decker's time was running out. Soon Bert Tolinson would begin to ask questions; Decker would run out of food; the local phone service and the power would be shut off; and sooner or later some computer security person would question the recent activity in his bank account or the calls made on his phone, and, one way or another, the police would be notified. He knew he'd have to leave soon. When he came to Derwood, he had hoped that with time he would be able to think things through, to find some answers. Instead, after a month, he found himself just as confused as when he arrived.

Thus it was that he had come to this point where his simple gut reaction to Christopher's broadcast would determine whether he would return to Babylon to serve at Christopher's side or flee into the night, living on scraps of garbage and fearing contact with any other human lest he be betrayed to the police.

"Friends," Christopher began simply, immediately setting the tone for the rest of the speech. "There has been a great deal of speculation as to my reason for waiting so long after the most recent plague to address you. The truth is simple: I believe that actions speak far louder than words.

"It is now Sunday evening in Babylon. It's a bit warmer than I care for," he said with a slight but sincere smile, "but, unlike the past five Sundays, the water has not turned to blood; there is no darkness seeping up out of the earth; there are no demonic locusts swarming overhead; no asteroids are heading in our direction; no nuclear wars; there are no reports of mass insanity, or murders, or suicides. In short, there are no plagues. And I pledge to you, there will be no more plagues!" Christopher pounded his fist to emphasize his point. It was a tactic he had used seldom in the past, which made it all the more forceful now.

"I have waited until now to speak with you," he continued, "because I wanted not only to tell you, but to *show* you—so that you would be able to see for yourselves—that the plagues have come to an end. We who have survived have weathered the storm, and though the loss has been great, I am here *not* to admit defeat, but to declare victory!

"Now, I fully recognize that this may seem like a typical politician's ploy to obscure the ugly truth with unfounded visions of hope. It has not escaped my attention that according to the polls a large number—in fact, an overwhelming majority of you, including many respected world leaders—have lost faith in my ability to lead us through this crisis. And yet I am certain that few of you would prefer to allow the fundamentalists and the KDP to impose their totalitarian controls on your lives.

"Still, in all honesty, I acknowledge that there is every reason for you to doubt me, and I would not be so presumptuous as to expect, or even to ask, you to abandon your skepticism based merely on what I say to you here tonight."

Christopher had every reason to be concerned. His approval rating had sunk below 10 percent. Many expected this to be his resignation speech, but there was no sign of desperation in his voice. Instead, his words and demeanor showed only confidence.

"Again, I believe actions speak far louder than words. In a moment, I'll present a simple proposal that outlines the actions I'll undertake and the means by which you may be absolutely certain that what I say tonight is true and that victory is finally ours.

"First, however, allow me to take a moment to set the events of the past few weeks in perspective.

"Seven years ago, famines and drought struck India and Pakistan, which led to a long war that killed 4.5

million people. The war spread and ultimately resulted in a nuclear exchange between China, India, and Pakistan, in which an additional 420 million people died. While these at first appeared to be tragic but natural events, we later realized that the planet had come under attack from outside, by a spirit known as Yahweh, and that he was acting in concert with and at the invocation of his*human mediums, the men John and Saul Cohen.

"Less than six months later, an asteroid entered the earth's atmosphere and, in a span of mere minutes, killed 175 million, including most of the population of central Canada and the midwestern United States, as well as nearly all of Mexico, Belize, Guatemala, Honduras, El Salvador, Nicaragua, Costa Rica, Panama, Colombia, Ecuador, Peru, Brazil, and Bolivia. Tens of millions were left injured and homeless. And one-third of the world's forests, including the once vast woodlands of North America and most of the South American rainforests, were reduced to funeral pyres.

"The same day, on the other side of the world, a second asteroid struck in the Pacific south of Japan, causing earthquakes, tsunami, and unprecedented volcanic activity that killed an estimated 206 million and left the ocean a blood-red pool of death as it totally destroyed all marine life in the Pacific.

"The two asteroids had the additional effect of so profoundly displacing the ozone layer that all grains and grasses throughout the world were destroyed, resulting in worldwide famine and an additional 50 million deaths.

"A third asteroid, far larger than the first two and capable of eliminating all life on the planet, was destroyed while it was still a safe distance from the earth, thanks to the cooperation of the member nations of the UN. But weeks later, as the dust of the third asteroid reached the earth, we learned that it contained a high level of arsenic, a deadly poison, which polluted much of the earth's water supply and killed 20 million more. Altogether from the asteroids, more than 450 million innocent men, women, and children died. Again, this was no natural disaster, but rather the vile handiwork of Yahweh.

"The following year, insects, genetically mutated by the design of Yahweh and whose coming was foretold by John and Cohen, swarmed over the earth for five full months, causing havoc and horrible suffering, and bringing agricultural production and most industries to a virtual standstill. UN estimates of the death toll from the resulting starvation are conservatively put at 155 million. While none died as a direct result of the locusts, the pain was so great that death would have been preferred by those who endured the excruciating torment of their stings. Many, perhaps most of you listening tonight, experienced that pain firsthand.

"Four months after the locusts died, a follower of the KDP, without provocation, shot me in cold blood and endangered the lives of hundreds of bystanders." Christopher paused to let those listening recall the tragic scenes of that day at the UN. The video of the assassination had been broadcast on television so many times it was doubtful there was anyone who had not seen it. The black patch that Christopher still wore over his right eye socket and his crippled left arm bore further witness to the suffering he had endured.

"Within minutes of my assassination, a savage madness swept over much of the planet, which caused neighbor to kill neighbor, spouse to kill spouse, and even parents to kill their own children. For three and a half days this madness continued unabated until, following my resurrection, I flew to Jerusalem and ended the madness by putting an end to John and Saul Cohen. In all, nearly 1.5 billion—a full one-third of the remaining population of the earth—died because of the madness. Had I not stopped these two agents of Yahweh, it is doubtful that anyone on earth outside of Israel would have been left alive.

"When John and Cohen were themselves resurrected three days later, they left a reminder of their infamous destructiveness: an earthquake that destroyed 10 percent of the city of Jerusalem and killed seven thousand people. Fortunately that was the last we would ever see of these men.

"Over the next three years, under my leadership, our planet experienced a period of unprecedented peace and prosperity. And in this environment of peace, as we entered the New Age of Humankind, which Yahweh had been unsuccessful in stopping, people throughout the world of all races, cultures, nationalities, and ages began to experience powers of the mind and spirit that had only been dreamt of before.

"Thirteen months ago, with the communion, the world witnessed the end of sickness, miraculous recoveries from injuries, and even a reversal of the aging process. Humankind was at last running full speed toward its glorious destiny.

"This brings us to the events of the past four weeks.

"Unable to control us any longer, as Humankind stood poised on the threshold of the New Age, Yahweh and his henchmen, the KDP and the fundamentalists, unleashed another set of plagues intended to frighten us into submission. First it was the lesions on those who had dared to make the first step into the New Age by taking the communion. Next he turned the seas and then the fresh water to blood. Each time, as Robert Milner halted one plague, a new one followed. Then it was the extreme heat, and finally the darkness. Altogether these last five plagues have resulted in an additional 510 million deaths.

"But now that is over. Let me repeat what I said earlier: There will be no more plagues!

"Yahweh's forces are like a three-legged stool, made up of the KDP, the fundamentalists, and Jews who inhabit Petra. Through the cooperative efforts of police and security forces around the world, the program to deal with the fundamentalist threat is working. We have splintered that leg of the stool and broken their power! *There will be no more plagues!*

"The KDP, the fundamentalists, the dwellers of Petra, and Yahweh have done all the damage that they can for now. And so, let the first proof that what I tell you is true be offered and confirmed on a daily basis, as no more plagues befall us.

"But it is not enough to remove the one leg of the stool. We must complete the goal by dealing also with the KDP and those in Petra. If we do nothing, they will learn to stand upon two legs and they will do even worse, to the point of destroying all of Humankind.

"I have been criticized for not dealing more harshly with the KDP and their supporters. I will admit that I have always held out hope that the KDP would see the error of their ways and join us. I do not regret having had that hope. I do, however, regret the toll in human suffering they have caused as we have held out to them the hand of peace. It is now clear that they will not travel with us. By their own choice, we must leave them behind. I know there may be some who fear that because of my patience with the KDP in the past, I may again be persuaded to offer the olive branch. Let me assure you that that will *not* happen. The KDP and the rest of the Cult of Yahweh have shown themselves to be maniacal, intolerant, narrow-minded fanatics, cruelly calling down plagues upon the earth as if for their amusement. We must now deal with them with equal fervor.

"They have assembled themselves in the ancient walled city of Petra, and it is ironically fitting, for their religion is an ancient one—old and brittle and ready to crumble down upon them. So let it be that the legend of Joshua will serve as a metaphor for their own destruction. In that legend, all the people of Israel, under the rule of Joshua, gathered around the walled city of Jericho.[81] So let us gather at Petra. But unlike the people of Israel who called on Yahweh to destroy Jericho, we will call out to no one. Neither will we bring with us any weapon. For by the very power of our combined will and inner strength, all the universe will bear witness that no walls of stone or self-proclaimed god can stand against a united Humankind. For just as the walls of Jericho in the legend fell, so shall the walls of Petra come down upon those who have rained terror down on us. Let us be rid once and for all time of Yahweh and those who would force us to our knees to worship him.

[81] Joshua 6.

"That is my proposal. But I offer more.

"I said that I would provide the means by which you could be certain that what I have promised—the end of the plagues, the end of Yahweh's dominion, and our victory—is at hand.

"The proof that I offer will not be a miracle at the hands of Robert Milner. Nor will I, myself, perform some miraculous deed. Instead the miracle will come from you, from Humankind, by the sheer will and power of each of you. For let me assure you," Christopher said, "that during these past three years since Humankind began experiencing the powers of the mind and spirit, evolution has not stood still.

"Within two weeks time, the first of three great signs will be given that will offer conclusive proof that Humankind has, over the past three years, taken a giant step in the evolutionary process. It is you, those who hear my voice and have joined with the rest of Humankind, who will perform the miracle. And you will see for yourself why Yahweh fears you!

"Humankind must be free to achieve its destiny. It was not mere chance that Professor Harold Goodman found the cells on the Shroud from which I was cloned. I have come into the world to act as the catalyst that Humankind may achieve its destiny. But it is not my place to carry Humankind into the New Age. Rather, each of you must go of your own accord and under your own power. And each of you must participate, for though we each must carry our own weight, we must all go together as one family.

"All of us have lost friends or family over the past few weeks," Christopher said, drawing his address to a close, "and it is understandable that there should be a healthy release of anger. And if much of that anger is directed at me, well then, so be it. I am well aware of the calls for my resignation and that many of you listening may hate me as much as you hate Yahweh for what has befallen you. But before you abandon the path that has brought us this far, realize that the plagues are not and have never been the result of animosity between Yahweh and myself. This began long before I was elected secretary-general and declared the beginning of the New Age. The plagues that afflict us have a simple and undeniable root cause: After thousands of years of stagnation, evolution has brought Humankind to the brink of a transformation that will take all who embrace it as far beyond the narrow confines of the present human form as Humankind is now above the simple one-celled amoeba!

"Join me for this final battle against the Cult of Yahweh and together let us forever throw open the door of the jail of evolutionary stagnation that has held us so long! Thank you, and good night."

❑

It wasn't there.

Decker had watched carefully, but the speech left him still uncertain. Whatever it was he had hoped to see wasn't there.

What *had* he hoped for, he wondered. Before the speech, he had thought he could look Christopher in the eye and instinctively be able to interpret his true motivation. Now that seemed an embarrassingly naïve assumption. He had known Christopher for twenty-three years. If he still had doubts after that long, how could he possibly expect to get a true read of the man now, simply by watching him on television?

As far as the speech itself was concerned, Decker considered the delivery first class. Apparently the public agreed. Christopher had stressed actions over words and said he expected the words of his address to convince few, but within fifteen minutes insta-polls showed his approval rating jumping from 8 to 21 percent. The speech was inspiring, and if Christopher did what he promised—if the three signs were given and there were no more plagues— then he might once again have the world's support.

There was only one problem: The evil people of Petra who Christopher described in his speech were not the people Decker had seen there. They were not "maniacal, intolerant, narrow-minded fanatics." Yes, they had a very different view of the world. And because of their belief in Yahweh and their trust in the KDP, many of them might even support the raining down of plagues for what they wrongly but sincerely believed to be the greater good of the very people who suffered. But Decker could not believe that any of the people he had met there would "cruelly call down plagues upon the earth, as if for their amusement," as Christopher had said.

Christopher obviously did not understand. Granted, it was a fine point to try to argue in light of the suffering that had occurred, but Decker had to do something. He thought of Rhoda, young Decker Donafin, Tom Jr., Rachael, and Charlie the "jailer," and the many others he had met. The battle that Christopher had described would leave them all dead. He had watched the speech to discover Christopher's true motives. Now that no longer mattered. Whether

Christopher was the embodiment of good or the epitome of evil, Decker could not sit still and let the people of Petra be killed. His course was set for him. He had to return to Babylon.

Somehow he needed to arrange for a flight. He couldn't simply buy a ticket, or even pay for taxis to and from the airports. Without the mark he couldn't buy or sell anything. Nor did he want to log on to the UN's secure web page to schedule a flight. That could set off alarms in the system. The only way was to get someone from his office to arrange for limousines and passage on a UN plane. It had been a week and a half since his long distance telephone service was cut off. He had expected to lose his local service by now as well, but the circumstances of the last two plagues, not surprisingly, had affected the phone company's efficiency and they had not yet disconnected him. The net result was that while he could not place a long distance call, he could still make and receive local calls, and he could probably still receive long distance calls placed to him. The solution was simple. He would ask Bert Tolinson to call his office at the UN and have them call him back. He'd tell him it was all part of the same mix-up as with the bank.

❑

Fifteen minutes after Decker called Tolinson, the phone rang. It was Kwalindia Oshala, Debbie Sanchez' administrative assistant. She was working late when she got the call. She was both helpful and very friendly to Decker and told him how much everyone had missed him around the office and they'd be glad to have him back. Decker explained what he needed, and she checked the scheduled UN flights from Washington to Babylon. There was only one, the first since the darkness. It was scheduled to leave Dulles Airport at 6:00 that evening. It would make three stops along the way, and arrive in Babylon at 6:30 P.M. the next day. Kwalindia booked the flight and arranged limousine service.

Decker went without luggage; he had none with him when he had arrived in Derwood. He wore loose-fitting clothes and bandages on his left cheek, the back of his neck, and on the back of his right hand where the mark should have been. All went as planned, and by 7:00 P.M. he was in the air on his way back to Babylon.

Home Free

17

DECKER WALKED THROUGH THE DARK, nearly abandoned halls of the UN Secretariat Building. It was late, and nearly everyone had gone home. Christopher would be there though; somehow Decker knew it. Opening one of the mammoth mahogany double doors that led to Christopher's spacious reception area, he was surprised to see Jackie Hansen still there.

"Come on in," Jackie said, as she preceded Decker into Christopher's office. "He's waiting for you." Jackie seemed placid in an almost surreal way. She said nothing of the fact that he had been gone for so long, and nothing in her voice hinted that she was at all surprised to see him.

As he walked into Christopher's office, it was strangely cold and dark, much as the halls had been. The air had a strange musty smell. Something . . . *everything* was wrong. He looked around him and saw no one. He had somehow lost sight of Jackie, and it now seemed that she had simply vanished. Looking about, he sensed movement to his right and turned to see the high back of Christopher's desk chair rotating away from him.

"Christopher?" he said. There was no answer. He approached the desk and called out again. Still, there was no reply.

As he neared the spot, he reached for the back of the chair to spin it around. Suddenly he jumped back in horror as he came face to face with his worst possible fear. It was Christopher. At least it was Christopher's face, but he was not at all as Decker remembered him. His eyes were cardinal red, the specific hue of which differed not one shade from the sticky liquid which trickled from the corners of his mouth and matted the hairs of his normally neatly kept beard. His skin appeared somehow scaly and iridescent green. His teeth, jagged and sharp, dripped pink with saliva and blood. His fingernails were long and clawlike.

And in those claws he held the source of the blood: the leg of Jackie Hansen, ripped clean from its socket and with several large bites already taken from it. On the floor beside his chair, Jackie Hansen lay naked and barely alive as the blood drained from her body. Decker struggled not to vomit. Deep gashes in Jackie's flesh revealed the tracks of Christopher's claws where he had torn away her clothes. On her face was the same serene smile Decker had seen earlier, and in her eyes as she looked up at Christopher was the unmistakable look of love.

"What do you want?" Christopher growled, spitting out his last bite of bloody flesh as he jumped to his feet and threw Jackie's dismembered leg to the floor, hitting her in the stomach and leaving the appendage lying across her body.

Decker turned and ran in terror, but Christopher charged after him. He looked for the door, but in his panic he simply could not find it. He looked desperately for a way—any way—out, but there was none. He ran like a man possessed, dodging and trying to stay ahead of his pursuer, but it was impossible. The younger and stronger Christopher stayed right on his heels. Every move Decker made, he seemed to anticipate. Struggling to keep going, he began to believe that Christopher was toying with him like a cat with a trapped mouse. Then suddenly, he spotted a window. It was open, but it was nineteen floors down. Still, he had to get away. Christopher was so close behind him he could feel his hot, foul breath. With all his strength, Decker ran and leapt for the open window just as Christopher reached out and caught the leg of his pants with the extended claws. Razor sharp, the nails dug deep into his leg, tearing long bloody stripes through skin and muscle, but it was not enough to slow his momentum. Free of Christopher, Decker looked below him to his chosen alternative: certain death.

Desperately, instinctively, he tried to grab at the air to slow his fall, and inexplicably his hand found something solid.

It was the seat in front of him. He was still on the plane, headed for Babylon. It had all been a dream, but he was covered with perspiration and his heart pounded as hard as if it had been real. He was exhausted.

Decker unfastened his seat belt, stretched, and walked to the restroom. He needed to get up and let the thoughts of consciousness—and perhaps a splash of cold water on his face—purge the dream from his mind. A few moments later, when he returned to his seat, he found that this had not been entirely successful because the dream, though exaggerated like a carnival mirror in its form, was nonetheless a reflection of the real fears he bore.

He shifted from side to side, adjusted his seat, added a pillow, removed a pillow, adjusted his seat again. He was very tired, and probably still several good nights of rest away from full recovery from the effects of the last plague. He needed to sleep, especially now, to be prepared to confront Christopher about Petra.

When he finally found a comfortable position and his mind began to relax, he thought back to the dream and how absurd it had been. He had not had a nightmare like that since he was a child. Still, he thought a moment later as he slipped closer to unconsciousness, he should be prepared, be ready, to defend himself. The most obvious means was a handgun, but he couldn't buy one because he didn't have the mark. Perhaps a knife. A large kitchen knife should be sufficient. Getting it in past security might be difficult, but . . .

Decker opened his eyes abruptly and sat up straight in his seat.

Is this how it was with Tom? he wondered. Had Tom had a similar dream that led him to shoot Christopher? Then another thought struck him: *Was* this just a dream at all, or had it been planted in his mind by the KDP, like a time bomb waiting for this exact moment to go off—to set him off? And if this failed to have the desired effect, would there be others? Had the KDP planted other dreams, other thoughts, other visions? When he got to Christopher's office would he see things as they really were or would reality be hidden behind a mask fabricated by those who wanted Christopher dead? What monster, he wondered, had Tom seen standing there on the dais at the UN the night he shot Christopher?

And what drove Decker to go to Christopher at this time, just as the KDP appeared to be losing power? Was it really to try to spare the lives of those in Petra, or was it to take the life of Christopher?

To the last question, at least, he thought he knew the answer. He wanted to try to spare the lives of those in Petra. Yet he knew that in going to Babylon he might be doing exactly what the KDP wanted. The feeling that he must go and see Christopher at this precise moment might have been their intent all along. If it was, then he was a pawn, again playing out the role of Judas, and believing it was his idea when he really had no choice.

It didn't matter.

Whether it was his own idea or one that had been planted in his mind by the KDP, he had to go.

Decker was not even sure if he truly controlled his own will, but to the extent that he did, he made one vow. Under no circumstances would he bring a weapon, *any* weapon, or anything that could be used as a weapon, with him to Christopher's office. Even if his worst fears about Christopher proved true, even if he appeared to be or really was a green scaly demon as he had been in his dream, Decker vowed he would do nothing to harm him or even to protect himself.

It was an easier decision than it might have seemed. If he was wrong about Christopher, then he must not allow himself to do anything against him. And if he was right, then he would just as soon die anyway.

Monday, July 13, 4 N·A·
Babylon

Decker's plane arrived at King Nebuchadnezzar
International Airport six minutes ahead of schedule. A
limousine was waiting, ready to take him wherever he
wanted to go. It would have been very easy to tell the
driver to take him to his apartment, but he knew what he
had to do and there was no use delaying it.

He took a deep breath. "The UN Secretariat
Building," he told the driver.

❑

Slipping the fake bandage from around his hand, Decker
placed his right palm on the identipad and stared at the
screen of the retinal scanner beside the door of the exec-
utive entrance to the Secretariat Building. "Decker
Hawthorne," he said clearly.

"Verified," a soft female-sounding electronic voice responded, as the lock clicked and the door opened.

Apparently no one had thought to tell the UN security
system to search the World Health Organization's database for UN executives who had not received the communion and to restrict their access to the building.

"Good evening, Mr. Hawthorne," the guard inside the
door said cheerfully.

"Good evening," Decker responded, a little startled. He
had been through that door a hundred times, at all times of
the night and day, and had always been greeted as cheerfully as tonight. What startled him was that it *was* just the

same. He had been so sure that somehow it would be different. The building was brightly lit with just the right level of shadow, and the air was refreshingly cool in contrast to the arid Iraqi night. Though it was nearly 7:30 P.M., a few employees and guests were still in the lobby, in the elevator, and walking down the halls as he made his way to the top floor and Christopher's office. Finally he arrived at the entrance to the offices of the secretary-general. He had been away for longer periods than this on UN business and always returned with a feeling as though he had never really been gone. That much at least *was* different; now as he stood outside the dark wood double doors, he had the strange feeling that he should knock.

As he stood there going over again in his mind what he was going to say, suddenly one of the doors opened. His heart seemed to stop in anticipation of seeing Christopher coming through the door toward him, and then start again as Jackie Hansen appeared. She was rushing off somewhere and was startled to see an unexpected face.

"Decker! How are you?" she said as she recovered her composure and wrapped her arms around him. Even with a large bandage on her cheek, she was a beautiful woman. The effect of the communion had continued its work and she seemed even younger and more vivacious than when he had seen her last, a little more than a month before.

"I'm fine," he answered, as he returned the show of affection.

"Oh, Decker. We need to talk, but I'm late for a class. Will you be here tomorrow?"

"Yeah, I guess so," he shrugged.

"Okay. I'll talk to you then," she said, and hurried down the hall.

"Is Christopher in?" he called after her.

"He's in his office," Jackie called back.

❑

Decker walked quietly across the carpeted floor toward Christopher's door. This was it. There was no turning back. He knocked on the door. There was a pause. "Come in," came a faint call from deep inside the large office. Decker opened the door. Christopher was sitting at his desk looking toward his door to see who was coming to see him this late in the evening. Suddenly the look in his eyes went from mild curiosity to rapturous joy.

"Decker! Oh, Decker, am I glad to see you!"

Decker stood expressionless as Christopher came to greet him with a long, firm hug.

"You don't know what it's been like around here without you. Debbie Sanchez is very competent, but she's no Decker Hawthorne when it comes to dealing with the press. I am so glad you're back!"

"I . . . uh . . . I'm glad to *be* back," Decker answered, not sure what else to say.

Christopher released his hug and backed up to get a better look at him. "So, how have you been?" he asked, almost absent-mindedly. "Oh," he said, as though he had just recalled the plagues and all that had happened in the past few weeks. "I'm sorry, Decker. Here I am just thinking of how happy I am that you're back. Are you all right?"

"I'm . . . I'm fine, I guess."

"You've lost a lot of weight."

"Well, it's been a tough few weeks."

Christopher nodded. "At least you're still alive," he said gratefully. "Here, come sit down." Christopher motioned toward a sitting area near the windows with a view of the hanging gardens. These were not the windows Decker had jumped from in his dream, and they were, of course, closed because the windows in the UN complex of buildings were not made to open.

"What can I get you to drink?" Christopher asked, starting toward the wet bar.

"Uh . . . just water," Decker answered as he sunk into one of the comfortable armchairs. He wanted so much just to forget about the last few weeks and accept Christopher's warm welcome and go on about his life. But by now the images of Rhoda Donafin and her family and the others in Petra were burned into his memory. He had to complete the task that had brought him here.

"I need to talk to you about your decision to march on Petra," he said resolutely.

"We can talk about all of that later," Christopher answered, as he returned with a glass of ice water, handed it to Decker, and then sat down across from him. "Tell me how you've been."

"You need to reconsider your decision," Decker insisted.

"Decker," Christopher entreated, taken aback, "it's late. You've been away for over a month. A lot has happened. Do we really need to have a policy discussion right now?"

"Yes. Please," Decker persisted.

"It will be a month before the first phase of deployment even begins. Why is it so important that we discuss it right this minute?"

"Because it's wrong," Decker responded bluntly.

Christopher raised an eyebrow, sighed, and leaned back in his chair. "Decker, this was not a decision I rushed into. The Security Council has been pushing me to do this since the plagues first began."

"Well, tell them you won't do it," Decker interrupted.

"I can't do that."

"Why not?"

"Because I agree with them. I didn't at first. You know I've always held out hope that the KDP and their followers would join us. I've done everything I can to get them to listen to reason."

"Have you?" Decker didn't intend for the question to sound like an accusation, but it did.

Christopher seemed surprised and a little hurt. "Decker, stop. I can understand the public losing their faith in me, but will you abandon me, too?"

"I haven't abandoned you."

"I don't like having to deal with Petra any more than you do. But it has to be . . ." Christopher stopped in mid-sentence as his expression suddenly changed to shock and then disbelief. Getting up from his seat, he crossed over to Decker, took hold of his forearm and tore away the bandage that covered the back of his right hand. Decker didn't resist.

"So *this* is why you question my decision! You *have* abandoned me! You, of all people!" Christopher backed away, shaking his head in disbelief. "You told me you'd receive the communion, and then you disappeared."

Coming near again, he looked Decker in the eye. "Bob Milner tried to tell me when you called here saying you needed a vacation that he sensed something was wrong. But I didn't want to believe it! I said you were probably just tired! I actually got angry with him for suggesting such a thing! But I see I owe him an apology." Christopher shook his head again. "You never went to get the communion. You were hiding . . . you were—" Christopher pulled himself up short and studied Decker's face. "No," he said more slowly, as a look of sympathy and understanding swept over him. "You were . . . you were kidnapped! Why didn't you tell me? Are you all right? Did they hurt you? How did you get away?"

Somehow Christopher realized what had happened.

The look of caring and concern was so real, Decker could no longer remain aloof. *This* was what he had hoped to see when he had watched Christopher's speech. Now he was sure. The relief swept over him like a flood, as he knew for certain his concerns about Christopher had been unfounded.

"I'm . . . I'm fine," Decker stammered, but it was obvious he was not. "Actually," he said, smiling in relief, "I feel terrible. The plagues have been hard on everyone. I'm exhausted, my teeth hurt, my head hurts, and my tongue and the inside of my mouth feel like I gargled with broken glass."

"So, you *did* go through the plagues. I thought maybe you had been held in Petra all this time."

"I was only there for a few days. When they released

me, I went back to the U.S. Actually, being kidnapped and held in Petra was a walk in the park compared to the past several weeks."

"I'm just glad you're back," Christopher said. "Did the KDP torture you?"

"No, they just scared me pretty good." Decker reached for the glass of water, which had thus far gone untouched. "You know what I really need?" he said, as he looked at the water.

"Just name it!" Christopher answered.

"What I really need is a beer."

"Hefeweizen Dunkel?" Christopher asked, referring to a German dark wheat beer that Decker was particularly fond of.

Decker's eyes lit up. "You have some?"

"I even have one cold."

Decker nodded eagerly and collapsed back into the chair. It was the first time he had *really* relaxed since before he was kidnapped, for it was not just his body that relaxed, but his mind as well. He wanted to apologize to Christopher for all the terrible things he had thought about him, but he realized that discussion could wait for another time.

Christopher poured the beer slowly into a tall glass and handed it to Decker.

"This is so good," Decker said, pausing only long enough to take a breath and lick the foam from his lips before drinking down another refreshing gulp. Christopher stood watching, apparently sharing his enjoyment.

"Decker, look, you're tired and you're . . . well, you're not as young as you used to be," Christopher said. "And like you said, it's been hard on everyone. Have you seen a doctor?"

"No. I guess I should."

"Why don't you go home and get a good night's rest. I'll have Jackie make an appointment for you tomorrow."

Decker nodded agreement. He was tired and thought it would be a relief to get back to his apartment.

"And while you're there you can finally take the communion," Christopher added, "*discreetly,* of course. It wouldn't be good to have anyone find out you had waited so long."

"Yes," Decker agreed. "I'll do that." Still, though he no longer believed Christopher to be a monster, he had come a long way and had not yet achieved his purpose. "But before I go," he added, "there are a few things we really must talk about." His expression made it obvious that he would not be swayed from his intent. He wanted to talk, and it had to be now.

"All right," Christopher smiled accommodatingly and sat back down opposite Decker. "What is it that's so important that it can't wait till morning?"

"Christopher," Decker began, sitting forward in his seat and setting his beer down so he could use his hands to express himself, "when I was taken to Petra, at first I just wondered whether or not I'd ever get out of there alive. They never tortured me, but for the first three days they tried their best to convince me that you're evil and Yahweh's good. After that, I guess they just gave up. They let me go wherever I wanted throughout the whole encampment. I had a chance to meet the people and talk to them, to listen to what they thought about what was happening. And I realized some things. Most of them are *not* KDP crazies, Christopher. They're just ordinary people who have been convinced by the circumstances that the KDP have their best interests at heart and that you are their enemy.

"On the plane to Jerusalem after your resurrection," Decker continued, "you told me that my role would be to serve as communicator of your message to people who were not familiar with the concepts of the New Age. Well, I served you in that role for three years, and I thought that job was pretty much complete. There's not a man or woman on the planet who hasn't been thoroughly familiarized with the message of the coming advance in the evolution of Humankind: movies, television, Internet, radio, newspapers, magazines, books, songs, plays, billboards, bumper stickers—your vision of the future is everywhere. There's not a child in school from age three and up who has not been trained in the ethics and tenets of the New Age. Even the younger ones learn the message through cartoons, toys, and games.

"The mission has gone so well, in fact, that I was beginning to think I had worked myself out of a job. But on my last night in Petra, I realized there was still much work that could be done. But it was with the least likely of audiences: the people of Petra, and maybe even the fundamentalists."

Christopher shook his head to indicate the hopelessness of what Decker was suggesting. His skepticism did not deter Decker. "Christopher, I'm convinced that we can reach these people—make them understand that you're not their enemy—that what you offer the world is not to be feared, but welcomed."

Christopher seemed unconvinced, but Decker continued, clarifying one point, "I'm not saying there's hope for the KDP. I think they probably *are* beyond the point where they can be persuaded by reason. But their followers—I'm certain that many of them can be persuaded if they're just presented with all the facts."

"Decker, believe me," Christopher answered, "more than anyone, I understand how you feel about this, but I think you're underestimating just how hard these people are to deal with. Don't you think I've tried? I've had the best cult deprogramming experts and psychiatrists in the world working on this with some of the fundamentalists in prison. They're still working on it, but they're getting nowhere."

Decker was well aware of this. His office had been responsible for distributing information on the program to the press. "But the psychiatrists and deprogrammers are missing the point," he responded. "They're never going to convince the fundamentalists of anything as long as the KDP continue to appear infallible. Everything that the KDP says is going to happen *does* happen. Everything they attempt, they accomplish. Sure, Bob Milner may come along later and stop what they've started, but in the meantime they've accomplished their purposes. But if just once we could alter events so that the KDP would fail in one of their prophecies, the whole foundation of their control would fall apart!

"In Petra," Decker continued, "they told me the plagues were coming. The KDP told their followers that in response to the plagues, you would act first against the fundamentalists and then assemble an army to march on

Petra. They even said when it would happen: September. They've told everyone. It's commonly known throughout the camp.

"But you can short-circuit the prophecy, prevent it from coming true! If you don't march on Petra, then the KDP and their followers will have to admit they were wrong. I believe you should go to Petra, but instead of assembling an army for war, you could send a peace envoy. Show your true face as peacemaker and benevolent leader instead of the demonic beast the KDP has made you out to be. The KDP took me to Petra to convince me that they were right and you were wrong. What I'm suggesting would allow us to turn that completely around, so that we could use what I learned while I was there to our own benefit, so that we can convince their followers of the truth about you and about Yahweh."

"Decker," Christopher reasoned, "all the KDP have done with their 'prophecy' about how I would respond is to state the obvious. It's like an accomplished chess player or a good military strategist. They can predict what their opponent will do several moves in advance because they know what their own moves will be and they know that, under the given circumstances, their opponent will have no choice in how he will respond."

"But can't we respond differently?"

Christopher shook his head. "It's not that easy, Decker, and the KDP knows it. That's why they can speak with such confidence. It's not a coincidence that each of the plagues has been worse than the one before. We must stop the KDP before they're strong enough to act again, or the next plague will kill everyone on the planet except the KDP and their followers in Petra. No one outside the walls of Petra, not even the fundamentalists, will be spared."

"I'm only asking for a brief delay. There are so many in Petra who simply have been misled by the KDP," Decker pleaded. "If you march on Petra in September, they will suffer the same fate as those who have misled them."

"I don't know what it is you think I'm going to do," Christopher objected. "Do you think we're going to go in there and kill everyone? The people of Petra will be given the same opportunity as the fundamentalists have been given to denounce Yahweh and the KDP. Anyone willing to leave Petra and reject the KDP will be allowed to do so."

"But they won't!" Decker insisted. "If you march on Petra in September, you'll be doing exactly what the KDP said you'd do. By your own actions you'll be giving credence to the KDP. What if you went *next* month, in August?"

Christopher shook his head. "We simply can't be ready that soon."

"Then, can it wait until October? You said yourself the KDP have been weakened enough that they won't be able to call down any more plagues for a while."

Christopher didn't answer, but it was obvious he hadn't changed his mind.

Decker tried another approach. "Christopher, when I recommended that you institute the mark, it was to use the biblical prophecies to our advantage. What I'm suggesting now is the same thing, except I think now we should do just the opposite of what the prophecies say."

Then another thought occurred to him. "Besides," he said, "if you march on Petra in September, you could be walking right into a trap."

The suggestion brought an uncharacteristically chilly stare from Christopher. "Odd, Decker, but I get the feeling it's not *me* you're concerned about."

"Not exclusively, no," Decker admitted quickly. "I'd be lying to tell you otherwise. But my motives don't make what I'm saying any less true. If you can wait just a month, the people in Petra will realize that the KDP are wrong and their stranglehold will be broken. We can accomplish our goals *and* avoid a massacre."

"Decker, don't you understand, every day of delay is like putting off the removal of a life-threatening cancer. In one month—a single month—these people you're trying to protect have killed over 500 million people and nearly every aquatic creature on the planet! I have no desire to kill anyone," Christopher continued, "but you are wrong. If I delay my plans, they will not see their error. They will simply find some way to reinterpret the prophecies to say that I'll be coming the next month, or the next, or the one after that. Do you have any idea how many times in the past these religious types have used exactly that kind of prophetic revisionism? The leaders of the Jehovah's Witnesses practically made an art of it—predicting numerous events that never happened,[82] including the end of the world in the 1870s and 1914,[83] and

---

[82] See David A. Reed, *Index of Watchtower Errors* (Grand Rapids, MI: Baker Book House, 1990).

[83] *Studies in the Scriptures*, vol. 3 (Allegheny, PA: Watch Tower, 1891).

again in 1975.[84] Time after time their leaders made their predictions, and time after time they failed. And when the predicted dates passed, they'd make up some story about how what they predicted actually *did* happen but only 'in the heavenly realm' or 'invisibly.'[85] Or else they'd claim that they never actually made the prediction and that what they said had just been misinterpreted or taken too literally by others. And yet, time after time their followers believed them. No amount of truth would shake them from what they wanted to believe."

Christopher shook his head to indicate the hopelessness of any attempt to convince the KDP's followers that they were wrong. "If I postpone the march on Petra for a month, the KDP will simply make up some excuse. They'll do exactly as the leaders of the Jehovah's Witnesses did. And their followers will go on believing their every word."

What Christopher was saying made sense. As Decker thought it through, the faces of Rhoda and Tom Jr. and Rachael and Decker Donafin and all the people of Petra seemed to blur in his memory. Maybe Christopher was right; maybe he *was* just tired and old. "But we can't just—" Decker tried to think of something, some new reason, but he seemed to be running out of arguments. Still, he couldn't just give up and let the people of Petra

---

[84] "Why Are You Looking Forward to 1975?" *Watchtower,* August 15, 1968, pp. 494–501. Also, *The Truth That Leads to Eternal Life* (Brooklyn: Watch Tower, 1968), p. 95; *Awake,* October 8, 1968, pp. 13–14; and *Man's Salvation Out of the World Distress at Hand!* (Brooklyn: Watch Tower, 1975), p. 75.

[85] *Golden Age* (Brooklyn: Watch Tower, 1930), p. 503.

die. There had to be a way . . . something he had not thought of yet.

"I'm sorry we can't agree on this, Decker," Christopher said, "but I have to do what I believe is best. Now frankly, I just don't have the time to continue to discuss it." He got up and went back to his desk, leaving Decker sitting there.

Had he not turned so quickly, Christopher would have noticed the sudden look of startled recollection that swept over Decker's face, and the expression of sheer horror that followed it: horror so great that all thoughts of Petra—the whole reason he had come here—were totally eclipsed in his mind.

Decker had seen something. It was no monstrous metamorphosis such as in his dream on the plane, but it was every bit as terrifying. It was the look on Christopher's face when he said he didn't have time to discuss it. It was *only* a look, but its meaning was inescapable. Decker had seen it just once before—exactly the same expression that had been on Christopher's face all those years ago in Lebanon when he was asked about Tom.

In that instant, the universe changed.

Then he said it.

"There's something else."

With those three words, Decker crossed a line of restraint he had maintained for more than twenty years. He had advised, even argued with Christopher, but never before had he challenged him. In reality, his words could have meant anything. He simply could have let it drop. But to Decker it seemed that he was caught in a swell that he could no longer navigate but only press through.

"There's nothing more to discuss." The look had not left Christopher's face.

"I'm not talking about Petra," he said, rising from his chair to face Christopher on even ground.

"Then what?" asked Christopher, apparently unaware of the tempest in Decker's mind and heart. "What else have I done that has not met with your approval?"

Decker sensed a thinly veiled sarcasm in Christopher's voice that he had never heard before. Then suddenly, he understood why Christopher hadn't called him during all that time while he was in Derwood. Christopher no longer needed him. He had served his purpose and was no longer of any use. In truth, Christopher no longer had time for Decker.

"You were going to leave Tom Donafin," he answered.

Christopher responded with a look of complete puzzlement. "What in the world are you talking about?" he asked, his voice showing not only confusion about the relevance of Tom Donafin to the current conversation, but growing anger as well. "Leave him where?"

"When Tom shot you," Decker began, "I was standing right next to him. When I realized what he had done, I asked him why. He started to answer, but all he had time to say before he was shot was, 'He was going to leave me.'

"It didn't make any sense at the time. I thought it was just the ramblings of a lunatic. Later I became convinced that the Koum Damah Patar had brainwashed him. But when I was at Petra I had the dream again." Decker paused to breathe and calm his pounding heart. He hadn't tried to, but he was beginning to sound more and more like a prosecuting attorney about to drive home his point to the jury.

Christopher didn't like being put in this position, and it was obvious that he didn't care for Decker's tone.

"What dream?" Christopher demanded, wanting to waste no more time at this game. "What are you talking about?"

"It was the same dream I had in Lebanon."

There was a long pause while Christopher studied Decker's face in confusion. "You mean," he asked, "when I rescued you from the Hizballah? That's what this is all about?"

"That's what Tom was talking about," Decker answered. "I never told anyone else about that dream except Tom and Elizabeth. In the dream you came into my room to get me. 'It's time to go,' you said. But when I was following you out, I stopped you to ask about Tom." Decker watched Christopher for any reaction. There was none. "I asked you where he was. You knew but you didn't care. If I hadn't insisted, you would have left him there to die."

"But that was just a dream!" Christopher interrupted, his good hand outstretched, appealing to Decker's reason.

"But it *wasn't* just a dream!" Decker shot back in anger. "In New York you told me that you used astral projection to come to Lebanon to rescue me. It was you! It wasn't just a dream!"

Unable to argue the point, Christopher dropped his hand to his side.

"You came there to rescue *me! Just* me! You had no intention of rescuing Tom! You were just going to leave him there to rot away and die! That's what Tom must have realized." Christopher's disposition suddenly seemed to change. His anger and defensiveness vanished, and instead he just waited and listened. "I don't know how Tom knew it was more than just a dream, but I'm sure that's what he meant when he said you were going to leave him. Somehow, Tom knew that it wasn't just a mistake or an oversight. You were going to leave him!

"You don't really care about Humankind—about people—at all. If you did, you would never have forgotten about Tom."

Christopher's composure had now become so incongruous with the situation that Decker had to pause. Not only was he undisturbed, he almost seemed amused.

"But he wasn't a part of your plan," Decker began again haltingly, growing more and more unsure as the look of amusement on Christopher's face became more and more pronounced. "You didn't need him to carry out your plans. You only needed me." Decker stopped, the last words falling from his lips merely from the momentum of the words that had gone before.

Christopher now smiled broadly, and it became painfully obvious that he was smiling to himself and not at Decker. Decker had expected denial or anger; certainly not this.

Finally the smile became outright laughter.

"Bravo!" Christopher said at last, almost shouting. "That's pretty good, Decker! Even if it did take you twenty-three years to realize it!"

Decker was stunned. Was this an admission . . . or just ridicule?

"Frankly, Decker, arguing with you is taking more time than you're worth anymore," he said. "To tell you the truth—something I do as seldom as possible," he added and then raised his hand in mock surrender, "it never even occurred to me to rescue Tom Donafin. As you said, I was there to get *you.*" Christopher shrugged. "Why should I have cared what happened to Tom Donafin?

"Of course, at the time, I had no idea who Tom was. I thought he had been killed along with the rest of his family in an auto accident. You see," Christopher explained, "Tom Donafin was supposed to have died years before in a little late-night meeting that was arranged for his family with a drunk driver. It was a beautiful sight—blood and broken glass everywhere," he digressed. "The drunk driver wasn't even scratched. He felt so guilty about it after he sobered up that he hanged himself in his jail cell. He left a wife and two sons nearly penniless. And the best part: When he hanged himself, the guard was watching. He didn't even try to stop him. It was perfect.

"Well . . . almost perfect. I thought the whole Donafin family had died. Apparently Yahweh's minions managed to hide your friend from us all those years." Christopher shrugged off any personal responsibility for the oversight. "I had no idea who he was when I came to get you out of Lebanon.

"You know," he said, pointing his finger in the air and shaking it slowly to emphasize his syllables as a realization dawned on him, "I'll bet that's why he let you think he was dead all those years! Donafin or Saul Cohen or somebody must have realized that the best way to hide him from me was to let you think he was dead. If the two of you had stayed in regular contact after I moved in with you, sooner or later I would have realized who he was and arranged another 'accident.' "

Then another thought occurred to Christopher. "The day I was shot—earlier, in your office—was Donafin standing there with you when you told me you wanted to introduce me to an old friend of yours?"

Decker nodded a nod that was more a question than an answer.

Christopher smiled, "Yahweh wasn't taking any chances," he said. "He must have had a whole legion of angels surrounding him. I sensed something, but I didn't even see Donafin. I just assumed the friend you wanted me to meet was waiting in your office." Christopher spoke as if this was just a normal, everyday conversation. Decker was stunned and confused—not at the specifics of what he was saying—but at the fact that he was saying it at all.

Christopher either interpreted Decker's expression as a request for additional explanation or just wanted to further his agony by continuing. "You see, Tom Donafin was the last of his line, the last blood relative of Jesus—or Yeshua, or whatever you want to call him. Anyway, according to an ancient law, a blood relative of one who is murdered has the right to seek out the killer and avenge the murder. I knew that I'd be killed; that was never in question. It's in the prophecy.[86] In fact, it fit perfectly into my plan. How else could I have staged such a dramatic resurrection with the whole world watching?

[86] Revelation 13:3.

But I had someone else in mind to actually pull the trigger."

Christopher laughed a contemptible laugh. "Poor Gerard Poupardin. The pathetic fool wanted to shoot me to avenge Albert Faure, a man who had used and betrayed him whenever it suited his purposes. It didn't really matter who killed me." He shook his head with the regret of a chess player who realizes he made the wrong move. "I just wanted it to be a murder. Instead it was an execution! It's a minor point in the larger scheme of things, but I spent a lot of time setting that up!" It was clear that Christopher did not like Yahweh beating him at his own game.

Christopher regained his composure. "No matter," he said, putting the defeat behind him. "It was rather sweet irony, though, that Poupardin was so determined to kill me that when Tom Donafin robbed him of the pleasure, he turned the gun on Donafin instead.

"Oh, and in all modesty," he added with a grin, "I think timing the beginning of the madness to coincide with my death and then ending the madness when I killed John and Cohen was a master stroke. Who would have suspected that the spirit beings who appeared at my call at the Temple in Jerusalem were the same ones who had wreaked bloody carnage with the madness only moments before?"

Christopher smiled and waited for Decker to respond, and the longer he waited, the bigger his smile became.

"Then it's all true?" Decker finally managed to ask, not only in disbelief that he had been right, but even more so that Christopher was admitting it. "All the things that the KDP say about you are true! You really are the Antichrist, the son of Satan!"

"In the flesh," Christopher said triumphantly, bowing grandly, and mocking Decker. "But don't act so surprised. I've never made a secret of it. I even told you as much on the plane to Israel after my resurrection and on several occasions since then. I've been saying it all along, but it didn't seem to matter to anyone. Of course, I've always couched the truth in stories of how evil Yahweh is."

Christopher shook his head in wonder. "It's always amazed me how eager humans are to believe that line. All I have to do is draw their attention to some pretty bauble or trinket that's just beyond their reach, tell them how unfair it is that they don't have it, and that if God were really good and loving, he wouldn't keep them from having it. Money, power, sex: It all works pretty much the same. Of course the most seductive temptation for humans has always been telling them they can be their own god, or at least be equal to God. It worked with Eve in the Garden of Eden—'You will be as God,'[87] Lucifer told her. It's worked throughout the centuries. And now the very same lie has worked with the New Age for all of *Humankind.*"

"So your entire life," Decker had to force the words from his lips, "your entire life has been an act?"

"Please, Decker, let's not trivialize my accomplishments with terms like 'act.' I prefer to call it a magnificently orchestrated, brilliantly executed lie."

[87] Genesis 3:5.

"And the prophecies about you in the Bible are all true?"

"Of course," Christopher said without emotion.

"But then you must know that if you go to Petra you will lose."

"Ah, true," Christopher agreed with resignation. "But even if I do not go, it will make no difference. The time of my end has been set. It does not matter where I am. For my purposes, going to Petra is simply the most favorable of the available options. It is to Petra that Jesus will come. I will not cower in fear in some dark corner when that day arrives. I will go there to meet him! I will stand defiant at his return, and I will bring with me those I have stolen from him! I will no more *fear* him in the end than I have *served* him in the past! I will never yield! I have set myself against him, and I will defy him until the end. And thereafter, I will curse him boldly from the flames of hell!"

"But why? If you know you will end up in hell, why go through with it?"

Christopher laughed. "Call it hatred of God. Call it independence. Surely you can understand that. I simply refuse to serve. The poet John Milton understood it. He put it quite succinctly back in 1667 in *Paradise Lost:* 'Better to reign in Hell, than serve in Heav'n,' he wrote, paraphrasing the Lord Lucifer.[88] *And,* to take others with me, of course! It's really quite simple. Man was made to rule and reign with God, to love and be loved. When I take those that God had intended for him-

[88] John Milton, *Paradise Lost: A Poem Written in Ten Books* (1667), Book 1: Line 263.

self, I anger him, I enrage him, and—most important—I *hurt* him!

"Do you have any idea," Christopher said in great earnestness, truly wanting Decker to understand, "what it's like to tweak the nose of God?" Christopher threw up his hand in exhilaration at the thought. "The rush of sheer, raw power that swells through you when you watch his face and know that you—" Christopher looked back at Decker and struck the air with his clenched fist to emphasize each point "—by your will! by your power! have intentionally made God, the one who created the Universe . . . *weep!*"

Decker was lost . . . defeated. Scott Rosen and the KDP had been right about Christopher, about everything. And whether Christopher called his life an act or a lie, Decker realized that his own life had been a sham. On that backdrop nothing really mattered anymore. Still, there was one thing Decker wanted to know.

"Christopher," he said. The feel of Christopher's name on his lips, the sound of it in his ears, shook Decker with the memory of all the years he had spoken it before and been deceived. "Just one more question."

Where before Christopher had no time for Decker, his expression now indicated an eagerness to answer. He was truly enjoying this.

"Why me?" Decker asked. "Why did you pick me?"

Christopher looked at Decker, momentarily surprised by the unexpected query. Then suddenly his cheeks expanded as he pressed his lips together, trying to control his response. Giving up and yielding to the impulse, Christopher exploded into riotous, prolonged laughter.

"Can you really be so stupid?" he roared with derision. "Can you really believe that you were so important to my plans that there has to be a reason that I picked *you?* I could just as well have chosen any of at least a thousand other people." Christopher paused to wipe a tear of laughter from his eye before he continued.

"Okay," he said, trying to sound serious but enjoying this far too much to conceal it, "I'll tell you why I chose you." Christopher stopped to savor the irony. It was a joke whose punch line had waited twenty-three years for just the right moment to be told.

"You," Christopher said, and then paused, struggling to deadpan the delivery of his response, but enjoying the sound of each syllable as it rolled off his tongue, knowing the effect it would have on Decker, "you just happened . . ." Christopher laughed despite himself, "to be in the right place . . . at the right time!"

Christopher now roared with laughter so uncontrollable that he had to take hold of the back of a chair to steady himself.

Decker's body went limp. Had he the presence of mind to notice it, he would have found it quite inexplicable that his heart continued to beat under the weight of his chest as he suddenly came to understand that the sum total value of his life had amounted to nothing more than a joke for Christopher's entertainment.

Up until this moment he at least had his anger. Now even that was gone. It was not satisfied; it was just finished. Now there was nothing. Nothing had meaning. For more than two decades he had built his life around Christopher. Now, not only was that gone, snatched out from under him, it had all been a farce. Not only had he been betrayed, he had been a fool! He was a joke!

Decker's arms felt heavy and his shoulders slumped, giving the impression that he had simply curled up to die but that someone had propped him up with a stick. He stood there for a long moment, unable to move while Christopher looked on in delight.

Finally, Christopher went over to the bar and poured himself another drink. "You've been quite a project, actually," he said. "I've brought you along; given you opportunities to advance your career." Pointing with his finger while holding the drink, he elaborated, "I'm sure you remember the boy in Jerusalem who ran from behind the Wailing Wall, the boy you brought home to *Jenin* after the riot. I arranged all of that.

"Getting you taken hostage to Lebanon served two purposes. First, it got you out of the way for a few years until I was ready for you. You were starting to ask too many questions. I couldn't risk having you publish a story that might expose my origin, and I couldn't be sure that dear Uncle Harry would be able to keep you quiet. I needed you locked away for a few years." Christopher took a drink and grinned. "A minute ago you said that I had come to Lebanon only to rescue *you*. In truth, I wasn't there to *rescue* you at all. It was more like getting you out of cold storage." Christopher shrugged. "Tom Donafin was of no consequence to my plan. He could have stayed there and rotted for all I cared.

"The second purpose for having you taken hostage was that it provided a means of getting you and Jon Hansen together. Of course, there were other ways I could have arranged for you to meet him. You could have met him while working on a news story. But this way, with him rescuing you just as you were about to collapse from hunger in Lebanon, you had a couple of days together and, because of the circumstances, strong emotional ties were built.

"Actually, the toughest part was getting you to accept the job with Hansen. I almost gave up on you there, but you finally came through, thanks to the behind-the-scenes work of Robert Milner and Alice Bernley. After that, it was pretty easy. I just had to play the perfect kid and, from time to time, make up some ridiculous story about dreams I had." Christopher's only purpose in telling Decker these things was to make him hate him more. It was working.

"But you helped along the way," Christopher said as though he was sharing credit, though in fact his point was to ridicule Decker. "When you suggested the idea about requiring that everyone who took the communion also take the mark, I nearly lost it trying not to laugh. Not only did you swallow my lies hook, line, and sinker, you even cut your own bait!"

"Then what you told me about Elizabeth and Hope and Louisa being reincarnated . . . ?" Decker asked like a fighter dropping his fists and leaving himself open to be hit.

Christopher just laughed and shook his head.

"And the story about the Theatans?"

"It's amazing what people will believe," Christopher answered smugly. "I didn't make it all up, though. I adapted the name from the teachings of one of the New Age groups. Of course, they got it from me originally."

"And the televised confessions and calls for God's wrath by the fundamentalists?"

"Contrived, for the most part. Of course, there is a lunatic fringe who actually do say such things."

Decker fell silent, closing his eyes for a moment to try to endure it all. "So what now?" he asked finally, helplessly, barely managing a whisper.

"Now I prepare a brilliant speech, an inspiring plea, whipping the people of the world to a fever pitch against Yahweh. I'll issue a bold challenge, appealing to their sense of pride, their incredible propensity to overestimate their own worth, and despite both, their inconceivable willingness to sell themselves and their birthright for a little temporary gratification. I'm certain I can depend upon their willingness to believe flattery, no matter how preposterous and insincere. It's always worked in the past. Then I'll gather all of the peoples of the world, *Humankind,*" he added with a snicker, "at Meggido and I'll lead them into 'glorious battle' at Petra."

"I meant," Decker stammered, "what about me? What do you plan to do with me?"

"I know what you meant!" Christopher answered scornfully. "That's up to you. You can either take the mark or you can die."

"You're not going to kill me?"

"There's no profit in that," he said. "Except for a few special exceptions like John and Cohen or Albert Faure, I never kill anyone myself. It's much more enjoyable when someone else does it. It just heaps one more burning coal of guilt on their heads.

"So, there you have it," Christopher said. "If you'd like, you can take the mark tomorrow and live until you die—which should be about three months. Oh, but of course, we wouldn't want you to get kidnapped again or lose your way to the clinic, so I'll have UN Security assign some bodyguards to stay with you just to make sure you get there safely tomorrow. Or if you prefer, I'm sure they can squeeze you in at the guillotines and you can have your head removed before the night is out.

"Take a few minutes to think it over," he said, as he turned to go back toward his desk. Then stopping and turning back, he added in an engaging tone that seemed totally out of place, "Actually, Decker, the next few months should be quite interesting for you. You've always enjoyed new experiences. Think of it! You have the opportunity to know the feeling I've experienced since before your world began: to know that with every passing second, you're moving a little closer to eternity in hell. First you'll feel the horror and dread, and then the denial, and the anxiety, and the nightmares—if you can sleep at all. Pretty soon," he said, now sounding philosophical, "you'll come to realize that there is really only one possible response." He paused as if to give Decker a chance to realize for himself what the one possible response was. "Hate!" he said finally, standing face to face with Decker.

"You'll hate me. You'll hate everyone around you. You'll even hate yourself. But most of all, you'll hate God. After all," he explained, "he's the one who put you here in the first place.

"Think about it, Decker. You never asked to be here. You'd be better off if you'd never been born! So who deserves your hatred more than God? He stacked the deck against you right from the start!"

Christopher smiled and turned to walk away.

"And if I tell anyone?" Decker asked.

Christopher laughed a pathetic laugh. "Who would you tell? Besides, no one would believe you. Of course, if you insist on being a nuisance, I'll just have to make an exception and kill you myself." Shaking his head, he added, "Don't be stupid, Decker. Unless, of course, you're in a hurry to see hell."

He looked at Decker and laughed once more before walking back across his large office to his desk. Finishing his drink, he pressed a button that slid back a wall panel, revealing a ninety-six-inch television screen. The set was already on, muted and tuned to a satellite feed of the executions. He had apparently been watching them before Decker came in. Turning the sound back on, he sat down to watch.

At first Decker took no notice of the scene portrayed on the screen but slowly the repetitious sound of the blade awakened his attention, and he could not help but look upon the melee of blood and death. To his surprise, Christopher appeared to take little pleasure in these deaths. Instead his focus was fixed on the faces of the executioners as they led the condemned to the guillotine, positioned them to die, and then released the blade.

As Christopher watched the proceedings, Decker thought back to what Scott Rosen had said about the plagues and the beheadings and about the coming battle at Petra. As the blades continually dropped and were raised again for the next victim, Decker began to comprehend the true significance of what had happened. To this point it had been quite enough to consider his own misery. His hopes and plans of helping to build a better world and a New Age had all turned out to be a lie. The promise that he would someday be reunited with Elizabeth and his daughters had been nothing but a ruse to lure Decker forever away from them. His whole life had been wasted. He had been played for a fool and had proven himself more than worthy of that designation. And now he was only weeks away from eternity in hell. And yet, it occurred to him that there was an even worse toll for his life: He had actually had a key role in bringing on the world's destruction.

"How many?" he asked.

Christopher did not need to ask for clarification; he understood the question. "If you look in the bottom right of the screen," he said, pointing, "you can see I've got a special feed connected to this set that gives a running count. Right now it's just a few shy of 3,058,000," he answered. "The second number is the estimate of how many are left. We got off to a slow start," he said almost apologetically. "You'd be amazed at the logistics that go into something like this. And, of course, we were at a complete standstill during the darkness, but my people are working around the clock at 114 locations with 22 more coming on line by Wednesday, each with at least twenty guillotines. They assure me the job will be completed by early September."

Decker looked at the second number on the screen. "You intend to decapitate 14 million people?" Decker asked, aghast.

"Oh, I'm sure there will be a few stragglers," Christopher acknowledged, "but the police and security forces are doing a great job of rounding them up. Of course, it would have been more, but several million of them died during the plagues."

Nearly 3 billion people had already died in the wars and other disasters over the past seven years. Christopher had given the numbers in his speech. Fourteen million more would die under the blade. Another 2 billion would die in and following the battle at Petra. For those, however, death was only the beginning of their miseries, for beyond the veil of death waited damnation. Their fate had already been sealed with their rejection of Yahweh and their acceptance of the seal of Christopher's communion on their hand or forehead, a seal that Decker had first proposed.

Christopher had said he could have picked any of a thousand other people and it was probably true: It didn't have to be Decker. If someone else had been chosen, then perhaps they would have come up with the idea for the mark, or else Christopher or Milner would have proposed it. It was a part of the prophecy, so one way or another it would have happened with or without Decker. But that was not much comfort, for it had not been someone else. He had been involved from the very beginning. He looked back and could now see clearly all the times he had been seduced by the vision of Christopher's New Age into justifying whatever Christopher said and did. And though he did not yet bear the seal of the communion himself, he was no less marked, for the blood of billions was on his hands and head. Time after time he had accepted whatever Christopher said, no matter how bizarre, without questioning. Day after day he had helped Christopher build a foundation of deceit. Lie after cursed lie, Decker had been a part of it all, and he had justified it as being for the good of Humankind.

Decker's words of just a few minutes earlier came back to haunt him. "There's not a man or woman on the planet," he had said, "who hasn't been thoroughly familiarized with the message of the coming advance in the evolution of Humankind: movies, television, Internet, radio, newspapers, magazines, books, songs, plays, billboards, bumper stickers—your vision of the future is everywhere. There's not a child in school from age three and up who has not been trained in the ethics and tenets of the New Age. Even the younger ones learn the message through cartoons, toys, and games."

My God, he thought, *what have I done*?

As a child in school, Decker had read with disbelief about the atrocities of history: the Nazis in World War II, Goebbels, Goering, Hitler; the mass slaughter of seventeen million Russians by Stalin. Later there were the genocides of Pol Pot, Idi Amin, Saddam Hussein, and the like. Now as he looked at his life, he realized he was no better than any of them. True, he had not administered the torture and death himself, but he had facilitated it. All of it.

Christopher had said the only possible response was hate, but Decker felt something far worse: the crushing weight of his guilt.

While Christopher watched the executions, Decker winced as each drop of the blade gave bloody demonstration of the result of his sin. Finally, but unexpectedly, his guilt found its voice in anger. There was hatred in his heart—Decker could not deny it—but it did not feel quite the way Christopher had described it. It filled his lungs with the frigid air of defiance. There was, he thought, yet something to be said.

"Christopher," he said softly, almost whispering.

"Yes," Christopher answered calmly, as though nothing the least bit unpleasant had occurred.

"What's hell like?" he asked.

Christopher muted the television and turned his chair to face him. "I'm afraid it's every bit as bad as you've heard," he said in a consoling tone. There was no real sympathy in his voice. It was just that he knew, for the moment, that there was no way left to hurt the old man. "Of course, I've never actually been there. It's just an ignorant myth that hell is Lucifer's home. That's a bit like suggesting that a criminal's headquarters was in prison because that's where he wound up at the end of his career.

"But as far as what it's like," he continued, very seriously, staring off into space as if he could actually see it there before him, "I believe it's a good deal like the darkness of the last plague . . ." He paused, revealing his significant discomfort with the thought, but finally concluded, ". . . only a lot hotter."

He had ended his description with a bit of dark humor, but there was something else in his voice. For just that brief moment, Decker could sense Christopher's terror.

"And you'll be there, too?" Decker asked.

Christopher was roused from his vision of hell by Decker's voice and now smiled enthusiastically. Rising from his chair, he walked back over to where Decker still stood. "That's the spirit!" he said, goading him on. "You want to see me in hell right alongside you!

"Vengeance!" he said.

"Anger!" he prodded.

"Hatred!" he urged.

"You're catching on faster than I expected! You'll fit right in!

"Oh . . ." Christopher paused, "but don't get your hopes up too high. I'll be there with you, but, well, in Lucifer's kingdom there are a number of different levels—ranks, I guess you might call them. And with rank comes power; in this case, the power to be feared and hated. And I'm afraid you're nowhere near high enough in the pecking order to do anything to me."

Decker did not respond.

"Does that make you hate me even more?" Christopher asked in a condescending voice.

"Yes," Decker answered truthfully. But it was not his hatred that he was thinking about.

"Good!" Christopher responded, delighted.

"When we get there," Decker continued slowly toward his point, "and when you're looking out over the flames of hell at all of those you've brought with you . . ."

"Yes?" Christopher pressed.

"You won't have any trouble finding me in the crowd."

Christopher laughed a hearty, cruel laugh and shook his head at Decker's attempt to distinguish himself even in hell. "Why?" he asked. "Will you be shaking your fist at me? Will you be shouting your curses at me?"

Decker didn't answer.

"Well, you'll have to be yelling pretty loud to be heard over the billions of others!" he said with a caustic chuckle. "You don't get it, do you?" he asked. "That's one of the few things I can actually look forward to. Every time someone curses me for their pain it will be confirmation that I have accomplished what I set out to do. I'll love it. I will thrive on it. And, you know, it's really ironic," he said, truly amazed and cheered at this fact, "funny really, but even though it will be obvious that I enjoy their curses, it won't stop the damned from cursing me. They'll be so enraged, they'll just do it all the more." He shook his head at Decker's feeble attempt and started back toward his desk.

But Decker wasn't through. "No," he said, pausing to reflect. "I won't be cursing you."

He dropped his eyes to the floor for a moment as his guilt briefly overpowered his anger. Biting his lower lip, he raised his eyes again and stared defiantly at Christopher, who had come back and now stood directly in front of him. Christopher waited, unsure what Decker had in mind, but eager for whatever amusement he was about to offer.

"You're not the one who's responsible for me going to hell," Decker said. "I am." Christopher was unimpressed by Decker's realization and rolled his eyes in disgust.

"So, when we get there," Decker continued, "if you ever decide you want to look me up, you won't have long to look."

He paused to take a final rebellious, recalcitrant breath. His moment was here. It was not much to make up for a lifetime that had been reduced to a bad joke, but it was all he had, probably all he ever would have that could be put on the other side of the scales. He would hold on to it for as long as he could. Every second he stalled put Christopher another second closer to hell, and that in itself seemed worthwhile.

Christopher waited.

Decker's stare grew surprisingly cold and steady. Finally, when he knew Christopher would wait no longer, he spoke. "I'll be the one down on my knees among the flames of hell, thanking God for giving me exactly what I deserve!"

Decker's words were slow and crisp and firm, but they had not been shouted. Still, in the sudden silence that followed, they seemed to echo through the languid air and shake the entire room.

Christopher's teeth clenched and his nostrils flared, and Decker saw the muscles in his neck tighten like bands of steel. Christopher's burning gaze felt as though he was looking right into Decker's soul. He was.

In a moment, Christopher seemed to find what he was looking for, and he did not like what he saw: Decker had not just said this to enrage him. He actually meant it.

Christopher breathed in deeply and exhaled audibly like a bull set to charge. His eyes were flames. His face was red, and his body stiffened and actually shook with rage.

Decker stood motionless, unable to take much pleasure in Christopher's reaction because of the awful weight of his own guilt. Christopher's brow was tightened in anger, the likes of which Decker had never seen in any man. His face was flush with fury. And then he did something that seemed very strange to Decker. He started to turn to the left as if he were going to simply leave.

Was he just going to turn back to the televised executions?

As Christopher's upper body turned, Decker assumed his feet would follow, but Christopher's feet were planted firmly on the floor. Swiftly, he raised his right arm up and to the left, his hand forming a fist. Decker held his ground in anticipation of a backhanded blow delivered against his face with Christopher's full weight. He determined not to move or flinch. He would not give Christopher the pleasure of seeing him cower. Then suddenly and totally out of place, his eye caught a strange glint of light. It was just above Christopher's head at a point about a foot and a half beyond his hand, which was now hidden from Decker's view by his leftward-turned body.

Christopher raised his heel and pivoted on the ball of his right foot, and then, turning with his full force and speed toward Decker, he straightened his arm at the elbow. Decker instinctively tightened his jaw in anticipation of Christopher's blow.

But, strangely, there was that glint of light again, and it was moving in perfect synchronization with Christopher's clenched fist.

As his fist came closer, Decker was suddenly dumbfounded by what he saw. It appeared that Christopher would actually miss him, his fist passing a good eighteen inches short of Decker's face. Christopher even seemed to be leaning back, as if to increase the certainty of a miss.

Then he realized Christopher had something in his hand. And again there was that strange glint of light.

Suddenly, Decker realized what it was.

From thin air . . . from nowhere, Christopher had drawn a brightly polished, double-edged sword and he was swinging it with incredible speed and all his might toward Decker's neck.

The entire incident took only a fraction of a second. There was nothing he could do. There was no time to duck or even blink. The blade was only inches from his neck. Swiftly it sliced through the air toward its mark. In an instant it was there, its cold edge pressing against his skin just before it penetrated.

Helplessly, Decker watched Christopher's hand, clutched tightly around the sword's grip, as it passed almost effortlessly before him, propelling the blade through his neck. The muffled crack of metal against bone as it separated his spinal column between the fourth and fifth vertebrae barely slowed the blade in its bloody path through skin and vein and muscle and sinew and nerve fiber.

Then it was through.

Decker's head had been completely severed from his body, and Christopher followed through with his stroke. Surprisingly, it had all been relatively painless.

Decker felt himself toppling as his head tipped and rolled to his left and off his shoulders. The room appeared to spin as his head tumbled freely to the floor. His forehead hit first, causing Decker to wince in pain as his head bounced and rolled, landing finally on his left ear. At that moment, Decker's body crumpled to the floor beside him.

From start to finish it had all taken little more than two seconds. In his last moments of consciousness, as the blood drained from his brain, Decker could see Christopher standing there, his rage satisfied as he smiled down at him, the sword raised above his head as Decker's blood spilled over its hilt and dripped down upon his hand. Beside Decker's head, but out of his line of sight, the blood pouring from his headless torso spurted erratically as his heart convulsed and stopped. Soon the flow would slow until it was drawn out by the force of gravity alone. The same was true of Decker's head. Because it had been severed from the heart, there was no pressure forcing the blood out, as would be the case with a normal wound; the only force draining blood from his head was gravity. The result, as Decker realized firsthand, was that a few seconds of life and consciousness remained after decapitation.[89] Even in death, Decker's curiosity had found some distraction.

"I was wrong, Decker. That was more fun than I realized!" Christopher said as he walked away. "I'll see you in hell!"

Decker could feel the blood draining from his brain and watched the room grow dark as he began to lose consciousness. At least it was quick, he thought.

Then Decker heard something . . . a voice. With the loss of blood to his brain, he had no idea where it came from, but he was certain it was talking to him. Then he remembered something and the realization hit him like a freight train. Despite his condition, despite his disorientation, no other thought in his life had ever been clearer. He knew what he had to do, and he could not help but muse (if his body were still a part of him, he would have laughed out loud) that it should come to this: Seconds from death, his head severed from his body, and yet he realized that it was for this very day and hour and moment that he had been born.

---

[89] Historically and in countries where decapitation is currently practiced, e.g., Saudi Arabia, it has been reported that the eyes and mouths of victims sometimes continue to move after beheading. The most notable case is that of Anne Boleyn, who after she was beheaded at the order of Henry VIII, continued to move her lips, silently uttering her dying prayer for several seconds. It is calculated that the human brain has sufficient oxygen for metabolism to persist for about seven seconds after beheading.

At once Christopher stopped dead in his tracks.

"Nooooooo!" he screamed, his voice exploding in a sound so terrifying that its source could only have been deep beneath the gates of hell. If Decker had still been able to hear, he would have recognized the voice from years before when he had been at a point near insanity. If he had still been able to see, as Christopher turned back and raised his sword again, he would have seen for the first time the true face of the man he had brought up as his own son. All the evil works and imaginings of mortal man and demons could not have shown more darkly than did the hatred upon this true face of death.

Charging to where he had left Decker's truncated head and body, Christopher grasped the sword, dropped to one knee, and with all his strength brought down the edge of the blade squarely, just in front of Decker's right ear, splitting his skull from side to side with a sharp crack and spilling his brains out upon the floor.

"Pull his hair!"

The Signs

18

"WHAT?" Christopher barked in response to the knock at his door. Robert Milner cautiously entered to find Christopher still seething, his muscles twitching with rancor.

"You said you wanted to see me . . . ," Milner began a bit sheepishly, even before spotting the decapitated remains on the floor.

Christopher took several deep breaths to compose himself. Still, the anger in his voice was unmistakable. "I want the World Health Organization, the military, the security forces, and the police to do whatever it takes to round up every last follower of Yahweh. I don't want *any* to escape—not one!"

Milner heard Christopher's words, but his attention was now clearly focused on the carnage at his feet. "What happened?" he asked. There was just enough of Decker's face showing for Milner to be relatively certain it was him.

Except for a glare, Christopher did not answer. "And tell the guards the prisoners must suffer before they die in order for the spiritual cleansing to be complete. They can do whatever they want to them. Beat them! Humiliate them! Rape them! Torture them! Mutilate them! But I don't want to see any more of them smiling before they die!"

"I'll take care of it immediately," Milner answered obediently, finally giving Christopher his full attention.

"And get someone up here to clean up this mess," Christopher scowled, finally acknowledging the existence of Decker's remains.

"I'll call Security. I'll tell them he attacked you," Milner said, and then looking at the two cleaved pieces of Decker's head separated by at least a yard of bloody carpeted floor, he added, "but I'm not sure how to explain the . . . uh . . . circumstances."

"Just get someone up here that we can count on to keep his mouth shut!" Christopher said, momentarily losing his composure and slamming his fist on the desk.

Milner nodded nervous agreement. "I'll tell him to dispose of the body at one of the involuntary life completion facilities," he said as he reached for the phone to make the call. Then he remembered something and stopped. "I talked to Jackie Hansen as she was leaving a little while ago. She knows Decker was here."

Christopher shook his head, discounting Milner's concern. "Jackie Hansen is mine," he said. "She's always been mine."

**Friday, July 17, 4 N.A.
Central Iraq**

Three miles north of Jadad, Iraq, along the banks of the Euphrates River, a small team of civil engineers completed the final steps to close the massive water gate and thus divert the flow of the great river through the Wadi Ghazila to the lake called Mileh Tharthâr. No one on the team was sure why they had been given this assignment. The gate had originally been put here to control flooding, but there was no risk of that at this time of year. The rainy season would not start for at least another month. If the gate remained closed for long, navigation farther down the river toward Babylon would become impossible. But there was nothing in the order that said when the gate should be reopened, only that it was to be closed. The order gave no reason for any of it. It said only to do it, and so they did.

Friday, July 24, 4 N.A.
Chongqing, China

Su Lien Chu finished her bath and began to dry herself, taking extra care not to irritate the numerous painful sores that scarred her body. As she stood naked before her mirror, she shook her head in disgust at the sheer ugliness of the open wounds. The largest formed a rough circle that had grown to about six inches in diameter at the base of her neck and spread out onto her right breast. "I hate you!" she said in her native dialect as she looked toward heaven, and began to weep. Holding her face in her hands until she was composed, she wiped the tears with the backs of her hands. When she looked in the mirror again she averted her eyes to try not to look at the large lesion. Nonetheless, she could not help but see that there had been a change: The sore seemed to be smaller. Staring in wide-eyed disbelief, she held her hand up to the sore to get a rough measure. It was clearly smaller, and she soon realized that so were all the other sores on her body.

It was absurd, but with nothing to lose, she decided to test for a connection. "I hate you," she said again, this time in a clinical manner without much feeling. There was no apparent change. "I hate you!" she yelled emphatically. Now the change was immediate; the sores shrank before her eyes. That was proof enough. Shaking her fist heavenward, she cursed, "I hate you, God! I hate you! I hate you!" Yelling as loud as she could, her eyes twinkled with delight as she watched the ulcerous maledictions diminish and finally disappear altogether.

❑

From a few similar events word spread quickly of the cure and within hours the reports reached the international news media. At about 2:00 P.M. Babylonian time, Robert Milner released a statement confirming that this was, indeed, the first of the three signs Christopher had promised. "As we curse Yahweh," Milner said in his release, "we take away his control over the earth. The most immediate result is the healing of our own sores. But as we join our voices," the statement continued, "and unite in our cry of liberation, we set in motion the greater process that will lead to Yahweh's ultimate downfall and to our own glorious ascendancy. We must curse him unceasingly, even when our sores are gone. We must join as one voice, continuing our defiance of the tyrant, and carry that defiance as our banner and our shield into battle against Yahweh and our enemies in Petra until all Humankind is free."

Milner's statement concluded with the promise that the second sign would follow in one week and the third, one week after that.

Friday, July 31, 4 N.A.

As morning rolled across the face of the planet and the people of the world awoke in turn, no one had long to wonder about the second sign. If the sudden and over-whelming feeling of strength and vitality were not enough to convince them, it took only one look in the mirror to confirm its reality. Five, ten, fifteen years of youth had been restored to older people in a single night. Pounds of useless fat had simply melted away, leaving the beneficiaries trim and strong. Those already in good health sensed new power rushing through them. A general outbreak of health, energy, and stamina, far exceeding what had resulted even from the communion, filled the people with the assurance that what Christopher had promised was true and gave them hope of victory over their foes in the coming battle at Petra.

Thursday, August 7, 4 N.A.
Petra

Chaim and Rose Levin walked the steep path up the mountain called Umm Al Biyara, from which they could view most of Petra. Below them, the rows and columns of tents, set off by interwoven strips of garden, formed a huge quilt pattern that seemed to stretch on forever.

Scattered throughout the lush valley, groves of fruit trees offered their harvest to all who came to pick. Bisecting Petra from east to west, the crystal clear waters of the Wadi Mousa flowed into their ringed refuge, directed there through an ancient tunnel cut through the mountain. And in the morning, they were sure, the life-sustaining manna would again settle upon their camp, just as it had six mornings each week for the past three and a half years. Neither Chaim nor Rose had said much since they set out on their trek—ostensibly for their evening walk—but both had the same thing in mind.

"It's all happening just as they said," Chaim whispered, as much to himself as to his wife as they reached the end of their journey and stopped to rest. "All of this," he said with a broad wave of his hand over the valley below, "the plagues, the extermination of the Christians. And soon, no doubt," he said nodding, "the armies of the world will be at our door."

Farnborough, England
(south of London)

Ian Wilder sat on the bare wooden floor leaning against his assigned bunk in the World War II vintage barracks. In his lap sat one of the four books he had been given to read about the New Age. After three weeks of waiting with literally nothing else to occupy his time, he decided to try to read one of them in earnest, instead of just flipping through the pages. Three weeks before he had been assured that this was not a prison and that he would only be here long enough for his paperwork to be out-processed and then he'd be returned to fulfill a useful role in society. He had taken the communion and the mark of his own free will, they reminded him, and that meant he was a citizen of the New Age, with all the associated rights and privileges. It did not matter, they had told him at the time, that he had made the choice only minutes before he was scheduled to die; only minutes, he remembered, before his wife——refusing to listen to reason and just too stubborn to see logic——had submitted to her own death. It was just as well, he supposed: She never would have let go of her old religious beliefs and never would have been happy in the New Age. Still, he was glad that he had not had to watch her die.

It all seemed like a dream now. In a single day they had been betrayed by his brother, arrested, loaded into the back of a cattle truck, and sent to be executed. When they arrived they were taken to a large holding cell and crammed in with a hundred others to wait. Next to them, another cell was being steadily emptied as its occupants were taken to the guillotine. There simply wasn't time to torture everyone as Milner had ordered and still keep to the quotas, so on the wall in front of the cells, television screens were showing close-ups of the guillotines and scenes of various prisoners, usually young boys and girls, being brutally beaten, sodomized, raped, and mutilated by guards before being taken to their deaths. The floor of the cell was puddled in urine, and the stench mingled with that of excrement and sweat, making the air almost unbreathable. Music blared over the prison's speaker system at ear-splitting volume to drown out any praying or singing of religious songs. Ian covered his ears but it offered only minor relief.

When the other cell was emptied, the guards came to Ian's cell and began taking those nearest the door. The executions progressed so rapidly that in minutes only about half the prisoners remained. At about this time, another truckload of people arrived and were put in the other cell to wait. Ian stayed close to his wife, though he could not help but feel resentment that she had gotten them into this by insisting that they not take the communion. Soon the guards came and took him and his wife and eight others from the cell. Going down a series of long corridors, the music finally faded and, though their ears were still ringing, they could now begin to make out the crack of the falling guillotine blades. The sound became more distinct as they were taken out a door into a poorly lit exterior passageway.

The air was heavy and putrid as, turning a corner, they came into the open courtyard where the decapitations were taking place. The scene was overpowering, and Ian's wife stumbled and nearly passed out. Several in their group vomited. Three rows of six guillotines each dropped head after head after head into blood-spattered gray-green plastic barrels until they could hold no more. Bodies were rolled or heaved by blood-soaked brawny men onto conveyors that deposited them unceremoniously into waiting dump trucks. Here and there, bodies that had missed their mark on the conveyor or heads that had bounced and rolled free from the overfull barrels were left where they fell until a convenient time for removal could be found. The cement floor of the courtyard was sloped with a drain in the center, but the blood poured so quickly from the victims' bodies it made a pool several inches deep and formed a continuous whirlpool that emitted a sickening sucking sound over the drain.

From four other doors, Ian could see other prisoners being led in. Apparently, the holding cells he had seen were just two of many in the prison. Ian could not believe that the number was so high. From the televised executions (which, unlike the direct satellite feed to Christopher's office, did not have a running tally) he had the impression that no more than a few hundred beheadings had taken place throughout all of England, and perhaps twenty thousand had occurred worldwide. At the current rate, he was certain that number would be exceeded at this one facility in a single day. He remembered watching the first one on television. The condemned was a particularly vocal fundamentalist from the States, a man who was admired by Ian's wife, but whom Ian had long thought the world would be better off without. The second and third had come a few days later. Ian was not familiar with these men, but they were said to hold beliefs similar to the first. The executions began to occur more often after that, and while it was now possible to watch the bloodletting from somewhere in the world any hour of the day, the novelty had quickly worn away and few paid much attention unless someone famous was to die.

What Ian Wilder could not have known was just how orchestrated the televised executions had been. Secretary-General Christopher Goodman had personally directed that the number should appear small in the beginning and increase incrementally until the full extent of the daily slaughter was shown. Just as in ancient Rome, it took time for some to build up a tolerance, and for others to build up an appetite, for the spectacle of so many deaths. And that, after all, was the real purpose for televising the butchery: that in their approval or at least in their tolerance, all were culpable, all were responsible, all shared guilt with the executioners— and with Christopher.

"Will you take the communion and the mark?" one of the guards asked Ian.

Between the shock at what he saw and the ringing in his ears, Ian barely heard the guard. "What?" he asked, and then realizing what the guard must have said, he nodded his head eagerly. "Yes! Yes!" he answered. From the corner of his eye he could see his wife's look of alarm.

"No! No!" she pleaded.

"Yes! I want the mark!" he insisted as they pulled her hands away, breaking her hold on him.

That was the last time he saw her. The guard took him to a clinic in the prison and the communion and mark were administered within minutes. He was then put in a van with others who had made the same choice and brought to this old military base and assigned to these barracks.

Now after three weeks the only reality he knew was the barracks, and he wondered if they'd ever get out. He had heard a rumor that someone in one of the other barracks had been told by someone else that orders had come through to move everyone out in the morning, but he had heard the same rumor two nights before, and still they waited.

Friday, August 8, 4 N.A.

This was it. A week had passed and now finally it was the day of the third sign. No one knew for sure what it was to be, but it promised to be big. Excitement was everywhere. The media was filled with predictions and guesses of what the sign would be, but even the psychics were not sure. Christopher had intentionally hidden it and even the best psychics could not—dared not—look beyond the veil to see the secret that lay there. But now it was Friday and soon the mystery would be revealed and the whole world would know.

The signs—both the fulfillment of the first two and the anticipation of the third—had had their desired effect. Not only did they give a foretaste of the promised magnificence to come, they also served by their contrast as a constant reminder of the suffering and plagues that had preceded. And together they served to focus attention on what Christopher said must be done at Petra so that even greater suffering would not follow.

Babylon

At exactly noon Debbie Sanchez, formerly Decker Hawthorne's second in command and now his replacement, came into the crowded briefing room. In her hand she carried a folder. "I have a statement from the secretary-general," she said as she took her place at the lectern and opened the folder.

" 'At its completion,' " she began reading, " 'the New Age will see the evolution of Humankind into pure spirit energy. In this form, matter will no longer place limits on our abilities. As evidence of what is to come, the third sign will be telekinetic abilities for all Humankind who have taken the communion and the mark. These abilities will not be fleeting, as were the psychic abilities that many experienced over the past three and a half years. Instead, they will be permanent and will grow stronger with time.

" 'Of necessity,' " she continued, " 'these capabilities will begin on a small scale so that Humankind will be able to adjust and deal with this power in a controlled fashion. Soon, however, as we learn to use the power wisely, it will increase until, ultimately, no power in the universe will be able to stand against it.' "

Debbie Sanchez closed the folder and looked up to answer questions. The brevity of the statement caught most in the room off guard. "Is that the whole statement?" one reporter asked without waiting to be recognized.

Another reporter apparently had the same question, and though he did not speak or even give second thought to his desire to look at Debbie Sanchez's folder, suddenly and to his great surprise, his wish was fulfilled as the folder flew from the lectern and into his hands. For a moment the room, as well as the millions who watched the briefing on television, fell silent until the reporter, in comic fashion attempting to appear unruffled, looked in the folder and answered the first reporter's question. "That's all," he said.

Suddenly, the folder flew again, this time back to Debbie Sanchez, who seemed to understand the power and showed relative comfort with its exercise. "Thank you for the demonstration," she said as she set the folder back down on the lectern and held it there with her hand.

The room exploded with questions, but before any could be answered other reporters began to experiment on their own, raising chairs off the ground, holding microphones suspended, one raising himself several feet into the air. "I wouldn't try that just yet," Debbie Sanchez said to the airborne journalist. "You'll wind up with a whopper of a headache if you're not careful."

"How long will this last?" a reporter shouted, not taking Christopher's written statement at face value.

"As the secretary-general's statement said," Sanchez answered, "it's permanent."

"And the power will grow stronger with time?"

"Yes, as you learn to use the power, it will increase. But you must use it responsibly, with forethought, not haphazardly."

"Is this the power that will be used to defeat the KDP at Petra?"

"Yes," Debbie Sanchez answered.

If Thy Right Hand Offend Thee

19

Thursday, August 27, 4 N.A. Petra

FOR THREE DAYS Chaim Levin, the high priest of Israel, had not eaten or drunk anything. Nor had he spoken. That in itself was not unusual for a rabbi seeking to know God's will, and so he was left alone to meditate and pray. Even his wife, Rose, did not disturb him.

No one wondered what he prayed about. They were as aware as he was of what was happening in the world outside Petra; no one with a radio or television could have missed it. The signs promised by Christopher were coming to pass, and very soon the armies of the world would assemble to march on this place of God's provision. Levin's followers in Petra wanted to know God's answer as much as the high priest did.

On the third day at about noon Chaim Levin rose to his feet, broke his fast, and bathed. He then called for Samuel Newberg, his assistant and confidant. Newberg was already waiting, having been notified by one of the common priests that Levin had ended his fast.

"Sam, I want to speak to the leader of the KDP," he said straight away.

Newberg looked confused. "Rabbi, I . . . uh . . . I don't think . . ."

Chaim Levin nodded reassuringly; he knew his request might be a bit surprising. "It's all right, Sam, just bring him to me." Noticing the expression on Newberg's face, a thought occurred to him. "Unless you don't think he'll come."

"No, it's not that. It's just that, well . . . I don't think they *have* a leader."

This was a possibility that Levin had not considered. He frowned, struck by how little he really knew about the other residents of Petra. Still, he wanted to talk with someone who could speak for the KDP and in their behalf. "Is there no one who is pre-eminent among them?" he asked.

"Not since the deaths of John and Saul Cohen," Newberg answered. The high priest looked perplexed, and Newberg blurted out the only suggestion he could think of. "I have heard that Cohen had a son," he said, immediately regretting the suggestion as he realized he had no idea how to contact Cohen's son.

The high priest stroked his beard as he quickly pondered the option. The idea had merit. "I would like to speak with him," he said.

Jerusalem

The Resistance in Jerusalem existed for one purpose only: to assist those who wanted to flee to Petra. As such their usefulness was nearly spent. It had been a month since anyone from outside the country had come through

Israel on their way to Petra. Only a few in Israel did not bear Christopher's mark, and most of them were part of the Resistance. With their work completed, the leaders of the Resistance gathered at an abandoned kibbutz outside Jerusalem to plan their own escape to Petra. There to meet with them was Benjamin Cohen, son of Saul Cohen, and a member of the KDP. When the meeting concluded, Cohen's long-time friend, Jim Carp, asked Cohen to wait. When everyone else had gone, Carp said he had someone he wanted Cohen to meet.

"Who is it?" Cohen asked.

"My brother, Asaph," Carp answered.

Cohen smiled in surprise. "As long as I've known you, I didn't even know you had a brother. Has he just arrived in Israel?"

"No," Carp answered. His voice revealed discomfort. "He's been in Jerusalem for several years."

"Why have I never met him?"

"Well, it's possible you have. Actually, he changed his last name when he first came to Israel."

"Really?" Cohen began, but before he could finish, Carp's guest came in.

Cohen was stunned. He looked back and forth between Carp and the other man. It seemed beyond belief but before him stood Asaph ben Judah, Mayor of Jerusalem, a man who had served for the last three and a half years as a puppet of the UN occupation government, a man who on every occasion had served as Christopher's pawn in the region. "You have betrayed us," Cohen told Carp.

"No," Carp insisted.

"Your brother is Asaph ben Judah?" Cohen exclaimed incredulously. The resemblance was less than obvious.

"He's changed his mind!" Carp said. "He realizes he's been wrong." Somehow talking about ben Judah in the third person, as though he were not there with them, made the conversation at least a little more endurable.

"He's changed his mind?" Cohen repeated, spitting out Carp's words as if they were some vile poison. "He's changed his mind!" The idea was preposterous.

"Yes, Mr. Cohen," ben Judah said, finally joining the conversation, "I have. I realize that I've been wrong, as do many of the people of Jerusalem."

"Well, that's all very nice," Cohen said contemptuously. "But I'm afraid you're a little too late." Cohen cast his eyes toward ben Judah's right hand and Christopher's number, which marked it. "You made your choice! You could have resisted. You could have left with those who went to Petra. You could have gone into hiding like your brother." Cohen looked back at Jim Carp, still in disbelief that the two men were related. "But you chose to go along with Christopher Goodman. Even after he defiled the Temple and destroyed the tablets of the law; even when he set up his image on the wall of the Temple, which was clearly the abomination that the prophet Daniel warned about;[90] still you went along! You even turned against your own people, betraying them to United Nations executioners if they refused to worship the image. How many have died because of you?"

Asaph ben Judah sighed and clenched his teeth. He did not answer the question. It did not need an answer.

[90] Daniel 9:27.

Even one death was too many, and in truth he did not know the number. "All that you have said is true. I have done all these things, and I realize it's probably too late for me. But the others—"

"You heard the angel's warning," Cohen said. "They all heard it: Anyone who receives the mark will drink of the wine of God's fury and will be tormented with burning sulfur forever. There will be no rest for those who worship the beast and his image, or for anyone who receives the mark of his name," he said, paraphrasing the angel's words.

"But there must be something that can be done. Most of these people never really rebelled against God. They took the mark only because if they had not, they would have lost everything."

"And so they have," Cohen responded. "They traded away their birthright as God's chosen people for the sake of their possessions, just as Esau traded his birthright to Jacob for a little food."[91]

Cohen's response was not unexpected, but that made it no less difficult for ben Judah to bear. "Please, there must be something."

"Even if I wanted to help you, there is nothing I can do. You've taken the mark and, as the angel warned, you will drink of the wine of God's fury. There is nothing in what the angel said, or anywhere in the Bible, to suggest that you can now change your mind. Just as Esau could not regain his birthright, neither can you or the others that you represent."

"But will you not at least pray for us?" pleaded ben Judah.

[91] Genesis 25:29–34.

"I cannot pray for the enemies of God," Cohen shot back.

"But we do not wish to be his enemies."

There was sincerity in ben Judah's voice and in his eyes. For a long moment Cohen silently studied his face. "No," he said finally.

"I beg you to at least pray and ask God if there is anything that can be done."

"I'm sorry," he said, his voice now showing at least a hint of regret mingled with his loathing.

"But there must be something."

"There isn't." His words had been final, but then something occurred to him. It startled him and it was obvious to the others in the room.

"What?" asked Jim Carp.

Benjamin Cohen shook his head, dumbfounded. It was absurd, he thought. But then perhaps it was not.

"Please, what is it?" ben Judah urged.

Cohen was not ready to answer, but he made an attempt to explain. "I do not know if this is from God or if it is only a random thought that has passed through my mind."

"Please, tell us."

"No," Cohen answered. "But I *will* pray about it."

"May I wait while you pray?" ben Judah asked.

"If you wish. But I do not know how long it will be."

"I will wait."

Jim Carp showed Benjamin Cohen to a room where he would not be interrupted, and then returned to wait with his brother.

❑

Two hours passed before Cohen returned. His expression gave no hint that God had provided him an answer. Ben Judah did not ask; he was afraid of what Cohen's response might be. Nevertheless, the question was obvious on his face.

Cohen shook his head. "God has not chosen to answer me," he said finally. "I still do not know if this is from God or from my own imagination, and he has not seen fit to reveal it to me."

"Please tell me," ben Judah pleaded.

"I don't think you will like the answer."

Ben Judah waited silently.

"You must understand, what I say is not by God's command, but by his permission. It may not be from God at all; it may be just my own wishful thinking."

"I understand."

"And you must also understand, if you choose to accept what I am about to tell you, it is not your action that will save you. God's forgiveness cannot be earned or bought, lest anyone should be able to boast. God's forgiveness has been purchased at the price of his son's own life. If you do what I am about to suggest, it is not your deed that will save you, rather it is because he has already saved you that you will do this. Still, I do not know how it is possible that you, bearing the mark, could be saved."

"God showed his love for us in this," ben Judah said, paraphrasing from the fifth chapter of the book of Romans, "that while we were still sinners, Messiah died for us."[92]

92 See Romans 5:8.

Cohen studied ben Judah, amazed that he could quote the Bible at all, much less find an appropriate verse from the New Testament. "Perhaps then you also know the verse in Matthew," Cohen replied, " 'If thy right hand offend thee, cut it off.' "[93]

---

[93] Matthew 5:30, KJV.

20

The Demonstration

**Friday, August 28, 4 N.A.
Farnborough, England**

"EVERYBODY UP!"

Ian Wilder shielded his eyes from the bright barracks light and quickly got out of bed so as to not risk the wrath of the guards.

"Up!" the guard shouted again, as he stomped toward one of the bunks whose occupant was known to be a very sound sleeper.

Ian was already half dressed.

The guard stood beside the bunk of the sleeping man and smiled sadistically down at him. Then grabbing the edge of the bed, he threw it over, toppling both upper and lower bunks and the man to the floor. Having witnessed this event several times before, the woman from the upper bunk had moved well out of the way as soon as the guard approached.

It was still dark outside, without even a hint of dawn. Ian could only guess at the time. No one in the barracks had a watch. Every bit of their personal property had been confiscated when they were arrested. All that most of them had was one change of clothes and the four books on the New Age. Their only currency was the sexual favors they might do for the guards, for which they would be given some extra portion of food or a piece of soap or some bit of information or rumor from the outside.

Perhaps they were finally leaving, Ian thought. The guard quickly confirmed his assumption. "Everybody get your stuff," he said as he headed for the door. "The trucks will be here to take you home in fifteen minutes."

A cheer went up from the whole barracks and people started shaking each other's hands and slapping each other on the back. Ian Wilder slipped through the celebratory crowd and made his way to the latrine.

◻

With only one brief stop for gas, the truck had been on the road for six hours, including passing through the Chunnel beneath the English Channel. None of the more than a hundred men and women crammed into the back of the truck had any idea where they were or where they were going but it was obvious that they were not, as the guard had told them, going home. The truck had no windows, and air was circulated through a beveled system that let in no light. The only illumination came from two fixtures in the ceiling. A third light had gone out when they hit a bump shortly after leaving the camp. The only facilities were crude toilets placed at each end of the truck over small holes in the floor from which the waste fell and through which came their only view of the outside.

They had had no breakfast before they left, and all were growing very hungry. Despite his hunger and the crowded conditions, Ian felt himself drifting off to sleep. When he awoke, he had no idea whether he had been asleep for only minutes or hours. Apparently they had reached their destination, for the truck had stopped and from his position near the door he could hear voices outside and the sound of the door being unlatched.

"Everyone out!" a very masculine woman's voice called in a French accent.

Ian was one of the first off the truck. He looked around as he got out but was unable to determine their location. Something about the place looked or perhaps felt like the region around Dijon and Mulhouse near the French border with Switzerland and Germany, though he could not have said why he thought so. Wherever they were, they were definitely on another military facility, though this one was far more modern than the one they had left in England.

Ian and the others were herded around to the front of the truck and told to make two lines. As the fresh outside air replaced the stuffy air from the truck in his lungs, the pungent smell of human sweat and unbathed bodies was replaced by the delightful aroma of food cooking. Directly in front of him was a building from which the flavorful smells came. It was, he hoped, their goal—a mess hall.

❑

Being one of the first in line, Ian was able to load his plate high and he eagerly ate everything. Quiet conversation was permitted but other than questions and guesses about where they were and where they were going, no one seemed to have much to say. This was not unusual. Over the past several weeks in the barracks no one had talked much. A few had spoken of their hatred for those who had betrayed them—friends, neighbors, relatives. But no one spoke of what they had seen—the horror of the executions—though the frequent screams and crying in the night suggested that all had been witness to similar events. And no one *ever* talked about the ones they had left behind—husbands, wives, children—when at the last moment, they like Ian, had accepted the communion rather than accompany their loved ones in death.

As Ian drank down the last of a glass of milk he felt a firm tap on his shoulder. Looking around, a guard motioned toward the building's back door, and then moved on, repeating the silent procedure as others finished their meals. Ian followed the guard's direction and was taken outside to a fenced yard and allowed to walk around until about twenty others joined him. The guards then led the group through a gate and around to the front of the building where the truck still sat. They did not stop at the truck, however, but continued down the road and toward a cluster of buildings about a quarter-mile away.

Continuing past the buildings, they came to a parade ground on which perhaps two or three thousand French troops stood silently in formation. At first Ian could see only their backs because they were all facing the center of the grounds. Considering all that he had been through, Ian knew that any fate was possible here. He was relieved, therefore, to see that the soldiers appeared to be unarmed and that there were no guillotines in sight. Even so, the situation did not appear hopeful.

In the center of the parade ground stood a reviewing stand to which the soldiers' attention seemed directed, and toward which Ian and the others were being taken. His heart sank as he realized what was happening. He did not know the specifics, but there was little doubt that they had been brought here to serve as some sort of spectacle. He wanted to run but there was nowhere to go. They were led onto the reviewing stand and directed toward a row of chairs. This seemed a rather congenial offer and Ian again wondered if his fear had been unfounded. After all, they had been provided with a good meal—the best he had had in months—and he was now certain the troops were not armed.

Suddenly there was a commotion to Ian's left. *"Viva la France!"* someone shouted. It was one of Ian's companions. *"Viva la Nouveau Époque! Viva la Christopher!"* the man added. Apparently he had the same fears as Ian and hoped his display might ingratiate him to his captors. The idea must have seemed like a good one to some of the others because presently half a dozen stood and repeated the chant. Others joined in. Not wanting to be left out, Ian was about to do the same but as he scanned the faces of the soldiers he saw no sign that the display was having the desired effect. There were a number of smiles, but they were not smiles of camaraderie, but rather of disdain and amusement. Ian held his seat.

Failing to arouse a positive response, one by one the others ceased their refrain and quickly took their seats as well, hoping that their indiscreet behavior might be overlooked. Within seconds only the first man remained standing. Being the first and therefore the most conspicuous, he was committed to the attempt and, hoping that some variation of his chant might yet evoke the desired effect, he briefly tried several variations. Still floundering, his voice seemed to fail as he stood there dripping with nervous perspiration. Ian did not look at him, nor did the others. No one wanted to be associated with him. The intense anxiety of the man's situation found its way to his stomach and he was gripped by uncontrollable nausea and began vomiting his lunch onto the stage. The scene had apparently amused the guards who had let it go this far, but now one grabbed the man's hair and jerked him back into his seat.

A moment later a car arrived, and someone called the soldiers to attention as a much-decorated United Nations general with French insignia got out of the car and approached the reviewing stand. He was followed by a military aide and two other men in civilian clothes. Coming up the steps, the general went directly to the lectern to address the troops. The older of the two men in civilian clothes turned and faced Ian and the others and announced that he would be their translator.

The general gave a command, which the translator did not relay but which obviously was calling the soldiers to *at ease*. He then began in earnest.

"As you are no doubt aware," the translator relayed, "over the next four weeks most of you will be deployed to the Middle East for what we believe will be a relatively short but strategically critical mission. I am certain that all of you will perform in a manner that will bring honor to this battalion and to France. As you know, each of you has recently acquired certain abilities which Secretary-General Goodman has said will be vital to the coming conflict."

Ian and his companions had been weeks without communication from the outside and so were unaware of the three signs. Nor had they received the benefit of the signs themselves except that most had not gotten the sores since receiving the mark, and of those who had, the lesions were only minor. Thus they did not understand the nature of the recently acquired abilities to which the general referred.

"It is no secret that our strategy will be to bring down the walls of Petra upon our enemies. We anticipate, however, that some will escape the destruction. Mr. Warren Sardon," the general continued as he motioned toward the younger man in civilian clothes, "who has just arrived from UN headquarters in Babylon, has come to demonstrate how your new abilities can be used when dealing with the KDP enemy in a one-on-one situation. I have not seen this myself," the general added, "so I'm looking forward to this as much as the rest of you." The general stepped away from the lectern and Sardon approached.

"Thank you, General Sonnier," Sardon said. "I'm sure you won't be disappointed." Then turning to the troops, he began. "With the help of the volunteers behind me," he said, obviously referring to Ian and the others. "We will . . ."

Sardon continued speaking but Ian did not hear him. His words no longer mattered. There was now no doubt: Ian knew he was about to die.

The man stopped speaking and signaled to the guards to bring forward one of Ian's companions. "Now, like the rest of you," Sardon continued, addressing the soldiers, "I'd much rather do this to one of the KDP, but since we don't have any KDP available," he joked, "these men and women have agreed to help us with our demonstration.

For those who may feel uneasy with this, let me note that all of these volunteers were until recently in collaboration with the fundamentalists. While they *did* accept the communion and the mark rather than face *le rasoir national*,[94] we *and* they have concluded that for their own betterment, they should be freed of the negative memories of this lifetime and be allowed to convey into their next incarnation with a clean slate."

The guards went directly to the man who had vomited. "No! No!" he cried, as they pulled him to the front.

"It appears our first volunteer is having second thoughts," Sardon said with a smile. The man was dragged weeping to a point about six feet to Sardon's left on the stage. To silence him, one of the guards finally held a gun to his head. "Can everyone see okay?" Sardon asked. When he was satisfied all could see, he continued. "In the technique I'm about to demonstrate, I'm going to use both telekinetic power and, to aid in visualization and concentration, I will use my hand in a corresponding physical action. While it is not necessary to use the physical aid, it is recommended, at least at first." With this, Sardon stepped away from the lectern, turned and faced the still whimpering "volunteer," and extended his right hand slightly. Concentrating as he visualized the man's heart, he began to close the fingers of his extended hand and twisted it slowly to the right. The volunteer abruptly ceased both his whimpering and his breathing as his face convulsed into a grotesque expression of pain. He would have collapsed altogether, but Sardon prolonged the performance and now

---

[94] "The national razor," one of many names for the guillotine, coined during the French Revolution.

used his telekinetic ability to hold the man erect so that no one would miss the demonstration. Sardon squeezed his fingers and continued the twisting action back and forth, as the man's head was thrown back, his body went limp, and blood began to pour from his mouth. Finally, when the man was obviously dead, Sardon released his telekinetic grip and let the body drop onto the stage.

It was an impressive display and General Sonnier could not help but applaud, which let the soldiers know it was all right to do likewise. Sardon appreciated the show of approval. "Now," he said, when the applause died down, "while we'd like to provide each of you with an opportunity to try this yourselves, we unfortunately have a limited number of volunteers. What we're going to do then is select . . . Let's see . . . ," he said, interrupting himself long enough to turn and count how many "volunteers" he had, ". . . eighteen, nineteen. Just nineteen?" he asked disappointedly, to no one in particular. "Okay," he continued, turning back to the troops, "we'll select nineteen of you to come up and try it yourselves one at a time. I'll stay here to comment and offer direction so that the rest of you can benefit from watching, even if you can't yet try it yourselves."

21

Dayenu

Saturday, August 29, 4 N.A. Babylon

THIRTEEN-YEAR-OLD AKBAR JAHANGIR peered from behind a pile of boxes and wooden pallets in the alley as the back door swung open and a woman emerged carrying a large black garbage bag. There was no telling what was inside, but it had been two days since he, his mother, and his little sister had eaten and he could only pray it contained some scraps of food. He would have had a better chance of finding food in the garbage behind one of the restaurants, but those places were more likely to be watched by the police. He knew people who had been arrested in such places. He and his mother assumed that was what had happened to his father. No one was sure. One day his father and another man went to try to find food and they simply didn't come back.

As the woman went back inside and the door closed tight, Akbar looked all around and then made a dash for the trash can. Attempting to be both silent and quick, he removed the lid and grabbed the bag. He would not examine its contents until he was better hidden, somewhere

where he was certain that no one would see that he did not bear the mark.

Sunday, August 30, 4 N.A. Petra

"I apologize for taking so long to arrive," Benjamin Cohen said as Samuel Newberg introduced him to Chaim Levin, Israel's high priest, "but I was in Jerusalem when I got the message that you wanted to see me."

Having finished the introductions, Newberg started to leave. "Please, Sam," the high priest said to his assistant and long-time friend, "stay." Then turning to his guest, "If that's okay with you."

"Certainly," Cohen said. And with that the three men sat down on wooden chairs around a table at which Rose Levin had set a pitcher of water, a bowl of strawberries, and a plate of manna cookies.

"Jerusalem, you said?" Levin's implied question was how Cohen, a member of the KDP, could have gone to Jerusalem and not been arrested. As soon as he said it, he realized it really didn't need explaining; the KDP had their ways.

"The Lord provides," Cohen answered anyway.

Levin nodded, then after an uncomfortable pause, he pointed at Cohen with his little finger. "I knew your father," he said.

"I know," responded Cohen.

"We both trained under Rebbe Schneerson.[95] We were

[95] Known as the Lubavitcher Rebbe, Rabbi Menachem Mendel Schneerson died June 12, 1994.

never very close," Levin added. "Your father was five years older than I—but I believe we respected one another."

"He always spoke very highly of you," Cohen said. "He was pleased when you became high priest."

Levin did not respond but raised his left eyebrow, smiled appreciatively, and nodded. After all these years, it was nice to know.

"How can I serve you?" Cohen asked.

Levin looked at the marking on Benjamin Cohen's forehead—the Hebrew letters spelling out the name Yeshua. "You know," he began, "I grew up hating Christians. My mother told me I shouldn't hate, but I had heard her weeping in the night. During the Second World War she spent two years in Belsen," he explained, referring to the Nazi death camp. "She weighed seventy-two pounds when the Allies liberated the camp. I blamed the Christians for what the Nazis did to the Jews, and most Christians I met when I was young did little to change my opinion. I had to adjust my thinking, though, when I met my wife. Her parents had also lived in Germany, near Würzburg. They spent most of the war hiding above the garage of a Christian family who risked their lives to protect them. I did not understand it then, but in time I came to realize that evil people—people like Hitler and the Nazis—frequently attempt to clothe themselves in righteous garments to hide their true nature. I also realized that not all who claim Christ actually follow his teachings. And I suppose it occurred to me that if I blamed all Christians for the acts of some, then I as a Jew must accept blame for every act of every Jew, all the way back to Jacob for deceiving Isaac and stealing Esau's birthright, as well as for the deaths of the prophets at the hands of my ancestors. Neither of us, Jews nor Gentiles, exactly has a spotless record."

"They are *my* ancestors, too," Cohen interjected.

Levin nodded, "Yes, but . . ." His reference to "my ancestors" was not intended to imply otherwise. He knew the KDP considered themselves Jewish and even followed all the laws and traditions—were it not so, he could never have allowed Cohen to sit at his table—but in truth, he *did* question how a person could be a Christian *and* still be a Jew.

"I sit before you a Jew," Cohen insisted, "nothing more and nothing less. When my father studied under Rebbe Schneerson, he believed Schneerson was the Messiah," Cohen said.

"As did I, as did thousands of his followers," Levin added.

"Did that make them, or my father, or *you*, not a Jew?"

Levin did not answer. It was a rhetorical question.

"And yet Rebbe Schneerson never even set foot in Israel, much less was he born in Bethlehem, the city of David, as the prophet Micah said Messiah would be.[96] So how is it that if a person believes that Yeshua—a Jew of the house of David, born in Bethlehem—was Messiah, they suddenly stop being a Jew?"

Levin had heard the argument before. He knew it made sense, but despite himself, despite even the purpose of this meeting, he was still uneasy with it. "For three and a half years," Levin said, letting Cohen's question pass, "we have been here together—we Jews and you KDP

---

[96] Micah 5:2.

and your Chris—" Levin caught himself. "What do you prefer they be called?"

"Christians is fine," Cohen answered, "but many prefer 'Jewish Believers' to distinguish themselves as believers in Yeshua as Messiah, while making it clear that they are still Jews."

Levin nodded and restated the question. "For three and a half years we have been here in Petra together—we Jews and you KDP and your Jewish Believers—and yet none of you have ever come to call, ever come trying to convince me that we are wrong about your messiah. Why?"

Benjamin Cohen thought for a second before answering. "What could we tell you that you do not already know?" he asked. "Shall I tell you of the signs given by John and my father? Shall I tell you how, after lying dead in the streets of Jerusalem for three and a half days, they were resurrected and taken into heaven as the whole world watched? Should I explain how Christopher Goodman's speech at the Temple and the setting up of his image exactly fulfill the words of the prophet Daniel?[97] Or would you have me show you the evidence of God's blessing on what we do—the manna and the fruit of the harvest from what had been a barren wilderness," he said as he pointed with open hands to the cookies and berries on the table.

"We know that no one could perform such miraculous signs if God were not with him," Chaim Levin immediately volunteered.

"Then shall I read to you the words of the prophets: Daniel, who said Messiah would come 483 years after the

---

[97] Daniel 9:27.

decree to rebuild Jerusalem after the Babylonian captivity.[98] Jeremiah, who said Messiah would be of the house of David.[99] Micah, who said Messiah would be born in Bethlehem in Judah, and yet his origin was from days of eternity.[100] Shall I quote for you Isaiah, who said Messiah would be called Mighty God, the Everlasting Father, and the Prince of Peace;[101] that his ministry would begin in Galilee;[102] that he would perform numerous miracles;[103] that though he had done nothing wrong, he would be tried, and at his trial Messiah would not defend himself, but would be led as a lamb, silent to the slaughter;[104] that he would be pierced for our sins and crushed for our iniquities;[105] but that after his death he would be resurrected;[106] and that what Messiah had done and said would be told throughout the world for generation after generation, forever.[107] Or should I read to you the words of Zechariah, who said Messiah would come into Jerusalem riding on a donkey,[108] and would be betrayed by a friend

[98] Daniel 9:25.

[99] Jeremiah 23:5.

[100] Micah 5:2.

[101] Isaiah 9:6.

[102] Isaiah 9:1–7.

[103] Isaiah 35:3–6.

[104] Isaiah 53:7.

[105] Isaiah 53:4–12.

[106] Isaiah 53:10–11.

[107] Isaiah 49:6.

[108] Zechariah 9:9.

for thirty pieces of silver.[109] Or shall I appeal to King David, who described Messiah's death in detail a thousand years before crucifixion was first used—the taunting of the crowds, the casting of lots for his clothing[110]—and who also said that Messiah would be resurrected."[111]

Sam Newberg, who had until now remained silent, finally spoke. "How could it be," he asked with some urgency, "if all you say is true, our fathers could have rejected him?"

"I'm afraid," Cohen answered, "we Jews have quite a history of rejecting the ones God has sent to rescue us. Did not our fathers reject their brother Joseph and sell him into slavery because his dreams said they would all bow to him someday?[112] And yet, years later, in accordance with God's will, they *did* bow to him and he rescued them from famine.[113] Moses was rejected at first, too.[114] He fled Egypt and went into the Sinai for forty years before he returned to free Israel from Pharaoh. But again we rejected him.[115] And even when Moses had freed them from Egypt, our fathers rejected him as their deliverer twelve more times.[116] Twice they were ready to stone

---

[109] Zechariah 11:12–13.

[110] Psalms 22:7–8, 16–18.

[111] Psalms 16:10; 30:3.

[112] Genesis 37.

[113] Genesis 43–47.

[114] Exodus 2:11–14.

[115] Exodus 6:9.

[116] Exodus 14:11–12; 15:24; 16:2–3; 17:1–4; Numbers 11:18–20; 14:1–5, 40–45; 16:1–3, 41–45; 20:2–5; 21:4–5; 25:1–9; Deuteronomy 1:26–27, 42–43; 9:9–17, 23–24.

him.[117] But it wasn't just Moses that they had rejected; Moses said that their grumblings were actually against God.[118] Did not our fathers reject both Moses and God and build for themselves a graven image—a golden calf—to worship?[119] Even Aaron and Miriam rejected Moses' leadership.[120]

"At the Passover in the song *Dayenu,* we sing that we would have been satisfied 'if he had merely rescued us from Egypt, but had not punished the Egyptians; if he had merely punished the Egyptians, but had not destroyed their gods; if he had merely destroyed their gods, but had not slain their first born . . .' But it's a lie! We only fool ourselves. It *should* have been enough, but even after all the things God did for us, still we did not cease in our rebellion. Did not the Lord say of us through the prophet Isaiah:

> All day long I have held out my hands to an obstinate people, who walk in ways not good, pursuing their own imaginations—a people who continually provoke me to my very face . . . who say, "Keep away; don't come near me, for I am too sacred for you!"[121]

"Is not the whole of the Bible the history of our rebellion and of God's forgiveness?

[117] Exodus 17:4; Numbers 14:10.

[118] Exodus 16:7–8; Numbers 20:13.

[119] Exodus 32:1–6.

[120] Numbers 12.

[121] Isaiah 65:2–5.

"Moses said that from the day they left Egypt our fathers were rebellious against the Lord.[122] Twice God would have destroyed all of Israel except that Moses pleaded with him not to.[123] Did not Aaron," Cohen said looking at Levin, "whose spiritual robes you wear, say of our fathers, these people are prone to evil?[124] And did not God himself call us a stiff-necked people?[125]

"And did we not reject and rebel against God when, though he had blessed us with his law, we went our own way time and again, breaking his law, ignoring his prophets, and bringing his wrath down upon us?

"Is it any surprise then, that when God sent the Messiah, our fathers—and we—rejected him, too? Indeed, it would have been out of character for us to have done otherwise!

"And just as Joseph, when he was rejected by his brothers, saved the Egyptians first[126] and then his own family, so also Yeshua, when he was rejected by our fathers, turned his attention to the salvation of the Gentiles. As it is written, 'I will call them "my people" who are not my people.'[127] And now, at last, the time has come for the salvation of Israel."

"You make us sound pretty awful," Samuel Newberg sighed, more as a confession than as a challenge.

---

[122] Deuteronomy 9:7.

[123] Exodus 32:9–14; Numbers 14:11–19.

[124] Exodus 32:22.

[125] Exodus 33:3–5.

[126] Genesis 41.

[127] Hosea 2:23; Romans 9:25.

"No worse than we are. There is no room for arrogance when we stand before a holy God. And yet, despite it all, God has told us through Moses that we are a people holy to the Lord, whom God has chosen out of all the peoples on the face of the earth to be his people, his 'treasured possession.'[128] It is just as you said," Cohen noted, recalling Levin's earlier comment, "neither we *nor* the Gentiles have a very good record. Both of us require God's forgiveness."

Chaim Levin folded his hands in thought. For a long moment no one spoke. Finally Cohen added, "In truth, I can tell you nothing that you do not already know. I cannot make your decision any easier. I cannot convince you further. Indeed, I suspect there is nothing of which to convince you. You know the truth. You have for some time."

The high priest took a deep breath and let it out slowly, staring deeply into Cohen's eyes as he considered what he had heard.

"The question is no longer one of finding the truth," Cohen concluded, "but of finding the courage to face the truth you have found."

Chaim Levin frowned and thought and nodded slowly, and then thought and nodded some more. Newberg and Benjamin Cohen waited silently. "I am not familiar with your book," Levin said finally. "What do the Christian prophets say must be done?"

"The answer," Cohen said, shaking his head, "is not in the *Christian* prophets. Look instead to the words of Zechariah:

---

[128] Deuteronomy 7:6; 14:2.

I will pour out on the house of David and the inhabitants of Jerusalem a spirit of grace and supplication. They will look on me, the one they have pierced, and they will mourn for him as one mourns for an only child, and grieve bitterly for him as one grieves for a firstborn son. "[129]

Thursday, September 3, 4
N.A.
Megiddo, Israel

The red light on the camera lit up, indicating that the feed was live to the network.

"Armageddon," the reporter began ominously, "a word that has struck terror in the hearts of Humankind for nearly two thousand years, a word that has become synonymous with the end of the world. This is Jane Reed, reporting from the ruins of the ancient city of Megiddo above the Valley of Jezreel in Israel. It is from this mountain, on which this ancient city is built—the mountain of Megiddo or, in the Hebrew *Har-Mageddon*—that the apocalyptic Armageddon takes its name.

"Behind me, stretching out for more than thirty kilometers, is the Jezreel Valley." The camera panned the vast expanse as the reporter continued. "It is this commanding view of the valley and the two major trade routes[130] that

---

[129] Zechariah 12:10.

[130] The Via Maris connecting Egypt and Mesopotamia, and the route linking eastern Palestine with the Mediterranean.

passed through it that made Megiddo a point of strategic importance in the ancient Middle East, and the scene of numerous battles between 3000 and 400 B.P.E.[131] It was here in 1460 B.P.E. that the Egyptian pharaoh *Thutmose III* led a successful preemptive strike against the princes of Megiddo and Kadesh to establish the western border of his empire at the Euphrates River.

"And it is here that New Testament prophecy said the final battle was to be fought.

"Ironically," the reporter continued as the camera focused again on her, "the valley beneath the mountain of Megiddo, or *Har-Mageddon, does* figure into what is touted as a final battle of sorts—a battle that even more ironically promises to bring to a conclusion both the religion that spawned the prophecy and even the religion that spawned the religion—but it is unlikely that either this mountain or the valley below will see any fighting. Instead the site has been chosen as the staging ground for what is expected to be by far the largest mobilization of international military forces in all of history. Soon military units from more than 150 member countries of the United Nations will gather here." The video feed went to a taped shot of a UN Corps of Engineers division marking out portions of the valley as the reporter's voice continued. "Already, advanced logistical teams are surveying the valley, and by tomorrow night trucks will deliver mess tents and sanitary facilities for the ground troops that are expected to begin arriving within five days.

"Although actual numbers have not yet been made available," she continued as the clip ended and the camera

---

[131] Before Previous Era, i.e., B.C.

returned live to her, "it is estimated that within two weeks this valley will shelter well in excess of six million troops. From here, some time in mid-month, the UN forces will travel south past Jerusalem and will cross the border into Jordan and advance to the area around the KDP stronghold of Petra. There they will be joined by additional units coming from China, India, Korea, Thailand, Mongolia, and other countries in the east. It is at Petra that the actual battle will be fought—and fought by what Secretary-General Christopher Goodman has explained will be very unconventional methods."

Thursday, September 10, 4 N.A.
Nine miles southwest of Babylon

The wheels of the small truck rolled on relentlessly, bringing the two men closer with each rotation to a confrontation, which, if they were discovered, would end in their deaths. Ed Blocher looked in the mirror one more time at the mark on his forehead. It looked real, so real it was difficult to tell how much of the churning in his stomach was due to nervousness and how much was the result of being sickened by the sight of it on his face. He looked over at his co-conspirator, Joel Felsberg, who was driving. Joel seemed so confident. He had done this all

[132] Antipater of Sidon (circa 130 B.C.).

before. His confidence was reassuring but not enough to ease Blocher's anxiety.

Even at this distance, they could see the great city ahead of them, its walls 120 feet high and 18 feet thick, a replica of what had in the earliest accounts[132] been considered one of the seven wonders of the ancient world, forming a perfect square fourteen miles on each side, encompassing the city. Inside the walls was everything Blocher detested, everything that his faith told him was sinful and corrupt. Joel Felsberg had warned him to be prepared to see and hear anything and everything: men, women and children selling themselves to satisfy the most perverse sadomasochistic whims of those with enough money; public displays of bestiality; widespread use of drugs; drunken parties that never ended as big screen televisions showed an uninterrupted blood-fest of executions. And yet, behind those same walls there were also some who still served Yahweh—people who had come here seeking work before the mark became mandatory and who afterward were unable to leave. A few were hidden in attics or basements by relatives who, though they had taken the mark and sworn allegiance to Christopher, were still reluctant to turn in members of their families. Most, however, slept in alleys and tunnels, hiding in sewers and recesses and behind crags along the river. They lived on scraps and garbage, insects and rats. The police caught as many as they could, but some still remained. It was to these that Blocher and Felsberg hoped to get this shipment of food and medicine.

They approached the checkpoint right on schedule, a little before 6:00 A.M., when the guards changed. The sentinels they would encounter had been working all night and were ready to be relieved. They were less likely to perform a thorough check than the security personnel coming on duty a few minutes later.

Joel Felsberg pulled the truck to a stop at the checkpoint and rolled down his window to hand the guard his manifest. The guard gave a cursory glance, saw that the two men inside both bore the mark on their foreheads, and took the manifest. It would have taken only a quick electronic scan of the marks to reveal that they were counterfeit, but that was an extra hassle and the guards used the scanner only if there was something suspicious. Their real responsibility was not to keep people or shipments out of the city, but to arrest anyone without the mark who tried to leave.

"I'll need you to open up the back," the sentry said as he checked the registration of the truck and manifest on his hand-held data link. It was a good system but not so foolproof that Joel Felsberg couldn't get into the network and add a few numbers or manifest records that weren't supposed to be there.

Joel got out and walked around to the back of the truck and opened it. The guard glanced in at the wooden crates of produce and climbed up on the bumper to have a better look. As long as he didn't make them unload the truck, there wouldn't be a problem. The medicine they carried, mostly tetracycline and metronidazole for dysentery, would give away their true purpose—for people in Babylon who had the mark and had taken the communion had no need for such medicines.

"Where is this from?" the guard asked about the produce, though its origin was clearly entered on the manifest.

"Ash-Shināfiyah," Joel Felsberg answered, referring to the city southwest of Babylon around which much of Babylon's food was grown. Inside the truck's cab, Ed Blocher tried to stay as calm as possible.

"And where's it going?" the guard asked, though that too was on the manifest.

"The UN cafeteria," Felsberg answered.

"You think they'll miss a couple of these melons?" he asked as he picked one from the top of a crate.

"I suppose they might not miss one or two of them," he answered.

"Okay," the guard said, taking two of the melons. "It looks like everything is in order."

22

The Gathering

Monday, September 14, 4 N.A.
Northeast of Ar-Ramādī, Iraq

ON THE BANKS OF THE GREAT RIVER EUPHRATES—the largest river in southwestern Asia even before it was dredged and widened as a part of the United Nations program to facilitate commerce in and out of Babylon—stood the advance units of the combined Asian forces en route to Petra in Jordan. Their journey to Jordan would be greatly expedited, for neither they nor the tens of millions that followed would need boats or pontoon bridges to cross the Euphrates. A month and a half before their arrival, on Christopher's orders, the river's waters had been redirected to flow into the Mileh Tharthâr, sixty miles northwest of Baghdad. Before them lay only dry river bed, solid enough to support the weight of their trucks and armored personnel carriers.

Wednesday, September 16, 4 N.A.
Bojnūrd, Iran

The first light of dawn glistened above the eastern horizon and at once the branches of the trees along the Elburz

Mountain range burst into life as countless thousands of birds awoke and took wing, flying toward the southwest.

Thursday, September 17, 4 N.A. Babylon

The skies above Babylon were clear and blue, and there was every indication that this would be a beautiful autumn day. Then without explanation or warning, the sky began to rumble. There were no rain clouds. No aircraft flew overhead. There was only the rumbling.

And then it stopped.

For most it was just a curious phenomenon.

But to some, perhaps a few hundred or more, it had not been a rumbling at all, but a warning.

Friday, September 18, 4 N.A. Megiddo, Israel

As the camera looked down upon a crowd that seemed beyond number, a woman's voice cryptically hinted at an explanation: "Two weeks ago no one could have conceived what has taken place here." The camera continued to pan the crowd and then faded to a female reporter standing on a natural rise high above the mass. "This is Jane Reed, reporting from atop the mountain of Megiddo, looking out over the Jezreel Valley in northern Israel. Two months ago," she said, playing on the contrast to her opening sentence, "as the world reeled from the effects of the plagues of blood and heat and darkness, few gave

Christopher Goodman one chance in ten of even lasting out the year as secretary-general. Then came his dramatic speech in which he did four things: first, he made clear that as bad as things were, there was no going back; second, he promised there would be no more plagues; third, he called on world leaders to join him in a final battle against the KDP and Yahweh; and fourth, he offered three signs by which the world would know that all that he had promised about the New Age was true.

"For anyone who has been in a cave or on some other planet," she said facetiously, "the first of those three signs occurred when, by cursing Yahweh, Humankind symbolically threw off the chains of spiritual bondage, refusing to submit to Yahweh's domination, and thus ended the plague of sores. The second sign was health and youth, a further effect of rejecting Yahweh's oppression. And the most dramatic sign of all, the third, was permanent telekinetic abilities. These abilities, which Christopher describes as evidence of Humankind's accelerated evolutionary process and a foreshadowing of things to come, figure prominently into the upcoming confrontation. The telepathic abilities of the KDP are well known and have allowed them to elude capture and avoid punishment for nearly seven years. Now, for the first time, it is possible to confront the KDP on a level playing field, matching their abilities one-for-one.

"Christopher's strategy for the upcoming battle has been known from the beginning: to march on Petra with as large a force as possible and, using the combined telekinetic energy of those gathered, bring down the walls of Petra, thus crushing the powers that would re-enslave Humankind. Conventional means of attack have been rejected for three reasons: first, such weapons would harm the environment—something that Christopher has vowed not to do; second, intelligence reports indicate that conventional weapons would likely prove futile against the KDP's telekinetic abilities; and finally, Christopher has said that as Humankind embarks upon its evolutionary journey, we must turn from our reliance upon the weapons of the past and learn instead to use the tools of the future.

"In a few moments, Secretary-General Goodman will address those gathered here and give the word for this great mass of humanity to begin its journey to Petra.

"There is no way to get an accurate count of those gathered here. There are simply too many. Millions—thirty million—perhaps far more. Among them are military units representing 162 nations, but the military make up only a small minority. Surprisingly, by far the largest contingent are civilians, ordinary citizens. They have come here from everywhere, by the busload, by the truckload, by plane, in cars, on motorcycles, in recreational vehicles; from all over Europe, from throughout the African continent, from the Far East and India, from Babylon, from England, Ireland, Scotland and Wales, from Iceland, from the Americas, from Australia and New Zealand. It seems there is not a country in the world that does not have a contingent of at least a few thousand. And tens of thousands more are arriving every hour.

"All have come to play a part, to have a role in this historic undertaking. Many, perhaps most, have come here in part to seek justice for their friends and family who died in the plagues, as well as for their own suffering. All have come to put an end to the KDP's reign of terror before they can strike again. An air of celebration fills the valley as they look forward to what most believe is certain victory.

"This site was chosen for its terrain and for its proximity to sources of food and water in order to simplify the logistics of supporting such a large number of participants, but moving a multitude of this size is no easy matter. The 175-mile trek to Petra will be led by the military, and the first contingent is expected to reach Petra sometime tomorrow afternoon. Their arrival is timed to coincide with the arrival of units from the Far East, China, and India, comprising a force every bit as large as, if not larger than, the one gathered here. Because of the sheer number of people involved, it is expected to be late Sunday evening before everyone has arrived.

"Earlier there was some concern expressed by those scheduled to arrive later, that by the time they reached Petra the battle would be over. To allay those fears, Christopher has gone out of his way to stress the importance of everyone joining their mental energy together to defeat the KDP in a single blow, and he has vowed that the battle will not begin until the last of those gathered here arrives at Petra. Additionally, we are told that half of the military will remain here to bring up the rear of the formation."

Jane Reed held her hand to her ear and placed a finger on an earphone. The motion was more to indicate to the audience that she was getting a message than it was to actually help her hear that message. "I understand that the secretary-general has arrived along with all ten members of the Security Council, who will accompany this expedition to Petra. The secretary-general is about to address those assembled," she relayed. "The word we are getting is that this will be a very brief statement. We'll take you there now."

The scene changed to a temporary stage set above the valley on the side of the mount of Megiddo, where Christopher was approaching the microphone. A deafening cheer erupted, and every conceivable noisemaker was employed to add to the sound of spontaneous celebration as people danced and laughed and reveled in the moment. It was more than fifteen minutes before the sound died down enough for Christopher to begin.

"I do not have words," Christopher began finally, speaking in the universal language the world had first heard when he spoke from the Temple in Jerusalem, "that can express the deep sense of appreciation and gratitude I feel that so many would come and join in this noble effort." Again the sound of sustained cheers reverberated across the valley as those in attendance celebrated their own participation and the participation of those around them. "Today we go to Petra!" Christopher said, not waiting for the applause to entirely wane. "By noon Monday we will have forever thrown open the doors of the prison that has held us, and nailed shut for all time the coffin of our jailers: the KDP, Yahweh, and their followers."

The crowd roared its approval, many sounding horns or beating drums or banging on whatever they could find to add to the din.

"Onward for Humankind!" Christopher shouted. "Onward for ourselves! And onward to victory!"

Petra

Inside the walls of Petra the high priest had called an assembly. This was the first time that *all* of the people of Petra—Jews, Jewish Believers, and KDP—had met together in the three and a half years they had been here. Emotions were understandably high. They were well aware of the immense armies from the east and west that were now marching to destroy them.

Chaim Levin had prayed and fasted and studied, and then prayed and fasted and studied some more in preparation for this day. On matters of great importance, normally he would talk with his council to seek their guidance on how to proceed. This time, he decided, was different. His decision could not be made based on majority rule: There was a right answer and a wrong answer, and he would have to trust God to reveal which was which. Nor had he discussed his decision with the council after he had made it: On such a decision, he would not be swayed by the words of men. The council would learn of his decision along with everyone else. Then they, like everyone else, could decide whether he had acted correctly and what their response would be. Still, he had not anticipated that when this moment finally came it would come under such circumstances—with more than sixty million people coming in his direction and bent on destruction. He could not help but draw the obvious comparison to Moses as he stood on the banks of the Red Sea with Pharaoh's army in pursuit. He did not know how his declaration would be received by those assembled here, but as he looked out over the sea of faces he wondered if like Moses, his leadership would be challenged in the face of this impending threat. Benjamin Cohen had tried to assure him that his words would be received well: "Prophecy demands it," he had said.[133]

It didn't really matter: He had to speak what he knew to be true.

Sam Newberg was firmly of the opinion that most of the people of Petra had already come to the same conclusion as their high priest. They had witnessed the same miraculous events unfolding for the past seven years. They had watched as John and Cohen were resurrected; they had eaten the daily manna; and they had witnessed the plagues falling on everyone but them. More important, they had lived here for nearly three and a half years, side by side with those who called themselves Jewish Believers in Messiah; they had seen the love and selfless kindness that these Jewish Believers lived out on a daily basis. They wanted what these people had, and they were only waiting for their high priest to say it was all right to accept it. These were not the faces of those who had challenged Moses; rather they were the faces of those who had followed Joshua across the Jordan into the Promised Land.[134]

So that his address could be seen and heard by all, Chaim Levin would speak from atop Umm Al Biyara, where a sound system had been set up to amplify his words. As all the appropriate formalities were concluded, Levin looked out over the silent assembly. He was suddenly more aware than he had ever been of the awesome responsibility that rested on his shoulders as high priest.

[133] Romans 11:25–32.

[134] Joshua 3–4.

Opening his Bible to the words of the prophet Isaiah, he began to read:

> *Who has believed our message and to whom has the arm of the Lord been revealed? He grew up before him like a tender shoot, and like a root out of dry ground. He had no beauty or majesty to attract us to him, nothing in his appearance that we should desire him. He was despised and rejected by men, a man of sorrows, and familiar with suffering. Like one from whom men hide their faces he was despised, and we esteemed him not.*
>
> *Surely he took up our infirmities and carried our sorrows, yet we considered him stricken by God, smitten by him, and afflicted. But he was pierced for our transgressions, he was crushed for our iniquities; the punishment that brought us peace was upon him, and by his wounds we are healed. We all, like sheep, have gone astray, each of us has turned to his own way; and the Lord has laid on him the iniquity of us all.*
>
> *He was oppressed and afflicted, yet he did not open his mouth; he was led like a lamb to the slaughter, and as a sheep before her shearers is silent, so he did not open his mouth. By oppression and judgment he was taken away. And who can speak of his descendants? For he was cut off from the land of the living; for the transgression of my people he was stricken. He was assigned a grave with the wicked, and with the rich in his death, though he had done no violence, nor was any deceit in his mouth.*
>
> *Yet it was the Lord's will to crush him and cause him to suffer, and though the Lord makes his life a guilt of-*

*fering, he will see his offspring and prolong his days,
and the will of the Lord will prosper in his hand. After
the suffering of his soul, he will see the light of life and
be satisfied; by his knowledge my righteous servant will
justify many, and he will bear their iniquities. Therefore
I will give him a portion among the great, and he will di-
vide the spoils with the strong, because he poured out his
life unto death, and was numbered with the transgressors. For he bore the sin of many, and made intercession
for the transgressors.*[135]

Lárnax, Cyprus

The eighty-mile flight over the Mediterranean from the
mainland of Turkey to the island of Cyprus was farther
than any of the birds had ever flown at a single stint.
Now, after resting the night, they continued their trek,
leaving the southeastern corner of the island. Had they
understood that it would be more than twice the first distance before they would see land again, they might have
turned back. But they did not understand, nor did they
know their destination or their purpose. All they knew
was that they must fly in this direction.

Babylon

The time for discretion had passed. The warning from the
sky to flee Babylon had come two days before, and no

[135] Isaiah 53.

one knew how much longer they had to make good their escape. Many had already been caught trying to leave and were promptly executed. Still, the thought of piling into the back of a produce truck and making a desperate attempt to go unnoticed past armed guards at one of the city gates seemed a pretty good one compared to the alternative. And so they took the risk, leaving their hiding places in broad daylight, coming to the meeting place, packing into the back of the truck like sardines in a can or commuters on a subway car.

Among those hoping to get on the truck, Akbar Jahangir, his sister, and mother struggled to stay together. At first it seemed impossible that there would be enough room for them, they were so far back in the line, but soon all three were on board.

"There's no more room," Joel Felsberg said, as he pulled shut the door on the truck and locked it.

"Please, please," called several voices from among those still in line.

"I'm sorry," Ed Blocher answered. "If we make it out of the city alive, we'll try to come back to get you."

"How will we know if you've made it?" someone asked.

"Listen for gunshots," Felsberg answered as he looked at the truck's tires and suspension and shook his head. If the guards were observant enough to notice, they'd know right away the truck wasn't empty and they'd all be dead. "If we make it out okay," Felsberg continued, "there won't be any gunshots. It will take us about two hours to get back for another load . . . assuming, of course, we can get back in." It was not the answer anyone wanted to hear, but for now they could only pray and wait and hope that they would not be discovered as they made their way back to their hiding places.

The truck lurched forward, and the weight of those inside shifted, pinning Akbar and his little sister against the back door. The shift was only temporary, and as everyone attempted to right themselves, compensating for the movement, the truck turned a corner, and the process was repeated, pinning those who were on the wall opposite the turn beneath the crush of human cargo. People looked for something to hold on to, but except for a few tie ends on the side walls, there was nothing. Those too young to understand what was happening inside the darkened vault began crying, while those who realized that the noise could get them all killed tried desperately to calm and quiet them.

As Joel Felsberg pulled the truck up to the checkpoint, he rolled down the window to speak to the guard. "Manifest," the guard said in a one-word sentence.

Felsberg handed him the document with its forged signature, showing that the produce they had brought in that morning had been delivered. The guard then checked the manifest in his hand-held system to ensure that the produce had in fact been delivered. Felsberg's computer hacking had included not only the entry of his false manifest: He had also included a triggering mechanism that would automatically create a record of the completed delivery one hour after the initial security check indicated they had entered the city. Three hours later, all records of the manifest would disappear from the system altogether.

So it was that the guard found everything in order. Nine out of ten times the next step for the guard was to have the driver open the back of the truck to show that it was empty. That is why no attempts had been made in the past to smuggle people out of the city. Felsberg, Blocher, and everyone in the back of the truck were praying this would be that one in ten times that the guards would forego that requirement and let them go on their way.

"Okay," the guard said in a tone that said their prayers had been answered. Joel Felsberg breathed a silent sigh. Ed Blocher could barely contain his relief. But then suddenly the guard's eyes shifted to the back of the truck. Had he heard something?

Inside, Akbar Jahangir cringed and put his hand back over his sister's mouth. "Shhhhh," he said, pleadingly.

"Wait a minute," the guard said. "Open the back."

Felsberg's foot twitched above the gas pedal. He knew this might happen and yet he was unsure what to do. What could he do? If he made a run for it, the guards would fire at the truck, killing many of those inside, and the chase vehicles would certainly catch them before those still alive could be let out to scatter and try to make it on their own. But if he opened the back, they would all be arrested, and most would be dead before sunset. The only hope—and it could hardly be called that at all—was that those inside, realizing the situation, might jump out and rush the guards, and though many would be killed, perhaps a few would survive to escape the city.

Felsberg got out of the truck. Though he prayed, his prayer did not consist of words. He prayed with raw emotion, his mind too busy planning what to do while trying not to let on by his actions that anything was wrong. Scanning the area for any path of escape, he was startled by the sight of four human heads displayed on poles next to a sign that read: "There is no escape for the enemies of Humankind." This had not been there a few hours before, and he guessed the victims had been caught in a recent failed attempt to flee the city. Certain that the same fate awaited him and those in his truck, he clenched his teeth for the conflagration to come, unlocked the door, and threw it open as quickly as possible to allow those who could fight a chance to get out.

Nothing happened.

The door slid open but no one jumped out to fight. There was no sound of gunfire, no shouting.

"Okay," the guard said.

Joel Felsberg was frozen, afraid to look at the faces of those he had gathered up only to deliver them to their executioners, faces that would soon be gruesomely displayed on staffs. But what had the guard said? "Okay"? . . . *"Okay"?*

The guard had already walked away. Felsberg did not understand. Had he not seen . . . ? At last he looked for himself. The truck was . . . the truck was empty. Empty! Felsberg closed his eyes and then looked again. It was still empty. Slowly, not knowing what else to do, he stepped up on the truck's bumper and pulled the door closed and locked it shut. As he started back to the front of the truck, he ran through the events that had led up to this moment, trying to understand. Had he just imagined loading all those people? Was he dreaming?

Then he noticed something: the tires. Acting as though he had dropped something, he leaned over and picked up a pebble while turning to look at the truck's suspension. The truck looked like it was loaded with lead.

"What happened?" Ed Blocher asked when Felsberg got back in the cab.

"I don't know," he answered. "I don't know."

◻

To keep from arousing suspicion, Joel drove the truck four miles from the city before he stopped. When he finally did stop, he literally jumped from the cab and ran to the back, followed by Ed Blocher. Unsure of what he would find, he unlocked the door and slid it open.

"Are we there already?" asked Akbar Jahangir.

Joel began laughing and crying at once. They were all there. "Not yet," he answered, dumbfounded. "Just a few more miles."

When they returned to the cab, Ed Blocher again asked what had happened at the checkpoint.

"I'm not sure you'd believe it. I'm not even sure I believe it myself. But right now we've got to deliver these people and go back for another load. I have a feeling this is going to be a very good day."

History's Penumbra

23

Saturday, September 19, 4 N.A.
Petra

As HIS FAMILY LISTENED QUIETLY, Michael Feingold, like thousands of other fathers and mothers in Petra, read them the words of the prophet Hosea:

> Then I will go back to my place until they admit their guilt. And they will seek my face; in their misery they will earnestly seek me.
> Come, let us return to the Lord. He has torn us to pieces but he will heal us; he has injured us but he will bind up our wounds. After two days he will revive us; on the third day he will restore us, that we may live in his presence. Let us acknowledge the Lord; let us press on to acknowledge him. As surely as the sun rises, he will appear; he will come to us like the winter rains, like the spring rains that water the earth.[136]

In accordance with the instruction of their high priest, the people of Petra clustered together in their family tents

[136] Hosea 5:15–6:3.

and sought forgiveness as they recalled their individual and collective rebellion against God. They recalled their animosity to others, their vanities and chasing after things of this world, their selfish acts, their lack of trust in their God.

They remembered too, the many false messiahs throughout the centuries that their people had followed:[137]

- Bar Kochba, who when he briefly recaptured Jerusalem from the Romans in about 130 A.D., was proclaimed Messiah by Rabbi Akiba, but shortly thereafter was captured and put to death;
- Moses of Crete, who promised the Jews of Crete he would part the sea and lead them back to Israel on dry land, but after failing to perform the promised miracle, quietly slipped into obscurity;
- Abraham ben Samuel Abulafia, who in 1284 proclaimed himself Messiah but whose prophecy of a messianic age that was to begin in 1290 died with him;
- Shabbetai Zevi, whose thousands of followers in the Middle East, Asia, Europe, and British Isles so ardently believed him to be the Messiah that his initials were inscribed in gold above the Torah shrines in synagogues and new prayer books were printed with his name appearing in place of the Messiah, but who, when challenged by the Muslim Sultan in Constantinople to prove he was Messiah by turning

---

[137] Information on each of these false messiahs and many others can be found readily on the Internet.

away arrows fired at him, instead chose suddenly to convert to Islam;

- the lesser false messiahs Asher Lemlein, Isaac Luria, Hayyim Vital, Baruchya Russo, Jakov ben Judah Leibovich, Moses Guibbory, Abu-Issa, Serenus;
- and in the 1980s and 1990s, Menachem Mendel Schneerson, some of whose followers continued for years after his death to insist that he would rise from the dead and establish his messianic kingdom.

All in all, Samuel Newberg's assessment had been correct. Many of the people of Petra had only been waiting for the word from their high priest before accepting Yeshua, Jesus, as their Messiah. Others, upon hearing the high priest's words and reasoning and reading from the prophets, wondered only how they had so long missed what now seemed so obvious.

Abū Zanīmah, Egypt

Some had come more than 1,500 miles. They flew endlessly it seemed, toward the northwest, in numberless flocks over the great continent of Africa. Stopping here to rest for the night on the eastern bank of the Gulf of Suez before continuing on in the morning, the famished birds scavenged for whatever they could find to eat. Soon there would be food enough, but they would not reach it if they could not maintain their strength for the journey.

Sunday, September 20, 4 N.A.
The Seir Mountains

From his sentry's position atop Gebal Haroun, on the Seir Mountains above Petra, Dennis Kreimeyer watched in amazement as the vanguard of the UN forces swept toward him from the east and west like two slow-moving storms. Peering through binoculars revealed only that the storms stretched on to the horizon and seemed to have no end.

For two days the people of Petra had confessed their sins. Now as their destruction bore down upon them, the high priest of Israel issued a decree that all prayer should become a call for deliverance from the enemies gathering at their door.

❑

By noon, Mount Seir and Petra within it had become an island, surrounded by the sea of their adversaries. And yet still the tide that had engulfed them stretched on forever in the direction of Israel in the west and the Euphrates in the east. There seemed no end to those who came to destroy them.

Babylon

Joel Felsberg and Ed Blocher had not slept in fifty-two hours. So far, adrenaline and concern for those trapped in Babylon had kept them going, but even that was beginning to fail them. They did not know how many trips they had made in and out of the city during that time; both had lost count somewhere in the middle of the first night. They could loosely estimate it based on the number of city gates—they had used them all twice so far, though never in the same eight-hour shift, and had started on their third cycle—but such a calculation was beyond them in their current state of exhaustion. Whatever the number, it seemed there were always more waiting to leave, and so Felsberg and Blocher continued to come back. This time, though, the truck was only about half full and there seemed to be no one else.

"What now?" asked Blocher.

"Let's give it a few more minutes," Felsberg answered. But as the minutes passed, no one else came.

"I guess that's it," Felsberg said finally, and as he did he noticed that the faint wisps of clouds overhead appeared to have noticeably darkened.

Looking up, Blocher nodded and responded, "That's definitely it!"

"Everybody hang on!" Felsberg said, as he reached to pull the door shut. In the few seconds it took to lock the back and for the two men to reach the front seat, a cool wind began to blow against their faces and the sky had begun to turn gray. As Felsberg started the engine, lightning struck a nearby building and thunder like a cannon blast shook the truck. "Okay," he said, looking up, "we're gone!"

But as he pulled his door closed, Blocher saw someone in the mirror. "Wait!" he shouted.

"Please, let me in!" a voice called to them. It was a teenage girl. "Please," she cried again as she ran to the driver's side of the truck. Felsberg looked out, and the girl threw back her hair away from her forehead and held up the back of her right hand so he could see she did not have the mark.

"Are there any others?" he asked.

"No," she answered and then changed her response to, "I don't know," as another bolt of lightning struck, this time a little farther away.

"Get in the other side!" he said, concluding there was no time to open up the back. He did not wait for her to get settled in or for Ed Blocher to close the door before throwing the truck into gear and pulling away; already lightning had struck twice more and fire rose from the first building that had been hit.

Blocher looked at the girl and thought about getting out the city gate. "It will be interesting to see this vanishing act up close," he said.

The fact that the truck was empty going in and appeared empty going out gave the security guards no reason to suspect they were doing anything illegal. But to keep questions to a minimum, they had been careful not to use the same gate too often. With the storm closing in there was no time to think about such things. They had to get out of the city fast and so they simply headed for the closest exit. Even so, by the time they approached the city gate, it had become as dark as late evening.

"Joel," Ed Blocher said, watching the girl beside him as they sped toward the gate, "I don't think she's going to disappear."

"It doesn't matter," Felsberg responded, as he pressed the accelerator closer to the floor. "We're not stopping anyway."

"Good idea," Blocher said under his breath as they

barreled through the gate. Apparently the environmental cataclysm, which included numerous lightning strikes nearby, was sufficient to distract the guards because no one fired a shot or even tried to stop them.

Having cleared the city walls, Joel Felsberg floored the gas pedal and accelerated down the straight flat road leading east from the city. In the back of the truck, the passengers held on as best they could and wondered what was going on outside.

Two minutes and three miles later the day had turned black as the darkest night, with the repeated bolts of lightning creating a strobe effect all around them. The wind whipped at the truck as Joel struggled to keep it on the road. The rumbling of thunder was a constant drumbeat, with new claps coming one after another. Then one of the beats did not die away, but grew quickly and steadily louder.

"This is it!" Felsberg shouted as he took his foot off the gas and hit the brakes, slowing the truck as quickly as he could. They had nearly stopped when the earth beneath them began to roll like a wave and then finally buckled, throwing the truck off the road and onto its side. Inside the truck, the passengers were tossed violently about, resulting in numerous abrasions and bruises, two concussions, several cracked ribs, and a dozen other broken bones.

But it was not over yet.

The ground continued to shake until it seemed the truck would be torn apart. Even a thousand miles away, the quake was beyond the instrumentation's capability to measure, but estimates put it at as high as 10.5 on the logarithmic Richter scale, or more than a hundred times stronger than the 8.1 quake that devastated Mexico City in 1985. Clearly the battle for the planet earth was about to reach its zenith.

❑

Inside Babylon, at the epicenter of the massive quake, buildings crumbled into enormous burning heaps, ignited by lightning and fueled by natural gas pipelines. The city's magnificent perimeter walls became an insurmountable mountain of rubble, sealing all avenues of escape. Along the dry bed of the Euphrates, the earth split open like an overripe fruit, leaving a gaping chasm a hundred yards wide and a mile deep. A second crack, running eastward from the first, passed directly through the UN complex and swallowed whole the ruins of the United Nations Secretariat and General Assembly buildings. Collectively, the chasms divided the city into three huge blazing sections consumed by raging fire.

❑

The quake's radius of destruction stretched for more than two thousand miles—from St. Petersburg to Somalia, from Nepal to Barcelona—collapsing buildings, devastating whole cities and crushing much of their populations. But the Babylonian quake was only the forerunner of death as it triggered major shifts of the African and Eurasian tectonic plates, causing a chain reaction that shook the Indian-Australian and Pacific plates as well. Thousands of islands in the Atlantic, Pacific, and Indian Oceans along the borders of the plates were shaken like a child's rattle, turning most signs of civilization to wreckage and creating massive tsunami to wash away what was left. The loss of life was in the millions, and tens of millions more were injured.

❑

Hundreds of miles from Babylon, along the route to Petra, the quake shook Christopher's armies, knocking many off their feet, but few were seriously injured. Primarily this was because they were in the open where there were no structures to fall on them (the cause of most quake injuries), but most credited their good fortune to their solidarity against Yahweh. Their bravado would be short-lived, however, for they had not yet seen the smoke of Babylon rising in the east or heard news reports of the damage that had occurred elsewhere.

❑

Three miles southeast of Babylon, with headlights shining through the dust and dark before it, the overturned truck's passenger door was slowly pushed open, revealing the only sign of life for miles. It was just after noon, but the clouds that still rained down lightning upon the city made it appear as night. Ed Blocher shielded his eyes from the wind and dirt as he groaned in pain and attempted to climb up through the door and then down from the cab to the ground. Close behind, their teenage passenger jumped the last few feet, followed next by Joel Felsberg who, not nearly as agile, landed hard and immediately wished he had not.

"Here," Felsberg said, wincing and handing Blocher the keys. "Go see how bad it is back there."

Ed Blocher took the keys and went to the back door.

"Is everyone all right in there?" he asked, yelling to be heard above the thunder. The cries from inside told him they were not.

"I don't think so," answered an adult female voice. "We've all been tossed about pretty badly. I think we've got some broken bones back here. What happened? Did we hit something?"

"An earthquake," Blocher answered.

The woman leaned forward to see beyond the open door. "Is that the city?" she gasped, only now coming into Blocher's view as the light of the raging fire reflected off her face.

It was a rhetorical question asked in stunned amazement, but Blocher answered anyway. "Yeah," he said, as he helped a not-so-badly-injured man to his feet.

For a long moment the moans and talking completely ceased as those inside looked on in disbelief at the burning ruins of the capital of Christopher's New Age.

"Now what?" asked the woman finally, spitting dust that had blown in her mouth.

From outside the back of the truck Joel Felsberg's voice answered her question, "Now we get everyone out of the truck, and if we can, we try to get it back upright. If we can't . . ." Felsberg stopped. He really didn't have an alternate plan.

"If we can't, what?" prodded Blocher as he climbed out of the back of the truck.

But Felsberg had something else on his mind. "Don't you think it's a little strange," he asked, leaning close to be heard, as he looked up at the black cloud covering, "that despite the clouds and the lightning, there's been no rain?"

The fact had occurred to him earlier, but with everything else that was happening, Blocher had not given it much thought. Now as he looked around, the ominous tone in Felsberg's question brought the matter clearly into focus. "What's happening?" he asked.

"In order for there to be lightning," Felsberg answered, "something has to be creating a static charge in those clouds. Since it's not raining, the movement that's causing the static must be in and above the clouds."

Blocher shook his head and gave Felsberg a confused look to say he still didn't understand what Felsberg was getting at.

"We've got to try to get these people to shelter," Felsberg said, still not explaining the reason for his concern.

"Most of them can't walk, especially in this storm," said the woman from inside the truck. "And unless you can turn the truck right side up with just the few of us that aren't badly hurt, you're going to have to come up with another plan."

Felsberg looked at the sky again, shaking his head.

"What is going on, Joel?" Blocher demanded.

"I don't claim to be an expert at interpreting either prophecy or meteorology," Felsberg answered, "and the Bible doesn't say exactly *when* it's supposed to happen, but unless I miss my guess, we're about to be—"

At that moment there was a muffled thud and the ground shook again. It was different than before: not even a fraction so strong as the quake but it felt somehow localized, closer. An instant later it was followed by a second thud, and then a third. "Quick! Back in the truck!" Felsberg ordered.

There was another thud closer than the previous ones, and Ed Blocher turned to look for the origin of the sound. At first he saw what appeared to be a boulder, light-colored and perhaps eighteen inches or two feet in diameter, rolling slowly toward the truck. Before his eyes could fully focus on the curious sight he realized there were thousands of such boulders. They were falling from the sky.

Two miles outside of Petra

Sand and dust flew in all directions as the helicopter set down near the headquarters tents of the UN encampment outside of Petra. Not waiting for the blades to stop, the helicopter's passenger, General Rudolph Kerpelmann, in charge of the UN peacekeeping forces in Israel, tapped on the window of the door with his baton to indicate to the crewman that he wanted it opened immediately.

Climbing from the chopper as the blades still rotated, Kerpelmann scanned the tents, and went directly to the one with the flag and seal of the secretary-general of the United Nations. The guards posted outside showed him in. Christopher was waiting for him.

"Thank you for coming, General Kerpelmann," Christopher said as the general tucked his baton beneath his left arm and saluted him. "Please sit down." Kerpelmann sat, and Christopher got right to the reason he had called him for this meeting.

"General, I've read your report on the large number of Jews in Jerusalem who oppose our efforts here. Is it true," Christopher asked with a grimace, "that they are actually cutting off their own right hands to remove the mark?"

"I'm afraid so, sir," Kerpelmann answered.

Christopher shook his head and sighed as if to say "poor fools," before getting back to the immediate purpose of the meeting. "I've also read your recommendation for dealing with the problem." Christopher leaned back in his chair. "I am inclined to agree with your assessment."

General Kerpelmann showed no change in his emotion, but inside he was celebrating. He had not expected Christopher's support.

"Have there been any changes since you submitted your report that would make you reconsider your recommendation?" Christopher asked.

"No, sir. In fact, in light of the upcoming action here, I believe my recommendation to be all the more sound." Christopher's silence urged General Kerpelmann to continue. "Sir, I don't pretend to understand exactly how all these psychic powers work, but it seems to me that if you've got an action taking place here, you don't want a millstone around your neck from a lot of interference coming from Jerusalem."

Christopher paused and seemed to be considering Kerpelmann's advice and then nodded agreement. "You've got your work cut out for you, General," he said. "I want this completed by noon tomorrow, before the action at Petra begins."

"My people can be ready in two hours," Kerpelmann assured him.

"Good!" Christopher said, and then after a pause added, "We've got six divisions under the leadership of General Novak at the rear of the procession coming from the Jezreel Valley. They should be reaching Jerusalem right about now. To speed things up, I'll direct Novak to transfer command to you until you complete your mission."

General Kerpelmann stood to attention, saluted briskly, and left the tent. "Finally," he said under his breath, and slapped his baton in the palm of his left hand. If only he had been given permission to do this three and a half years ago when they had first occupied Israel, he thought, before the rest of them had had an opportunity to go to Petra, the world would never have suffered the plagues. He knew the Jews. Growing up in Austria he had learned to hate them. As a youth he had studied the Second World War and would lie awake at night agonizing over missteps and miscalculations that had led to Hitler's defeat. It seemed a deliciously ironic vindication of Hitler's convictions that so many years after the defeat of the Third Reich, the UN, the very organization formed by those who defeated Germany, had finally realized the necessity of completing the work that the Reich had begun.

Three miles southeast of Babylon

As hailstones two feet in diameter, each weighing a hundred pounds or more, rained down all around them, those in the truck huddled together and prayed for deliverance. Suddenly there was a loud crash and the sound of shattered safety glass. The truck's cab had been hit. A moment later a hailstone hit the truck's upturned rear wheel, tearing it from the hub, separating the differential from the drive train, forcing the axle through the wheel on the ground, and driving it fourteen inches into the dirt. Two more stones demolished the cab. Additional stones rolled against the back door after striking the ground nearby.

The storm continued for another twenty minutes as various parts of the truck were pummeled, but, miraculously, none hit the compartment directly.

❑

When the storm was over, Ed Blocher and Joel Felsberg and every other able-bodied person in the truck had to work together to force open the back door. Even then, they could open it only about a foot and a half. Accumulated hailstones around the truck left only a small hole, large enough for one person to climb through at a time. Ed Blocher was the first. As he emerged to look around, he saw the full impact of the hail. As far as he could see, the earth was covered six to eight feet deep with the massive hailstones, and the city of Babylon had become a crushed, smoldering wasteland.

Eighty miles northeast of Petra

High overhead a large flock of crows winged their way eastward above the advancing columns. Those below on their way to Petra took no notice of the birds' flight: Their eyes were drawn four hundred miles to the east, where a huge dark cloud rose from beyond the horizon. Nor did they hear the birds, for the air was full of cursing. The first reports of the destruction of Babylon and the damage to other cities from the earthquakes were being broadcast to the world.

In the concern of the moment, no one remembered the words of the second angel, who had appeared at the dedication of the UN complex two years earlier.

Jerusalem

The steel-toed combat boot found its mark squarely in the middle of the wooden front door, breaking the lock and throwing the door open. Cautiously but quickly, two uniformed men rushed in and began to search the apartment. Carefully proceeding from room to room, they checked under and behind furniture, in closets, and behind full-length curtains. Coming at last to the master bedroom, one slid open the closet door as the other pointed his rifle. Inside a woman stood against the back wall, her eyes closed as she tried in vain to hide behind the clothes that hung before her.

"Get her," said the man with the rifle. The other man reached in and took hold of the woman's hair and pulled her out as she bit her lip to keep from screaming.

"Not bad," said the other as he lowered the rifle. "But let's get a better look." With that, he tore the clothes from her body until she stood before them naked, attempting to cover herself—a task made all the more difficult by the fact she had no right hand.

"Hold this," he said, as he handed his rifle to his companion.

"Hold it yourself," the other answered as he dropped both their weapons on the carpeted floor.

The two men grabbed the woman to force her down on the bed, but she resisted, scratching the first across the face.

The man jerked back and felt his face where she had scratched him. The blood on his hand revealed the extent of the wound. "You dirty slut!" he said, and grabbed her left hand and twisted it behind her back. Taking hold of the bandaged stump of her right wrist in his other hand, he twisted both of her arms and gave a hard sharp jerk downward, dislocating her left shoulder and making that arm useless. Her missing right hand had fouled his grip on that arm and so as the woman screamed in agony, the man shifted his hold to the other arm. With the stump in one hand and her elbow in the other, he countered the one against the other and, with a nauseating snap, broke her right arm at the joint. Quivering with unbearable pain, she prayed she would lose consciousness as she was thrown to the bed and the two men dropped their pants.

Suddenly there was a flash of motion from behind as the woman's husband who had been hiding elsewhere in the house, crazed with anger, ran into the room toward the two men. In his left—and only—hand was a large claw hammer, the only weapon he could find. With a single stroke, he drove the claw of the hammer deep into the skull of the first soldier. Then, ripping it from the man's head, he attempted to do the same to the second but instead hit the man's arm raised in defense. The force of the blow knocked the soldier back, and being unable to catch himself because his pants were down around his knees, he fell to the ground and became easy prey for the relentless blows of the hammer.

Down on his knees, the adrenaline of his rage compelling him to continue beating the soldier though he was already dead, the woman's husband nearly missed the sound of others coming into the apartment. At the last

moment, he dropped the hammer and reached for one of
the rifles on the floor. Having been right-handed, aiming
the rifle was nearly impossible, but at this range it would
be difficult to miss. Not suspecting what had happened,
two more UN soldiers appeared at the door. As four shots
rang out, the two men collapsed as their blood spilled out
upon the floor.

Barely able to stand, the man tried to help his wife. He
did not notice a moment later as two more soldiers entered the apartment. They came through the bedroom
door shooting. When it was over, the woman's husband
lay with the four soldiers, dead on the floor. Unseen in the
other side of the closet from where she had hidden, a
stray bullet had pierced the closed door and the small
body of their four-year-old daughter. The woman had
been wounded in the side, but she did not feel it for the
pain in her shoulder and arm . . . and for the pain in her
heart.

As blood ran from her side, the two soldiers completed what the first two had started, raping her, and when
they were done they put a bullet through her head.

❏

From the battle headquarters atop the Mount of Olives
outside Jerusalem, General Kerpelmann peered through
his binoculars down at the city of Jerusalem. What he saw
did not please him, and the reports he was receiving
pleased him even less. The Jews were fighting as people
possessed. Even the frail and elderly had proven difficult
to deal with—and this though most had only one hand.
Now as he cast his view toward the Temple, he saw three

men on the pinnacle at the base of Christopher's statue, planting explosives.

"I want those men killed," he shouted, pointing in their direction with his ever-present baton. But it was too late. Before marksmen could be dispatched, the sound of the explosion echoed in the hills around them. As Kerpelmann watched in horror, knowing how upset this would make the secretary-general, the statue fell to the street below and crumpled into a heap.

General Kerpelmann screamed irately and cursed God. His cursing had nothing to do with any belief that in doing so he would weaken Yahweh's control of the situation. Rather he cursed, as he always had, in anger. "Colonel," he shouted to his second in command, "direct the artillery to target the Temple. Notify our people and give them two minutes to get out of there, and then I want that entire structure turned into a blazing crematorium! I want to smell their flesh burn!"

24

The Epic of Eight Millenia

Outside of Petra

"WHAT IS GOING ON HERE?" American Ambassador and Security Council member Jackson Clark demanded. Secretary-General Christopher Goodman sat calmly and confidently despite the verbal challenge. "You didn't say anything about this! Or didn't you think the destruction of Babylon and cities throughout Asia, Africa, and Europe, and nearly every island on the planet was important enough to mention?"

"I understand your concerns," Christopher responded calmly. "And in truth I am surprised that Yahweh would use this tactic. It makes no sense, except perhaps as a distraction."

"A distraction?!" Clark howled incredulously. "You consider a storm that rains down fire and boulder-sized hail, and an earthquake that decimates your capital city and destroys cities around the globe a *distraction?!*"

"All that Yahweh can possibly hope to accomplish is to use this to distract us from our real mission here."

"Well, it's working!"

Christopher looked unfalteringly into the eyes of

Jackson Clark and answered firmly, "When this battle is over tomorrow, I will restore Babylon: every*thing* and every*one* in it. And within three days time I will do the same for every other city that has been destroyed. By the end of three days, no evidence will remain that there ever was an earthquake, or fires, or hail."

Clark and all those around him were momentarily struck dumb by Christopher's bold claim. Despite its magnitude, from all they had seen, they could not help but wonder if Christopher was, indeed, capable of fulfilling this promise. "If we're not all dead!" Clark ventured finally. There was not much else he could say.

The sudden look of fury that swept over Christopher's face made Clark and everyone else in the tent wish he had said nothing. As Christopher clenched his teeth, apparently holding back a torrent of anger like a dam about to break, the tent quickly emptied without another word being said.

The Mount of Olives, overlooking Jerusalem

When the bloodbath in Jerusalem and the surrounding areas ended, nearly half the Jewish population had been killed; hardly a girl or woman had not been raped at least once. Those who had not been killed were held captive, with half taken from the city to execution facilities and half temporarily held in the Kidron Valley below General Kerpelmann's headquarters on the Mount of Olives. On the hill between Kerpelmann and the captives, the construction of guillotines brought in for the occasion went on at a feverish pace. General Kerpelmann had vowed before the fight that the Kidron Valley would flow with the blood of the Jews, and flow it would. Other forms of execution were quicker and neater, but beheading had become quite popular with the troops, and General Kerpelmann was always conscious of the importance of maintaining troop morale.

At gunpoint, Asaph ben Judah, the mayor of Jerusalem, beaten and with his arms tied behind his back, was marched by two blue-bereted soldiers up the hill to where General Kerpelmann waited, relishing the moment. Soon the two stood face to face. Heaving a sigh of disgust, Kerpelmann looked over his captive, paying particular attention to the stump that had been his right hand. Kerpelmann had given some thought before their meeting to what he might say, but realized now that whatever he said would be a waste of his breath. He did not want to communicate with the Jew; he wanted to humiliate him, to crush him. He would no more have anything to say to ben Judah than one would have to say to an irritating insect before smashing it.

Finally, when Kerpelmann was satisfied with his examination of his enemy, he set his footing, and with all the strength his anger and disgust could marshal, he hit ben Judah on the right side of the face with his baton, knocking him to the ground. Kerpelmann laughed and shared a smile of accomplishment with the two UN soldiers who had escorted ben Judah to him.

Bleeding and dazed, with his arms still tied behind him, ben Judah struggled to get to his feet. Having accomplished the task, he stood and faced Kerpelmann again. For a long moment the two men looked each other in the eye. And then, without speaking, ben Judah turned his head and offered the latter-day Nazi his other cheek also.

"Get him out of my sight!" Kerpelmann said to the soldiers.

Petra

Inside Petra, word of the destruction of the Temple and the fall of Jerusalem reached Chaim Levin, who immediately called for the people to assemble for prayer. Addressing the gathering, he read from the Psalms:

> O God, the nations have invaded your inheritance; they have defiled your holy temple, they have reduced Jerusalem to rubble. They have given the dead bodies of your servants as food to the birds of the air, the flesh of your saints to the beasts of the earth. They have poured out blood like water all around Jerusalem, and there is no one to bury the dead. We are objects of reproach to our neighbors, of scorn and derision to those around us.
>
> How long, O Lord? Will you be angry forever? How long will your jealousy burn like fire? Pour out your wrath on the nations that do not acknowledge you, on the kingdoms that do not call on your name; for they have devoured Jacob and destroyed his homeland. Do not hold against us the sins of the fathers; may your mercy come quickly to meet us, for we are in desperate need.
>
> Help us, O God our Savior, for the glory of your name; deliver us and forgive our sins for your name's

*sake. Why should the nations say, 'Where is their God?'
Before our eyes, make known among the nations that
you avenge the outpoured blood of your servants. May
the groans of the prisoners come before you; by the
strength of your arm preserve those condemned to die.*

*Pay back into the laps of our neighbors seven times
the reproach they have hurled at you, O Lord. Then we
your people, the sheep of your pasture, will praise you
forever; from generation to generation we will recount
your praise.*

*. . . O Lord God Almighty, how long will your anger
smolder against the prayers of your people? You have
fed them with the bread of tears; you have made them
drink tears by the bowlful. . . . Return to us, O God
Almighty! Look down from heaven and see! . . . Let your
hand rest on the man at your right hand, the son of man
you have raised up for yourself.*[138]

The Mount of Olives

General Kerpelmann looked down from the Mount of
Olives on the row of guillotines and the captive inhabitants of Jerusalem who would shortly feel the blades
upon their necks. To his right and left on the hillside, his
soldiers stood by in raucous anticipation of the bloodletting. The exhilaration of the moment filled Kerpelmann
with power and faith in his own destiny.

Farther up on the hillside, about a hundred yards behind Kerpelmann, where no one had been a moment be-

---

[138] Psalms 79 and 80.

fore, a man clothed in a white robe stood silently looking down on the scene.

Suddenly, Kerpelmann felt his knees buckle beneath him and his entire range of vision began to shake violently. Trembling with the massive quake, the guillotines jerked from side to side and then toppled, many of them falling on those who had been assembling them. UN soldiers and Jewish captives alike struggled to stand and were thrown from their feet. Kerpelmann's headquarters tent collapsed, bringing down with it the flag of his rank and the flag of the United Nations. And then, as he rode out the quake, a small crack began to form in the dirt at Kerpelmann's feet. At first it was not even noticeable with all else that was happening around him, but quickly it grew to a span of several inches. He attempted to right himself on one side of the split or the other, but the quake was so strong it proved impossible to shift his weight entirely to either side. And still the crack continued to grow. Watching as it did and yet unable to compensate for the shaking, Kerpelmann called out for help.

Immediately two aides tried to reach him, first attempting to run and then finally crawling on hands and knees, but neither came close enough. At his feet, the split became wide enough that he could see that it ran to a depth of more than a hundred feet. A moment later, unable to hold his footing any longer, he toppled and fell headlong into the chasm, tumbling as the breach swallowed him. Coming down with nothing to slow his fall, Kerpelmann landed with tremendous force against a large jagged rock. The wind knocked from his lungs, Kerpelmann realized he could not move: He had broken his back.

The stone ramparts of the city tossed with the quake and then finally collapsed, rolling huge stones down upon the soldiers in the Kidron Valley who had assembled there for the executions. Those who were not crushed were forced to flee the valley to the east and west, leaving the captives nearly unguarded.

General Rudolph Kerpelmann caught his breath, but he could no longer feel his body as it shook with the mountain around him. The fracture into which he had fallen was now more than ten feet wide and it continued to expand. Despite his situation, Kerpelmann felt himself begin to grow tired. Unaware of the massive internal bleeding, which drained him of his strength, and only vaguely sensing the warmth of the flow of blood from his mouth and down his neck, he was at a loss to understand his sudden fatigue. Slowly his eyes drooped shut, but opened again when he heard voices coming toward him. Rescue had come; he was sure of it. But it was not rescue; those approaching were escaping Jews. The gulf had swollen to fourteen feet, entirely cleaving the mountain from east to west, and as the earth continued to heave, the split grew wider. Suddenly the paries of dirt next to Kerpelmann collapsed, covering his body with earth and rocks. Only his face remained exposed, and it was so concealed that those approaching did not see him.

At first only a few passed, then scores ran past him, fleeing through the canyon that had formed. Buried only a bit prematurely, his mission thwarted, Kerpelmann looked up at those passing by.

He did not call out for help. Even if they had offered, he did not want their help. He desperately tried to hold on to consciousness, and though it sickened him to watch the

Jews escaping, there was something he hoped to see before he died. Finally, his patience paid off as he saw Asaph ben Judah running through the valley toward him. On his face, a huge bloody welt had formed where Kerpelmann had hit him. Kerpelmann smiled to himself, spit up some blood, and died.

Monday, September 21, 4 N.A. Petra

Inside Petra, prayers for deliverance and rescue continued throughout the night. Now, forty-five minutes before dawn, Chaim Levin ended his prayers and called for Sam Newberg and Benjamin Cohen. "It's time," he told them, though they knew it as well as he. The whole of Petra seemed to know, for they rose as one and followed Levin, Cohen, and Newberg as they started up the steep winding path toward the top of Gebal Haroun, where, according to tradition, Aaron the brother of Moses is buried. It was a long hard climb on this warmer than usual September morning, but no one thought twice about going.

"*Yom Tov,*" Levin told his companions, for the day was Yom Kippur.

"*Yom Tov,*" Newberg and Cohen answered.

❏

Robert Milner woke early and breathed deeply of the air of victory's dawn. This was the day of the end and the beginning. By nightfall, Christopher and those who followed him would utterly destroy the final remnant of the

Cult of Yahweh, and at last the earth would be free. Never again would shadows of conscience or whispers of guilt enter into his mind. Never again would his feelings, his desires, his thoughts, or his actions be measured by any standard but his own. Soon the world would forget there ever was a Yahweh. It was the work, the dream, the quest of his lifetime, and today it would all come to pass.

❑

As those who followed Levin, Cohen, and Newberg reached the summit of Gebal Haroun, many saw for the first time in the predawn light the incredible size of the force that Christopher had led against them. Their camp spread like a blanket around Petra, twenty-two miles wide. To the east and northwest the procession of those coming against them seemed to stretch on forever.

And there was one other thing—birds, hundreds of millions, perched still and silent on every branch and rock of the mountains around them for as far as the eye could see.

Finally, with all assembled, Chaim Levin began to read from the prophet Isaiah. He did not read to the people but faced away from them, looking toward the east.

> *Oh, that you would rend the heavens and come down, that the mountains would tremble before you! As when fire sets twigs ablaze and causes water to boil, come down to make your name known to your enemies and cause the nations to quake before you! For when you did awesome things that we did not expect, you*

came down, and the mountains trembled before you. Since ancient times no one has heard, no ear has perceived, no eye has seen any God besides you, who acts on behalf of those who wait for him. . . . Oh, look upon us, we pray, for we are all your people. Your sacred cities have become a desert; even Zion is a desert, Jerusalem a desolation. Our holy and glorious temple, where our fathers praised you, has been burned with fire, and all that we treasured lies in ruins.[139]

At that moment in the UN camp below someone spotted the assembly on the mountain. "Jump!" someone yelled in jest, and it quickly became a chant that filled the camp. "Jump! Jump! Jump!" they urged. Robert Milner laughed.

❑

Turning back to the people, Chaim Levin opened and read from the Psalms.

Give thanks to the Lord, for he is good; his love endures forever. . . .

The Lord is with me; he is my helper. I will look in triumph on my enemies. It is better to take refuge in the Lord than to trust in man. It is better to take refuge in the Lord than to trust in princes.

All the nations surrounded me, but in the name of the Lord I cut them off. They surrounded me on every side,

[139] Isaiah 64.

but in the name of the Lord I cut them off. They swarmed around me like bees, but they died out as quickly as burning thorns; in the name of the Lord I cut them off.

I was pushed back and about to fall, but the Lord helped me. The Lord is my strength and my song; he has become my salvation. . . .

I will not die but live, and will proclaim what the Lord has done. The LORD has chastened me severely, but he has not given me over to death. . . .

This is the day the Lord has made; let us rejoice and be glad in it.

O Lord, save us; O LORD, grant us success. Blessed is he who comes in the name of the Lord. . . . Give thanks to the LORD, for he is good; his love endures forever.[140]

Then as the sun crested the horizon in the east, Levin closed his eyes and spoke the words of Jesus from the New Testament,

For I tell you, you will not see me again until you say, "Blessed is he who comes in the name of the Lord."[141]

Then without urging, but as if on cue, the people shouted, "Blessed is he who comes in the name of the Lord! Blessed is he who comes in the name of the Lord!"

---

[140] Psalm 118.

[141] Matthew 23:39.

At that moment the light of the sun, which had just begun to rise, suddenly changed from golden to sullen gray. The moon, still high but lacking the sun's light to reflect, disappeared from the sky altogether. The day, which had started normally, now seemed to be turned back to late twilight.

❑

In the encampment, fear that this might mark the beginning of some new plague swept through the camp with screams and cries of terror, which woke any who were not already awake. Their screams were muted however, when from the northwest, in the direction of Jerusalem, there came a roar so loud that the entire earth shook and even the sky seemed to tremble.

Robert Milner shook his head in disbelief as he stood his ground. He found it beyond comprehension that so many were so quickly frightened. They were fools—the result of being born into the old age. He wondered if even a thousand years would be enough for some to be completely purged of their old superstitions and fears.

❑

From above the scene of panic in the camp, looking down from the summit of the Seir Mountain range, Chaim Levin, the high priest of Israel, raised up his hands toward the darkened sky and cried, "Behold the salvation of our Lord and Messiah. Blessed is he who comes in the name of the Lord!"

High overhead in the east, the infinite distance of the

universe seemed to shimmer as if from heat and in a moment began to ripple. Seconds later, there appeared the impossible: a rip in space, a tear in the very fabric of heaven, as though a rift between dimensions was opening. The fracture was more than illusion, for as it widened, rending the sky as if it were a paper panorama, the stars themselves rolled back and fell away.

From within or behind the tear there appeared a distant flaming light that cast upon the earth a cruciform image as if to remove all doubt of the meaning of the event.

The panic that gripped the camp now became outright frenzy as the light grew so intense that the sun itself, had it been visible, would have appeared as just another star in the cosmos.

Then from the midst of the blazing light, there emerged a human form seemingly dressed in the light that surrounded him and sitting upon a large white beast that appeared most closely to resemble a horse. And at that moment there erupted the prolonged sound of trumpets, and behind the first figure there assembled a countless entourage similarly attired and mounted.

Many in the camp froze in place. Others ran foolishly for the cover of the nearest tent. Robert Milner steadied himself and held firm. He knew this moment would come and he, for one, refused to be frightened.

Then there came to those in the camp and those along the way who had not yet reached Petra, a shout that pierced the dread in their souls and gave them hope. "Stand fast!" Christopher commanded in the universal language, speaking directly to the minds of all who followed him. "*Stand fast!*" he roared. "Stand fast and see the destruction of our enemy!"

From east of the Euphrates to Petra, from Petra to the Jordan, a spontaneous cheer went up that filled the camp and stretched east and west the entire length of the procession. Christopher's words so filled Robert Milner with excitement and expectation that he found it hard to breathe.

Borne up by the spirit beings who had delivered him safely to the ground when he leapt from the pinnacle of the Temple three and a half years earlier, Christopher rose from the earth to meet his challenger in the air. As he did, the other figure descended, coming near enough to the ground that those closest could see that he was dressed in a white robe that appeared to have been dipped in blood. Milner savored every moment of this final confrontation. He would remember this time forever.

Still a hundred yards away, Christopher began to address his foe. As before, he spoke in the universal language so that all who followed him could hear and understand. "Yeshua," he called, "follow me."

The other did not answer.

"There is no need for us to oppose one another. My fight is with the Father. Join me."

Those who followed Christopher struggled to understand the scene that unfolded before them. Was it truly possible that the meeting they watched could result in an alliance between Jesus and Christopher against Yahweh?

But why not?

Were they not, after all, the same, this Jesus and Christopher? Whatever resulted from this meeting, there was a sense of hope in just the fact that Christopher did not appear frightened by the man.

"Join me! Join us!" Christopher shouted.

Jesus still did not answer.

"Pity," Christopher said finally. "Still, it was worth a try." Suspended above his anxious audience, Christopher turned and waved his right arm above the mass of people. "Well," he said, looking back at Jesus, "what do you think of my little gathering? There would have been many times more but that last set of plagues made quite a mess of things. Still, quite a turnout, wouldn't you say?" Christopher laughed a forced laugh. "And they're all here to see you. Gathered here to *oppose* you, that is. To take what is rightfully theirs: their freedom, their inheritance, their destiny!"

Christopher's followers began to feel foolish for ever doubting him. Obviously he was standing up for them, defending them to this representative of Yahweh. And was this not, after all, what they had come here to accomplish?

A deafening cheer of excitement and approval rose from those on the ground. Robert Milner was exuberant. The foretaste of victory was sweet upon his lips. "Curse him," Christopher told his followers. "Scream your curses so the whole universe will hear!"

The masses responded as one, exploding in blasphemies, jeers, and taunts, each shouting to be heard above the rest. Fists were shaken and obscene gestures made. All had cursed him a thousand times before, while at the same time denying he even existed. But now to see the object of their hatred, now to know he heard their denunciations and imprecations, now to know that his defeat was theirs to force upon him, engulfed them in a sense of dark gratification few of them had ever known. The feeling was of power, accomplishment, vengeance, and intemperance. The cursing of their comrades and Christopher's unwavering contempt for the one so many had called "God" gave each a sense of belonging in the family of Humankind, and of dominance over any who would stand in his way.

Christopher understood exactly what they were thinking and feeling. This was his moment. "Over sixty million," he said as he turned back to face Jesus, "here of their own accord. And there are hundreds of millions more all around the planet. All have willingly followed me." He paused for a long moment as the anticipation of his followers grew, and then continued almost in a whisper. "Those you died for. Those you intended for your bride. All, by their own free choice, *have become my whores!*"

The millions who watched fell into sudden paralyzed silence. What had he said? His "whores"? Could they have misunderstood? Could this be just some kind of taunt at the representative of Yahweh? Though they struggled to find some other meaning, though they longed to deny it had even been said, the meaning was intrusively clear to all, including Milner. It began as a stifled murmur, but in that brief moment the veil was lifted and, as Christopher roared with laughter, there swept over the entire conclave and oncoming procession an atmosphere of tumult, which was at once supremely macabre and hopelessly pathetic. They had not been brought to this place for a battle between Humankind and Yahweh. They were not here to bring down the walls of Petra on the enemies of earth's glorious destiny. They were brought here as trophies, insanely paraded out by Christopher and put on display. This was not about winning liberation from

Humankind's oppressors. This was about spite, vindic-
tiveness, malevolence, and hate. Suddenly all of
Christopher's lies became grossly transparent, revealing
the ugliness of not only the lies, but also of the liar. And
suddenly Milner realized his fate.

A new panic consumed the camp.

And from the eye of the one upon the horse, a tear appeared.

"All these and hundreds of millions more," Christopher
boldly boasted, "have rejected you and freely chosen to
follow me to hell. All have taken my mark. All have eagerly cursed you and the Father. All have—"

"*ENOUGH!!*" thundered the one upon the horse, his
eyes becoming like flames.

And with that single word Christopher was surrounded
by a score of magnificent heavenly beings. Those spirit
beings who had raised him from the ground now released
their hold and fled in arrant terror. Christopher's inability
to resist made it painfully clear to any who doubted, that
instead of being Jesus' equal and opposite, he was merely
an impotent imposter.

"The false prophet also!" Jesus said, pointing at Milner.

By now the multitude below, understanding that they
had been betrayed, turned and fled. In utter disarray
borne of absolute hysteria they stampeded, shoving or
climbing over any who got in their way. In only moments
the health and strength they had been given as
Christopher's third sign leached from their bodies and
was replaced by a burgeoning fatigue and thirst, followed
quickly by debilitating throbbing soreness throughout
every member of their bodies. In deranged dread and torment, many in the horde ceased their attempt to flee and

in their anger turned instead on one another, seeing in each of their comrades an accomplice to Christopher and a conspirator who had encouraged and helped push them down the road to damnation.

In their agony, each hoped as much to be killed and freed from the present pain as to kill.

Every conceivable object became an instrument of torture. Everything sharp was used to stab or hack; everything hard became a tool to bludgeon; every article of clothing became a cord with which to strangle. Every part of the body became either a weapon or a target. Hands were alternately fists to hit or claws to gouge and tear or choke. Elbows and knees flew against nose and jaw and fleshy body part. Feet were used to kick those who stood or to trample those who had fallen. It was not an efficient way to kill, but it was an effective way to create carnage.

Finally, with excruciating tyranny, the pain consumed them and they could flee or fight no longer. Overcome by their infirmity and fear, they cursed God and watched helplessly as blood began to seep from the pores of their flesh. In mere minutes their skin wrinkled and turned as gray as the day and then began to stink and rot away. Streams of blood rolled down their cheeks and exuded from every opening in their bodies, soaking and matting their clothing. And at the same time, with a taste so vile and foul it caused most to wretch, their tongues began to wither and decompose in their mouths.

The fatigue and thirst and pain and rotting of flesh did not consume them all at once, but overtook the fleeing masses like a cold, crawling wave of death, starting with those closest to Christopher and Milner and reaching out to swallow up each of the millions in its path.

Then, with a cacophonous screeching and the roar of a billion wings, there descended suddenly from the skies a half a billion birds, so starved by their long journeys that they did not wait for death to take the fallen, but rather swooped in upon their prey and began to claw and tear the raw flesh from the bones.

Watching the melee, Christopher and Robert Milner, now cursing their captors and their captors' king, were restrained, as below them there was opened a dimensional breach from which there rose a terrible stench and the heat of a blazing furnace. Six years before, Milner had told Decker that his ability to see into the future was limited by a veil beyond which he was not permitted to look. He had explained that there was something beyond the veil that he believed would be very painful and from which the spirit that shared his body was protecting him. Now the veil was gone, and he realized the spirit who possessed him had not been protecting but deceiving him. Milner's spirit guide had led him straight into the jaws of hell.

Christopher fell silent in stark terror as he began to comprehend the vastness of the flames that would be his eternal destiny. Faced with the imminent reality of his fate, the carefully crafted facade of detachment that hid his fear with defiance began to crumble. His strength borne of hatred for all that belonged to Yahweh was lost as he felt his body tremble with cold sweat. It seemed that all he was, all he had lived for, was suddenly being undone. He had always known this moment would come, but now he found it worse than he had ever imagined. In another second he might even have begged for mercy, but Milner spoke first.

"I trusted you, you lousy son of a . . . ," Milner screamed. "You said this wouldn't happen! I trusted you. I trusted you!"

Suddenly Christopher felt restored. The suffering of others made it all worthwhile. "You made your own choices," Christopher answered, laughing. "So did they all."

When the hole was opened sufficiently, Christopher and Milner were hurled into the lake of fire and the dimensional fault was sealed.

❑

All that day, from the Euphrates to the Jordan and around the world, the dark current of death flowed until none of Christopher's followers remained alive. Some who fled west got as far as Jerusalem and the Kidron Valley, where their blood filled the ravine to as much as three feet deep. For four hundred miles, the birds of the air feasted on the rotting carcasses of over sixty million people. By late afternoon, the sun shone again.

❑

Thus it was that in a single day, the epic of eight millennia came to an end.

Epilogue

The Right Place at the Right Time

"PULL HIS HAIR!" the voice called again.

This time Decker recognized it as the voice of his older brother, Nathan. The sound was coming from behind him, and Decker strained to look back at him. There was no time to understand what his brother had meant. Seven-year-old Decker Hawthorne felt his mother's grip on his arm loosen.

As the fingers of her left hand slipped from his arm, the muddy slope slid upward against his chest and stomach and he slipped down into the gaping sinkhole. But the fall was short; she had only let go of him with one hand; her other hand still held firmly to his arm, pulling upward, as his hands remained locked around the root he had clung to for over an hour. His eyes closed briefly. Then suddenly, without explanation, Decker felt as though scalding water was being poured over his scalp. The pain seemed unimaginable to a boy not yet eight years old.

Decker's mother understood what Nathan meant. She had let go of her younger son's arm with one hand and had taken hold of his hair. As she pulled up, she heard her son's cry of anguish but she did not let go. She pulled him toward her, letting most of the weight of his body hang from his hair. It took only a second before it had the desired effect. With every fiber of his being distracted by the pain, Decker's fingers released their hold on the root, and his mother was able to finally pull him free. He felt the mud against his cheek and felt his body move again. He was being pulled upward. Holding tightly to his right arm, his mother quickly released her hold on his scalp and, with hundreds of uprooted hairs clinging to her damp, muddy fingers, took hold of his other arm.

He tried to help lift himself by digging his fingers into the slope but had no control of his blood-starved arms and hands. Nathan moved around behind his mother and took hold of her feet to keep her from sliding in as she lifted Decker out. When she had finally pulled him to her, she rolled to her right side to try to pull him from the hole, but that was as far as she could lift him. He tried to help, but he could not get a foothold on the muddy slope. For a moment they just held that position before Nathan realized the problem.

"Help me!" his mother cried.

Nathan moved up beside her and grabbed one of Decker's lifeless hands. Nathan was sixteen, and it had always seemed to Decker that he was remarkably strong. That strength proved useful now as, with a loud grunt and a single heave, he pulled his younger brother from the sinkhole.

Nathan dragged Decker from the side of the hole and tried to stand him on his feet but the legs of the exhausted boy could not hold the weight.

Quickly, his mother crawled away from the hole to join them. Still on her knees, she held Decker tightly and finally let herself cry. He felt her shake from the fear she had held inside while she tried so long to pull him free. He cried with her, his arms hanging limp and lifeless beside him.

Behind his mother, Decker saw the glow of the sun setting in the west. The shadows in the pit had made it seem much later than it was, and he felt an added warmth in knowing the day had not ended without him. As his mother held him and he watched the sunset over her shoulder, blurred by his tears, he could feel the tingle of blood returning to his arms and hands. The feeling itself was odd, but it seemed that something even odder was happening. The sun appeared not to be setting, but rising.

Could he have been in the pit the whole night? Was this the sunrise? No, he knew that was west by the position of a large oak tree where he had built a tree house. Then, as he watched, the sun grew in size until it seemed to fill the sky. The brightness should have been blinding, but he could not look away. There was no pain in looking at it, only warmth. Decker closed his eyes briefly, not because of the light but rather to reorient himself. When he opened his eyes again, he had the strange sensation that he was somewhere else. As his eyes adjusted to the light, he realized that there were people around him.

There was his brother Nathan, but he was older. And standing near him was Scott Rosen, his forehead marked with the sign of the Koum Damah Patar. Next to Rosen were his parents, Joshua and Ilana. A few feet away stood Tom and Rhoda Donafin and their children, Tom Jr., Rachael, and young Decker. As his eyes cleared he could see there was a very large crowd, perhaps a thousand or more people, around him. There were some that he knew well and others he had seen only once or twice before. With remarkable clarity, he remembered every face and what involvement each one had in his life. It was as though somehow he had total and complete access to the memories of every event in his life. Then he saw someone that he did not recognize: a boy about four years old standing with a woman. He had seen the woman before; twice, but only briefly. Decker remembered. It was in Turin. She was the woman from the restaurant whose son had been ill.

As unexpected as all of this was, he then saw something that made no sense at all. Standing there among the others was his mother! But it was his mother's arms he felt around him, wasn't it?

His senses seemed to be reemerging one by one, and he became aware that the people around him were cheering. Decker Donafin was laughing and clapping, and others were dancing as if in celebration. He realized that he was back in his own body, fully grown, but he felt youthful and strong.

Finally he looked down to see who was holding him and to his utter disbelief and rapture saw his beloved Elizabeth looking up at him, tears in her eyes. Beside him were their daughters, Hope and Louisa, with their arms around both of their parents. They appeared just as they had the day before the Disaster.

Only now did the meaning hit him. He had made it. He hadn't gone to hell. Decker held his family to him and wept openly with joy. His family cried with him, as did many of those around him.

He was drawn again to look into the light, but the light was no longer in the distance. Instead, it was right before him, and the light was a man. He was standing there, smiling warmly, with his arms open wide. In his life before, Decker would have curiously studied the strange similarities and yet stark differences between this man and the pretender, Christopher. But that was before. Now he simply understood, and dropped from Elizabeth's hold and fell flat on the ground at the man's still-scarred feet.

No sooner had he done so, than the man reached down to lift him up. Decker was afraid, but he didn't feel that he could resist him; he didn't truly want to. But how could he look his rescuer in the eye? His suddenly perfect memory now seemed more a curse than a blessing as he recalled every dark detail of his life. How could he let one so loving look at his life of self-love and the guilt that he knew would be written on his face? Tears of loss and shame welled up in his eyes.

Then suddenly he became aware of the cool, sweet freshness of the air around him. As the man lifted him to his feet, Decker felt fearfully drawn to his eyes. Slowly he raised his head and looked at him through his tears. In the eyes where he had expected to find anger, there was only understanding. Where he had expected to find wrath, he found only forgiveness. From the one who should have condemned, there was only love. In that moment Decker felt all of the fear, guilt, and pain of seventy-four years melt away, replaced by a glow of peace.

He was drawn to look deeper and as he did, he realized that the love of the man was the source of the light around them.

"Well done," Jesus said.

Decker buried his face in Jesus' shoulder and wept. "I'm so sorry," he sobbed.

"I know, Decker. I know," Jesus said as he wept with him. "All is forgiven," he said, stroking Decker's hair, still holding him in his arms.

Decker felt strength and comfort and healing surround him and fill him as it flowed from his savior. Soon his tears stopped, and instead of the sting of guilt, he felt the tender warmth of a child in his father's arms. A little longer and it seemed to him that he could stand again. It was only a few moments but it seemed an eternity, for in those few moments Decker's eternity had changed.

"I must go now, Decker," Jesus said.

"But I have so many things to ask you," he appealed, shocked at his own boldness.

Jesus smiled and nodded. "We will have time to talk later," he said. "Right now there are many others waiting for their resurrection. And your friends and family are here. But do not be concerned, I am always with you."

Then he was gone. For a long moment Decker did not move. It seemed incredible but he had momentarily forgotten that there was anyone else there.

"Sit down, Decker," Elizabeth said from behind him.

Decker looked back, and Elizabeth was standing next to an outcropping of rock that seemed a perfect height for sitting. He did not recall seeing it there a few moments before but assumed it had been hidden by the press of people. As he sat, Hope, Louisa, and Elizabeth gathered closely around him but left his view unobstructed so others could greet and speak with him.

Decker suddenly realized that the number of those around him had dropped to only those few to whom he had been closest in life. "What happened to the others?" he asked Elizabeth, assuming she would understand his reference.

"They have gone on to be at some of the other resurrections. You'll have plenty of opportunity to see them later."

Decker looked around him at the incredible beauty. Everywhere there were lush plants and flowers and trees. Birds of great variety flew overhead or rested on tree limbs. Nearby a creek gurgled, filling the air with a soft peaceful sound. In the distance perhaps a hundred miles off, green rolling hills gave way to an immense mountain, higher than any he had ever seen before. From the temperature he guessed it to be late spring. The air was so pure and fresh it was almost sweet in his lungs.

"Is this heaven?" Decker asked.

"No," his brother Nathan laughed. "This is earth. Though it's not at all the same as you remember it. Things have changed quite a bit."

"But I thought that when you died . . ."

"You went to heaven?" Ilana Rosen said, finishing his sentence.

Decker nodded.

"This is what is known as the Millennial Kingdom," Joshua Rosen interjected. "In the book of Revelation, it says that with his blood Messiah purchased us from every tribe and language and people and nation, and that we will reign with him on the earth for one thousand years."[142]

"But what about heaven?"

"Oh, well, you can certainly go there. In fact you can go anywhere in God's creation you want: any place, any

---

[142] Revelation 5:9–10. See also 20:1–4.

time, anywhere in the universe, and to dimensions you've never even dreamed of. But this is home. The earth has been restored to the way it was in the time of the Garden of Eden."

This was not at all what Decker had expected. The images that had been painted in his imagination of sitting around on a cloud and playing a harp had never been very appealing, and he found this much more to his liking—though he would not have complained otherwise, greatly preferring harps and clouds to the flames of hell.

"The last thing I remember was . . ." Decker paused as he reached up to touch his neck. He did not expect to find anything, but his fingers quickly came to rest on the scar of his decapitation. Immediately he reached up with his other hand to confirm his finding: The scar ran all the way around his neck. His eyes filled with wonder—not that the recollection of his death was correct, but that he bore the scar. It seemed terribly incongruous to him that having been restored to youthful form, he would yet retain the scar of his beheading. "I don't understand," he said.

"It's sort of a badge of honor," Tom Donafin answered. "All who were executed by Christopher bear it. It marks you as one who gave his life rather than bowing to Christopher. All martyrs bear some mark of their martyrdom—" Decker raised his eyebrows, surprised that, considering the circumstances of his life and death, he should be counted worthy of that distinction, "—though not to the point of being disfigured," Tom concluded.

All at once Decker realized that Tom's appearance had changed significantly from what he remembered. He was not just young again; his head was no longer disfigured. "Tom, your head," Decker said as he jumped to his feet.

"Oh, yes," Tom commented. "Do you like it?" he asked in jest.

"You look great!"

"Thanks. But continue your story," Tom insisted.

Decker thought back to where he had left off. "After Christopher cut off my head," he continued, as he sat back down on the rock, "I remember discovering that there were a few seconds of consciousness before I actually died. My awareness was fading when, clear as day, I heard a voice. I didn't know where it was coming from, but I was certain it was talking to me. It sounded like Christopher, but at the same time it was very different from Christopher's voice. I know now it was Jesus. He said, 'Come.' That's all. Just, 'Come.'" Decker looked up at Scott Rosen. "Then suddenly I remembered what you told me about the thief on the cross."

"I'll have to introduce you to him later," Rosen remarked.

Decker was a little caught off guard by the fact he would have such an opportunity, but did not let it distract him from his account. "In that instant, I understood it was not too late for me. I remember thinking how ironic it was that after almost seventy-four years, there I was, decapitated and seconds from death, and I finally understood why I had been born."

"God is never too early nor too late, Decker, but always right on time." The speaker was a beautiful brown-haired woman with a melodic Scottish accent whom Decker had never met, but who he somehow knew was his great-great-grandmother.

He was just about to go on with his story when the sound of the woman's voice and her accent abruptly caused him to realize that she had not been speaking English. She and everyone else, including Decker, had been speaking in the universal language.

"Go on," said the woman. "You'll get used to it." Somehow she knew what Decker had just realized about the language.

He complied, though still surprised. "I understood that, like the thief on the cross, all I had to do was ask and, despite all I had done, God loved me enough to forgive me."

"So you asked?" Joshua Rosen urged.

Decker nodded. "I asked."

"Of course he asked," Ilana said. "He's here, isn't he?"

Decker continued. "The next thing I remember, I was dreaming—I guess it was a dream—about something that happened to me when I was a kid. I was running and had fallen into a sinkhole and was holding on to an exposed tree root to keep from falling farther in. My mother was there trying to pull me out, but I couldn't let go of the root. Then I heard Nathan yell, 'Pull his hair.'" Decker looked over at his brother who was nodding to indicate he remembered the incident from their childhood. Decker looked at his mother, who also indicated she recalled the event. "You let go of me with one hand and grabbed my hair. The sudden pain was so intense it caused me to release the root so you could pull me out. In my dream, after I was out of the hole, somehow I found myself here."

For a brief moment everyone seemed puzzled and then Joshua Rosen said, "What you remember is a dream that began as you slipped into unconsciousness before you actually died. A little of that dream came with you and was played out in your mind at your resurrection."

It might just have been a guess, but somehow it seemed

obvious to Decker that Rosen's explanation was correct. It appeared that everyone else around him agreed.

"But what happened to me? How long ago did I die?"

"About four months," Tom Donafin answered.

Decker was surprised and let the answer settle in for a moment before continuing. "But it seems like it all happened just a moment ago."

"It did," Tom confirmed.

"But you said I was dead for four months," Decker persisted, speaking to the whole group, for it seemed they were all in accord on the matter. "How can they both be true?"

"God is not bound by time," Scott Rosen answered, "and when you died, neither were you."

"So," Decker said haltingly, trying to understand the point, "what you're saying is that between my death and resurrection it was like I was asleep—I just wasn't aware of the passage of time?"

"Well, no, not exactly," Rosen insisted. "From our perspective it would *appear* that you were asleep in death during those four months. But from your perspective and God's perspective, no time passed at all."

Decker shrugged. "I don't see what the difference is. If I died four months ago, that means that for four months I was dead, whether I noticed it or not."

"Decker," Tom Donafin interjected, "do you remember that old movie *The Time Machine* with Rod Taylor?"[143]

Decker listened to Tom's question but then burst out laughing. It was good to know that some things had not changed. After all these years, and even after dying and being resurrected in this paradise, Tom was still using

[143] 1960, MGA/UA.

movies to help explain his thoughts. Decker's laughter was infectious, and the others laughed as well. Finally, he managed to answer. "Yes," he said. "I remember, Tom. Go ahead."

Smiling but in full blush, Tom continued. "From his time machine Rod Taylor watched what was going on around him in fast motion because he traveled *through* time. Well, it's not like that when you die. Of course, I mean in the past. In our new bodies we are not bound by aging or sickness or death. But, anyway, what happened to you is more like the movie *Back to the Future*.[144] When Marty McFly and Doc Brown traveled forward in the DeLorean, they traveled instantly, jumping *across* time, from one point to another without experiencing any passage of time themselves."

Decker continued to chuckle, both at Tom's unorthodox method of explanation and because despite its unorthodoxy it was obviously effective. He was beginning to understand.

"As Scott said," Tom continued, "God is not bound by time. He exists outside of it. When you died, you exited time, jumping immediately from the point of your death to the point of your resurrection. I did the same after I was shot. I got here just a few days ago."[145]

---

[144] 1985, MGA/Universal.

[145] Concerning what happens to the dead, the Bible presents a paradox. From the following verses it is clear that the dead are unaware until their resurrection: Psalms 6:5; 115:17–18; Isaiah 38:18–19; Daniel 12:2; Job 14:12; 19:25–27; Luke 14:13–14; Acts 2:29–34; and 1 Corinthians 15:22–23, 51–52. And yet the following verses indicate an immediate or near–immediate transition into God's presence: Luke 23:43; Philippians 1:23. The theory presented here offers a possible explanation for that paradox.

"And everyone else?" Decker asked.

"Those who died in the past—from Abel to the last person to die before the Rapture—if they accepted God's forgiveness, they went immediately from their deaths to their resurrection at the Rapture. Those like Joshua and . Ilana, and Elizabeth, Hope, and Louisa, who served God and were alive at the time of the Rapture, did not die but were instantly changed. They simply sloughed off their old bodies and were given new ones just as though they had been resurrected from the dead. Those who died after the Rapture and who trusted God and did not take the mark or worship Christopher or his image are like you and me, going from death immediately to their resurrection in the Kingdom. Most have already been resurrected, but there are still several million who were executed after you on Christopher's guillotines who are being resurrected even now, in the same order in which they died.[146] Those who served God and did not take the mark and managed to survive until the Kingdom were also changed just as those who were taken at the Rapture, for as the Bible says, '. . . flesh and blood cannot inherit the kingdom of God.' "[147]

"And those who took the mark?"

"They made their choice. No one was forced to take the mark. No one could take it by accident or without understanding the consequences. God even sent an angel to warn the world what was at stake. In fact, the mark had to be voluntary because Satan has never been able to take

---

[146] This ordered approach is suggested by 1 Corinthians 15:20–23, especially by the use of the Greek word τάγμα (tagma).

[147] 1 Corinthians 15:50.

anyone against their will. Along with the rest of the people throughout history who have chosen hell and refused God's forgiveness, those who took the mark will be resurrected at the end of the thousand years of the Millennial Kingdom and will be judged by God."

Decker sighed at the loss. His great-great-grandmother understood his feelings. "Decker," she said, with melodic Scottish inflection, "God was not willing that any should perish but that all would come to repentance."[148]

"Hmm," Decker responded, which meant only that he was willing to let the subject pass.

"If anyone is not here it's because they've chosen not to be here," another woman said. At first Decker could not see who had spoken, but the others moved aside to allow her to be heard. It was Martha Goodman, "Aunt Martha," as Christopher had called her. "They'd never be happy here anyway," she said. "A wheel can have only one center. The universe can only have one God. Otherwise you have chaos, hatred, bigotry, war—the world as we knew it. You take my husband, Harry, for example. He'd be miserable here (though he won't like the other place any better, I'm sure). He never could live by God's rules—even though all of them can be summed up in the simple phrase 'Love your neighbor as yourself.'

"Now, mind you, I'm not talking about being able to follow the rules—even such simple rules. If we could have followed them on our own, then we wouldn't have needed God's forgiveness. I'm just talking about being willing to accept that God has the right to make the rules

[148] 2 Peter 3:9.

and acknowledging that the rules he has made are good. If a person cannot accept that, then he would never be happy here." Her voice showed no sign of anger at her husband, just resigned recognition of the truth. "Harry was simply unwilling to let God be God," she concluded.

Decker sighed again, this time in sympathy and understanding, for Martha Goodman and for all the others whose loved ones had refused forgiveness.

"Is the whole world like this?" Decker asked, changing the subject as he again surveyed the beauty of his surroundings.

"Almost, but not all," Joel Felsberg, Rhoda Donafin's brother, answered. "There are some places, like Babylon, that were left desolate as a reminder of the evil that grew there." Though Joel had never met Decker before, he certainly knew of him as Christopher's confidant. He was also aware of the close relationship that had existed between Decker and Joel's brother-in-law, Tom Donafin.

"Will it be like this forever?" Decker asked.

"Not forever, Decker," Joshua Rosen answered, "but for a thousand years. After that will be the judgment Tom talked about. Then God will create a new heaven and a new earth. We don't know very much about the details, but we do know it will be even better than this world."

"What part of the world are we in, exactly?"

"Israel," Scott Rosen answered. "From the Euphrates to the Nile, just as God promised to Abraham."[149]

Decker raised his eyebrows in surprise. This didn't look at all like the Israel he remembered. Things really *had* changed. "And that mountain?" he asked.

---

[149] Genesis 15:18.

"That is Zion, the highest mountain in the world. On top of it is a plateau measuring fifty miles square, on which sits Jerusalem and a new Temple, built according to the plan given to the prophet Ezekiel."[150]

"A new Temple? What happened to the old one?"

"It was destroyed by Christopher's armies," Scott Rosen answered.

"And the Ark of the Covenant?"

"There is none. There's no need for one.[151] The Ark was the vessel for the physical evidence of God's covenant with his people. Now the evidence of God's covenant is within us and all around us. This is God's promise fulfilled."

Decker nodded. He had more questions, but his more immediate interest was in being with his wife and daughters. Surprisingly it was Scott Rosen, the once-blustering egocentric, who was first to discern this. "There's something else you might be interested in," Scott said. "There is a river that flows out of the Temple across the plateau and then divides, with half of the river running into the Mediterranean and the other half into the Dead Sea. I think you'll be amazed at the changes there. As for the rest of us, I'm sure there are lots of other resurrections we'd like to attend. Perhaps Elizabeth and the girls would like to show you the river."

Decker looked at Elizabeth, Hope, and Louisa, who smiled and nodded. "You'll love it, Dad," Louisa said.

Decker smiled in return, and when he looked up an

---

[150] Ezekiel 45:1–3; 48:8–10.

[151] Jeremiah 3:16.

instant later he was alone with his family. "What happened? Where'd they go?" he blurted in surprise.

"They had places to go," Elizabeth said. "Shall we go see the river?"

Decker's eyebrows raised and stayed there as his eyes shifted from side to side, marveling at everyone's sudden exit. "I don't suppose you intend to *walk* there."

"Well, we could, but it's quite a long way. We could run or we could fly. Or we could just be there."

"What do you mean?"

"C'mon, Dad," Hope chimed in as she took hold of his hand. "Just think about where you want to go . . . and here we are."

Decker sensed no movement, but in that instant their surroundings changed. He now found himself near the base of the mountain that a moment before had been a hundred miles distant. A great cataract of roaring water sparkled like diamonds as it fell more than eight thousand feet down the mountain's steep rock face and emptied into an immense glassy clear pool. The spray from the falls rose nearly half as high as the ledge from which the water fell and, carried by a gust of wind, settled drops of cool mist upon Decker's face. It felt wonderful, and the taste as he licked the mist from his lips was fresh and clean and more satisfying than anything he had ever tasted. Hope's eagerness to come here with her father had apparently caught Elizabeth and Louisa off guard, for they were not with them, but arrived a second later.

Decker took a deep breath and swallowed hard. "So, uh . . . , this must be the river," he managed, not wanting to spoil his family's fun by his apprehension: This form of travel would take a little getting used to.

From the pool at the bottom of the falls flowed the river they had told him about. On its banks grew fruit trees of every kind he had ever seen and many he had not. The air was filled with the sweet smell from the many varieties of trees that were in flower. Others were laden with fruit ripe for harvest.

"The trees bear year-round," said Elizabeth, who watched as her husband surveyed his surroundings.

"The, uh . . . way we got here from where we were, can we go anywhere like that?"

"Anywhere we want. Is there somewhere else you'd like to go?" she asked, eager to please her husband.

"No," he answered quickly, concerned that he might again find himself unintentionally somewhere else. "Maybe later. This is fine for right now."

"So what exactly is it we do here?" Decker asked.

"Pretty much anything we want as long as we abide by the two commandments: love God and love your neighbor as yourself. Of course, you'll find that it's a lot easier to follow those rules here. Satan has been locked up until the end of the thousand years, so temptation has been greatly reduced. Of course, humans are capable of quite a bit of evil on their own and so there is still the need for a government, with Jesus as the head. Soon, after all the others have been resurrected, we will all gather, and he will place us at different levels in his government under him, based on how we lived our lives before the Kingdom."

Decker was certain that in such a government he would have no position at all, but it didn't matter.

"After that there will be a huge banquet, called the Marriage Supper of the Lamb, to celebrate the founding of the Kingdom and God's love for us."

"But after that," Decker probed, "what will we do on a daily basis?"

"Decker," Elizabeth said shaking her head to emphasize that there were no limits other than the ones she had already mentioned, "anything you want. You can do anything from farming to exploring the universe. You can learn to play a musical instrument, a hundred musical instruments. You can write that novel you always used to talk about. And whatever you decide to do, as long as you're willing to put in the time and effort, there is no failure here."

Decker looked over to where Hope and Louisa sat playing with a litter of month-old lion cubs as the mother lion looked on. The sight, which before would have been so startling, felt entirely natural to him as he grew more accustomed to his circumstances and surroundings. "Hope and Louisa," he said, thoughtfully, "they're the same age as when they died."

"We didn't die," Elizabeth insisted. "We were raptured."

Decker nodded, acknowledging his brief lapse. "Will they stay the same age?"

"No, now that we're back on earth, they'll grow naturally."

" 'Back on earth'? Where have you been since the Rapture?"

"We were all taken into heaven for a time. In heaven there is no aging. Now that we're back on earth, the girls will grow naturally. They'll never grow old, but they will reach maturity. They'll take husbands,[152] have children of their own. You'll have grandchildren. In fact, you'll have great-grandchildren and great-great-grandchildren, and you'll live to bounce them all on your knee, never aging but staying young and in perfect health, just as you are today."

"No sickness, no physical defects, no poverty, success dependent only on our effort. Strange, but it sounds a little like what Christopher promised," Decker said.

"A little," Elizabeth agreed. "Except Christopher could never have kept that promise."

"How was it that Christopher was able to give people the things he did—health, youth, psychic abilities?" Decker asked.

"Youth and health did not come from what Christopher gave, but rather from what Satan ceased to take. By reducing the parasitic power of evil over the physical

---

[152] While few question the perpetuity of family relationships or friendships in the Millennial Kingdom, Jesus' answer to the Sadducees' question (Matthew 22:23–33; Mark 12:18–27; Luke 20:27–40) calls into question the exact nature of marriages following the resurrection. Alfred Edersheim (*The Life and Times of Jesus the Messiah*, Book 4, Peabody, Massachusetts, Hendrickson Publishers, 1993, pp. 750–751) concludes that Jesus' words do not intend the dissolution of the husband and wife relationship but rather that in the Kingdom legal matters such as those addressed by the Sadducees' question will be of no consequence. That is, while the marriage relationship alone (unlike other familial relationships or friendships) is built around a legal contract, it is not the legal contract that makes the marriage. On this it should be recalled that though Adam and Eve were never ceremonially wed (i.e., there was no "marrying or giving in marriage"), they were nonetheless husband and wife, as well as father and mother. The author plans to address this issue as well as many others in a prophecy study guide companion to *The Christ Clone Trilogy*. To be notified when a publication date has been set, send an e-mail to StudyGuide@ChristClone Trilogy.com.

bodies of those who took the communion and the mark, he allowed their bodies to return to a state closer to what existed in the Garden of Eden, where there was no disease or death."

"So taking the communion really didn't do anything?" Decker asked.

"No," Elizabeth confirmed. "As for the psychic abilities, those were the deceptions of the fallen angels."

"What about Robert Milner's powers? How was he able to stop the plagues?"

"Many of the things Milner did, like calling down lightning in Jerusalem, were the result of real powers he had that came from Christopher and ultimately from Satan. But stopping the plagues wasn't Milner's doing. Christopher and Milner simply waited for each plague to run its course and then Milner showed up to take the credit as the plague was lifted."

He pondered the response for a moment and then moved on to another thought.

"There is something else that is very, very different about this place," he said. "I noticed it from the first moment, though I still can't begin to explain it. It's as though my whole life up until the time I arrived here was a dream—clearly and perfectly remembered—but a dream nonetheless. I might even believe it *had* all been a dream except that dreaming presupposes having lain down to sleep the night before—" he shook his head, "—and I can remember no such lying down. In truth, I cannot recall ever being truly awake before, not as I am now. It's not just that *now* my old life seems like it was a dream, but rather, looking back at it, I realize that even *then* I sensed the dreamlike quality of it, but I was unable to break free or even to fully comprehend it." Even after having said this, Decker felt compelled to ask, "Was it a dream?"

"No," Elizabeth answered, smiling.

"And there's more," he continued. "It's as though, well, it may sound a little crazy, but it's as though the physical limits of my body no longer confine me, no longer limit me, and everything around me, the grass, the trees, the earth itself, even the air have become a part of me and I a part of them." Decker shook his head. Even in the universal language it was a struggle to find the right words to adequately express himself. "It's a little like going up in an airplane, and you don't really notice the air pressure changing until your ears pop, and then suddenly you can hear better. Well, it's as though my whole life was under that pressure, and now finally my ears have popped. I can hear and taste and see and feel and smell and sense as I never before imagined possible." Decker paused. "And it's you as well. I feel now so much a part of you and you a part of me that I know I could never have felt before. I feel for you a love so strong that even all my years of missing you cannot compare to one moment of the love I have for you now."

Decker continued his explanation, describing a beauty, an awakeness, an awareness so acute that it is impossible to describe it in words used on this side of the event. But well it is, for were it to be described here, all who read it and are bound for it would die from longing. And yet I will here attempt in these earthly words to express what I can of it, and do so without fear of causing any harm but that sweet stab of pain and longing which C. S. Lewis described as "Joy,"[153] which was so cheaply forsaken for the satisfaction of Eve's desire to know good and evil, and Adam's desire for his wife.

Lewis is said to have called it "real life," something that has not yet begun for anyone now "living" as we know it. The gurus and Eastern mystics call it "unity consciousness." It is a clear-headedness, a "higher level of consciousness"—though that terminology is so often misused—that makes what is called "normal life" and "normal experience" seem like nothing more than a drunken stupor. It is a consciousness that the gurus and yogis have only dreamed of, though they *and we* instinctively know is there, but which always—save for fleeting moments, and then only in clouded pastel hues—exists just beyond our human reach. It is, as best it can be described here, truly being a part of nature, in tune with all creation, synchronized with the mind of God. And it is only for the lack of this faculty that things imaginary such as novels can seem to take on life. For who, having experienced a single moment of *real* life could ever have conceived to question one's own existence, or could have been forced to rely on the logic of "I think, therefore I am"[154] to be certain of it.

"Real life has just begun, Decker," affirmed Elizabeth, who was familiar both with C. S. Lewis' writings and, in this Kingdom, with Lewis personally. "The rest seems like a dream, an illusion, a nightmare. Most of the things that Christopher promised were merely the things

---

[153] C. S. Lewis, *Surprised by Joy: The Shape of My Early Life.* (London: Geoffrey Bles, 1955; New York: Harcourt, Brace & World, 1955).

[154] René Descartes, *Discours de la Methode.* Descartes reasoned further in this book to prove the existence of God.

mankind gave away when he fell in Eden," she continued. "In a real sense, Adam and Eve *did* die on that day they ate the fruit, and all of us with them. It's only in our new lives that we can begin to see just how real that death was."

Decker nodded his understanding and complete agreement. "When will I be able to see Jesus again?" he asked. "There is so much I want to tell him; so much I want to ask him."

"Just a few minutes ago he told you that he is always with you," Elizabeth reminded him. "He meant it. He is with you even now. You can tell him whatever is on your mind. Ask him anything and he will answer. Before the words have fully formed in your mind, he will answer."

"That must be how Joshua Rosen was able to explain my dream, and what Scott meant when he said that the Ark of the Covenant was no longer necessary because the evidence of God's covenant is within us and all around us."

"Ask him yourself," Elizabeth urged.

Decker considered the suggestion for a second and then began to compose the question. No sooner had he done so than the answer became clear. And he also understood that the rock upon which he had sat after his resurrection but which he did not recall seeing a moment before had been provided in response to his wife's unspoken prayer.

Decker sighed and bit his lip as he looked into the loving eyes of his wife, overcome with all that he had been given. To him it had been less than an hour since he stood in Christopher's office, faced with the fact that his life was a waste and his sins were comparable to those of

Hitler and Stalin. God's forgiveness overwhelmed him. Decker took his wife in his arms and held her. Neither spoke for several minutes, but both of them understood.

"Scott said the river flows into the Dead Sea," he said finally.

"Yes, but you'd hardly call it dead anymore," Elizabeth answered. "Because of the river, the sea has been made alive. It's teeming with fish and waterfowl. Would you like to go there to see it?"

"I'd like that," he said, "but let's just walk for a while."

Elizabeth smiled, and the two headed off in the direction of the sea. As they walked together beside the gently flowing river, the sounds of songbirds filled the softly floral-scented air. Without speaking, Elizabeth reached down and slipped her small hand into his. Decker closed his fingers around her hand and held it tenderly as he took a deep breath and drank in all that was around him.

❏

Once again, Decker had managed to be in the right place at the right time. He was home.